ACTS

TSO/E CLISTS

TSO/E CLISTS

Basics, Applications, and Advanced Techniques

HALLETT GERMAN

VNR VAN NOSTRAND REINHOLD
New York

The following terms mentioned in this book are known to be trademarks at the time of publication

Registered Trademark of the SAS Institute Inc: SAS

Registered Trademarks of International Business Machines Inc.:
CMS, DB2, DCF, IBM, ISPF, PDF, RACF, SDSF, TSO, TSO/E, VM/SP

Trademark of Information Builders Inc.: FOCUS

Registered Trademark of ATT: Unix

Trademark of Computer Associates: ACF2, Top Secret

Trademarks not known to be such that may have been used inadvertently in this book are the property of their respective owners.

The author has tested all examples to the best of his ability and neither he nor the publisher is responsible for problems resulting from their use by the reader.

Library of Congress Catalog Card Number 89-28503
ISBN 0-442-31867-7

Printed in the United States of America

Van Nostrand Reinhold
115 Fifth Avenue
New York, New York 10003

Van Nostrand Reinhold International Company Limited
11 New Fetter Lane
London EC4P 4EE, England

Van Nostrand Reinhold
480 La Trobe Street
Melbourne, Victoria 3000, Australia

Nelson Canada
1120 Birchmount Road
Scarborough, Ontario M1K 5G4, Canada

16 15 14 13 12 11 10 9 8 7 6 5 4 3 2 1

Library of Congress Cataloging-in-Publication Data

German, Hallett.
TSO/E clists: basics, applications, and advanced techniques/by Hallett German.
p. cm.
ISBN 0-442-31867-7
1. Time-sharing computer systems. I. Title.
QA76.53.G47 1990
004'.32—dc20 89-28503
CIP

To Raquel and Alessandra,
with Metta

Contents

List of Figures

Preface

It does not seem that long ago that a young man began his first clist assignment of building an interactive full-screen application using ISPF. Confronted with ten bulky manuals and a poorly documented clist, he somehow successfully got that first application off the ground. Several years later, after talking to other programmers, he realized there was a real need for a book on TSO and its related environments that would serve as both a reference and a tutorial. This book is a result of that education, providing the first comprehensive overview of using the current command language of IBM's Time Sharing Option—clists. It provides the necessary information for beginning and intermediate clist programmers to build well-documented efficient applications, front-ends, and system utilities. By using the same application across several chapters, you get a sense of how to modify and maintain clists.

There are many wonderful people who contributed to this book and I am pleased to acknowledge their efforts. The major contributor both in letter and in spirit to this text is Charles Hoffman. His approach to data processing, which is to explain things in a nonthreatening and enthusiastic way, is the underlying philosophy of this book. His contribution goes far beyond the original sections he provided (Chapter 5 on where to find more TSO commands and Chapter 9 on the DEMO dialog). Charles also reviewed and gave insightful comments on many of the chapters. Tom Buonomo, Mark Scherfling, and Robert Virgile allowed some of their clists to be included in the book. Mike Murphy, Gerry Pauline, Scott Russell, Otto Stolz, and Bob Thompson went out of their way to provide information about TSO's version of REXX. Dave Carter gave insightful comments on SDSF. Cicely, Stanley, and Robbyn German provided ongoing support. Sakyamuni Buddha kept me going with excellent inspirational teachings. Dianne Litwinn at Van Nostrand Reinhold was a wonderful editor, and the anonymous reviewers gave insightful comments. Alessandra Rose German, my two-year-old daughter, allowed me to use her computer for other things besides "ABDs." Most of all, Raquel German, my wife, who patiently supported this eighteen-month effort, has my deepest appreciation.

1

A Quick Tour of TSO

WHAT IS TSO?

Dataset, Program, Background (Batch), and Other Operations

TSO is an acronym for **Time Sharing Option,** an available selection for the MVS/370, MVS/XA, and MVS/ESA operating systems (MVS stands for Multiple Virtual Storage, XA is Extended Architecture, and ESA is Enterprise System Architecture). You can find the MVS operating system on IBM 370-class mainframes such as the 308X, 3090, 303X, some 43XXs and 9370s. TSO's major feature is its time sharing capabilities.

> Time sharing (Corbato 1982, 1521) is a technique of organizing a computer so that several users can interact with it simultaneously. The term *time sharing* also usually refers to those multi-user systems in which arbitrary general-purpose computation is performed and users operate independently of each other, often at locations remote from the computer itself.

This definition highlights some of the advantages of time sharing.

1. Nearly immediate execution of commands—eliminating the need for scheduling command processing.
2. Because the computer's processing time is so fast, unsuspecting users think they have exclusive use of the time sharing system.
3. Multiple remote terminals are supported, with nearly all of the capabilities of a local terminal.
4. Time sharing supports an interactive command language. Clist (pronounced "see-list") or *command list* is the most common command language for TSO where the user responds to the computer's prompts in real time.
5. Time sharing teamed with today's large and efficient data storage systems allows storage of and access to any number of files at a moment's notice.

Table 1-1. Overview of Time Sharing

Strengths	Weakness
• Near-immediate execution • Multiple remote terminals supported • Interactive command language • Large data storage capability with near immediate file access	• Slow response time if too many users are logged on or if computer is inefficient

There is one large disadvantage to time sharing systems. If many users execute commands at the same time or the computer is not running efficiently, then the response time is longer. Users will feel unhappy because their computer is "busy" and thus they cannot do anything else. Table 1-1 summarizes the strengths and weaknesses of TSO.

MAJOR COMPONENTS OF TSO

The capabilities of TSO can be divided into four major areas:

1. Dataset Operations
   - Allocating a dataset
   - Deleting a dataset
   - Freeing a dataset
   - Listing dataset information
   - Renaming a dataset
   - Copying a dataset
   - Editing a dataset
   - Listing a dataset
   - Printing a dataset
2. Program Operations
   - Assembling a program
   - Debugging a program
   - Link editing a program
   - Testing a program
   - Compiling a program
   - Executing a program
   - Loading a program
3. Batch (Background) Job Operations
   - Canceling a batch job
   - Displaying a batch job's output
   - Routing a batch job's output to a printer
   - Displaying a batch job's status
   - Submitting a batch job

4. Other Operations
   - Information center facility (TSO/E)
   - Micro-mainframe communications (MVS/XA, MVS/ESA)
   - Logging on and off a terminal
   - Session manager
   - Command language (clists and REXX (Version 2))
   - On-line help facility

Dataset operations are the various tasks that modify the contents of one or more datasets. *Program operations* help create, compile, and execute programs written in such languages as COBOL or FORTRAN. *Batch (background) operations* can submit a job for background execution and route the results to a terminal or printer. *Other operations* include communications, interactive language, and on-line help facilities of TSO. Chapter 2 discusses the specific commands used for performing all of the above operations.

WHAT IS TSO/E?

TSO/E (the E stands for "extensions") is an enhanced version of TSO that runs under later releases of MVS. Its major features include improved performance, significantly enhanced commands, and many new facilities. Since IBM is directing their plans to TSO/E and not TSO, the emphasis in this book is on TSO/E. However, to help TSO users know what is available to them, this book notes TSO/E features and commands. TSO/E Version 1 Release 4 does work with all later versions of MVS and is the only release supported for MVS/370 (i.e., non-MVS/XA or MVS/ESA). The latest release, TSO/E Version 2 Release 1 runs only under MVS/XA or MVS/ESA. The MVS/XA Version 2 TSO/E will not receive any future enhancements. All future enhancements are only available for sites having MVS/ESA.

Unfortunately, this book cannot cover all the aspects of TSO (IBM covers them in 10 to 15 large books!). The following features are either used infrequently or are beyond the scope of this book.

- Host to PC communications (MVSSERV)
- Information center facility
- TSO commands and VSAM datasets
- TSO program operations (TSOSERV, LINKEDIT, TEST, language compilers)
- Creating and maintaining a command processor

WHY LEARN TSO?

There are three major reasons why you should learn TSO:

1. TSO, through its commands and clists, provides an easy and flexible means to (*a*) perform routine tasks, (*b*) create self-contained applications, (*c*) manage applications written in other languages, and (*d*) use other languages (such as PDF's edit macros). *Thus TSO is a gateway for building numerous ad hoc and production applications because of its ties to many languages and products.*

To begin to understand the power of TSO, here are some of the languages and products you can use it with.

- JCL (batch jobs)
- ISPF (full-screen application)
- PDF (customized editing facilities)
- DB2 and FOCUS (database)
- All mainframe languages (including assembly language)
- QED editor with or without full-screen capabilities
- RACF, ACF2, and Top Secret (security systems)
- SAS (statistical product)
- REXX (in TSO/E Version 2)

Chapters 7, 9, and 10 explore TSO's ties with other products.

2. Learning TSO commands provides beginning programmers a means for quickly learning important programming concepts (i.e., conditional logic, subroutines, functions, and file operations). Because TSO is interactive, users can immediately verify that their TSO commands or clists are correct.
3. TSO is heavily used at many mainframe sites, so knowledge of TSO is a marketable skill.

TSO is a popular and powerful product that you can use for creating programs to meet your special needs. Chapter 2 reviews the syntax used by TSO commands and the major commands used for the dataset, batch, and other operations areas of TSO.

HOW SHOULD I READ THIS BOOK?

This book addresses the needs of many different audiences. To get you to the sections that will help the most, I am including the following suggested reading plans.

Beginners: Chapters 1 to 5 (clist style), 7 (session manager, edit), 9 (PDF section), and Appendix B
Intermediate and Advanced: Chapters 5 to 8, 11, and Appendixes A and C
Interfacing with Other Software: Chapters 7, 9, and 10
Latest Features: Chapters 4 (flow control), 6, 8 (subprocedures), 9 to 11, and Appendixes A and C
Background Processing: Chapters 2, 7

A SPECIAL NOTE

Due to the typeface being used in the clist listings, program built-in functions (such as &DATATYPE(1)) and TSO keyword operand values (such as DSN('INFO.TEST.DATA')) will appear to have a blank space between the function/keyword and its value in parentheses. *Please ignore this blank space when typing in the clist!*

SUGGESTED READINGS

Corbato, F.J., 1983. Time Sharing, in *Encyclopedia of Computer Science and Engineering*. Anthony Ralston and Edwin D. Reilly, Jr. (eds), New York: Van Nostrand Reinhold, pp. 1520–1526.
Katzan, Harry Jr., and Tharayil, David, 1984. *Invitation to MVS*. New York: Petrocelli Books, pp. 1–18.
Lowe, Doug, 1984. *MVS TSO*. Fresno, Calif.: Mike Murach and Associates, pp. 6–39.

2

Getting Started with TSO

In Chapter 1, we reviewed four major areas of TSO.

1. *Dataset operations,* which are the various tasks that modify the contents of one or more datasets.
2. *Program operations,* which help create, compile, and execute a program written in a language such as COBOL or FORTRAN.
3. *Batch (background) operations,* which can submit a job for background execution and route the results to a terminal or printer.
4. *Other operations,* which include communications, interactive language, and on-line help facilities of TSO.

This chapter discusses the TSO commands for performing the above operations (except program operations) and concludes with an example that serves as an introduction for a discussion on clists in Chapters 3 through 5. Chapter 3 presents an overview of clist features, and Chapters 4 and 5 follow up by reviewing clist commands and concepts.

THREE WAYS TO INVOKE TSO COMMANDS

You can invoke TSO commands by entering them at a terminal, including them in a submitted batch (background) job, and executing a clist or, in TSO/E Version 2 and later, a REXX exec. This book has examples of all three ways. TSO commands can also be invoked from within a program (such as one written in COBOL.)

TSO COMMAND SYNTAX

Figure 2-1 shows four examples of TSO commands. It is not important to understand at this point what the commands do, but just observe the command syntax.

Figure 2-1. TSO Command Syntax

```
1. logon uid1/pword size(1024)
   1     2     3     4   5
2. logon uid1/pword s(1024)
   1       2     3  4  5
3. logon uid1/pword -
   1       2     3  6
   S(1024)
   4 5
4. listalc history /* Get history of each +
   1         4     7                     6
     dataset */
```

KEY
1 = TSO command
2 = Positional operand
3 = Multiple positional operand
4 = Keyword operand (with or without abbreviation)
5 = Keyword operand value
6 = Continuation flag (+ or −)
7 = Comments

Command Components

The following are the general rules used in creating the above TSO commands:

1. TSO commands may contain up to three components: the *command,* one or more *positional operands,* and one or more *keyword operands* with a possible operand value. Enter commands in *any case.* TSO commands may have an *alias,* or an alternate name (e.g., an abbreviation), for a command.
2. Separate operands with *commas* or *blanks.* Note LOGON's password operand and dataset names can use / as a delimiter.
3. You can *abbreviate* or fully spell operands. So, both S and SIZE are valid LOGON operands. Abbreviations need only the minimum number of characters to be different from other operands. For example, you need only S for identifying size if no other LOGON operand starts with that letter. However, if another operand starts with SI, then use SI to identify SIZE. You can use abbreviations and fully spelled operands together.
4. TSO treats a text string starting with \ * and ending with * \ as a *comment.* Even if placed after a TSO command, the comment does not execute when the command is processed. Note that a * \ is optional if it is the last character in a command.
5. If a command ends with a + or −, then it *continues* on the next line. The + also *eliminates leading blanks.* Example 4 places "dataset" one space after "each" and retains no leading blanks. However, example 3 retains the

leading blanks between PWORD and S(1024K). You can use comments and continuations in the same command, such as in example 4 in Figure 2.1.

6. A positional operand must be entered in a *particular sequence*. In examples 1 to 3, if typing just LOGON and pressing enter, TSO prompts for the USERID and PASSWORD operand values. The computer always "thinks" the first operand after LOGON is your USERID and the second is your password.
7. Keyword operands are "flags" for the computer to enable an option when executing a command. You may place keyword operands *in any order after positional operand*. Many keyword operands have default, or preassigned values, which you may be able to change. Some keyword operands have an additional value. (In the above examples, the keyword operand of SIZE has an additional value of 1024K.)

TSO COMMAND SUMMARY

Table 2-1 lists the TSO commands discussed in this chapter and their functions:

Table 2-1. Summary of TSO Commands

Function	Command/Alias	Typical Usage (can also be uppercase)
	Dataset Operations	
Allocate a dataset	ALLOCATE/ALLOC	alloc f(d1) da(book.text) – shr
Set a dataset's attributes	ATTRIB/ATTR	attrib dtest lrecl(80) – blksize(3120) alloc f(d1) da(book.text) new space(1,1) using (dtest) tracks
Copy a dataset	COPY	copy book.text–book1.text
Delete a dataset	DELETE/DEL	delete book.text
Editing a dataset	EDIT*	edit book.text old
Free a dataset	FREE	free f(d1) da(book.text)
List a dataset	LIST	list book.text
List dataset history	LISTALC/LISTA	lista status
List cataloged datasets	LISTCAT/LISTC	listc level('uid1')
List dataset characteristics	LISTDS/LISTD	listds d1
Print a dataset	†	†
Rename a dataset	RENAME/REN	rename book.text – newbook.text

Table 2-1. Summary of TSO Commands (*continued*)

Function	Command/Alias	Typical Usage (can also be uppercase)
	Batch Operations	
Canceling a batch job	CANCEL	cancel job1111
Displaying batch output	SDSF	sdsf h‡
Printing a batch job	SDSF	sdsf o‡
Status of a batch job	STATUS/ST	status job1111
Submitting a batch job	SUBMIT/SUB	sub book.text
	Other Operations	
Executing a clist	EXEC/EX§	exec cleanup
Accessing help	HELP/H	help allocate
Listing system bulletins	LISTBC/LISTB	listbc
Logging on to a terminal	LOGON	logon uid1/pword
Logging off a terminal	LOGOFF	logoff
Sending a message to another user	SEND/SE	send 'Hi' user(hhg1)
Session Manager commands	¶	¶
Display the current time and date	TIME	time

* You may use EDIT, QED, or PDF to edit datasets; see Chapters 7 and 10.
† Use PDF, PRINTDS (TSO/E Version 1 Release 4 for laser printers only.), the IBM-supplied ICQCPC10 clist, and PRINTOFF or DSPRINT commands for printing datasets. (Not all TSO sites have PRINTOFF/DSPRINT installed.)
‡ Although the OUTPUT command can both display and print a batch job, this chapter instead discusses the easier and more powerful SDSF (system log display and search facility).
§ Chapter 3 presents the EXECUTE command as part of an introduction to clists.
¶ Chapter 7 discusses Session Manager commands (i.e., commands starting with SM).
Note: Most commands may display a message and return to READY.

OTHER OPERATIONS COMMANDS

Getting On-line Help (HELP)

There is on-line help available for nearly every TSO command statement covered in Chapters 3 to 5. (However, see Appendix A for a third-party vendor offering this service.) Many TSO sites have their own help text that can be just informational and not associated with a command. The following are general guidelines for using the HELP or H command.

1. Entering HELP HELP from READY displays instructions and examples for using the HELP command.
2. Entering just HELP or H usually displays a list of valid TSO (non-clist)

commands. This is a good way to learn what system and local commands run under TSO at your site.

3. Entering HELP command name operands provides information about a desired TSO command or subcommand. (This is the command name positional operand.) The following keyword operands, in any order after the command name, specify what the HELP command displays.
   - ALL (the default) displays *all* of the information for a specific command or subcommand.
   - FUNCTION displays the tasks a command or subcommand performs.
   - OPERANDS displays all of the operands for a command or subcommand. Placing one or more operand names in parentheses displays information about just the specific operand. (Separate these operands by blanks or commas.)
   - SYNTAX displays all valid command formats.

EXAMPLES

1. / * *Display all help for LOGON command:*
   `help logon` *or* `help logon all` *or* `h logon all`
2. / **Displays all operands for the LOGON command:*
   `help logon operands`
3. *Displays help just on SIZE operand:*
   `help operands(size)`

Listing System Bulletins (LISTBC)

TSO usually keeps both system bulletins and messages sent to you with the SEND command (and the LOGON operand) in the SYS1.BRODCAST dataset. Both display after you log on. Note that your computer center staff creates and deletes system bulletins, *but TSO deletes personal messages from the SYS1.BRODCAST dataset after displaying them.* LISTBC can display system bulletins and unread personal messages any time during a TSO session. With TSO/E Version 1 Release 4 and later, you can save messages and bulletins to a log dataset.

If specifying LISTBC or LISTB without either the MAIL/NOMAIL and NOTICES/NONOTICES keyword operands, then TSO uses the defaults of MAIL and NOTICES. (Note that LISTBC has no positional operands.) The MAIL default displays your unread messages and NOTICES displays any system bulletins whether in SYS1.BRODCAST or a log dataset. (Log datasets are in TSO/E Version 1 Release 4 and later.) NOMAIL or NONOTICES does not display them.

EXAMPLES

1. *Displays all system bulletins and any unread messages:*
   `listbc` *or* `listbc mail notices` *or* `listb`
2. *When you want to display your unread messages only:*
   `listbc nonotices` *or* `listbc mail nonotices`

Entering and Exiting TSO (LOGON and LOGOFF)

You must know how to enter and exit a TSO session before using any TSO commands or writing clists. Here are some tips on doing this using the LOGON and LOGOFF commands.

Logging on to TSO

To log on, you must first get a userid and password from your computer center (and possibly other information such as account number). On entering a LOGON command, a cataloged procedure with JCL (Job Control Language) statements initiates the following steps.

1. Checks your userid, password, and region size against a master userid dataset that your computer center's security system (e.g., RACF, ACF2) defines or against SYS1.UADS.
2. Possibly checks your userid for an expired password. (If your site has a security package, you may have to change your password every 30 days.)
3. A line then connects to the mainframe with the default or user-specified region size.
4. Display any new mail or system bulletins if using the MAIL and NOTICES operands.
5. If accidentally "unplugged," you can reconnect to your previous session if you are on the same terminal.
6. A start-up file then executes and allocates appropriate files (such as IS-PFPROF for ISPF).
7. Finally, the READY prompt of TSO appears and you can enter TSO commands.

Your site determines if you enter LOGON operands as part of a command or as choices on a panel (or "full screen.") Full-screen LOGON operands are quicker to enter because of many preset choices and you need only enter an S (for select) rather than typing the entire operand. Figure 2-2 is a sample of a full-screen LOGON panel:

Figure 2-2. A Typical Full-Screen LOGON Panel

```
                --------TSO/E Logon--------
PF1/13 => Help  PF3/15=> Logoff  PA1 => Attn  PA2 => Reshow
You may request specific HELP information by entering a ' ? ' in any entry field.

ENTER LOGON PARAMETERS                    RACF LOGON PARAMETERS:
BELOW:
  USERID       ===> UID1
  PASSWORD     ===> PWORD                 NEW PASSWORD ===> PWORD2
  PROCEDURE    ===> LOGONA                GROUP IDENT   ===>
  ACCT NMBR    ===> 2358
  SIZE         ===> 1024
  PERFORM      ===>
  COMMAND      ===>
ENTER AN 'S' BEFORE EACH OPTION DESIRED BELOW:
-NOMAIL        -NONOTICE        -RECONNECT        -OIDCARD
```


You may also use the LOGON command for entering any operand appearing on the LOGON panel. Those operands that you, and not the security system, provide are discussed below. Here are some tips about LOGON:

1. To begin a different TSO session and end the current one, enter a LOGON command in the current session. Be certain that the next session retains the current settings of the TERMINAL command. (Terminal settings include attention, break, and clear screen manipulation.)
2. LOGON has two operands, positional and keyword

The positional operand consists of:

1. Userid—the one- to eight-alphanumeric-character TSO user account you use to access TSO. The eighth character is for batch job identifiers.
2. Current password is a one- to eight-alphanumeric-character "secret word" you now use to access TSO. You *must* correctly enter this password and have your center's security system (i.e., RACF or ACF2) recognize it.
3. New password is the secret word that overwrites the current password and is used from the next time you logon to TSO. A slash (/) separates new and old passwords.

Keyword operands consist of:

1. MAIL/NOMAIL and NOTICES/NONOTICES. These are the same as under LISTBC. See LISTBC above for further information.
2. RECONNECT, which logs on again if your line cuts off. The LOGON command ignores all other operands but userid and current password if using RECONNECT.
3. SIZE (size) sets the region size for the current TSO session. If not included, then TSO uses a default value from the master userid dataset. The SIZE operand is ignored if the set is larger than allowed by the master userid dataset.

EXAMPLES

1. *To log on as UID1 with a region size of 1024K and a password of PWORD:*
   `logon uid1/pword s(1024)` *or* `logon udi1/pword size(1024)`
2. *To log on as TRY1906 and change your password from APRIL to MAY:*
   `logon try1906/april/may`
3. *To receive all unread messages and system bulletins for UAX5698:*
   `logon uax5698/thatsme mail notices`
   or
   `logon uax5698/thatsme`

Logging Off TSO

When wanting to end a terminal session, enter LOGOFF. The LOGOFF command frees all allocated datasets and cuts off the line connected to the mainframe. Once processing the LOGOFF command, a message displays (usually very quickly) that you logged off at a certain time. (Other information such as CPU time and actual time used may also be displayed.) To begin a different TSO session and end the current one, enter a LOGON command in the current session.

EXAMPLE

1. *Ends your TSO session and to have no operands. A message saying that you logged off the display:*
   logoff

Sending a Message to Another User (SEND)

Sending messages to other users can be helpful in reaching several people or the console operator quickly. However, some use the SEND command for lengthy two-way informal conversations. (This is discouraged at many TSO sites.) Here is a summary of the SEND command:

POSITIONAL OPERANDS

1. **Text to send**—A message (enclosed in single quotes) of up to 115 characters.

KEYWORD OPERANDS

1. **USER(userid)**—A list of userids separated by commas or blanks to receive your message. *Messages with unspecified userids go to the console operator.*
2. **NOW**—Sends your message immediately. However, the message is lost if the user is not logged on. *NOW is the default value if not using the NOW or LOGON operands.*
3. **LOGON**—Saves your message until the user logs on and then sends it immediately. Messages are saved in the system broadcast dataset, SYS1.BRODCAST, or the user log dataset (TSO/E Version 1 Release 4 and later).

EXAMPLES

1. *Sends a message to another user immediately. (If he or she is not logged on at the time, the message is lost.) Note the abbreviation for the USER operand.):*
   ```
   send 'Learning TSO is a lot of fun' u(gru6)
   ```
2. *Send three users a message with the LOGON operand. (TSO saves the message if not logged on and then sends it immediately when the user(s) log on. The example uses the SE alias.):*
   ```
   se 'Our meeting is in room 2A' us(hfg1,yds6,jan0) l +
   ogon
   ```
3. *Sends a long message to the console operator, therefore no*/ userid is needed. (Note the continuation delimiter of –.):*
   ```
   send 'Can you cancel my current print job? I sent the -
   wrong job to the printer. Thanks'
   ```

Getting the Current Time and Date (TIME)

If your watch is unavailable, use the TIME command to display the current date, time, and CPU time usage since you logged on. It is also one of the easiest commands to learn.

1. TIME has no positional or keyword operands and displays in HH:MM:SS format with AM or PM also noted. Also use TIME to display both the CPU and actual time since you logged on.

EXAMPLE

1. *Displays the current local time of day and date:*
   `time`
   TSO displays something similar to this:
   ```
   TIME-10:00. . . .SESSION-00:03:45
   MARCH 15, 1990
   ```

TSO DATA TERMINOLOGY

This section reviews basic TSO dataset concepts that you must understand before discussing TSO dataset and batch operation commands. Further information can be found in the *TSO/E Primer, TSO/E User's Guide,* and *TSO User's Guide*.

What Is a Dataset?

Datasets are electronic "file folders" containing related information such as clist or Job Control Language (JCL) statements. One or more users during a TSO session may access a dataset, whether it is on tape or disk. Datasets used under TSO can have many formats, but many are 80 columns of data with columns 73 to 80 identifying the line numbers. However, datasets are often much larger. (Note that most text editors can only edit up to 251 columns.)

Dataset Organization (DSORG)

Dataset organization (DSORG for short) is how the dataset is physically arranged, providing a standardized means for access and processing. Two common file types are:

- *Sequential datasets* or *Physical sequential (PS) datasets*. These are datasets containing one large segment that is not separated into partitions. Sequential dataset records are arranged and read sequentially. (A *record* is one or more lines of data with information on a unique entity such as a person or a company. Note that you can go back to a previous record or the state of the file.) A typical use of sequential datasets is the large files of data and temporary datasets that TSO, clists, and batch operations create. Because sequential datasets are one large segment, there is no need to *compress* them to recover wasted space.

- *Partitioned datasets* (PDS for short) or *partitioned organization datasets* (PO) are datasets containing many segments or partitions called *members*. A member is similar to a sequential file because records are sequentially read once selected. A PDS directory keeps track of all members with information such as when created and last used. A typical use for partitioned datasets is storing related programs such as JCL, clists, language programs, and text files. Since a partitioned dataset usually saves all updated and deleted versions of its members (and these versions take up space), occasionally you must compress your dataset to recover the wasted space. (*Note:* Until compressing, a member is *logically,* but not physically, deleted. Thus, you can restore an accidentally deleted member if you have not yet compressed the dataset.)

Logical Record Length (LRECL) and Block Size (BLKSIZE)

The *logical record length* (or LRECL) and *block size* (or BLKSIZE) help determine the space needed for creating a TSO dataset. Logical record length is the length of the largest record in the dataset (i.e., the number of columns a record takes up or "how wide the record is").

A *logical record* is a piece of data to be processed as a unit. The *physical record* or *block* is an aggregate of data stored on a disk or tape to be read or written to the computer. (Many logical records may make up a physical record.) The result is:

> The block consists of one or more records, which are grouped together in a block for more efficient storage, and faster input and output processing. When the user requests a record from the supervisor, the supervisor reads the block, then doles out the logical record from the block one at a time. (Struble 1984b, p. 296) (*Author's note:* The MVS supervisor is responsible for obtaining the needed devices to read and write datasets and performing any dataset operations.)

Therefore the block size (or physical record size) is the length of the largest block (or data control block) in a dataset that a computer can read or write to. The record format decides both the logical record length and the block size.

Record Format (RECFM)

Record format (or RECFM) tells TSO how the dataset's records will look. Figure 2-3 summarizes the common record formats and their limitations on logical record length and block size:

Figure 2-3. Record Formats

Record Format	Description	Logical Record Length (LRECL)	Block Size (BLKSIZE)
F	Fixed	Equal to BLKSIZE	
FB or FBA	Fixed blocked	Total length of all fields	Integral multiple of LRECL (e.g., LRECL = 80, BLKSIZE = 8000)
V	Variable	Average length of record. No greater than BLKSIZE − 4	Equal to or greater than LRECL + 4
VB or VBA	Variable blocked	Same as V	Same as V

KEY
A = First column is reserved for ANSI carriage control characters
B = Records are in a blocked format
F = Records have a fixed length (i.e., always the same number of columns)
V = Records have a variable length (i.e., different-sized records)

File Disposition

File disposition gives the status of a dataset (i.e., does it exist or not), and what to do with it for normal and abnormal termination. The section on the ALLOCATE command includes file disposition types and their meanings. Knowing file dispositions is very important for background (batch) processing so that you can detect what happened to a dataset if a job abnormally terminates. Good batch users trace the disposition history of their JCL code, anticipating problems that occur during abnormal termination. One common file disposition mistake made by beginning JCL programmers is not realizing an abnormal termination defaults to the same setting as a normal one, so the computer could accidentally overwrite a dataset. Again, understanding file dispositions frees many hours of anguish.

File Space

To allocate datasets, use any of these units—*blocks* (BLKSIZE), *tracks* (TRK), *cylinders* (CYL) (from smallest to largest). The amount of data a track or cylinder stores depends on the storage device used. (Therefore, you use fewer units on a larger storage device.) The standard storage device (a disk or disk pack) can be thought of as collection of several "platters" on top of each other. Each pair of platters has a head to read or write data. Knowing this helps in understanding the following three space units.

- A *block* is an aggregate of data stored on a disk.
- A *track* is a concentric circle on the disk. (It does not always have the same circumference as other tracks.)
- A *cylinder* is a vertical set of tracks (or "taking a piece of a certain area of all platters").

You can allocate datasets with both *primary* and *secondary* allocations in the same unit. If the primary allocation is not large enough, the dataset overflows into the secondary allocation. (Allowing up to 16 "extents" or overflow space that may or may not be next to the dataset. *You should always have a large enough primary allocation and minimize overflow*.)

Dataset Names (DSNAME)

Dataset names must be unique for the computer to choose the correct dataset. *They should also be understandable to help you and others easily find the right dataset* (e.g., UID1.JUN88.GOLF.SCORES rather than X2386.DATA).

How to Name a TSO Dataset

TSO datasets usually have three parts:

1. Your userid or some prefix you have access to as determined by your security system.
2. A unique name you specify.
3. A valid descriptive qualifier.

Between each of the three parts are periods. Note that each part is called a *qualifier*. Figure 2-4 provides an example of a dataset name, and Table 2-2 lists common dataset descriptive qualifiers:

Figure 2-4. Dataset Name Example

```
     HHG1.SAMPLE.DATA
     1     2      3
1 =  Userid or an allowable prefix.
2 =  A unique name that you supply.
3 =  The descriptive qualifier.
```

Table 2-2. Common Dataset Descriptive Qualifiers

Name	Use
CLIST	Clists that contain TSO and clist statements, ISPF PDF edit macros
CNTL	JCL programs
COBOL	COBOL source programs
DATA	Data for programs and uppercase text files. (Data also can be in mixed case.)
FORT	FORTRAN source programs
HELP	Help library
LIST	Program listings, ISPF listings
LOAD	Load modules
MSG	ISPF message library
OBJ	Object modules
PANEL	ISPF panel library
SKEL	ISPF skeleton library
TABLE	ISPF table library
TEXT	Mixed-case text and data files

The following are the rules and conventions used in creating TSO dataset names:

1. Use as many qualifiers as needed as long as they are between 1 and 8 characters and the total dataset name is *no more* than 44 characters (with periods included). The following are invalid dataset names:
   `hhg1.badqualifier.text`
   Badqualifier is too large a qualifier (12 characters instead of 8).
   `hhg1.invalid.dataset.name.too.long.tobe.a.valid`
   46 characters in dataset name (only 44 allowed).

2. Valid qualifier characters are A to Z, and $, #, @, 0 to 9. *However, you cannot begin a qualifier with a number.* The following is an invalid dataset name:
   `1rr6.today.text`
   because it starts with a number.

3. You do not have to put the dataset name in quotes if using your default prefix or userid. However, if *accessing someone else's dataset,* then put the dataset name in *single quotes*. This is called a fully qualified dataset. If using your userid or prefix, *always* place it in single quotes or the computer will append a prefix to your dataset name. The system security software must

give you permission to access another person's dataset. The following examples show entering dataset names with both your userid and someone else's:

a. HHG1 is my userid. To access my own dataset called calendar.yr88, I use

`calendar.yr88` *or* `'hhg1.calendar.yr88'`

not

`hhg1.calendar.yr88`

TSO thinks this is hhg1.hhg1.calendar.yr88.

b. UIC1 is my userid and I am trying to access a dataset of CAHO's.

`'cah0.status.text'`

Always in quotes

DATASET OPERATIONS COMMANDS

Allocating a Dataset (ALLOCATE)

ALLOCATE, which creates temporary or permanent datasets, is one of the most powerful commands available to a TSO user. Some uses include creating datasets containing a clist or COBOL program and generating a SYSOUT dataset for printing reports or program output. ALLOCATE is the equivalent of the DD (data definition) statement in JCL.

For TSO/E users, you can specify the DCB (data control block) parameters in an ALLOCATE command as well as an ATTRIB command. TSO creates a data control block at execution time that serves as an input for opening a dataset. Most examples shown do not include an ATTRIB statement.

A major part of the ALLOCATE command is the use of dynamic allocation. *Dynamic allocation* is the process that automatically allocates datasets (including concatenated datasets), removes datasets from a concatenation, and performs dataset attribute tasks. *Concatenated datasets* are one or more datasets linked to the same filename or ddname (data definition name). An important point is that you must specifically free any dynamically allocated datasets—ALLOCATE does not do it for you. Table 2-3 lists common ALLOCATE operands.

Positional Operands

Enter *at least one* of the following:

1. **DATASET(dsname or *)** or **DA(dsname)** or **DSNAME(dsname)** or **DSN(dsname)**—The dataset or datasets (linked to the same file or ddname) to be allocated. Follow these rules when naming datasets (dsname).

   a. Look at TSO Data Terminology for general rules on dataset names.

Table 2-3. Common ALLOCATE Operands

Command/Alias	Positional Operand	Keyword Operand
ALLOCATE/ALLOC Operands	You must enter at least one of the following: 1. DATASET(dsname or *) or DSNAME(dsname or *) 2. FILE(ddname) or DDNAME(ddname) 3. DUMMY	*DCB* (data control block) BLKSIZE(size) REUSE TSO/E Only: DSORG(PO or PS) LRECL(lrecl) RECFM(A,B,F,V) *File Disposition:* MOD,NEW,OLD,SHR and CATALOG, DELETE KEEP, UNCATALOG DD (data definition) DIR(number) SPACE(p,s) su su = one only: BLOCK(blks) CYLINDERS TRACKS UNIT(utype) VOLUME(volnum) *Output:* COPIES(*number*) DEST(*location*) FORMS(*formname*) SYSOUT(*class*) Existing DCB: LIKE(dsname) or (for TSO/E Only) USING(attlnm)

b. Output written to the terminal files uses a dsname of *. It is allocated to the terminal in blocks and uses the DCB characteristics of any previous temporary files. You can use ATTRIB for specifying DCB attributes.

c. Dataset names for both single or concatenated files can include member names.

d. For *concatenated datasets:*

(1) *Do not use uncataloged datasets* or have more than 255 sequential datasets in a concatenation. PDSs are site-dependent.

(2) They must all have the *same record format* (RECFM) and ideally the same block size (BLKSIZE). If not including a BLKSIZE operand, TSO takes the block size of the first dataset. This causes problems if this is not the largest block size in the concatenation. *Therefore, a good programming practice is having concatenated datasets with the same block size or placing the dataset with the largest block size first.*

(3) To *deconcatenate a dataset,* use the FREE command with the same filename or data definition name (DDNAME) used by ALLOCATE to concatenate the datasets.

(4) Check your TSO or TSO/E command reference for the current available list of operands to use with concatenated datasets.

2. **FILE(ddname)** or **DDNAME(ddname)** assigns a filename or ddname (data definition name) to one or more datasets specified by the DATASET or DSNAME (operand). If not including file or ddname, TSO uses a system-supplied default. MVS reserves certain ddnames for special uses. These are listed below.

JOBCAT Specifies a catalog not in the user library for a batch job.

JOBLIB Performs dataset operations on members of a private library (a PDS) for a batch job. JOBLIB may include concatenations. STEPCAT and STEPLIB override it.

STEPCAT Specifies a private catalog to use in a batch job step and overrides JOBCAT.

STEPLIB Performs dataset operations on members of a private library (a PDS) in a batch job step and overrides JOBLIB. STEPLIB may include concatenations.

SYSABEND Produces a formatted dump of both system and user areas for a batch job. You can send SYSABEND output to any printer.

SYSCHK Sets a checkpoint where the batch job writes data into a checkpoint dataset and then restarts the program.

SYSCKEOV Sets a checkpoint at the end of volume (EOV) of a multivolume dataset (usually tapes) where the batch job writes data into a checkpoint dataset and then restarts the program.

SYSMDUMP Produces an unformatted dump of system areas that can be sent to any printer (after formatting).

SYSUDUMP Produces a formatted dump of user areas (i.e., your program) that can be sent to any printer.

It is only important that you understand that the above ddnames are reserved and not what they do. The *MVS/XA JCL Reference* or *MVS JCL* has more information on these ddnames.

3. **DUMMY**—Assigns a dummy or null dataset used by a batch job for testing steps and eliminate including some DD (data definition) parameters. Do not use a dummy dataset for input or output operations including any disk or tape device allocation and file disposition tasks.

Keyword Operands

DCB (Data Control Block) Operands. See the previous section for a more detailed explanation of these DCB parameters:

1. **BLKSIZE(size)**—The length of the largest block in a dataset to be read or written to by the computer. The size value cannot be larger than 32,760 and is also decided by the record format (RECFM) and logical record length (LRECL). Use Figure 2-3 as a guide in assigning BLKSIZE.
2. **DSORG(PO or PS)**—The type of dataset to allocate. *Physical sequential datasets* (PS) are datasets containing one large segment not separated into partitions. *Partitioned organization datasets* (PO) are datasets containing many segments or partitions (called *members*). *DSORG is in TSO/E only.*
3. **LRECL(lrecl)**—The average length of records in a dataset, i.e., the number of columns a record takes up. The record format (RECFM) and the block size help decide LRECL, which is based on bytes. Use Figure 2-3 in setting LRECL. *LRECL is in TSO/E only.*
4. **RECFM(A,B,F,or V)**—The record format specifies how records look. See Figure 2-3 for common record formats and their limits on logical record length and block size. *RECFM is in TSO/E only.*
5. **REUSE**—Used mostly for concatenations, the REUSE operand frees and then reallocates a currently allocated dataset. This does not work if another user has exclusive use of the file.

DISP (File Disposition) Operands. Select *one* from BOTH groups of file dispositions.

GROUP ONE

MOD Appends data at the end of a dataset while retaining existing data. You must give a dataset or dsname value. Also, you can use MOD for creating a dataset. This changes the file disposition to NEW when created.

NEW Creates a "fresh" dataset to be cataloged and kept if giving a dataset or dsname operand (otherwise it is deleted). Creation of a partitioned dataset requires a DIR operand.

OLD Allow *only* you to use an existing dataset (if uncataloged, add a VOL operand). You must give a dataset or dsname operand value.

SHR Allows you and others to use an existing dataset (if uncataloged, add a VOL operand). You must give a dataset or dsname operand value.

GROUP TWO

CATALOG Catalogs the dataset.
DELETE Erases and uncatalogs a dataset.
KEEP Holds onto the dataset.
UNCATALOG Erases but not deletes a dataset from a catalog.

DD (Data Definition) Operands. See TSO Data Terminology for additional information on space units.

1. **DIR(number)**—This operand specifies the number of directory blocks when creating a partitioned dataset with a NEW or MOD file disposition. Each block holds directory information for 4 to 21 members and takes up 256 bytes.
2. **SPACE(p.s) su (su = BLOCK(blks), CYLINDERS, or TRACKS)**—The disk or tape storage amount to use in allocating a dataset. Datasets allocations include both *primary* (p) and *secondary* (s) values in the same space units. If the primary allocation is too small, the dataset "overflows" into a secondary allocation of up to 16 extents. This is "overflow space" which may or may not be next to the dataset. *(You should always have a large enough primary allocation to minimize overflow.) Note:* If not giving a SPACE operand, then TSO uses a default space unit and allocation. Datasets are allocated by three different units: *tracks, cylinders,* and *blocks.* (The block value (blks) is multiplied by the primary allocation.)
3. **UNIT(utype)**—The device to allocate the dataset to. Unit names (utype) may be site-supplied (IBM3380) or generic (i.e., TAPE or DISK).
4. **VOLUME(volnum)**—1 to 255 tape or disk volume serial numbers that indicate where to find a dataset. Use a VOLSEQ operand (not discussed) to specify the starting volume of a multivolume dataset.

Output Operands. These ALLOCATE operands work only with the SYSOUT datasets. A SYSOUT dataset is allocated by the SYSOUT operand. Most of these operands were first available in TSO/E Version 1 Release 2. Those output operands not discussed are used to create sophisticated reports.

1. **COPIES(number)**—The number of copies of a SYSOUT dataset. If using COPIES, you must also give the number of copies because there is no default.
2. **DEST(location)**—A remote, never local, printer or device to send a SYSOUT dataset to. Locations are 1 to 8 characters.

3. **FORMS(formname)**—A standard form to print a SYSOUT dataset on. *Form names* are 1–4 non-integer characters.
4. **SYSOUT(class)**—Creates a SYSTEM OUTPUT or SYSOUT dataset used to print reports and program results. *Class* decides the output class and the available devices for display or hardcopy. TSO uses its own internal dataset name for SYSOUT datasets, so do not use the DATASET or DSNAME operands. SYSOUT datasets are deleted after processing.

Using Existing DCB Operands. ALLOCATE provides two different means for using preset DCB values. LIKE uses existing datasets and USING uses attribute lists created by the ATTRIB command. You can use one or the other, *but not both.*

1. **LIKE(dsname)**—Uses an existing dataset with some desired dataset attributes for creating a new dataset. You can only use LIKE for datasets with a file disposition of NEW and having a dataset or dsname value. If not wanting to use the LIKE dataset's DCB value, then overwrite it with the desired operand value.
2. **USING(attlnm)**—An attribute list name (attlnm) created by the ATTRIB command containing DCB values to be used in creating a new dataset. The attribute list must be created *before* the ALLOCATE command. *USING is in TSO/E only.*

EXAMPLES

1. *Allocates a new physical sequential dataset (For TSO/E only; TSO users use ATTRIB instead):*

```
alloc da('uid1.survey.data') fi(newdata) new +
dsorg(ps) +
block(13200) space (5,0) recfm(f,b,a) lrecl(132)
```

   a. Filename of new data is tied to the dataset name of uid1.survey.data and both operands are abbreviated. Single quotes and the uid1 first qualifier are not needed if uid1 is the default userid or prefix for this user.
   b. The space unit is BLOCKS and space quantity allocated is the block value (13200) multiplied by the primary space units (5), or 66,000. A secondary space unit of 0 indicates that no overflow units are allowed. TSO uses the default operands STORAGE UNIT and VOLUME because there are no UNIT or VOLUME operands. This is a NEW dataset to be cataloged.
   c. The record format is fixed-block (FB) and the first column is for carriage control characters (A). The dataset organization is a physical sequential (PS) dataset and the logical record length is 132 columns. A continuation symbol (+) joins the two lines.

2. *Allocates an existing sequential dataset:*
   ```
   alloc file(olddata) dataset(stat18.data) +
   unit(ibm3380) +
   vol(g38002) old
   ```
   a. Note filename can come before dsname.
   b. Local disk storage unit of ibm3380 and disk volume g38002 are specified because the dataset is uncataloged; otherwise they are not needed. OLD means only you can use this dataset while allocated.

3. *Allocates a new partitioned dataset (For TSO/E only: TSO users use ATTRIB instead):*
   ```
   alloc da(letter.text) f(letters) mod catalog dsorg(po) +
   space(10,10) tracks dir(10) lrecl(255) +
   blksize(259) + recfm(v b) retpd(25)
   ```
   a. The space unit is TRACKS and 10 primary and secondary tracks are specified. The secondary tracks use up to 16 extents. Ten directory blocks are allocated to hold information for between 40 to 120 members.
   b. Because the dataset does not exist and the file disposition operand is MOD, the disposition then resets to NEW. The dataset is also cataloged (CATALOG).
   c. The record format is variable-block (VB) and the block size is 4 plus the logical record length. The dataset retention period is 25 days. Note spaces or commas separate record format values. The dataset organization is a partitioned organization dataset (PO or PDS) and the logical record length is 255 columns.

4. *To allocate an existing dataset.*
   ```
   alloc dsn(memos.text(octstat)) dd(notes) shr
   ```
   a. Ddname of notes is tied to the dsname of memos.text and the member octstat. (Remember you can specify member name.) DDNAME or DD is an alternative to FILE or FI and you may use DSNAME or DSN instead of DATASET or DA. SHR states other users can use this existing dataset while you have it allocated.

5. *Allocates a SYSOUT dataset*
   ```
   alloc f (report99) sysout(a) forms(bigp) copies(5)+
   dest(prt1)
   ```
   a. A filename of report99 is tied to a SYSOUT (output) dataset. *You cannot specify a dataset name for a SYSOUT dataset.* The SYSOUT operand shows it is a SYSOUT dataset with an output class of A. Five copies of the output are made with the BIGP SYSTEM FORM. The output is sent to the remote location of PRT1.

6. *Allocates a dummy dataset*
   ```
   alloc f(dummy1) dummy block(1000)
   ```
   a. A filename of dummy1 is tied to a dummy dataset. *You cannot change the TSO-assigned NULLFILE dataset name.* The space unit is BLOCKS and the block value is 1000 (the *only* valid unit for dummy datasets). TSO ignores PAGE and FILE DISPOSITION operands for dummy datasets.

7. *Allocates a time sharing terminal.*
   ```
   alloc f(temp1) da(*) block(5000)
   ```
   a. A filename of temp1 is tied with the user's terminal. TSO assigns a name of TEMPFILE or TERMFILE to this operation. The space unit is BLOCKS and the block value is 5000 (the *only* valid unit for TEMPORARY datasets). TSO ignores SPACE and FILE DISPOSITION operands for temporary datasets.

8. *Concatenates datasets*
   ```
   alloc f(qtr1) da(jan.data,feb.data,mar.data) shr
   reuse
   ```
   a. A filename of qtr1 is tied to a concatenation of three datasets (jan.data, feb.data,mar.data). *The datasets are all the same block size or the largest block size is placed first.* The REUSE operand frees and then reallocates a currently allocated dataset. The concatenation fails if someone has exclusive use of the file.

9. *Using an ATTRIB attribute list*
   ```
   attrib list1 dsorg(po) recfm(f,b) blksize(3200) +
   lrecl(80)
   alloc f(fort1) da(plotit.fort) dir(6) +
   using(list1) new
   ```
   a. A filename of fort1 will be associated with the dataset of plotit.fort (a FORTRAN dataset). ATTRIB creates an attribute list called list1, which is used for creating a partitioned dataset (PO) with a fixed-block (FB) record format and a logical record length of 80 columns. Also specified is a block size of 3200.

   b. ALLOCATE creates this new dataset using the DCB operand value stored in the attribute list list1. The USING operand shows that an ATTRIB attribute list is used. If your system does not have default SPACE UNITS and SPACE QUANTITY, you are prompted for them.

10. *Using an existing dataset (TSO/E only)*
    ```
    alloc f(cl1) da(y.clist) blksize(8000) like(x.clist)
    ```
    a. A filename of cl1 is tied to the dataset y.clist. Since NEW is the only valid file disposition with LIKE, it does not need to be specified. The LIKE operand says ALLOCATE uses the DD and DCB parameters

from the model dataset x.clist in allocating y.clist. However, the default block size changes to 8000.

Creating a Dataset Attribute List (ATTRIB)

The ATTRIB command allows building "preset" lists of data control block (DCB) values for use by any ALLOCATE for new or existing datasets. After using an attribute list in an ALLOCATE command, you must unallocate it with the FREE command. Because ALLOCATE can now specify DCB values (since Version 1 Release 3), use of the ATTRIB command has declined. Table 2-4 lists common operands used by ATTRIB.

Positional Operands

1. **attlnm** is a unique attribute list name. The name follows the same rules as dataset qualifiers (i.e., 1 to 8 characters, start with A to Z, #, @, or $). To use a created attribute name list, place a USING operand with the attribute list name in an ALLOCATE statement.

Keyword Operands

See TSO Data Terminology for a further explanation on these DCB parameters:

1. **BLKSIZE(size)**—The length of a dataset's largest block. Size is not larger than 32760 and is also decided by the record format (RECFM) and logical record length (LRECL). Use Figure 2-3 in choosing a BLKSIZE.
2. **DSORG(PO or PS)**—The type of dataset to allocate. Physical sequential datasets (PS) are datasets with a large segment not separated into partitions. Partitioned organization datasets (PO) are datasets with many segments or partitions called *members*.
3. **EXPDT(yyddd)**—The first date a disk file can be deleted or overwritten. The EXPDT (expired date) value of yyddd is the deletion date (*YY is the last two digits in a year* and is between 00 to 99, while *ddd is the day of the year*

Table 2-4. Common Operands Used by ATTRIB

Command/Alias	Positional Operand	Keyword Operand
ATTRIB/ATTR	attlnm	BLKSIZE(size) DSORG(PO or PS) EXPDT(yyddd) LRECL(lrecl) RECFM(A,B,F,V) REPDT(days)

and is between 1 to 366). Deletion dates of 99365 and 99366 create permanent datasets. MVS/XA allows a deletion date up to the year 2155 with the format yyyy/ddd.

4. **LRECL(lrecl)**—The average length of records in the dataset, i.e., the number of columns a record takes up. LRECL is decided by the record format (RECFM) and the block size and is expressed in bytes. Use Figure 2-3 as a guide in determining LRECL.
5. **RECFM(A,B,F,or V)**—The record format specifies how the records look. Figure 2-3 lists common record formats and their limits on logical record length and block size.
6. **RETPD(days)**—The number of days to keep a dataset, with days being a value between 0000 and 9999. After that period of time, a dataset is erased or overwritten.

EXAMPLE

1. *Using an attribute list to create a dataset*

```
attrib pslist lrecl(255) blksize(25500) +
retpd(30) + dsorg(ps) recfm(f,b)

allocate f(tryit) da(trial1.data) using(pslist) +
space(10,10) tracks new
```

   a. ATTRIB creates the attribute list pslist. If called by ALLOCATE with the USING operand, it specifies a physical sequential dataset with a fixed-block record format, a retention period of 30 days, and a logical record length of 255 columns. ALLOCATE adds space and file disposition values to those set by ATTRIB.

Copying a Dataset (COPY)

A frequent task of TSO users is the copying of datasets (i.e., PDS member to a sequential file, sequential file to a PDS member, or a PDS to a PDS). The COPY command allows you to do this and more (such as copy to a new dataset, and reblock or renumber a dataset). *Note:* You must have exclusive use of the target ("to") dataset while copying with the COPY command.

Many TSO users do not realize that the COPY command is not a standard TSO command and therefore is not listed in the *TSO/E* or *TSO User's Guide*. Each site's COPY command may be "homegrown," public domain, IBM's version from the TSO Data Utilities (this is not recommended for TSO/E), or a third-party software package (such as Applied Software's Superset Utilities). Table 2-5 lists common COPY command operands.

Table 2-5. Common Operands Used by COPY

Command/Alias	Positional Operands	Keyword Operands
COPY	fromdataset todataset	ASCII BLOCK(blksize) LRECL(lrecl) NONUM NUM(bc1 length) *NUM is default.* NUM2(bc1 length) RECFM(A,B,F,V) RENUM(n1 incr)

Positional Operands

1. **fromdataset**—The source dataset or dataset to copy "from." The dataset name uses conventional TSO name syntax (see section titled "TSO Data Terminology"). The dataset may be a physical sequential file or a partitioned dataset.
2. **todataset**—The target dataset or dataset to copy "to." The dataset name follows the conventional TSO name syntax (see section titled "TSO Data Terminology"). The dataset may be a physical sequential file or a partitioned dataset.

Keyword Operands

See TSO Data Terminology for further information on block size, logical record length, and record format.

1. **ASCII**—Copies the target file and converts the source file from EBCDIC to ASCII. This is useful for exporting to microcomputers or minicomputers.
2. **BLOCK(blksize)**—The block size of the target dataset. Blksize cannot be larger than 32760 and is also decided by the record format (RECFM) and logical record length (LRECL). Use Figure 2-3 in choosing BLKSIZE. *Use BLOCK for reblocking a dataset or creating a target dataset with a different block size than the source dataset.*
3. **LREC(lrecl)**—The average length of records of the target dataset, i.e., the number of columns a record takes up. LRECL is decided by the record format (RECFM) and the block size and is expressed in bytes. Use Figure 2-3 as a guide in choosing a LRECL.

4. **NONUM**—Says the target dataset does not contain sequence numbers. *Use this for copying load modules.*
5. **NUM(bc1 length)**—Tells where the sequence numbers are in the source dataset. *BC1* is the starting column for sequence numbers and *length* is the sequence number's length. NUM is the default.
6. **NUM2(c1 length)**—Tells where the sequence numbers are to be in the target dataset. BC1 is the starting column for sequence numbers and length is the length of the sequence number.
7. **RECFM(A,B,F,or V)**—The record format specifies how the records look. Figure 2-3 lists common record formats and their limits on logical record length and block size.
8. **RENUM(n1 incr)**—Renumber the target dataset starting at line n1 with an increment of incr.

EXAMPLES

1. *Copy a dataset and convert to ASCII:*
   ```
   copy vers1.data vers2.data ascii
   ```
2. *Change the LRECL from 80 columns to 255:*
   ```
   copy olddata.data newdata.data lrecl(255)
   block(25500) + recfm(fba) renum(10 10)
   ```
   a. Copies olddata.data to newdata.data, changing the logical record length and block size. Also specified is a fixed-block record format with carriage control characters. Some COPY commands have DIR, SPACE UNITS, and DSORG operands. Unlike ALLOCATE, NO COMMAS OR BLANKS are needed to separate record format values. Renumbers the target dataset's sequence numbers starting with line 10 with an increment of 10.
3. *Copy from a PDS to a sequential file:*
   ```
   copy stat.fort(prog1) prog1.fort
   ```

Deleting a Dataset (DELETE)

One of the "house-cleaning" tasks TSO users perform is deleting unnecessary datasets. DELETE is a powerful command controlling the degree of deletion for both VSAM, non-VSAM datasets, and special cases (e.g., generation data groups, aliases, and user catalogs). *If the dataset is currently allocated, then you must issue* a FREE command before deleting—DELETE will not free it! However, if a deleted dataset is reallocated, it is not necessary to use FREE command; DELETE does the freeing for you.

Table 2-6. DELETE "Wildcard" Example

Command	Will Delete	Won't Delete
del 'uic1.*'	'uic1.text'	'uic1.letter.text'
del 'uic1.help.*'	'uic1.help.text'	'uic1.help.text.y1988' 'uic1.help2.text'

Use wildcards to delete a group of datasets "on the fly." (Wildcards are designated by an asterisk.) However, wildcards only work up to qualifier level specified. Thus, if you have two qualifiers and a wildcard in the second qualifier, datasets with three qualifiers are not deleted. This is clearly shown in Table 2-6. Table 2-7 shows common operands used with DELETE.

Positional Operand

1. **datasetname**—The dataset name may be a VSAM dataset, non-VSAM dataset, or special case (such as a user catalog, alias, or generation data group) and *the only required operand* (see the section titled "Dataset Names" earlier in this chapter). Multiple dataset names are allowed if in parentheses. You may also use wildcards to delete multiple datasets but they cannot be the first qualifier. (Only use fully qualified names with wildcards.)

Keyword Operands

1. **ALIAS**—Notes the dataset name is the alias for a member of a PDS. The ALIAS entry is deleted from the directory, but the main entry is kept.
2. **FILE(filename)**—The filename or ddname of the dataset to delete.
3. **NOPURGE or NPRG**—If the dataset's retention date has not passed, then do not delete the dataset. *This is the default.*

Table 2-7. Common Operands Used by DELETE

Command/Alias	Positional Operand	Keyword Operands
DELETE/DEL	datasetname	ALIAS FILE(filename) NOPURGE or NPRG *(NPRG is default)* NOSCRATCH or NSCR PURGE or PRG SCRATCH *(default)*

4. **NOSCRATCH or NSCR**—Does not delete the dataset from the disk volume's VTOC (volume table of contents). Only the catalog entry will be deleted. This is useful when a dataset has physically been removed from a volume, but the catalog entry has not yet been deleted.
5. **PURGE or PRG**—Deletes the dataset whatever the retention date.
6. **SCRATCH**—Scratches the dataset from the disk volume's VTOC. *SCRATCH is the default.*

EXAMPLES

1. *To delete a PDS with the defaults NOPURGE and SCRATCH:*
   `delete 'uic1.letter.text'`
   displayed:
   `IDC5001 ENTRY(A) UIC1.LETTER.TEXT DELETED`
   a. The dataset is purged only if the retention date has not passed. Also, the dataset is deleted from the disk volume's VTOC.

2. *To delete a sequential file whatever the retention date:*
   `delete jan11.data f(jandata) purge`
   a. The dataset is tied to the filename or ddname of jandata and is deleted whatever the retention date. The dataset is also deleted from the disk volume's VTOC. The computer gives a response similar to the first example.

3. *To delete more than one dataset with defaults:*
   `delete ('uic1.*.text' 'uic1.march.help')`
   a. The datasets are purged only if the retention date has not passed. Also the datasets are deleted from the disk volume's VTOC (volume table of contents). The computer gives a response similar to the first example. The following datasets are deleted: (1) All datasets starting with uic1 and ending with text. (Remember wildcards require fully qualified dataset names.); and (2) uic1.march.help.

Printing a Dataset (DSPRINT)

TSO offers many different ways to print datasets. Of these, PRINTDS (TSO/E Version 1 Release 4 and later) is a standard TSO/E command and has the best features of all other print commands. However, DSPRINT is more commonly used. (ISPF's foreground print functions use DSPRINT). So, the operands and syntax of DSPRINT are presented. Table 2-8 provides a summary of each command. Table 2-9 lists the operands used with DSPRINT.

Table 2-8. TSO Print Commands

Command	Advantages/Uses	Disadvantages/Limitations
DSPRINT	Line printers Print line ranges Margin setting Single/double spacing Carriage control characters	No portrait/landscape operand No enhanced laser printer support Cannot print an entire PDS No multiple copies No script (DCF) files
ICQCPC10	Laser printer Features Number of copies	No single/double space No carriage control characters No script files No portrait/landscape operand
PRINTDS	Print an entire PDS or just directory Carriage control Characters Single/double spacing Margin setting Print script files Print line ranges Title on each page Laser printer features	Must have TSO/E Version 1 Release 4 or TSO Version 2. No portrait/landscape operand
PRINTOFF	Print an entire PDS or just directory Single/double spacing Multiple copies Print line ranges	No landscape/portrait operand No carriage control characters No enhanced laser printer support No script files

Table 2-9. Common Operands Used by DSPRINT

Command/Alias	Positional Operand	Keyword Operand
DSPRINT	datasetname printername	BMARGIN (margin) CCHAR COL(c1:c2) DOUBLE LINES(l1:l2) NONUM PAGELEN(plen) SINGLE TMARGIN (margin)

Positional Operands

1. **datasetname**—Dataset names follow TSO dataset qualifier naming conventions mentioned in TSO Data Terminology. *This is a required operand.*
2. **printername**—A line printer name known to TSO. *This is a required operand.*

Keyword Operands

1. **BMARGIN(margin)**—Overrides the default number of empty lines at the bottom of a page (usually site- or printer-dependent).
2. **CCHAR**—Recognizes most carriage control characters if in the first column of a FBA or VBA dataset.
3. **COL(c1:c2)**—Prints a range of columns with c1 as the "from or start" column and c2 the "to or end column." Up to 32 pairs of c1:c2 may be used. The default for c2 is the last column.
4. **DOUBLE**—Prints the output with double spaces.
5. **LINES(l1:l2)**—Prints only a range of the dataset with l1 as the "from or start" line and l2 the "to or end" line. The default for l2 is the last line of the dataset.
6. **NONUM**—Prints dataset as if each line does not contain numbers.
7. **PAGELEN(plen)**—Overrides the default (usually site- or printer-dependent) page length.
8. **SINGLE**—Prints the output with single spaces
9. **TMARGIN(margin)**—Overrides the default number of empty lines at the top of a page (usually site- or printer-dependent.)

EXAMPLES

1. *DSPRINT with just dataset and printer name:*
   ```
   dsprint test1.data prt1
   ```
   a. Prints test.data at system line printer prt1. The printer or site margin defaults are used.
2. *DSPRINT with set margins, page length, and spacing, for a specified range of rows and columns.*
   ```
   dsprint letter.text(sales1) prt1 pagelen(66) +
   tmargin(5) +
   bmargin(5) lines(5:61) col(2:5) single
   ```
   a. Prints member sales1 of letter.text at prt1. *Only lines 5 through 61 and columns 2 through 5* are used. The page length is 66 and the output has a top and bottom margin of 5 blank lines. The output is printed in single space.

Editing a Dataset—An Overview

Like printing, there are many different ways in TSO to edit a dataset. These are listed in Figure 2-5. A complete discussion of TSO editors is available in Chapters 7 and 10.

Freeing a Dataset (FREE)

The best way to start a discussion on the FREE command is reviewing why it is used:

1. The TSO ALLOCATE command uses dynamic allocation to automatically allocate its datasets. However, you are currently responsible for freeing dynamically allocated datasets; ALLOCATE does not this for you.
2. The TSO DELETE command does not free a currently allocated dataset before deleting it.
3. The TSO ALLOCATE command also does not free an attribute list after processing it. This list is specified by the USING operand.

Therefore, until some future release of TSO/E has dynamic frees to take care of the above conditions, you are stuck with using the FREE command. FREE also changes the output class, disposition, or destination of a SYSOUT file. Table 2-10 lists common operands used with FREE.

Positional Operands

1. Enter at least one of the following:
   a. **ATTRLIST(attlnm)**—Frees an ATTRIB-created attribute list.
   b. **DSNAME(dsname) or DATASET(dsname)**—Names one or more datasets to free. Member names can also be used.
   c. **DDNAME(ddname) or FILE(ddname)**—Frees one or more datasets tied to a filename or ddname.

Figure 2-5. A Summary of TSO Editors and Their Capabilities

EDIT	Line editor; can be used by clists.
PDF	Part of ISPF; full-screen editor with macro capabilities. Edit macros can be used by clists.
QED	Line editor with optional full-screen capabilities; can be used by clists.

Table 2-10. Common Operands Used by FREE

Command/Alias	Positional Operands	Keyword Operands
	Enter at least one:	ALL TSO/E only
FREE	ATTRLIST(attlnm)	DEST(location)
	DSNAME(dsname)	
	DATASET(dsname)	Use only one:
	DDNAME(ddname)	CATALOG
	or	DELETE
	FILE(ddname)	KEEP
		SYSOUT(class)
		UNCATALOG

Keyword Operands

1. **All**—Frees all currently allocated unused datasets, SYSOUT files, and attribute lists (*TSO/E only*).
2. **DEST(location)**—Frees a remote location (usually a printer that is identified with one to eight characters). If not using DEST when freeing a SYSOUT dataset, TSO uses the location set at allocation time (whether by you or by the system, based on output class or default values).
3. Only one of the following may be selected:
   a. **CATALOG**—Catalogs a dataset after freeing.
   b. **DELETE**—Erases and uncatalogs a dataset after freeing. This is the only valid file disposition for SYSOUT datasets. The DELETE file disposition is invalid for datasets currently allocated as SHR or a PDS member.
   c. **KEEP**—Holds onto a dataset after freeing.
   d. **SYSOUT(class)**—Frees a SYSOUT file of a specific output class.
   e. **UNCATALOG**—Erases the dataset name entry from the catalog but does not delete it after freeing.

EXAMPLES

1. *Frees all currently allocated, unused datasets (TSO/E only).*
```
free all
```
   a. FREE ALL also frees currently allocated unused SYSOUT files and attribute lists.
2. *Frees multiple datasets, but does not delete them.*
```
free da(report1.cobol,report2.cobol) keep
```

3. *Frees an attribute list.*
   `free attrlist(atlist1)`
4. *Changing the output class of a SYSOUT dataset.*
   `free sysout(x)`
   a. Changes the output class of all currently allocated SYSOUT files to x. Remember DELETE is the only valid file disposition for SYSOUT datasets. You may be prompted for the names of the SYSOUT files.

Listing a Dataset

Like COPY, your site's LIST command may be homegrown, public domain, part of the IBM TSO Data Utilities, or a third-party command. Because LIST is not a standard TSO command, it is not described in the *TSO/E User's Guide*. LIST, like DSPRINT, can output just part of a sequential file. Table 2-11 gives common operands used with LIST.

Positional Operand

1. **datasetlist**—The list of datasets, separated by commas to be displayed. Datasetlist may include members (but not the complete) partitioned dataset. *This is a required operand.*

Keyword Operands

1. **COL(c1:c2)**—Displays a range of columns with c1 as the "from or start" column and c2 the "to or end column." Up to 32 pairs of c1:c2 may be used. The default for c2 is the last column.
2. **r1**—The first record number to display. If using r1 alone, then the default for r2 is the last record in a file. r2 is the last record number to display.
3. **NONUM**—Displays dataset as if each line does not contain numbers.

Table 2-11. Common Operands Used with LIST

Command/Alias	Positional Operand	Keyword Operand
LIST	datasetlist	COL(c1:c2) r1 r2 NONUM NUM(bc1,length) num is default SNUM(bc1,length)

4. **NUM(bc1,length)**—Tells where the sequence numbers are in a dataset. bc1 is the column where the sequence numbers start and length is the sequence number's length. This is similar to the SNUM operand, but NUM displays the sequence number at the beginning of a record.
5. **SNUM(bc1 length)**—Tells where the sequence numbers are in a dataset. bc1 is the column where the sequence numbers start and length is the sequence number's length. This is similar to the NUM operand, but SNUM *does not* display the sequence number at the beginning of a record.

EXAMPLE

1. *Displaying a dataset for selected columns and records*
   `list comm.data 2 10 snum(1 8) col(10:80)`
   a. Display the numbered dataset comm.data for records 2–10 and columns 10–80. The dataset does include sequence numbers starting in column 1 with a length of 8, but they are not shown.

Listing Allocated Datasets (LISTALC)

While using TSO, users often must display their currently allocated datasets (e.g., dynamically allocated, temporary, and attribute list datasets) and see information about the datasets. The LISTA or LISTALC command easily performs this task. Table 2-12 lists common operands used with LISTALC.

Positional Operands

1. There are no positional operands for LISTALC. *However, if entering LISTALC or LISTA, TSO displays a list of files now allocated.*

Table 2-12. Common Operands Used with LISTALC

Command/Alias	Positional Operands	Keyword Operands
LISTALC/LISTA	None	HISTORY MEMBERS STATUS SYSNAME

Keyword Operands

1. **HISTORY**—Lists the dataset organization (DSORG), the dates when a file was created and to be deleted (retention or expiration date), and if the file is password-protected.
2. **MEMBERS**—Lists members of partitioned datasets (PDS) having your userid or default prefix as the first qualifier. It also indicates if a member name is an alias.
3. **STATUS**—Lists filenames or ddnames, and the normal and abnormal file dispositions of datasets now allocated.
4. **SYSNAMES**—Lists the complete dataset names of system-created datasets (such as temporary files.)

EXAMPLES

1. *Lists just all currently allocated files except those with system-generated temporary names.*

   ```
   lista or listalc
   ```
   displayed (partial listing) :
   ```
   NULLFILE
   TERMFILE
   UIC1.LETTER.TEXT
   ```

2. *Lists members of partitioned datasets beginning with your userid or default prefix and the history of all currently allocated datasets.*

   ```
   Lista members history
   ```
   displayed (partial listing):
   ```
   ---DSORG---CREATED---EXPIRES---SECURITY
   UIC1.LETTER.TEXT
      PO      01/26/88    00/00/00    NONE
      LETTER1
      LETTER2
   ```
   a. Lists creation and retention dates, dataset organization (e.g., PO for partitioned datasets), and password protection flag for all currently allocated datasets. Also displays the members of datasets starting with your userid or default prefix.

3. *Lists the normal and abnormal file dispositions of datasets now allocated and the names of system-created datasets.*

   ```
   listalc status sysnames
   ```

displayed (partial listing):

```
--DDNAME---DISP---
UIC1.LETTER.TEXT
 SYS00028 KEEP,KEEP
```

a. In the above example, uic1.letter.text is tied to the system name of SYS00028 and has a KEEP status for normal and abnormal termination.

Listing Cataloged Information about Datasets

LISTCAT or LISTC easily displays information from a catalog on non-VSAM and VSAM datasets. In addition to the abbreviations from the minimum number of identifying characters, many LISTC operands have preset abbreviations (i.e., OFILE for OUTFILE). Table 2-13 lists common operands used with LISTCAT.

Positional Operand

1. There are no positional operands for LISTCAT. *However, if entering just LISTCAT or LISTC, TSO displays a list of all entries in the master catalog.*

Keyword Operands

1. **ALIAS**—Lists cataloged dataset aliases.
2. **CREATION(days)**—Lists cataloged datasets if created *before* the number of days specified by the days value. An example is CREATION(5), which lists those cataloged datasets created before 5 days ago.

Table 2-13. Common Operands Used with LISTCAT

Command/Alias	Positional Operands	Keyword Operands
LISTCAT/LISTC	None	ALIAS CREATION(days) EXPIRATION(days) LEVEL(lvl) or LVL(lvl) OUTFILE(ddname) or OFILE(ddname) Select only one: ALL ALLOCATION HISTORY NAME (the default) VOLUME

3. **EXPIRATION(days)**—Lists cataloged datasets if expiring *before* a number of days from now (specified by the days value). An example is EXPIRATION(10), which lists those cataloged datasets expiring during the next 10 days.

4. **LEVEL(lvl) or LVL(lvl)**—The criteria of the cataloged datasets to list. The lvl value uses one or more dataset qualifiers and may include wildcards (*) for the second or greater qualifier. (An example is listc lvl('uic.*.data'), which looks for cataloged datasets starting with UIC1 and have DATA as a third qualifier.) *If not using LEVEL, then only datasets starting with your userid or default prefix are listed.*

5. **OUTFILE(ddname) or OFILE(ddname)**—Sends a catalog listing to a file instead of the terminal. Ddname is the filename or data definition name of a dataset created by ALLOCATE. The default outfile dataset is a VBA (i.e., column 1 is used for carriage control characters) file with a logical record length of 125 (but 121 columns in the dataset) and a block size of 629. The dataset name is SYSPRINT.

6. Select *only one* of the following:
   ALL—Gives the same listing as using the ALLOCATION, HISTORY, NAME, and VOLUME operands together.

   ALLOCATION—Gives the same listing as VOLUME plus allocation information.

   HISTORY—Lists the dataset name, the creator's userid, the creation, and expiration dates. ALL, VOLUME, or ALLOCATION operands list the same information.

   NAME—Lists the dataset name and is the default operand. ALL, LOCATION, HISTORY, and VOLUME list the same information.

   VOLUME—Gives the same listing as HISTORY plus the entry type, volume serial number, and device type. The ALL and ALLOCATION operands list the same information. Figure 2-6 lists how much information the five operands give.

EXAMPLES

1. *Lists names of cataloged datasets for your userid or default prefix.*
   `listcat uic1` *or* `listc uic1`
   displayed (partial listing):
   IN CATALOG: SYS1.GTOL.CATALOG
   UIC1.CLIST
   UIC1.FORT

Figure 2-6. Relative Amounts of Information Given by LISTCAT Keyword Operands

Most Information	ALL
/ \	ALLOCATION
|	VOLUME
|	HISTORY
\ /	NAME
Least Information	

2. *Lists cataloged COBOL partitioned datasets for HHG1 created before 6 days ago.*

```
alloc f(sysprint) da(list.it) new space(1,1) +
   lrecl(125) tracks recfm(v b a) blksize(629)
listc lvl('hhg1.*.cobol') creation(6) ofile(sysprint) +
   all
list list.it
```

displayed (partial listing):

```
IDCAMS SYSTEM SERVICES + TIME: 08:10:11 08/22/88
Page 1
NONVSAM----HHG1.OLD.COBOL
IN-CAT ---SYS1.GTOL.CATALOG
 HISTORY
   OWNER-IDENT------(NULL)      CREATION----87.303
   RELEASE--------------2     EXPIRATION--00.000
 VOLUMES
   VOLSER------------S0001
```

   a. Note the datasetname is in quotes because the first qualifier is not your userid or default prefix.
   b. The catalog listing is sent to a SYSPRINT file. This information includes catalog name, dataset name, file creator, creation and expiration date (in a yy.ddd format), and volume serial number.

3. *Lists history information for selected datasets.*

```
listcat expiration(10) history
```

   a. Lists cataloged datasets starting with your userid or default prefix that expire during the next 10 days. This includes catalog name, dataset name, file creator's userid, creation and expiration dates (in a yy.ddd format), and volume serial number.

List Dataset Attributes (LISTDS)

The LISTDS or LISTD command displays information about selected datasets. Table 2-14 lists common operands used with LISTDS.

Table 2-14. Common Operands Used with LISTDS

Command/Alias	Positional Operand	Keyword Operands
LISTDS/LISTD	datasets	HISTORY LEVEL MEMBERS STATUS

Positional Operands

1. **datasets**—The search criterion of datasets to display attribute information. Dataset names may include member names (for listing directory information) or one or more dataset qualifiers if used with LEVEL. Wildcards (*) may be used for the second or greater qualifier. An example is listds 'uic.*.data', which displays attribute information for cataloged datasets starting with UIC1 and having data as the third qualifier. *No aliases can be in the datasets list.* If using no keyword operands, LISTDS lists the volume serial number, logical record length (LRECL), block size (BLKSIZE), and dataset organization (DSORG) for selected datasets.

Keyword Operands

1. **HISTORY**—Lists a dataset's creation date, expiration date, and password protection indicator.
2. **LEVEL**—Notes the values of the positional operand are one or more dataset qualifiers rather than complete dataset names. *No multiple datasets and wildcards (*) for the positional operand when used with LEVEL.*
3. **MEMBERS**—Lists the members and aliases of a partitioned dataset (PDS).
4. **STATUS**—Lists the dataset's filename or ddname, and the normal and abnormal file disposition (valid disposition values are CATALOG, DELETE, KEEP, and UNCATALOG).

EXAMPLES

1. *List the attribute of a selected dataset:*
   `listd help.text`
   displayed:
   UIC1.HELP.TEXT
   --RECFM-LRECL-BLKSIZE-DSORG
   FB 80 6160 PO
   a. Lists the volume serial number, logical record length, block size, and

dataset organization of a dataset. UIC1.HELP.TEXT is a partitioned, fixed-block dataset with a logical record length of 80 and a block size of 6160.

2. *List history, file dispositions, and member names for multiple datasets selected by a wild card.*
   `listds 'uicl.*.text' status history members`
   displayed (partial listing)

```
  UIC1.HELPDOCS.TEXT
--RECFM-LRECL-BLKSIZE-DSORG-CREATED---EXPIRES-SEC-
DDNAME-DISP
 VB     255    6160     PO    03/03/87      * *    NONE
SYS052  KEEP
--VOLUMES--
S008
--MEMBERS--
HELP1
HELP2
```

   a. The selected datasets begin with UIC1 and have TEXT as the third qualifier. STATUS, HISTORY, and MEMBERS show the dataset's ddname, normal/abnormal file disposition, creation/expiration dates, password protection flag, member, and aliases.

3. *Using the LEVEL operand:*
   `listds 'uicl.status' level`
   displayed:

```
UIC1.STATUS.TEXT
--RECFM-LRECL-BLKSIZE-DSORG
  FB     80     6160     PS
```

   a. One sequential dataset starting with UIC.STATUS is displayed.

4. *Listing directory information for a PDS member:*
   `listds 'rtg4.plotxy.fort(run1)'`
   displayed:

```
RTG4.PLOTXY.FORT
--RECFM-LRECL-BLKSIZE-DSORG
FB     80     6160     PO
--VOLUMES--
S008
--MEMBER---TTR-----ALIAS-TTRN-CNT-DATA
  RUN1       000120   YES    0     00
```

   a. The member listing shows RUN1 is an alias.

Renaming Datasets and Dataset Members

Suppose you want to copy a file into a member of a partitioned dataset but that member name now exists. All you would have to do is rename the existing member to a different name and then proceed with the copy. Other use of RENAME are creating an alias for a partitioned dataset member and changing the name of an entire cataloged dataset. Table 2-15 lists common operands used with RENAME

Positional Operands

1. **olddsn**—The current (''before renaming'') dataset name. The dataset name may use wildcards (*) or member names. Note that renaming does not change the current wildcard qualifier name.
2. **newdsn**—The latest (''after renaming'') dataset name. The dataset name may use wildcards (*) or member names. Note that renaming does not change the current wildcard qualifier name. An alias or member name, but not the complete dataset name, is allowed *if in parentheses*.

Keyword Operand

1. **ALIAS**—NEWDSN value is an alias for a member of a partitioned dataset (PDS)

EXAMPLES

1. *Renames a physical sequential or partitioned dataset:*
   `ren 'gr00.stat88.text' 'gr00.oldstat.text'`
   a. Changes the second qualifier for a TEXT dataset. Depending on the user's other dataset names, wildcards could be used.

2. *Rename a PDS member:*
   `rename 'metx.subr.fort(oldprog)' (newprog)`
   a. Renames a member from OLDPROG to NEWPROG. Note for the NEWDSN operand, you just specify the member name if in parentheses.

Table 2-15. Common Operands Used with RENAME

Command/Alias	Positional Operands	Keyword Operand
RENAME/REN	olddsn newdsn	ALIAS

3. *Creating a member alias:*
   `ren info.text(report) (rpt1) alias`
   a. Creates an alias of RPT1 for member REPORT. Note for the NEWDSN operand, you just specify the alias name if in parentheses.

4. *Using wildcards to rename datasets.*
   `rename 'jpd2.*.help' 'jpd2.*.text'`
   a. Renames all files with HELP as the third qualifier to TEXT. The second qualifier is unchanged after renaming.

A QUICK LOOK AT BATCH PROCESSING AND JCL

This section reviews batch processing, Job Control Language (JCL), and the TSO and ISPF commands you can use with batch processing.

What Is Batch Processing?

Batch, or *background, processing* offers users a means to submit one or more jobs to be scheduled for later execution. When a job executes depends on the job's size, the resources needed by the job, and also what other batch jobs are scheduled. The major advantage of batch processing for users is that by running in background, the user can still perform interactive processing. Its major disadvantage for users is the long time it takes to debug a batch job using trial and error.

Under MVS, JES (or job entry subsystem) performs many of the "behind-the-scenes" activities of batch processing, including:

1. Reading the batch job into the computer
2. Determining the priority of a batch job
3. Controlling the output processing
4. Deallocating resources

Because it is the resource and scheduling manager of batch processing, all batch jobs begin and end with JES.

What Is JCL?

JCL (job control language) is the way you "talk" to JES and control batch processing. Here are some things you can do with JCL:

- Set how JES prioritizes, selects, and ends your batch jobs.
- Choose the resources a batch job uses, such as datasets, tape devices, or disk devices.

- Control the normal/abnormal file disposition of datasets.
- See if all parts of a batch job (called *job steps*) are processed.

What Is the Syntax of JCL?

JCL statements are stored in 80-byte records as datasets using the descriptive qualifier CNTL. This is only a brief overview of JCL syntax and I encourage you to look at the *MVS/XA JCL User's Guide* or *MVS JCL* for further help. The most popular non-IBM text on JCL is Gary DeWard Brown's *System/370 Job Control Language* (1977).

1. *JCL statements begin in columns 1 and 2* with a // (JCL command), or /* (end of a data stream). A comment statement starting with //* is allowed. Columns 3 to 71 are used for the remaining JCL statement.
2. To *continue* a statement, stop after an appropriate parameter, begin the next line with // and *start the remaining JCL statement in columns 4 to 16.*
3. JCL statements have the following format:
   //NAME TYPE OPERANDS COMMENTS
   a. **NAME**—Starts in column 3 with 1 to 8 characters and follows standard TSO qualifier name syntax (see TSO Data Terminology).
   b. **TYPE**—Generally one of the three following types:
      (i) JOB—Job card containing accounting, security, resource, and priority information.
      (ii) EXEC—Run a program or procedure. This starts a *job step.*
      (iii) DD—Data definition card similar to TSO's ALLOCATE.
   c. **OPERANDS**—Operands may contain multiple *parameters* (separated by commas) and *subparameters* (usually in parentheses). Note that embedded blanks or special characters must be in single quotes, and many parameters and subparameters have default values. There are two types of parameters and subparameters—*positional* (where the parameter's meaning is based on its order) and *keyword* (which can be placed in any order and has the format of *operand = parameter*).
   d. **COMMENTS**—Comments may start at least with one blank space after the last parameter and in a comment (//*) statement.

To clarify this, let us look at a simple (one-step) JCL job (JCL statements are numbered to explain the job.) in Figure 2-7. Line 1 is the *JOB statement* and contains your *JOB ID,* which is your userid or default prefix plus a letter or @, #, $. The two positional parameters are *accounting information* (site-dependent and 1 to 142 characters long) and *programmer's name,* which is also site-dependent and uses 1 to 20 characters to identify who is submitting the job. The programmer's

Figure 2-7. Simple JCL Job

```
Columns
                          1
   1  4                   6
 1. //TAG1708A JOB (13666), 'JCL EX.',TIME=2,CLASS=A,
 2. //   MSGCLASS=H,REGION=1024K,MSGLEVEL=(1,1),NOTIFY=TAG1708
 3. //*********************************************************************
 4. //*SIMPLE JCL PROGRAM                                                  *
 5. //*********************************************************************
 6. //STEP1       EXEC PGM=IEFBR14
 7. //DATA01      DD DSN=TAG1708.TEST1.DATA,   COMMENT
 8. //               DISP=(NEW,CATLG,DELETE),
 9. //               DCB=(DSORG=PS,RECFM=FB,LRECL=255,BLKSIZE=25500),
10. //               SPACE=(CYL,(2,2)),UNIT=SYSDA
```

name is in quotes because of an embedded blank. The two keyword parameters are *time* and *class*. The time parameter states the batch job can run no longer than 2 minutes and will run in job class A. (At some sites, JES selects the job class based on the time and number of tapes used by the job.) The comma after class means the JCL statement continues.

```
JOBID       = TAG1708A
ACCOUNTING  = 13666
PROGRAMMER  = 'JCL EX.'
TIME        = 2
CLASS       = A
```

The JOB statement continues into line 2 in column 4 and sets these keyword parameters. MSGCLASS=H puts the job log in output class H. (But not program output, unless SYSOUT=* is in a DD statement. Again this is site-dependent, but usually a hold class.) REGION=1024K gives the batch job 1024K of virtual storage. NOTIFY=TAG1708 sends TAG1708 a message when the batch job is completed.

```
MSGCLASS = H
REGION   = 1024K
NOTIFY   = TAG1708
```

Lines 3 to 4 are comment statements. Use "flowerboxes" (boxes of asterisks) to easily find your comments. Line 5 is a comment statement that "closes" the flowerbox.

Line 6, the EXEC statement, marks the start of job step STEP1 and uses the program IEFBR14. IEFBR14 is a JCL utility and is called the "do-nothing utility." IEFBR14 does catalog maintenance, allocates files (like the example), and conditions code or program statements.

```
JOBSTEP = STEP1
PROGRAM = IEFBR14
```

The *DD statement,* line 7, allocates a new file called TAG1708.TEST1.DATA and a ddname or filename of DATA01. An example of adding a comment at the end of a JCL statement is provided. This statement continues on the next three lines. *Note:* To improve clarity of your DD statements, always code each DD parameter on a new line and place each new line under the first DD statement.

```
DATASET
 NAME    =  TAG1708.TEST1.DATA
DDNAME   =  DATA01
```

Line 8 gives the file dispositions of the new dataset. This line says that the *status* is new (dataset does not exist), and if the batch job ends *normally* (with a zero condition code), then CATALOG the dataset, otherwise DELETE it. This statement continues on the next two lines.

```
STATUS        = NEW
NORMAL
DISPOSITION = CATLG
ABNORMAL
DISPOSITION = DELETE
```

The *data control block* (DCB) parameters are set on lines 9 and 10. The dataset is a *physical sequential, fixed-block* file with a *logical record length* of 255 and a block size of 25500. The *space units* are *cylinders* (CYL) with two primary and secondary cylinders (up to 16 extents.)

Canceling a Batch Job

Although the CANCEL and STATUS commands are mostly replaced by SDSF (System Log Display and Search Facility), they are still useful. CANCEL ends execution of a batch job and deletes output from an output queue. CANCEL does not delete jobs already printing. If a job has been canceled, READY is displayed. Table 2-16 gives common operands used with CANCEL.

Table 2-16. Common Operands Used with CANCEL

Command/ Alias	Positional Operand	Keyword Operand
CANCEL	joblist	NOPURGE (default) or PURGE

Positional Operand

1. **joblist**—A list of one or more batch jobs to cancel. Typical joblist formats are (a) jobname; (b) jobname(jobid); (c) jobname, jobname(jobid); and (d) jobname, jobname. Jobname is up to eight characters long, including your userid and a suffix composed of the characters A to Z, @, #, or $. Jobid is up to eight characters and uniquely identifies a job (i.e., J68) and may be unique for your site. Note multiple joblists are always placed in parentheses and are separated by commas or blanks.

Keyword Operand

1. **NOPURGE**—Cancels the job but keeps the output (this is the default).
2. **PURGE**—Cancels the job and deletes its output.

EXAMPLES

1. *Canceling a batch job but not delete its output:*
   `cancel tag1708a`
2. *Canceling multiple jobs and deleting their output:*
   `cancel (tag1708a, tag1708@, tag1708c(job822)) purge`
   a. Multiple jobs enclosed in parentheses and separated by commas are deleted. Note TAG1708C also has a jobid to differ it from other TAG-1708C jobs. The output from all of the canceled jobs is deleted.

Viewing Batch Output

Since the OUTPUT command is all but replaced by SDSF, only an overview will be given here. Some uses of OUTPUT are

1. Redirecting output to your terminal, a different output class, or a dataset
2. Deleting the output for a batch job

3. Directing a batch job to a HOLD status
4. Printing batch job output.

OUTPUT has a subcommand level where additional processing may occur.

Checking the Status of a Batch Job

Batch users need to check the status of one or more batch jobs periodically. This can be done with SDSF or the STATUS command. Table 2-17 lists common operands used with STATUS.

Positional Operand

1. **joblist**—A list of one or more batch job for displaying their status. Typical joblist formats are (a) jobname; (b) jobname(jobid); (c) jobname, jobname (jobid); and (d) jobname, jobname. Jobname is up to eight characters long, including your userid and a suffix made up of the characters A to Z, @, #, or $. Jobid is up to eight characters long and uniquely identifies a job (i.e., J68). Note multiple joblists are placed in parentheses and are separated by commas or blanks. If specifying no joblist, the default is your userid plus one additional character (A to Z, @, #, or $).

EXAMPLE

1. *STATUS with the default JOBLIST.*
   `status or status (tag1708a,tag1708b)`
   displayed:
   ```
   IKJ56211I JOB TAG1708A(JOB06789) EXECUTING
   IKJ56192I JOB TAG1708B(JOB03470) ON OUTPUT QUEUE
   ```

Submitting Batch Jobs

Batch jobs are started by a SUBMIT command. Many of the full-screen and line editors allow use of SUBMIT while editing a dataset. Table 2-18 lists common operands used with SUBMIT.

Table 2-17. Common Operands Used with STATUS

Command/Alias	Positional Operand	Keyword Operand
STATUS/ST	joblist	None

Table 2-18. Common Operands Used with SUBMIT

Command/ Alias	Positional Operand	Keyword Operands
SUBMIT/ SUB	dsname	HOLD or NOHOLD (default) JOBCHAR(char) or NOJOBCHAR (default) NOTIFY (default) or NONOTIFY

Positional Operand

1. **dsname**—The name of one or more datasets or PDS members containing JCL statements. Multiple datasets are enclosed in parentheses and separated by commas.

Keyword Operands

1. **HOLD**—Puts the batch job output in a hold output class.
2. **NOHOLD**—The batch output is not put in a hold output class. This is the default.
3. **JOBCHAR(char)**—If your JCL does not begin with a JOB statement, one is generated. The job name is the userid and one character (A to Z).
4. **NOJOBCHAR**—If your JCL does not begin with a JOB statement, the computer prompts you for one or uses a job default. (Userid and one character A to Z.). This is the default.
5. **NOTIFY**—Sends a message when the job completes. If logged on with a NOMAIL operand, then NOTIFY messages are put in the broadcast or log dataset. Using LISTBC allows viewing these messages. This is the default.
6. **NONOTIFY**—You receive no message when a job completes.

EXAMPLE

1. *Submits a batch job and receives a NOTIFY message:*
   `submit base.cntl(job1) jobchar(a)`
   displayed:
   IKJ56750I JOB TAG1708A(JOB08897) SUBMITTED
   READY

```
11.18.10 JOB 8897 TAG1708A ENDED CN(00) MAX CON
CODE(00)
```

Appends an A to the end of the JOBNAME. NOTE CN(00) is *not* a condition
Appends an A to the end of the JOBNAME. NOTE CN(00) is *not* a condition code but console 0. MAX COND CODE lists the highest condition code returned by the program (a number higher than 00 to 0000 generally means the job did not execute successfully.)

SDSF—An Emerging Standard

Most TSO and TSO/E sites use SDSF for viewing their output and monitoring the status of their batch jobs. SDSF is accessed through ISPF and is usually, but not always, option S on the ISPF main menu. So, at most sites if you enter pdf s from the READY prompt, you will see the following options:

DA—Shows users currently logged in
END—Ends SDSF and returns to TSO or ISPF/PDF
H—Shows jobs in the hold queue
I—Shows jobs in the input queue
INPUT—To view SYSIN control cards and other trace information when using SDSF
O—Shows jobs in the output queue
PREFIX—Assigns prefix (userid) of jobs to display
REMOTE—Will show jobs in the output queue for only this printer
WHO—Shows your userid and other information

This section briefly discusses displaying and processing jobs for the I (input), O (output), and H (held) batch queues. A complete reference describing all options and use of PF (program function) keys is *System Log Display and Search Facility's User's Guide*.

Displaying Input Queues

Entering I or DA displays a list of the jobs that are executing for a particular userid. (The default, your userid, can be changed with the PREFIX option.) Figures 2-8 and 2-9 display what you might see in the I and DA screens after submitting the batch shown in Figure 2-7.

In Figure 2-8, the batch job is currently executing. The *job number* (needed for a CANCEL or STATUS command), *job name* (specified by the programmer's name parameter of the JCL JOB statement), and *job class* (A) all display. The top line of Figure 2-9 lists a paging rate of 47.44 pages per second, a start input/output rate of 155.30 per second, and a CPU utilization of 85.30% during the last CPU second. Like the *input* (I) screen, the DA screen displays the job name, job number, and job class. In addition, the now executing job step and PROC step, the current total

Figure 2-8. SDSF Input Queue (I) Screen

```
SDSF INPUT QUEUE DISPLAY ALL CLASSES                                LINE 1 TO 3 OF 1
COMMAND INPUT ===> _                                              SCROLL ===> PAGE
NP   C   JOBNAME                            CLS PRIO POS STAT   DEST NAME/TITLE
     TAG1708A    JOB 1060    A                                         JCL EX.
```

number of CPU Seconds used, and your *job-swapping status* are given. (IN means the job is processing now and OUT means another job is now processing with your job being put in a temporary hold status.)

For nearly all SDSF screens, there are two types of commands users can enter.

1. **Screen Commands**—These are commands entered at the command line or by pressing a PF key affecting the format for a particular screen. For example, after pressing PF8, the screen scrolls down to the next screen of jobs (so that jobs 18 to 24 might be viewed instead of jobs 1 to 17). *You may also use the command line to switch to another SDSF option (such as input to output) and do not need to return to the SDSF primary option menu.*
2. **Job Commands**—These are commands or values entered in the NP or other fields for a particular job. For example, placing a B (or some other value) in the CLASS field for a particular job changes the job class. Also, placing a certain letter in the NP field cancels or places a job in hold. *The availability of commands is very much site-dependent.*

Viewing Held Output

Two popular uses of Hold Queue (H) option of SDSF are viewing held output and requeuing held output to print. Both uses are shown in Figure 2-10.

The held queue displays the job name, priority, output class, form used, and total number of lines for each job. (If allowed, more fields are seen by scrolling right.) To view job output, place an S in the NP field. Additional commands (such as LOCATE) are available to ease your viewing of the job output. By entering an O in a job's NP field and an output class (such as A) in the output class or C field, you can requeue a held job to print. Other actions could be purging a held job or changing the output printer.

Figure 2-9. SDSF Display Active Users (DA) Screen

```
SDSF DA SOU PGING 47.44 SIO 155.30 CPU 85.3%                       LINE 1 TO 3 OF 1
COMMAND INPUT ===> _                                             SCROLL ===> PAGE
NP JOBNAME                          CLS JOBSTEP PROCSTEP CPU TIME %CPU SWAP
   TAG1708A JOB 1060                A   STEP1   IEFBR14  1.58     0.10 IN
```

Figure 2-10. SDSF Held Queue (H) Screen

```
SDSF HELD OUTPUT DISPLAY ALL CLASSES                 LINE 1 TO 3 OF 5
COMMAND INPUT ===> _                                 SCROLL ===> PAGE
NP  C  JOBNAME                PRIO  OUT  FORM  STAT  DEST  TOTAL
O   A  TAG1708A  JOB  1060    1     H    STD               33
S      TAG1708B  JOB  1061    1     H    STD               22
```

Viewing the Status of a Job Printing

Using the output queue (O) tells if your job is now printing. A typical display is shown in Figure 2-11.

The output queue screen displays for each job a job name, job type (usually JOB), job number, output class, forms used, total number of pages, printer ID, and job title. (Set by the programmer's NAME parameter of your job statement.) Since the STAT or STATUS field is not HOLD, the job is queued to print. Each site uses different fields to show if the job is now printing. *Most users are unable to cancel a batch job currently printing.*

AN EXAMPLE OF TSO IN ACTION

To reinforce the concepts and commands discussed in this chapter, let us review a possible TSO session. Garfield Lemay has work to do in TSO. His major task is to find and print a FORTRAN program someone else created and submit it in batch (background). Chapters 4, 5, and 7 show how to write a clist to "automate" this process.

```
Line

1. LOGON GRL1/WEEKDAY MAIL NONOTICES
2. ALLOC F(NEWFORT) DA(NEW.FORT) NEW DSORG(PO) DIR(5) +
   LRECL(80) BLKSIZE(16000) SPACE(10,10) TRACKS RECFM(F B)
3. READY
4. SEND 'WHO HAS THE PLOTIT PROGRAM?' USER(UIC1,RAS33) LOGON
   READY
```

Figure 2-11. SDSF Output Queue (O) Screen

```
SDSF OUTPUT CLASS A FORM STD                                    LINE 1 TO 3 OF 9
COMMAND INPUT ===> _                                            SCROLL ===> PAGE
NP  JOBNAME   TYPE  JNUM  OUT  FORMS  STAT  DEST  TOTAL  PRT  NAME
    TAG1708A  JOB   1060  A    STD                9      P1   JCL EX.
```

```
 5. LISTC LVL('UIC1.*.FORT') ALL
 6. NONVSAM----UIC1.FORT.FORT
    IN-CAT ----SYS1.ATOE.CATALOG
    HISTORY
      OWNER-IDENT -------UIC1
      CREATION ----------88.092
      RELEASE--------------2
      EXPIRATION--------99.001
    VOLUMES
      VOLSER------------SYS23
   NONVSAM----UIC1.MOVE.FORT
   IN-CAT----SYS1.ATOE.CATALOG
    HISTORY
      OWNER-IDENT -------UIC1
      CREATION----------88.092
      RELEASE --------------2
      EXPIRATION--------99.001
    VOLUMES
      VOLSER------------SYS23
    READY
 7. LISTDS 'UIC1.*.FORT' MEMBERS
 8. UIC1.FORT.FORT
    --RECFM-LRECL-BLKSIZE-DSORG
      FB      80      6160      PO
    --VOLUMES--
      SYS23
    --MEMBERS
      PAGE
      PLOTIT
      WEIGHT
    UIC1.MOVE.FORT
    --RECFM-LRECL-BLKSIZE-DSORG
      FB      80      6160      PO
    --VOLUMES--
      SYS23
    --MEMBERS
      MOVE3
    READY
 9. COPY 'UIC1.FORT.FORT(PLOTIT)' NEW.FORT(PLOTIT)
    READY
10. ITS IN RAS33.PLOT.FORT(PLOTIT) UIC1
11. DEL NEW.FORT(PLOTIT)
```

```
12. IDC0549I MEMBER PLOTIT DELETED
    READY
13. COPY 'RAS33.PLOT.FORT(PLOTIT)' NEW.FORT(PLOTIT)
    READY
14. RENAME NEW.FORT PLOT.FORT
    READY
15. HELP LIST
16. FUNCTION
    THE LIST COMMAND PRINTS OUT ALL OR PART OF A
   SEQUENTIAL  DATASET OR MEMBER OF A PARTITIONED DATASET.
   (More help text)
   READY
17. LIST PLOT.FORT(PLOTIT) NONUM
18. IKJ52827I PLOT.FORT(PLOTIT)
    DATA PI/3.141592654
    C      CALL INITT(120)
           CALL TERM(3.4096)
     (more FORTRAN statements)
           END
    READY
19. DSPRINT PLOT.FORT(PLOTIT) PRT1
20. PROCESSING HAS BEEN COMPLETED FOR DATASET:
    GRL1.POLT.FORT
      MEMBER:
    PLOTIT
    READY
21. TIME
22. IKJ56650I TIME-1:15:10 PM CPU-00:00:15 SESSION-
    00:07:14
    READY
23. not shown
24. SUBMIT CNTL(PLOT)
25. IKJ56250I JOB GRL1A(JOB0388) SUBMITTED
    READY
26. STATUS GRL1A
27. IKJ5692I JOB GRL1A(JOB0388)EXECUTING
    READY
28. LISTA
29. NULLFILE
    TERMFILE
    PLOT.FORT
     (more datasets)
```

```
    READY
30. LISTBC MAIL NOTICES
31. ***********************************
    * SYSTEM GOES DOWN AT 3:30 PM TODAY *
    ***********************************
    READY
32. LOGOFF
```

Explanation

A line-by-line explanation of the preceding TSO session follows by line number.

1. Garfield log ons to TSO with userid GRL1 (his initials). By using the NONOTICES operand, no system messages are displayed after logging on, but his messages display because of the MAIL operand.
2. This line allocates a new partitioned dataset to hold the FORTRAN program Garfield is seeking. The dataset name is NEW.FORT and has a logical record length of 80 and a block size of 16,000. This fixed-block dataset is allocated initially with both 10 tracks and overflow tracks allowed. Five directory blocks are allocated.
3. After completing each command, READY appears.
4. Garfield knows one of two users has a FORTRAN program called PLOTIT. He sends a message to both (this is retained until they log on), asking which one of them has the program.
5. While waiting for an answer, Garfield does some detective work. He does a LISTC command with a wildcard to display UIC1's FORTRAN datasets. (The example assumes that FORT is the third qualifier.) The ALL operand lists all available information.
6. The listing shows UIC1 has two FORTRAN datasets. (Usually a user has many more.) The dataset names and volume serial numbers are displayed.
7. A LISTDS command with a MEMBERS operand is entered, displaying all members for the two FORTRAN datasets.
8. A sample member listing from the two FORTRAN datasets is displayed. (Usually the listing is larger.) The listing shows a member named PLOTIT is in UIC1.FORT.FORT.
9. Thinking this is the desired program, Garfield copies the program into the dataset created on line 2.
10. However, UIC1 sends a message that the desired program it is in RAS-33.PLOT.FORT.
11. The PLOTIT program copied from UIC1 is deleted.

12. A confirmation message for the deleted dataset displays.
13. The PLOTIT program of RAS33 is copied into NEW.FORT. (Usually you copy the entire dataset to get all of the subroutines.)
14. So that other users may recognize his dataset in the future, the dataset is renamed to PLOT.FORT.
15. Garfield wants to display the PLOTIT program, but has forgotten the LIST command's syntax. He requests the HELP text for the LIST command.
16. A partial listing of the HELP text is shown here.
17. LIST is entered with NONUM, ignoring sequence numbers.
18. A partial listing is shown here.
19. Liking what he sees, Garfield prints the PLOTIT program at local printer PRT1.
20. A message similar to this is displayed showing the dataset and member have printed. (The message may be different for your site.)
21. Garfield wants to check how much time before his 2:15 meeting.
22. An hour is plenty of time to complete what's left to do.
23. What is not shown is Garfield editing a JCL file called GRL1.CNTL(PLOT) that will run PLOTIT; editing a dataset is discussed in Chapters 7 and 10.
24. The JCL job is submitted.
25. A confirmation message is given.
26. After a few minutes, Garfield does a status check on the job.
27. The program is still executing. Garfield will check on the output tomorrow.
28. After all the steps, Garfield is confused as to which datasets are allocated. He enters a LISTA to make sure.
29. A long listing of permanent and temporary datasets is displayed. PLOT. .FORT is one of the datasets.
30. Garfield checks for system messages with a LISTBC command.
31. The computer is going down at 3:30 P.M. . . . right in the middle of Garfield's meeting. He had better let his boss know right away there will not be a "live" demo and they will have to use the slides backup.
32. Time of log off. Logoff confirmation messages (different for each site) are displayed.

SUGGESTED READINGS

Brown, Gary Deward, 1977. *System/370 Job Control Language*. New York: John Wiley & Sons.

Desmond, Ralph, 1984. *Basic JCL/Advanced JCL & Utilities*. Unpublished course notes

Hoffman, Chuck, 1984. *TSO Fundamentals for Application Programmers*. Unpublished course notes

IBM Corporation, 1987. *MVS/Extended Architecture JCL User's Guide*. GC28-1351

IBM Corporation, 1984. *OS/VS2 MVS JCL,* GC28-0692

IBM Corporation, 1984. *OS/VS2 Terminal User's Guide*. GC28-0645

IBM Corporation, 1986. *TSO Extensions Command Language Reference*. SC28-1307 (TSO/E Version 1 Releases 3 and 4).

IBM Corporation, 1986. *TSO Extensions User's Guide*. SC28-1333 (TSO/E Version 1 Releases 3 and 4)

Katzan, Harry, Jr., and Tharayil, David, 1984. *Invitation to MVS*. New York: Petrocelli Books, pp. 4–6.

Northeast Utilities, 1982. *TSO-User Introductory Guide*. Unpublished in-house user's guide.

SAS Institute, 1984. *SAS Companion for OS Operating Systems and TSO,* 1984 ed. Cary, N.C.: SAS Institute. pp. 21–44, 107–122

Struble, George, 1984a. *Assembler Language Programming for the IBM System/370 Family*. Reading, Mass. Addison-Wesley, pp. 290–340.

——1984b. *Assembler Language Programming for the IBM System*. Reading, Mass.: Addison-Wesley, p. 296. Reprinted with permission.

3

An Introduction to Clists

WHAT ARE CLISTS?

A *clist* (pronounced "see-list") is a sequential or partitioned dataset of executable *TSO commands* (see Chapter 2), and *clist statements* (see Chapters 4 and 5). The clist language is a *high-level interpretive symbolic programming language* made up of clist statements. Clists may execute in either interactive or batch mode. To give you a better understanding of the clist language, let us further examine the above definition.

Clist Is a High-level Language

As a high-level language, clist statements use English-like commands instead of binary code or assembly language's two-three-letter mnemonics (e.g., ST for store). The result is a "more natural," easier-to-learn programming language, but one that is also slower and less powerful than assembly language.

Clist Is an Interpretive Language

The clist interpreter's two execution phases consist of checking for syntax, performing symbolic substitution on each variable, and executing a clist. This happens during every run of a clist. For large clients, the result is sluggish performance when compared with program load modules written in assembly language, C, COBOL, FORTRAN, and Pascal. This reveals the strength and weakness of the clist language. An interpretive language runs and reruns a program without compiling. This allows "real-time programming" (immediately confirming if a clist works) and memory savings since no object code is maintained. The result is slower execution than compiled programs, which a compiler and linkage editor processes, producing compiled or machine-executable code.

Clist Is a Symbolic Language

The foundation of the clist language is the creation and modification of *symbolic variables*. They start with an ampersand and hold a character string value. The clist language Interpreter resolves symbolic variables by making multiple passes of each clist statement, performing several levels of *symbolic substitution* (i.e., translating the symbolic variable to the correct value). Chapter 5 presents a more complete discussion of symbolic substitution.

Clist Is a Programming Language

As a programming language, clist offers an easy-to-learn means of performing string manipulation, file or input/output operations, error handling, subroutines (Version 1 Release 4 and later), and conditional logic. These concepts can be transferred to other interpreted and compiled languages (such as REXX in Chapter 11.)

CLIST DATASET ATTRIBUTES

DCB Characteristics of CLISTS

A clist dataset is either *partitioned* or *sequential* with a record format of FB (fixed blocked) or VB (variable blocked). *Do not use FBA or VBA as a record format since TSO ignores the first column of the clist and produces unpredictable results and hard to debug errors.* The default DCB parameters assigned to clist datasets are variable-blocked record format (RECFM), logical record length (LRECL) of 255, and block size (BLKSIZE) of 3120 (but you can modify these). Lower maintenance, ease of locating, and more efficient access to other clist members are three reasons for storing clists in partitioned datasets.

File Names and Concatenating Clist Datasets

Clist datasets generally are allocated with the filename or ddname of SYSPROC. This is done by an ALLOCATE command in your system/personal "startup" clist, by JCL during LOGON processing, or entering ALLOCATE at the READY prompt. An allocation of SYSPROC can concatenate several datasets.

```
alloc f (sysproc) da(mylib.clist -
                     'sys1.system.clist' -
                     'uic1.graph.clist') share reuse
```

In the above example, three datasets are concatenated. A personal clist dataset is placed first, followed by a system clist dataset, and a graphics application clist dataset. (Why the personal clist goes first is explained in the next section.) The SHARE operand allows other users to allocate these datasets and REUSE frees any currently allocated datasets before allocating. Concatenations should have datasets with similar record formats and block sizes. If different block sizes are used, the dataset with the largest block size is placed first or the BLKSIZE operand of ALLOCATE is used.) *Before allocating a SYSPROC concatenation, use LISTA STATUS to see what is currently allocated to SYSPROC, then include those files in your concatenation. Otherwise, you may lose access to some TSO commands and clists you are now using!)*

Search Order of the SYSPROC Concatenation

Whether a clist is invoked at the READY prompt of TSO or the COMMAND ===> line of ISPF or PDF, TSO searches the datasets of the SYSPROC concatenation for the member name entered. This search starts with the first dataset in the SYSPROC concatenation and ends with the last dataset in the concatenation. (TSO/E Version 2 searches the SYSEXEC concatenation first. SYSEXEC is for REXX programs.) So, to have your clist execute before a system command or clist of the same name, place your personal clist datasets *before* the system clist datasets. This is why the example in the previous section has the personal clist *before* the system clist. However, it is not a good idea to assign system names to personal clists because of the difficulty in debugging. See Chapter 11 on how TSO/E Version 2 searches for REXX programs and clists.

INVOKING A CLIST (THE EXEC COMMAND)

You can invoke a clist either implicitly or explicitly. The explicit method uses the EXEC command, while the implicit does not. Use either method at TSO's READY prompt or the COMMAND ===> line in ISPF or PDF. See Chapter 11 on implicitly or explicitly invoking a REXX program or clist for TSO/E Version 2.

Implicitly Invoking a Clist

If a CLIST dataset is a member of a dataset that is part of the SYSPROC concatenation, the EXEC command (discussed in the next section) is not needed. There are two different formats to implicitly invoke a clist:

FORMAT 1: MEMBER NAME ONLY (IMPLICIT FORMAT)

```
cleanup help.text
```

Using only the member name results in more system overhead. The reason is that TSO searches all the system libraries and program areas to see if CLEANUP is a TSO command and *only then* searches the SYSPROC concatenation. Thus, a TSO command with the same name is executed before a clist! Note that HELP. TEXT is an operand value and is not in single quotes.

FORMAT 2: % MEMBER NAME (EXTENDED IMPLICIT FORMAT)

```
%cleanup help.text
```

The percent sign (%) before the member name tells TSO to search only the SYSPROC concatenation (resulting in considerably lower system overhead). Again, the operand value HELP.TEXT is used and is not in single quotes.

Explicitly Invoking a Clist

The explicit method of invoking a clist uses the EXEC command to process the SYSPROC concatenation dataset members and datasets not part of the SYSPROC concatenation. There are four different formats to explicitly invoke a clist:

FORMAT 1: A FULLY QUALIFIED DATASET NAME

```
exec 'uic1.runit'
```

This sequential dataset is not part of the SYSPROC concatenation and belongs to another user (thus the fully qualified name). Use Format 1 for datasets that do not have a name qualifier of clist. The example has no operand values.

FORMAT 2: PARTITIONED DATASET AND MEMBER WITH A DATASET NAME QUALIFIER OF CLIST

```
ex utility(testit) '15 notrace'
```

This program executes a clist called TESTIT that is a member of the user's UTILITY.CLIST dataset. Two operand values of 15 and NOTRACE are provided in single quotes. Note that EX is a valid abbreviation of EXEC.

FORMAT 3: SEQUENTIAL DATASET WITH A DATASET NAME QUALIFIER OF CLIST

```
ex startup "'no'"
```

This example executes a clist in a sequential dataset named STARTUP.CLIST. It also passes an operand value of 'NO'. (To do this, the single quote is contained within quotes. So use three quotes to produce one, six quotes to produce two, etc.)

FORMAT 4: A MEMBER OF THE PARTITIONED DATASET USERID.CLIST

```
ex (calculat)
```

This invokes the member CALCULAT of the dataset uic1.clist (or whatever the user's default prefix is named). The example has no operand values.

TYPES OF CLIST APPLICATIONS

There are three types of clist applications:

- Utility clists
- Application clists
- Language front-end clists

With the release of TSO/E, a fourth type of application is available—the interaction of clists and other languages. Like all typologies, some examples may fit in more than one category. Let's briefly examine each of these.

Utility Clists

These clists (created and maintained by your computer or information center staff) will archive a file, restore file allocations, and perform many other tasks. Clists in this category may contain a mix of JCL statements, TSO commands, clist statements, and other programming language statements executed in either interactive or batch mode. This front-end to a TSO command or JCL saves you time in entering a command or from needing to learn command syntax.

Application Clists

These clists (created by the computer or information center staff or end users) are self-contained applications such as completing a travel report or generating a pie chart. They may be written using the full-screen capabilities of ISPF (i.e., field validations). Chapter 9 shows examples of these screens. Both TSO and ISPF/PDF may be used with a variety of written languages. Many of these applications use multiple clists, which Chapter 8 discusses.

Language Front-end Clists

A clist can access other programming languages such APL, ASSEMBLY LANGUAGE, BASIC, C, COBOL, FORTRAN, and PASCAL. Thus, you do not have to know APL to access and to execute a statistics program.

Clists that Interact with Other Languages

Clists interact with other languages in three different ways:

1. Executing clists within another programming language program. (Read the user's guide for each language on how to do this.)
2. Mixing clist statements directly with another language. (Examples of this are PDF's edit macros and TSO session manager.)
3. Calling clists from REXX programs or vice versa under TSO/E Version 2 as Chapter 11 discusses.

CLIST SYNTAX AND TERMINOLOGY

A Comparison of Clist Statements and TSO Commands

Table 3-1 highlights the syntax similarities and differences between clist statements and TSO commands.

Other Concepts

Other clist concepts are reviewed here: (1) Clist operators and their order of precedence, and (2) the relation between clists, clist statements, TSO commands, major components of the clist language, and clist limitations.

Mathematical Operators

Mathematical operators allow adding, subtracting, and other operations of two or more *numeric* clist variables. Table 3-2 lists the clist mathematical operators and their order of precedence. The following list gives additional notes on clist mathematical operators.

Table 3-1. A Comparison of Clist Statements and TSO Command Syntax

Feature	Clist	TSO
Abbreviations	Statements may not be abbreviated.	Commands may be abbreviated.
Blank lines	May be included between clist statements and does not slow down clist execution time.	May be included between TSO commands (in a clist) and does not slow down command execution time.
Case	Clist statements, but not variable and built-in function names, must be in uppercase.	TSO commands may be in upper- or lowercase.
Comments	May be on its own line or at the end of a clist statement.	May be on its own line or at the end of a clist statement.
On-line help	None available for clist statements.	Available for each TSO command.
Operands	Clist statement is separated from operands by blanks. Both keyword and positional operands are separated by blanks or commas.	TSO command is separated from operands by blanks. Both keyword and positional operands are separated by blanks or commas.

Table 3-2. Clist Mathematical Operators and their Order of Precedence.

Operator	Function	Example
**	Exponentiation	&y**2
/	Division	&y/2
//	Modulo (remainder)	&y//5
*	Multiplication	&x * &y
+	Addition	&x + &y
−	Subtraction	&x − &y

1. You may place a space between an operator and a clist variable.
2. Negative exponents are always equal to zero. The value of exponent is zero, making the value of that part of the expression one.

3. Parentheses determine what is evaluated first and override the default order of precedence.

```
10-5*2 = 0 (5*2 is multiplied first. Then
            10 minus 10 equals 0.)
(10-5) * 2=10 (Parentheses performed first--10
               minus 5. Then the result (5)
               multiplied by 2 equals 10.)
```

4. Use of the modulo (remainder) operator gives the integer remainder from an integer division:

```
5//2=1 (5 divided by 2 is 2, with an integer
        remainder of 1).
```

5. The following is the order of precedence after mathematical operators:
   a. Any relational operator
   b. The AND logical operator
   c. the OR logical operator
6. All mathematical operations round the result, since clist variable values are whole numbers (i.e., no decimals.)

Relational Operators

Relational operators compare two *numeric* or *string* clist values and have a *lower order of precedence than mathematical operators but a higher priority than logical operators*. Table 3-3 lists the clist relational operators. The following list gives additional notes on clist relational operators.

1. A space may *not* be placed between combined relational operators (i.e., < = and > = are both invalid).
2. Relational operators use either symbolic or character form. Both forms may be used together in a clist statement with more than one relational operator.

Table 3-3. Clist Relational Operators

Operator	Function	Example
EQ or =	Equal to	&x = &y
NE or ¬=	Not equal to	&x ¬= &y
LT or <	Less than	&x < &y
GT or >	Greater than	&x > &y
LE or <=	Less than or equal to	&x <= &y
GE or >=	Greater than or equal to	&x >= &y
NL or ¬<	Not less than	&x ¬< &y
NG or ¬>	Not greater than	&x ¬> &y

Table 3-4. Clist Logical Operators

Operator	Function	Example
AND or &&	Logical AND	&x = &y && &x = &z
OR or |	Logical OR	&x = &y | &x = &z

3. All relational operators have the same order of precedence.
4. Relational operators return a value indicating if the relation is true or false. Based on this result, you can specify where a clist goes next. This is also called *clist flow control* and *conditional branching or logic*.

Logical Operators

Logical operators logically evaluate two or more clist variables and have the lowest order of precedence. (Logical operators are also called Boolean operators. Note that a logical AND has a higher priority than a logical OR.) Table 3-4 lists the clist logical operators.

1. Logical operators may use either the character or symbolic form. Both forms may be used together in a clist statement using more than one logical operator.
2. A clist statement may use an almost unlimited number of logical operators. However, this produces a complicated statement that slows down processing. (A clist statement may be as long as 32,756 bytes.)
3. Like relational operators, logical operators also return if a condition is true or false. They also can be used for clist flow control.

MAJOR COMPONENTS OF THE CLIST LANGUAGE

Listed below are the major components of the clist language; many are discussed in the next several chapters.

1. Trace facility
   - Check symbolic substitution
   - Check clist flow control
   - List TSO commands
2. File operations
   - Open a file
   - Close a file
   - Put a record to a file
   - Read a record from a file

3. Terminal operations
   - Read a value from the terminal
   - Write a value to the terminal
   - Read an input stream from a terminal
4. Exception handling
   - Attention key routine
   - Error routine
   - Exit routine
5. Built-in functions
   - String/numeric operations
   - Other operations
6. System variables
   - Return current date or time
   - Return information about the processing of a clist
   - Turn the trace facility on or off (TSO/E Version 1 Release 4 and later)
   - List information about a dataset
7. Clist symbolic variables
   - Set a symbolic variable
   - Concatenate symbolic variables.
   - Set a symbolic variable array
   - Nest a symbolic variable
8. Clist flow control (conditional branching)
   - Evaluate a relation of one or more clist variables
   - Nest flow control statements
   - Loop through a series of clist statements
9. Using other clients
   - Call a subprocedure (TSO/E Version 1 Release 4 and later)
   - Pass information from the procedure to a clist (TSO/E Version 1 Release 4 and later)
   - Nest clists

LIMITATIONS OF CLISTS

Like all programming languages, clists have their own limitations. The following is a discussion of these shortcomings. Please keep these in mind when reviewing the REXX language in Chapter 11.

Data Values

This is probably the biggest deficiency of clists—which values a clist variable can have:

- Unless you use a built-in function, a clist is unable to read character data (such as blank spaces in the data, JCL characters, or ampersands) and double-byte characters.
- Clist have limited date and time manipulation as well. Character values cannot be easily parsed.
- Clists cannot read in mixed data strings (such as the double-byte characters and alphanumeric characters). *This is not true for TSO/E Version 1 Release 4 and later.*
- Clist variable values and operations must be in the range $+2^{31} - 1$ through -2^{31}. Most programming languages have a double-precision type of variable with a far larger range.
- Clist variables cannot contain integers with decimals. Rounding ("integer math") takes place for all mathematical operations.

Clist Is an Incompletely Structured Language

This criticism is less true for TSO/E Version 1 Release 4 and greater, which have case logic, iterative DO, compound DO, and DO UNTIL statements. More information on each of these statements can be found in Chapter 4. However, the clist language still lacks the speed and the power of a compiled language. Clists include a GOTO statement and can allow some sloppy programming practices, such as entering or exiting a DO loop.

In spite of its faults, clists are a good way to handle many TSO programming needs. As was said in Chapter 1, TSO is a gateway for building numerous ad hoc and production applications because of its ties to many languages and products. Chapter 4 reviews many of the available clist statements complete with examples, and Chapter 5 discusses some advanced clist topics.

SUGGESTED READINGS

Hayden, Peter, 1985. The IBM TSO Clist Command Language. *Computing* (England) August 15, p. 22.

IBM Corporation, 1987. *TSO/E Programming Guide*, SC28-1363.

IBM Corporation, 1987. *TSO Extension Clists*, SC28-1304.

Kusnierz, Thomas E., 1986. CLIST Tips and Techniques. *SHARE 67 Proceedings*, pp. 1–19.

Sammett, Jean E., 1983. Programming Languages, in *Encyclopedia of Computer Science and Engineering, Second Edition*. Anthony Ralston and Edwin D. Reilly Jr. (eds.). New York: Van Nostrand Reinhold, pp. 1228–1232.

4

Clists: Capabilities and Commands

This chapter covers most of the topics discussed in a typical one- or two-day clist course. The approach used is to first review the functions of a clist statement and then reinforce this by building up a utility clist that is a front-end to some TSO commands. The book stresses learning clist language basics rather than revealing clist "tricks." Although the book provides useful information throughout, Chapter 5 especially reviews advanced and miscellaneous clist topics. The problem with clist "tricks" is that they may not work at all sites or be unsupported in a future release.

OVERVIEW OF CLIST STATEMENTS

Chapter 3 presented a summary of the major components of the clist language. Table 4-1 shows the clist statements matching to each components. Chapter 5 covers control variables and Chapter 6 reviews built-in functions.

Clist (Symbolic) Variables

A *clist (symbolic) variable* starts with an ampersand (&) and is assigned a character or numeric value. The interpreter substitutes this value after making several scans of a clist statement. This is also called *symbolic substitution*. (*Note:* All symbolic variables in this chapter are translated after the first scan of the interpreter. Chapter 5 reviews second-scan symbolic variables or double ampersand (&&) variables.) So, if &NAME is set (equal) to JOE, then the interpreter substitutes JOE each time finding the variable &NAME. The clist assumes that a symbolic variable's value is character unless a value is completely numeric (i.e.,

Table 4-1. Clist Statement Overview

Function	Statement	Typical Usage
	Trace Facility	
Clist Trace	CONTROL	CONTROL CONLIST SYMLIST MSG
	Dataset Operations	
Open a dataset	OPENFILE	OPENFILE FILE1
Close a dataset	CLOSFILE	CLOSFILE FILE1
Get a record from a dataset	GETFILE	GETFILE FILE1
Put a record in a dataset	PUTFILE	PUTFILE FILE1
	Terminal Operations	
Read a value from the terminal	READ READDVAL	READ READDVAL PHONE STATE ZIP
Write text to the terminal	WRITE WRITENR	WRITE WHAT DAY IS IT? WRITENR ENTER YOUR–CHOICE:
Allow a temporary exit from a clist	TERMIN*	TERMIN QUIT,END,BYE
	Exception Handling	
What to do when the user presses the ATTN key	ATTN	ATTN DO WRITE LEAVING CLIST GOTO EXIT END
What to do when an error occurs	ERROR	ERROR DO WRITE ALLOCATE – FAILED RETURN END
	CONTROL	CONTROL MAIN/FLUSH
Resume normal processing after an error or attention routine.	RETURN	ERROR DO SET &LCC = 100 RETURN END
Exit clist with return code	EXIT	EXIT CODE(&LCC)
Process non-clist statements	DATA† ENDDATA†	DATA EDIT NEW.DATA NEW ENDDATA
Answers prompts to TSO commands	DATA PROMPT† ENDDATA†	DATA PROMPT 1 ENDDATA

Table 4-1. *(continued)*

	Clist (Symbolic) Variable	
Setting the value of a symbolic variable	SET	SET &PHONE = 5085551212
Set dataset information to clist variables	LISTDSI*	LISTDSI HELP.TEXT WRITE &SYSLRECL
Pass values to a clist	PROC	PROC 2 LIST + DS('HELP.TEXT')
	Clist Flow Control	
Condition	IF-THEN-ELSE	IF &OPT = 1 THEN + DELETE &DSN1 ELSE DELETE &DSN2
Testing	SELECT-WHEN-END	SELECT (&YEAR) WHEN (0:50) SET + &HLF = 1 WHEN (51:99) SET + &HLF = 2 OTHERWISE SET + &HLF = 3 END
Loop testing	DO-WHILE-END	DO WHILE &CNT <= + &LCNT SET &CNT = &CNT +1 WRITE &CNT END
	DO-UNTIL-END	DO UNTIL &CNT = + &LCNT SET &CNT = &CNT + 1 WRITE &CNT END
	Iterative DO	DO &CNT = 1 TO 100 BY+ 10 WRITE PHONE&CNT END
	Compound DO	DO &CNT = 1 TO 100 BY+ 10 WHILE &AREACODE =+ 212 END
Move to a label	GOTO	GOTO ONE
Condition testing for CALL	WHEN§	CALL 'SYS1.LOAD(FORT77)'

Table 4-1. Clist Statement Overview (*continued*)

	Clist Flow Control	
		WHEN &SYSRC(=0) WRITE PASSED WHEN &SYSRC(>0) WRITE FAILED
	Using Other Clists	
Passing clist parameters to other clists	GLOBAL¶ NGLOBAL¶ SYSREF¶	GLOBAL VAR1 VAR2 NGLOBAL VAR1, VAR2 SYSREF &VAR1
Calling a subprocedure	SYSCALL¶	SYSCALL SUB1 VAR1

* Chapter 5 discusses this statement.
† Chapter 7 discusses this statement.
§ Chapter 5 discusses WHEN and CALL.
¶ Chapter 8 discusses this statement.

255 is a numeric value, but 3 + 5 and 3.25 are both character variables because the plus and period are character values). Chapter 6 explains how built-in functions override this limitation.

Symbolic Variable Syntax

The following are some guidelines for creating symbolic variables.

Symbolic Variable Names

Symbolic variable names follow similar rules as TSO dataset names:

1. The names must start with letters A to Z (in either upper- or lowercase), or $, #, _, and @.
2. The rest of the name may use all characters previously mentioned and the numerals 0 to 9.
3. A variable name may have a maximum of 251 characters.
4. Variable names cannot use reserved words (such as label names, clist statement or TSO command names, and the character form of clist operators such as OR, AND, LT).
5. Use variable names that are meaningful.

Symbolic Variable Values

Symbolic variable values follow these rules:

1. The total length of a variable value (including the clist statement) is 32,756 bytes (characters).
2. A character value cannot end with a mathematical operator (e.g., +, −) or parentheses unless processed by a built-in function (see Chapter 6).
3. A variable value can contain any keyboard character plus special characters (such as line feed, hexadecimal 25. Do not use hexadecimal values 00 to 3F).

Clist Labels

Using a *clist label* ties a name with the location of one or more clist statements. Clist labels "point" to which part of the clist executes if a condition is true or specified by an active GOTO statement. (Also called *flow control* or *conditional branching*.) A *condition* is a mix of symbolic variables, clist operators, and values (i.e., &SEX = "M"). Label names are up to 8 characters (31 characters in TSO/E Version 1 Release 4 and later) and can use the same characters as symbolic variables. A label name always ends with a colon. Labels take one of two formats:

Format 1: *label: command*
Example: LABEL_ONE: EXIT
Format 2: *label:* + or *label:* −
command
Example: LABEL_ONE: −
EXIT

Label Syntax

Avoid unnecessary label problems by following these guidelines:

1. If you are using the second label format, *the command cannot be a comment or a blank line*. This stops the clist from executing and produces nonrelated error messages (which are hard to debug).
2. Use meaningful names for labels to aid ease of maintenance.
3. Label names cannot be reserved words (such as symbolic variable names, clist statement or TSO command names, and the alpha form of clist operators such as "OR," "AND," "LT").

STARTED WITH CLISTS

Passing Values to a Clist (PROC)

A clist usually begins with a PROC statement. (Put only blank lines or comments before a PROC statement.) This statement passes the value entered by the user when invoking the clist to one or more symbolic variables. (Covered in "Invoking a Clist" in Chapter 3.) Like TSO commands, the PROC statement can have both keyword and positional operands. (In this case, operands are the same thing as with clist variable values or symbolic variable values.)

Operand Names

Operand names used in a PROC statement follow these rules: (1) Variable names start only with uppercase A to Z and go up to 252 (positional) or 31 (keyword) characters. (2) The underscore is *not* a valid symbolic variable name character.

Positional Operands

Positional operands are entered in a *particular sequence,* have no default values, and usually prompt if not entered. The *number* after the PROC statement shows how many positional operands to expect.

EXAMPLE: TRYIT CLIST:

1. `PROC 2 DATASET_NAME DATASET_TYPE`
   From READY (TSO):
2. `EXEC TRYIT 'HELP.TEXT PDS'`
   or (3-5)
3. `EXEC TRYIT`
   displayed:
4. *`IKJ56700A ENTER THE POSITIONAL PARAMETER DATASET_NAME:`*
5. `HELP.TEXT`
   `PDS`

Following is an explanation by line number:

1. This appears in the TRYIT clist. It shows TRYIT has two positional operands named DATASET_NAME and DATASET_TYPE. When invoked, TSO expects to get both values. If not supplied, the interpreter usually

prompts the user for the values. (Read the line 4 note. If invoking clists is new to you, please review the appropriate section of Chapter 3 before proceeding further.)

2. From the READY prompt of TSO or the COMMAND ===> line of ISPF/PDF, the user enters this, explicitly invoking the clist. The clist is a dataset named in the user's TRYIT.CLIST dataset. Once entered, a symbolic variable with the same name as the operand is set with the inputted values. So, the interpreter assigns the value HELP.TEXT to the variable &DATASET_NAME and PDS to &DATASET_TYPE. This specifies that HELP.TEXT is a partitioned dataset.

3. Here is an alternate form (statements 3–5) explicitly invoking the clist without any positional operands.

4. The clist prompts the user for the operand value (e.g., HELP.TEXT). You are prompted *only* if:
   a. Your PROFILE dataset is set to PROMPT. (This is done by entering PROFILE PROMPT (a TSO command) at the READY prompt of TSO or the COMMAND ===> of ISPF/PDF), and
   b. You enter an EXEC command with the PROMPT operand (e.g., EXEC STARTUP 'DATA1' PROMPT. The default is NOPROMPT) *or* there is a CONTROL PROMPT statement in the clist. (More on prompting in Chapter 5.)

5. The user gives the values for the operands DATASET_NAME and DATASET_NAME after prompting.

Keyword Operands

Keyword operands are entered in any sequence, may have default values (including none), and do not prompt if the operand is not entered. To provide a default value, place it in parentheses immediately after the operand (the maximum length of a default value is 32,756 bytes). In the following example, the clist assigns the variable &LRECL (logical record length) the default of 80 and no default value to &RECFM (record format).

```
PROC 1 DATASET_NAME LRECL(80) RECFM()
```

To override these defaults, just specify new values:

From READY (TSO):

```
EX TRYIT2 HELP.TEXT LRECL(133) RECFM(F B A)
```

If invoking a keyword operand with no default value, then the operand name is assigned as a value. If not invoked, the operand is not assigned a value. In the following example, the keyword operands BATCH and LIST have no default values. When invoking the TRYIT2 clist, the BATCH operand is specified. As a result, the clist assigns &BATCH a value of BATCH and a null value to &LIST (since it was not specified).

```
PROC 1 DATASET_NAME BATCH LIST
EX TRYIT2 HELP.TEXT BATCH
```

Remember, a PROC statement may use any mix of positional and keyword operands (with or without default values).

Assigning Values to a Symbolic Variable (SET)

Use the SET statement to

1. Initialize a symbolic variable
2. Redefine a symbolic variable
3. Nest a symbolic variable
4. Concatenate two symbolic variables or a symbolic variable and a character string
5. Perform mathematical operations.

Each of these is reviewed.

Initialize a Symbolic Variable

Assigning a value to a clist symbolic variable or *initializing* a symbolic variable decreases the chance of abnormal termination or getting an ''undefined variable'' message. The format of the SET statement is as follows:

```
SET &symbolic variable = value
or
SET symbolic variable = value
```

Value is a number, character, other symbolic variable, or any mix of numbers or characters symbolic variables and built-in functions. For example,

SET &STATE = GA *or* SET STATE = GA

Many clist users do not realize that clist variables initially has a null value and a length of zero. The result is a clist filled with unneeded initialization statements assigning variables a value of blank (e.g., SET &Y =). See the first portion of this chapter for valid symbolic variable names and values.

Redefining a Symbolic Variable

To redefine a symbolic variable, simply issue a new SET statement:

```
SET &Y = 10
SET &Y = 20
```

&Y is reset to 20 by the second SET statement.

Nesting a Symbolic Variable

Nesting is when a symbolic variable is set to the *value* or *name* of another symbolic variable. (Chapter 5 examines nesting when assigning a name.) In the following example, &X assigns the value of a symbolic variable &Y which is 100.

EXAMPLES

SET &Y = 100
SET &X = &Y

Concatenated strings use nested symbolic variables to produce complex symbolic variable values (such as a dataset name) and mathematical operations.

Concatenating Symbolic Variables

Symbolic variables may be concatenated to each other or to a character string. Use concatenations to produce complex symbolic variable values and double ampersand symbolic variables (discussed in Chapter 5.) The following examples show the major types of symbolic variable concatenations.

EXAMPLES

1. SET &X = MERRY
2. SET &Y =
3. SET &Z = CHRISTMAS
4. SET &Q = &Y&Y&Z
5. SET &Q = &X &Z

In this example, lines 1 to 3 initialize the symbolic variables &X, &Y, and &Z. Line 4 concatenates the variables by assigning &Q the values of &X, &Y, and &Z. The interpreter removes any trailing blanks in the value resulting in MERRYCHRISTMAS (with no blank space between MERRY and CHRISTMAS). Line 5 shows one way of adding a blank space between symbolic variables (and producing MERRY CHRISTMAS).

Concatenating a Symbolic Variable and a Character String

Three different cases are shown below.

1. SET &S = HA, and
   SET &Y = &S.RRY
2. SET &R = HA&S
3. SET &NEW = N,
   SET &STATE = &NEW..Y.

In line 2, &Y is assigned the concatenation of the symbolic variable &S and the character string RRY (resulting in HARRY.) Note that *there must be a period between the symbolic variable and the character string only if the symbolic variable is first*. In line 3, *no period is needed since the character string is first*—the result is HAHA. To produce the value N.Y. in line 5, *place an extra period between the symbolic variable and character string*.

Performing Mathematical Operations

Symbolic variables help perform mathematical operations. These operations are useful for looping (explained later) and other clist tasks. The following are examples of mathematical operations with symbolic variables.

1. SET &COUNT = &COUNT + 1
2. SET &B = 10
3. SET A = (10 + &B)/(2 * &B)

Line 1 is often used in clist loops to increment a counter symbolic variable by 1. Line 3 uses a nested symbolic variable (&B) assigned in line 2 to perform a mathematical operation. The interpreter assigns &A the result of adding 10 and the value of &B (10) and then dividing it by 2 times the value of &B. In other words, 10 + 10 divided by 2 × 10, resulting in 20 divided by 20, or 1.

Writing Text to a Screen (WRITE and WRITENR)

To the user, the most visible parts of the clist are the prompts and messages generated by the WRITE and WRITENR statements. Use these two statements: (1) To give friendly prompts to enter texts (including menus), (2) to send confirmation messages after performing an operation, and (3) to debug clists. The difference between WRITE and WRITENR is the location where the user enters input. For WRITENR (or WRITE NO RETURN), the input is on the same line as the message, and for WRITE, it is on the next line. (WRITENR is ineffective under TSO's and TSO/E's Session Manager because the input begins on the line following the prompt. Also, to process a null value, the user must press the Erase to End of Field or EOF key and then the RETURN key. Therefore, WRITENR should be used conservatively with Session Manager.) The following examples show the major uses of WRITE and WRITENR statements:

EXAMPLES

1. WRITENR What is your name?:
   displayed:
   What is your name?: *Mark*
2. WRITE What is your home state?:
   displayed:
   What is your home state?:
   TN
3. ```
   WRITE **********************************************
   WRITE * Please Select One of the Following:        *
   WRITE *  1 - TRAVEL EXPENSE REPORT                 *
   WRITE *  2 - WORD PROCESSOR                        *
   WRITE *  3 - STATISTICAL ANALYSIS                  *
   WRITE **********************************************
   WRITENR Enter Your Choice (1-3):
   ```
   displayed:
   ```
   **********************************************
   *  Please Select One of the Following:       *
   *    1 - TRAVEL EXPENSE REPORT               *
   *    2 - WORD PROCESSOR                      *
   *    3 - STATISTICAL ANALYSIS                *
   **********************************************
   Enter Your Choice (1-3): 1
   ```
4. WRITENR The report has been queued for printing at
   WRITE Printer &PRT
   displayed:
   The report has been queued for printing at Printer PRT1
   ```

An explanation by example number follows:

1. This is a common one-line prompt using the WRITENR statement. The user's input is placed on the same line as the prompt.
2. This is a typical one-line prompt using the WRITE statement. The user's input is placed on the line FOLLOWING the prompt.
3. This is a possible menu format using a combination of WRITE and WRITENR statements. The user's input is placed ON THE SAME LINE as the prompt.
4. This example produces a long message using both a WRITE and WRITENR statement. The confirmation message also writes the values of the symbolic variable &PRT. (Creating ad hoc messages at execution time.)

Reading a User-Entered Value (READ and READDVAL)

Use a READ or READDVAL statement to retrieve user input and pass it to one or more symbolic variables that it creates. The READ statement obtains one or more values from the user's input and READDVAL from an input buffer assigned to the control variable &SYSDVAL. (Chapter 5 discusses control variables.) For both statements, the values are positional, so the first symbolic variable stores the first value and so on.

READ and READDVAL Syntax

The following are guidelines or rules when creating READ or READDVAL statements:

1. The formats of the READ and READDVAL commands are:
   `READ variable1 variable2...`
   `READ`
   `READDVAL variable1 variable2...`
2. Multiple values are separated by commas, blanks, or tabs.
3. Use two commas or single quotes to set a value to null in a READ statement:
   `READ VAR1,VAR2,VAR3`
   entered by user: (null middle value)
   `3,,2 or '3' '' '2'`
   Note: `'3'"'2' results in 3''2`
4. If a user does not specify a value for a READDVAL or READ symbolic variable, then it is set to null. If a user has more values than symbolic variables, then the extra values are ignored.
5. Ampersands are optional for symbolic variables used in READ and READ-DVAL statements.
6. If using READ without any variables, then the input is placed in the control

variable &SYSDVAL. &SYSDVAL retains any value delimiters such as spaces. (When using READ with variables, &SYSDVAL is assigned a null value.)

```
READ
```
entered by user:
```
1 2 3
```
stored in &SYSDVAL as:
```
1 2 3    /*If delimited by commas would be 1, 2, 3.*/
READDVAL VAR1 VAR2 VAR3
WRITE VAR1 = &VAR1, VAR2 = &VAR2, VAR3 = &VAR3
```
displayed:
```
VAR1 = 1, VAR2 = 2, VAR3 = 3    /* &VAR1 has the first*/
                                /* value, etc.        */
```

7. You can assign a value to &SYSDVAL by (a) a READ statement with no variables, (b) user-entered input through a TERMIN command (see Chapter 5), and (C) a SET statement.

EXAMPLES

1.
```
WRITE PLEASE ENTER YOUR AGE:
READ AGE
WRITE YOUR AGE IS .. &AGE
```
displayed:
```
PLEASE ENTER YOUR AGE:
25
YOUR AGE IS .. 25
```
2.
```
WRITE PLEASE ENTER UP TO FIVE LANGUAGES THAT YOU
SPEAK
READ
READDVAL LANG1 LANG2 LANG3 LANG4 LANG5
WRITE YOU SPEAK &LANG1, &LANG2, &LANG3, &LANG4,
&LANG5
```
displayed:
```
PLEASE ENTER UP TO FIVE LANGUAGES THAT YOU SPEAK
ENGLISH, FRENCH, SPANISH, PORTUGUESE, CHINESE
YOU SPEAK ENGLISH, FRENCH, SPANISH, PORTUGUESE,
CHINESE
```

Example 1 is a common use of the READ statement. The user is prompted for his or her age, which echoes back to them. &SYSDVAL does not store the age. In example 2, the user is prompted to enter up to five languages. &SYSDVAL stores these values and READDVAL takes the first value and assigns it to the first symbolic variable and so forth.

Processing a Character String (&STR)

This section provides a brief look at the &STR built-in function (see Chapter 6 for a more complete review). We have already talked about how clists cannot directly read certain character strings. &STR allows character strings to keep their current value during symbolic substitution (so that blanks and leading zeros stay intact). The following is the format of the &STR function.

SET &variable = &STR(argument)

The argument may be any valid mix of symbolic variables and their values and clist operators. Let us look again at an earlier example using the &STR function.

```
SET &X = MERRY
SET &Y = &STR(   )
SET &Z = CHRISTMAS
SET &Q = &STR(&X&Y&Z)
```

Because we are using the &STR function, the blank space value of &Y is retained and &Q = MERRY CHRISTMAS. (Remember, without the &STR, the blank space in &Y is eliminated!)

Our First Clist—SENDMSG

We are now ready to look at our first clist—SENDMSG. SENDMSG is a simple user-friendly front-end to TSO's SEND command. It is later added to the clist utility program TSO5COM (short for TSO 5 commands.) The clist is presented with line-by-line explanations and sample runs.

SENDMSG Clist

```
PROC 0 VERIFY(NOVERIFY)
WRITE WHO WILL RECEIVE THIS MESSAGE?
READ
READDVAL USID
WRITE WHAT IS YOUR MESSAGE?
READ
SET &NOTE = &STR('&SYSDVAL')
IF &VERIFY = VERIFY THEN WRITE YOUR MESSAGE IS &NOTE
WRITE MESSAGE IS BEING SENT
SEND &NOTE U(&USID)
```

Two Sample Runs

With Verify On

```
/*Entered by UIC1 at READY or the ===> COMMAND line of*/
/*ISPF/PDF. SENDMSG is in UIC1.CLIST. &VERIFY has a
   default*/
/*value of NOVERIFY, so no operand value is required.
   But.*/
/* VERIFY is specified anyway*/

ex (sendmsg) 'verify(verify)'
displayed:
WHO WILL RECEIVE THIS MESSAGE?
HHG1
displayed:
WHAT IS YOUR MESSAGE?
A SAMPLE MESSAGE WITH VERIFY ON
displayed:
YOUR MESSAGE IS 'A SAMPLE MESSAGE WITH VERIFY ON'
MESSAGE IS BEING SENT
displayed on HHG1's terminal:
A SAMPLE MESSAGE WITH VERIFY ON UIC1
With Verify Off
/* entered by UIC1 at READY or the ===> COMMAND line of*/
/*ISPF/PDF. SENDMSG is in UIC1.CLIST. &VERIFY has a
  default*/
/*value of NOVERIFY, so does not need to be specified.*/

ex (sendmsg)
displayed:
WHO WILL RECEIVE THIS MESSAGE?
CAH0
WHAT IS YOUR MESSAGE?
A SAMPLE MESSAGE WITH VERIFY OFF
displayed:
MESSAGE IS BEING SENT
displayed on CAH0's terminal:
A SAMPLE MESSAGE WITH VERIFY OFF UIC1
```

SENDMSG Explanation by Line Number

1. A keyword operand of VERIFY (giving the &VERIFY variable a value of VERIFY) enables reviewing the entered message. The default value is

NOVERIFY. Because the clist is so small, no labels are used. An alternate approach is assigning the message and userid through a PROC statement.
2. A WRITE statement prompts the user for the receiver's userid.
3. Uses a READ statement with no variables. User input is stored in the control variable &SYSDVAL.
4. READDVAL assigns &USID the value of &SYSDVAL (This includes everything entered up to the first comma or blank.)
5. A WRITE statement prompts the user for the message.
6. A READ statement with no variables is used storing user input in &SYSDVAL.
7. A SET statement assigns the entire &SYSDVAL value to the symbolic variable &NOTE. Using the &STR built-in function, retains the blank spaces in the message. &STR places the message in quotes to be used "as is" by the SEND command.
8. Here is a "preview look" at the IF statement. This IF statement WRITEs the user-entered message to the screen if the VERIFY keyword operand was invoked. Otherwise, the message is not displayed. More on IF is found later.
9. This WRITE statement is a confirmation note that the message is now being sent to the user.
10. SEND the message using the clist-generated values for receiver userid and message.

DEBUGGING A CLIST

The Clist Trace Facility (CONTROL)

Control Statement Overview

The clist product provides a trace facility which:

1. Displays the result of symbolic substitution (including intermediate results)
2. Shows execution of conditional and looping logic
3. Shows where a clist branches
4. Displays executed TSO commands in a clist
5. Displays any informational messages while the clist is processing.

Table 4-2 lists the CONTROL statement operands you use to access the trace facility. Chapters 5 and 7 discuss other operands of the CONTROL statement.

Table 4-2. CONTROL Statement Trace Facility Operands

Operand	Function
CONLIST	Displays each clist statement *after* symbolic substitution plus the output from WRITE and WRITENR a user would see.
LIST	Displays TSO commands *after* symbolic substitution plus the WRITE and WRITENR messages a user would see.
MSG	Display any informational and error messages (such as dataset allocated or deleted) plus the WRITE and WRITENR messages a user would see.
SYMLIST	Display each clist statement *before* symbolic substitution plus the WRITE and WRITENR messages a user would see.

Control Statement Syntax and Guidelines

1. CONLIST, SYMLIST, and LIST show clist statements *before* execution, whereas MSG displays messages *after* execution.

2. SYMLIST and CONLIST does not display:
   - GLOBAL and NGLOBAL statements
   - Clist labels
   - Comments
   - PROC statements

3. When more of these operands are used in combination with the CONTROL statement, more information is given. My personal preference is CONTROL CONLIST MSG LIST so I can see the clist statements and TSO commands only after symbolic substitution.

4. If you do not wish a trace operand "on," place a NO in front of it. (e.g., CONTROL NOCONLIST NOLIST NOMSG NOLIST). Use any combination of on and off CONTROL trace operands (e.g., CONTROL CONLIST NOLIST MSG NOSYMLIST).

5. If using no CONTROL statement, then the defaults are NOCONLIST, NOLIST, MSG, and NOSYMLIST. The CONTROL statement has no default operands. Therefore, a CONTROL statement with no operands uses existing operand values (i.e., from a previous CONTROL statement, an EXEC command, or TSO default values).

6. Many sites require a sequence similar to the following for clists used by the public:

```
PROC 0 CTEST
IF &CTEST=CTEST THEN CONTROL CONLIST SYMLIST LIST MSG
```

Table 4-3. Control Variables to set CONTROL Operands

Control Variable Name	Function	Example
&SYSCONLIST	Turns ON/OFF CONLIST ON = CONLIST OFF = NOCONLIST	IF &SYSCONLIST = ON IF &SYSCONLIST = OFF
&SYSLIST	Turns ON/OFF LIST ON = LIST OFF = NOLIST	IF &SYSLIST = ON IF = &SYSLIST = OFF
&SYSMSG	Turns ON/OFF MSG ON = MSG OFF = NOMSG	IF &SYSMSG = ON IF &SYSMSG = OFF
&SYSSYMLIST	Turns ON/OFF SYMLIST ON = SYMLIST OFF = NOSYMLIST	IF &SYSSYMLIST = ON IF &SYSSYMLIST = OFF

So, you can go to any clist and easily put trace on. By using the same trace operand name in all clists, you will never have to search for the trace on operand name.

7. Do not assign CONTROL operands to symbolic variables. (If CONTROL &TRACE was in your clist, you would get an error message similar to the following: *IKJ56261 Stmt 3 - Invalid Keyword - &TRACE.*) However, in TSO/E Version 1 Release 4 and later control variables (or reserved system symbolic variables) can reset the current CONTROL operands. Table 4-3 lists the control variables.

8. When debugging a clist, use CONLIST and SYMLIST only on the parts of the clist causing problems (and not the entire clist). The trace facility significantly slows down the execution of a clist and can be hard to read.

9. Study all messages—they are useful clues to debugging your clist. *TSO/E Messages* provides further information on messages. (Note that most of these messages start with the letters IKJ.)

Trace Facility Examples

To demonstrate the differences between the various CONTROL trace facility operands, Table 4-4 presents each operand on using the SENDMSG clist. The following list discusses the table.

Table 4-4. A Comparison of the Four Clist Trace Operands

CONLIST	LIST	SYMLIST
WRITE WHO WILL + RECEIVE THIS MESSAGE?	WHO WILL RECEIVE THIS + MESSAGE ?	WRITE WHO WILL + RECEIVE THIS MESSAGE?
WHO WILL RECEIVE THIS MESSAGE ?	HHG1	WHO WILL RECEIVE THIS MESSAGE ?
READ	WHAT IS YOUR MESSAGE ?	READ
HHG1	Testing LIST	HHG1
READDVAL USID	MESSAGE IS BEING SENT	READDVAL USID
WRITE WHAT IS YOUR + MESSAGE ?	SEND‘Testing List’’U(HHG1) + LOGON	WRITE WHAT IS YOUR + MESSAGE ?
WHAT IS YOUR MESSAGE ?	READY	WHAT IS YOUR MESSAGE ?
READ	*MSG and Normal Display*	READ
Testing CONLIST		Testing SYMLIST
SET &NOTE = ‘Testing + CONLIST’	WHO WILL RECEIVE THIS + MESSAGE ?	SET &NOTE = + &STR(‘&SYSDVAL’)
IF NOVERIFY = VERIFY + THEN	HHG1	IF &VERIFY = VERIFY + THEN
WRITE MESSAGE IS BEING + SENT	WHAT IS YOUR MESSAGE ?	WRITE MESSAGE IS BEING + SENT
MESSAGE IS BEING SENT	Testing MSG	SEND &NOTE U(&USID) + LOGON
READY	MESSAGE IS BEING SENT READY	READY

1. Since there are no informational messages, the MSG display and what a user would see are identical.
2. The LIST display is similar to MSG and additionally shows the SEND command after symbolic substitution.
3. Remember CONLIST shows clist statements *after* symbolic substitution—so substituted values of &NOTE, &SYSDVAL and &VERIFY display. In contrast, SYMLIST shows the values *before* substitution. Remember, the trace facility does not display the PROC statement.

Debugging Techniques

The following is one approach for debugging a clist (or a program in any other language.)

1. *What is the error ?*
   a. What happened? (e.g., The clist sent a blank message using the SENDMSG clist.)
   b. What error messages are given?

2. *Learn more about what caused the error.* (Using the trace facility and the methods described below.)
   a. Where did it happen? (Before the clist starts executing? At a certain label? When executing another clist or program?)
   b. This may also include reconstructing what happened.
3. Based on step 2, *make an educated judgment about what caused the error.*
4. *Suggest a way to test your solution.*
5. *Perform the test.* If successful, you have a working program. If not, it is back to step 2. Steps 2 to 5 are sometimes done together.

To learn more about what caused the error (step 2), you can use the clist trace facility (see above), set up breakpoints with a WRITE statement, and trap return codes. These techniques can determine (1) The value of a symbolic variable. (2) If a clist flow control statement executed. (3) The result of executing a clist statement and the version number of TSO/E used. Let's look at each technique.

Using the WRITE Statement

Use the WRITE statement to set up a BREAKPOINT for displaying the value of a symbolic variable at a particular point in the clist. Two examples with the SENDMSG clist are provided.

Technique #1: Displaying the Value of a Symbolic Variable. Janice Marco created a version of the SENDMSG clist and ran into a problem—only the first word of her message prints. What is wrong? Here is her version.

```
PROC 0 VERIFY(NOVERIFY)
WRITE WHO WILL RECEIVE THIS MESSAGE?
READ
READDVAL USID
WRITE WHAT IS YOUR MESSAGE?
READ TXT                        /* The problem*/
SET &NOTE = &STR('&TXT')
IF &VERIFY = VERIFY THEN WRITE YOUR MESSAGE IS &NOTE
WRITE MESSAGE IS BEING SENT
SEND &NOTE U(&USID)
```

Explanation. The problem is assigning the message to &TXT instead of a &SYSDVAL with a READ and no symbolic variables. &TXT assigns all input up to the first blank or comma. In contrast, &SYSDVAL assigns all input until the RETURN key is pressed. Let's help Janice debug this problem.

1. Janice tries finding out what is assigned to &NOTE. She puts a WRITE &NOTE breakpoint after SET &NOTE and reruns the clist. The WRITE statement displays only the first word of her message.
2. Is there something wrong with assigning a value to &TXT? Janice places a WRITE &TXT breakpoint after READ TXT—displaying only the first word of her message. Aha—the culprit is the READ statement! After going back through the TSO/E book, Janice reads about using &SYSDVAL and meets success.

Technique #2: Diagnosing Flow Control Logic. A major part of clist debugging is finding out if the flow control statements (used for condition and loop testing) executed successfully. In a complex clist, a WRITE statement can give as much information as the trace facility. Using a simple example from the SENDMSG clist shows this. Suppose you were not sure if the clist executes statements after the SET &NOTE. To find out, place a *WRITE GOT PAST SET STATEMENT* after the SET &NOTE. If the message displays, the clist is executing correctly, otherwise it is not. WRITE statements are helpful in any clist for pinpointing the problem.

Technique #3: The Result of Executing a Clist Statement (Using Return Codes.). A *return code* or *condition code* is a value (usually from 0 to 999) showing the execution status of a clist, TSO, REXX, ISPF, or PDF statement. A return code of 0 says a clist statement executed correctly. The general rule is the higher the return code, the more serious the error.

Using the control variable &LASTCC gives a clist statement's return code. A common practice is assigning a symbolic variable the value of &LASTCC. (Since &LASTCC changes after the execution of *every* clist statement, this is the only way to "freeze" a return code value.) The following example shows this:

```
SET &NAME = MARK
SET &RCD = &LASTCC
IF &RCD = 0 THEN WRITE IT WORKED
ELSE WRITE WHOOPS BACK TO DEBUGGING
```

By assigning &RCD the return code of the SET &NAME statement, it is now available to the remaining clist (such as the two IF statements) and is not updated (until overwritten by another SET statement). If not done, &LASTCC's value is lost after the execution of the next clist statement. Some of the common names used for "return code holders" are &LCC, &LCD, &RC, &RCD, &CD, and &CODE. Standardizing these variable names makes it easier for another person to understand your clist. Appendix B provides a list of common clist return codes.

Technique #4: TSO or TSO/E Version Number Used. When debugging clists at an unfamiliar site, *always* first check the version number. The following shows a simple way to do this:

WRITE MY TSO/E VERSION IS &SYSTSOE

displayed:

MY TSO/E VERSION IS or an error message /*TSO*/
MY TSO/E VERSION IS 1010 /* Version 1 Release 1*/
MY TSO/E VERSION IS 1020 /* Version 1 Release 2*/
MY TSO/E VERSION IS 1030 /* Version 1 Release 3*/
MY TSO/E VERSION IS 1040 /* Version 1 Release 4*/
MY TSO/E VERSION IS 2010 /* Version 2 Release 1*/

By knowing the TSO or TSO/E version number, you can determine:

- If enhancements made or statements are available.
- Any known bugs and fixes (through IBM's INFO/SYSTEM database and other sources.)
- Appropriate documentation.

CLIST FLOW CONTROL

Since TSO/E Version 1 Release 4, clists have a fairly complete set of *flow control* (or *structured programming*) statements. These statements tell the interpreter what to execute next based on certain conditions or to loop so many times (each loop is called an *iteration*) until a condition is true or false. *Labels* (i.e., a name assigned to one or more clist statements) easily identify a clist location for the interpreter to find when a condition is true or false.

Moving Around the Clist (GOTO)

The GOTO statement provides a two-edged sword. On one side, it is the sole means for moving to different parts of the clist. However, a GOTO statement can bypass other logic, forcing an unlucky programmer to spend time flow-diagramming a clist! When coding GOTO statements, ask yourself these questions:

- Do I really need this GOTO ?
- Can I restructure my clist in such a way so that I do not need this GOTO?
- If the GOTO is unconditional (''stand alone''), can it become a conditional GOTO statement (e.g., IF..THEN GOTO)?

GOTO Syntax

The following are guidelines for creating GOTO statements:

1. Do not use a GOTO statement to access a subprocedure (TSO/E Version 1 Release 4 and later) or another clist. Going from another subprocedure or clist to the "main" clist is also invalid. (Chapter 8 discusses alternatives to doing this.)
2. The general format of the GOTO statement is:
   `GOTO location`
   where *location* is the label name or a *symbolic variable* assigned a label name as a value
3. Try to use only conditional GOTOs by putting GOTO part of a conditional or logic statement. (e.g., IF..THEN GOTO..)

GOTO Examples

Examples for both unconditional and conditional GOTOs are listed below. The first example goes to the appropriate label (which is the first four characters of a day of the week). However, if someone enters a value that is not a label, what happens? The clist displays an error message on not finding the label and abnormally ends—unconditional GOTOs produce unexpected results. (The exact error message is *IKJ56541 THIS STATEMENT HAS REFERENCED AN INVALID OR UNDEFINED LABEL.*

Unconditional GOTO

```
WRITE What day is today (FIRST 4 CHARACTERS ONLY) ?
READ TDAY
GOTO &TDAY
MOND: WRITE Start of a long week
TUES: WRITE Two days till pay day
(other clist statements)
```

The second example shows how a conditional GOTO may handle unexpected input. The IF statement reprompts a user to enter a value when the first value is not an existing label name (i.e., the first four characters of the day of the week). Other error-detection and -handling techniques are discussed later in this chapter and in Chapters 5 and 6.

Conditional GOTO

```
LABEL1:
  WRITE What day is today (FIRST 4 CHARACTERS ONLY) ?
  READ TDAY
  IF &TDAY = MOND OR &TDAY =TUES THEN GOTO &TDAY
  ELSE GOTO LABEL1
  (Other clists statements.)
```

Condition Testing (IF-THEN-ELSE, SELECT-WHEN-END)

The IF and SELECT (Version 1 Release 4 and later) statements both evaluate if one or more conditions are true and then perform the specified task for that condition. A *condition* is a valid mix of symbolic variables, built-in functions clist operators, and values (i.e., &SEX = "M"). A specified *task* consists of one or more TSO, clist, or ISPF/PDF statements.

The IF Statement

The IF statement is the backbone of the TSO and TSO/E clist language for building complicated (and too often incomprehensible) condition-testing structures. Table 4-5 shows the most common formats of the IF statement.

IF Statement Syntax. The following are guidelines for creating IF statements:

1. To execute multiple tasks, enclose them in a DO-END structure.
2. IF statement components may continue on multiple lines. However, this method is less readable and takes up more lines.

WITH CONTINUATION

```
IF &OPTION=Y THEN+
  DO
  WRITE Dataset Deleted
  GOTO DELETEIT
END
ELSE+
  DO
  WRITE Dataset not Deleted
  GOTO EXIT
  END
```

WITHOUT CONTINUATION

```
IF &OPTION=Y THEN DO
  WRITE Dataset Is Deleted
  GOTO DELETEIT
E D
ELSE DO
  WRITE Dataset not Deleted
  GOTO EXIT END
```

3. If you have TSO/E Version 1 Release 4 and later and use an IF statement with three or more conditions, then consider using the SELECT statement. SELECT is generally easier to debug and maintain.

Table 4-5. Common Formats of the IF Statement

Format	Example
One condition	IF condition THEN perform task

One condition, multiple tasks (NULL ELSE)	IF condition THEN DO
	  perform task
	  perform another task
	END
	ELSE /*optional*/

One condition, multiple tasks (NULL THEN)	IF condition THEN
	ELSE DO
	  perform task
	  perform another task
	END

Two conditions (STANDARD)	IF condition THEN perform task ELSE perform another task

Two conditions, multiple tasks	IF condition THEN DO
	  perform task
	  perform another task
	END
	ELSE DO
	  perform yet another task
	  perform yet another task
	END

Three + conditions, multiple tasks (NESTED IF)	IF condition THEN DO
	  perform a task
	  perform another task
	END
	ELSE IF . . . THEN DO
	  perform yet another task
	  perform yet another task
	END
	ELSE IF . . . THEN DO
	  perform yet another task
	  perform yet another task
	END

4. An IF condition may include multiple logical operators (i.e., AND, OR). Use the symbolic variable name for each condition in a statement.

RIGHT FORMAT	WRONG FORMAT
`IF &SEX = M AND &SEX= F . . .`	`IF &SEX = M AND= F . . .`

5. For multiple IFs, make sure that you cover all possible cases:

   ```
   IF &A = 6 THEN SET &G = 10
      ELSE IF &A<6 THEN SET &G = 4
   ```

   If &A is greater than 6, then both statements are ignored (since neither condition is met) causing unpredictable results. A third IF statement setting &G to null eliminates this problem:

   ```
   ELSE IF &A<6 THEN SET &G =
   ```

6. Indent subordinate statements (i.e., tasks in a DO-END structure, secondary IFs) for ease of reading. Also, indenting makes it easy to know which DO belongs to which END.

   HARD TO FOLLOW

   ```
   IF &OPT = 1 THEN DO
   IF &MODE = BATCH THEN DO
   SUBMIT CNTL(RUN1)
   END
   END
   ```

   EASY TO FOLLOW

   ```
   IF &OPT = 1 THEN DO
      IF &MODE = BATCH THEN DO
         SUBMIT CNTL(RUN1)
      END
   END
   ```

7. Use a NULL THEN when you want to perform a task only if ELSE condition is true

   ```
   IF &TASK = NOEXIT THEN
      ELSE GOTO EXIT
   ```

If &TASK equals NOEXIT then perform no task and bypass the ELSE statement. IF &TASK equals anything other than &NOEXIT, the execution ends.

IF Statement Example

```
PROC 1 FNAME
 LBL1: -
  WRITE ****************************************
  WRITE * The following options are available:  *
  WRITE * 1 - DELETE A FILE                      *
  WRITE * 2 - ALLOCATE A FILE                    *
  WRITE * 3 - LIST A FILE                        *
  WRITE ****************************************
  WRITENR Please enter your choice (1-3 only):
  READ OPT
  IF &OPT LT 1 AND &OPT GT 3 THEN GOTO LBL1
```

```
12.    IF &OPT NE 1 AND &OPT NE 2 AND &OPT NE 3 THEN GOTO +
       LBL1
13. OPTION1: -
14.   IF &OPT = 1 THEN DO
15.     DELETE &FNAME
16.       IF &LASTCC = 0 THEN WRITE &FNAME DELETED
17.   END
18. OPTION2: -
19.   ELSE IF &OPT = 2 THEN DO
20.     FREE F(NEWFILE)
21.     ALLOCATE F(NEWFILE) DA(&FNAME) NEW TRACKS SPACE
        (1,1)+
22.     RECFM(F B A) LRECL(255) BLKSIZE(25500) DSORG(PS)
23.       IF &LASTCC = 0 THEN WRITE &FNAME ALLOCATED
24.   END
25. OPTION3: -
26.   ELSE IF &OPT = 3 THEN DO
27.     LIST &FNAME
28.       IF &LASTCC = 0 THEN WRITE &FNAME LISTED
29. END
```

IF Example Explanation. The following is an explanation of the IF statement example by line number.

1. This clist is a front-end for three TSO commands. The file name (&FNAME) is passed as a positional variable. Chapters 5 and 6 discuss checking if a dataset exists or is a fully qualified name.
2. LBL1 is the first label. It provides a location to return to for invalid input. (See statements 11 and 12.)

3–8. The menu displays the option choices.

9–10. The user enters his or her choice on the same line as the prompt. (Note the reminder on the valid choices.) Line 10 reads the user's input.

11. If the input is a number and is not in the range of 1 through 3, then reprompt for input. (An optional way is assigning a label to line 9 and returning to the prompt instead of the entire menu.)
12. If the option is not a number, then reprompt the user for input. (Chapter 6 has a better way of doing this.)

13–17. If selecting option 1, then deleted the user-specified file. This task has a label of OPTION1. The clist gives a confirmation message if the file deletes successfully.

18–24. If selecting option 2, then allocate the user-specified file with preset operand values. This task has a label of OPTION2. The clist gives a confirmation message if the file allocates successfully.

25–29. If selecting option 3, then list the user-specified file. This task has a label of OPTION3. The clist gives a confirmation message if the file lists successfully.

The SELECT Statement (TSO/E Version 1 Release 4 and Later)

You should strongly consider using the SELECT statement instead of multiple IF statements. Table 4-6 shows common formats of the SELECT statement.

SELECT Statement Syntax

The following are guidelines for creating SELECT statements:

Table 4-6. Common Formats of the SELECT Statement

Format	Example
No SELECT condition 1 task per WHEN	SELECT WHEN condition perform task WHEN another condition perform another task OTHERWISE perform yet another task END
No SELECT condition, more than 1 task per WHEN	SELECT WHEN condition DO perform task END WHEN another condition perform another task OTHERWISE perform yet another task END
SELECT condition, one task per WHEN	SELECT condition WHEN condition perform task WHEN another condition perform another task OTHERWISE perform yet another task END
SELECT condition, more than one task per WHEN	SELECT condition WHEN another condition perform task WHEN yet another condition DO perform another task END OTHERWISE perform yet another task END

1. A *condition* is a valid mix of symbolic variables, clist operators, and values (i.e., &SEX = "M.") and is always enclosed in parentheses. A specified task consists of one or more TSO, clist, or ISPF/PDF statements.

2. Valid conditions in a WHEN substatement include:
   a. A single number or character (e.g., WHEN (A) . . .)
   b. A range of values separated by colons (WHEN (18:20)). Note WHEN (1:1) and WHEN (1) are equivalent.
   c. The OR and | operator which executes if at least 1 value in the condition is matched.

   The next example creates an AGE_TYP variable based on the value of &AGE. Note the third WHEN sub-statement where two value ranges are separated by an OR operator:

```
WRITENR PLEASE ENTER YOUR AGE:
READ AGE
SELECT (&AGE)
  WHEN (0:18) SET &AGE_TYP = YOUNG
  WHEN (19:50) SET &AGE_TYP = MIDDLE
  WHEN (50:59 OR 60:99) SET &AGE_TYP = &STR(YOUNG +
  AT HEART)
  OTHERWISE WRITE THAT IS AN INVALID AGE
END
```

3. If meeting a WHEN condition, (i.e., Exact match or falls in a certain range.), then perform the matching task and then the clist moves to the END statement. (Some languages scan each remaining WHEN condition.) If not matching a WHEN condition, the clist checks the remaining WHEN sub-statements and performs the task the OTHERWISE statement specifies.

4. If you use a WHEN command (see Chapter 5) with a WHEN in a SELECT, enclose it in a DO-END structure.

SELECT Statement Example. Here is the example used earlier now with SELECTs. The result is easier to follow and takes two fewer statements. (You could instead use a SELECT condition.)

```
PROC 1 FNAME
  LBL1: -
    WRITE ***************************************
    WRITE * The following options are available:  *
    WRITE * 1 - DELETE A FILE                      *
    WRITE * 2 - ALLOCATE A FILE                    *
    WRITE * 3 - LIST A FILE                        *
    WRITE ***************************************
```

```
WRITENR Please enter your choice (1-3 only):
READ OPT
SELECT
  WHEN (&OPT = 1) DO
    DELETE &FNAME
      IF &LASTCC = 0 THEN WRITE &FNAME DELETED
  END
  WHEN (&OPT = 2) DO
    FREE F(NEWFILE)
    ALLOCATE F(NEWFILE) DA(&FNAME) NEW TRACKS SPACE(1,+
    1) +
    RECFM(F B A) LRECL(255) BLKSIZE(25500) DSORG(PS)
      IF &LASTCC = 0 THEN WRITE &FNAME ALLOCATED
  END
  WHEN (&OPT = 3) DO
  LIST &FNAME
    IF &LASTCC = 0 THEN WRITE &FNAME LISTED
END
  OTHERWISE GOTO LBL1
END
```

Loop Testing (DO-WHILE or UNTIL-END Iterative and Compound DO.)

The DO Statement

To repeatedly execute a series of TSO, clist, or ISPF/PDF statements, use the DO statement. This statement executes a specified number of times or while or until a condition is met. One execution of these series of statements is an *iteration* or *loop*. A common mistake is thinking that the DO-END structure performs looping; it actually executes the enclosed statements only once. Table 4-7 shows some common looping formats of the DO statement.

DO Statement Syntax. The following are guidelines for creating DO statements:

1. For TSO and TSO/E non-Version 1 Release 4 and later sites, simulate an iterative DO by initializing and incrementing or decrementing a COUNTER variable (i.e., a symbolic variable that keeps track of the number of loops or iterations). In the following example, a counter variable (&CNT) is set initially to 1 and increments by 1 each iteration until it is greater than or equal to 5.

Table 4-7. Common Looping Formats of the DO Statement

Format	Example
Conditional DO:	
Loop while a condition is true.	DO WHILE condition perform task END
Loop until a condition is true.	DO UNTIL condition* perform task END
Iterative DO:	
Loop by a certain increment so many times	DO counter = start TO end BY increment * perform task END *Note: counter* = Counter variable used increment the loop. *start* = Starting value of counter. *end* = Ending value of counter. *increment* = Value to increment or decrement the counter (default = 1).
Compound DO:	
Loop by a certain increment so many times (and/or a while or until a condition is true)	DO counter = start TO end BY increment + * WHILE condition + UNTIL another condition + perform action END (Note continuation (+) signs at the end of DO, WHILE, and UNTIL statements because all are viewed as one large statement.)

* Available only TSO/E Version 1 Release 4 and later.

```
SET &CNT = 1
DO WHILE &CNT LE 5
   SET &CNT = &CNT + 1
END
```

2. For sites earlier than TSO/E Version 1 Release 4, simulate a DO-UNTIL by using a DO-WHILE with a "not equal" condition. The following examples of a DO-WHILE and DO-UNTIL are equivalent. The example initially

assigns &MODE a value of NOEXIT and executes the DO-WHILE or DO-UNTIL loop until &MODE equals the value of EXIT. This reassignment depends on the value of the &BYE variable.

DO-WHILE

```
PROC 0 BYE
SET &MODE = NOEXIT
DO WHILE &MODE NE EXIT
 (Other clist statements)
 IF &BYE = BYE THEN SET &MODE = EXIT
END
```

DO-UNTIL

```
PROC 0 BYE
SET &MODE = NOEXIT
DO UNTIL &MODE EQ EXIT
 (Other clist statements)
 IF &BYE = BYE THEN SET &MODE = EXIT
END
```

3. Without ERROR routines, the error handling of a DO-WHILE structure depends on the TSO or TSO/E release used. Sites earlier than TSO/E Version 1 Release 4 give a warning message and the structure continues processing for one iteration. In later TSO/E releases, the processing of the DO-WHILE structure ends and continues with the first statement after the structure.

4. Multiple conditions are allowed in all DO statements. In the example, processing continues until &AGE is greater than 25 *and* &EXIT has a value of YES:

```
DO UNTIL &AGE > 25 AND &EXIT = YES
(Other clist statements)
END
```

5. Use DO-UNTIL for processing user input. TSO/E rechecks the DO UNTIL condition *after* getting the input.

```
DO UNTIL &AGE GT 0
  WRITENR PLEASE ENTER YOUR AGE:
  READ AGE
END
```

6. The iterative DO continues processing until the *counter* variable is outside

the range specified by the *start* and *end* values. In the following example, TSO/E loops three times (&CNT equals 1, 3, and 5):

```
DO &CNT = 1 to 5 by 2
  (Other clist statements)
END
```

7. The following bad programming practices do work in both TSO and TSO/E but are discouraged because they produce unexpected results.

   Transfer into a DO Structure

   ```
   SET &VAR = BAD
   IF &VAR = BAD THEN GOTO LOOPTEST/*DROP INTO LOOP*/
   SET &CNT = 1
   DO WHILE &CNT LT 10
     LOOPTEST: SET &CNT = &CNT + 1
   END
   ```

   Transfer out of a DO structure before Completion

   ```
   SET &CNT = 1
   DO WHILE &CNT LT 10
        IF &CNT = 5 THEN GOTO PRINTIT/*DROP OUT OF LOOP*/
        SET &CNT = &CNT + 1
   END
   PRINTIT: WRITE GOT TO PRINTIT
   ```

8. The following steps are how a compound DO statement processes:
   a. The counter variable is assigned the begin value.
   b. TSO/E checks if the counter variable value is in the range specified by the begin and end values. If not, then the compound DO processing ends.
   c. If meeting the condition of the WHILE statement, then continue processing the clist, otherwise end the compound DO processing.
   d. Execute all tasks in the WHILE structure. (Between the WHILE and the END.)
   e. If not meeting the condition of the UNTIL structure, then continue processing the clist, otherwise end the Compound DO processing.
   f. Increment or decrement the counter variable value by the increment/decrement value and return to Step 2.

9. An alternative to a Complex DO structure is a *nested DO* (i.e., using two or more DO structures). Another bad programming practice is jumping from an outer (second) DO loop into an inner one. Figure 4-1 shows a valid and invalid nested DO. For the invalid DO, you will never exit the outer loop! The next section has an example with DO statements.

Figure 4-1. Valid and Invalid Nested DOs

Valid DO	Invalid DO
1 DO &CNT1 = 1 TO 20	1 DO &CNT = 1 to 20
2 DO UNTIL &AGE > 0	2 DO UNTIL &AGE > 0
WRITE YOUR AGE:	LB1: WRITE YOUR AGE:
READ &AGE	READ AGE
END	END
END	GOTO LB1/*Inner Loop*/
	END

The TSO5COM Clist

TSO5COM is a utility clist providing a front-end for five TSO commands. It will be expanded to include error handling, file operations, and double-ampersand symbolic variables in Chapters 5 and 6. Suggestions for making this a fully functional clist are given. Two versions of the clist are shown to take advantage of the TSO or TSO/E release you have.

TSO5COM Clist (All Versions of TSO and TSO/E)

```
PROC 0 CTEST VERIFY(NOVERIFY)
IF &CTEST = CTEST THEN CONTROL SYMLIST CONLIST LIST -
MSG
  ELSE CONTROL NOSYMLIST NOCONLIST NOLIST MSG
MAINMENU: -
  WRITE ****************************************
  WRITE * The following options are available:  *
  WRITE * 1 - Create a New File                 *
  WRITE * 2 - Delete an Existing File           *
  WRITE * 3 - List an Existing File             *
  WRITE * 4 - Rename an Existing File           *
  WRITE * 5 - Send a Message to Another User    *
  WRITE ****************************************
  WRITENR Please enter your choice (1-5 only):
  READ OPT
 VALID: -
  IF &OPT LT 1 AND &OPT GT 5 THEN GOTO MAINMENU
  IF &OPT NE 1 AND &OPT NE 2 AND &OPT NE 3 AND -
   &OPT NE 4 -
   AND &OPT NE 5 THEN GOTO MAINMENU
  IF &OPT = 1 THEN SET &DESCRIBE = CREATE
    ELSE IF &OPT = 2 THEN SET &DESCRIBE = DELETE
    ELSE IF &OPT = 3 THEN SET &DESCRIBE = LIST
```

```
        ELSE IF &OPT = 4 THEN SET &DESCRIBE = RENAME
        ELSE IF &OPT = 5 THEN SET &DESCRIBE = SEND
        ELSE GOTO MAINMENU
   FILEGET: -
     IF &OPT GE 1 AND &OPT LE 4 THEN DO
         WRITE How Many Files to &DESCRIBE ? (1 or 2)
         READ FILENUM
         IF &FILENUM NE 1 AND &FILENUM NE 2 THEN GOTO +
               FILEGET
         SET &CNT = 1
         DO WHILE &CNT LE &FILENUM
            SET &FILENAME =
            WRITE WHAT IS THE NAME OF FILE &CNT :
               READ FILENAME
               IF &CNT = 1 THEN SET &FILE1 = &FILENAME
                  ELSE IF &CNT = 2 THEN SET &FILE2 = +
                  &FILENAME
               SET &CNT = &CNT + 1
         END
     END
     IF &OPT EQ 1 THEN GOTO ALLOC_IT
      ELSE IF &OPT GE 2 AND &OPT LE 4 THEN GOTO OTHER_IT
      ELSE IF &OPT EQ 5 THEN GOTO SEND_IT
      ELSE GOTO EXIT
 ALLOC_IT: -
  SET &CNT = 1
  DO WHILE &CNT LE &FILENUM
      IF &CNT = 1 THEN SET &FN = &FILE1
       ELSE IF &CNT = 2 THEN SET &FN = &FILE2
      FREE F(FILE&CNT)
      WRITE ********&FN*************************
      ALLOCATE F(FILE&CNT) DA(&FN) NEW TRACKS +
      SPACE (1,1) +
      RECFM(F B A) LRECL(255) BLKSIZE(25500) DSORG(PS)
      IF &LASTCC GT 0 THEN WRITE ALLOCATE FAILED.
      SET &CNT = &CNT + 1
 END
  GOTO EXIT
 OTHER_IT: -
  SET &CNT = 1
  DO WHILE &CNT LE &FILENUM
    SET &NEWFILE =
    IF &OPT = 4 THEN DO
```

```
        WRITE WHAT IS THE NEW FILENAME?
         READ NEWFILE
    END
    IF &CNT = 1 THEN SET &FNN = &FILE1
       ELSE IF &CNT = 2 THEN SET &FNN = &FILE2
    WRITE *******&FNN*******************
    &DESCRIBE &FNN &NEWFILE
      IF &LASTCC GT 0 THEN WRITE &DESCRIBE FAILED
    SET &CNT = &CNT + 1
   END
   GOTO EXIT
  SEND_IT: -
   WRITE WHO WILL RECEIVE THIS MESSAGE?
   READ
   READDVAL USID
   WRITE WHAT IS YOUR MESSAGE?
   READ
   SET &NOTE = &STR('&SYSDVAL')
   IF &VERIFY = VERIFY THEN WRITE YOUR MESSAGE IS &NOTE
   WRITE MESSAGE IS BEING SENT
   SEND &NOTE U(&USID)
     IF &LASTCC GT 0 THEN WRITE MESSAGE FAILED
   GOTO EXIT
  EXIT: WRITE &DESCRIBE IS COMPLETED
```

TSO5COM Clist (TSO/E Version 1 Release 4 and Later)

```
PROC 0 CTEST VERIFY(NOVERIFY)
IF &CTEST = CTEST THEN CONTROL SYMLIST CONLIST LIST +
MSG
   ELSE CONTROL NOSYMLIST NOCONLIST NOLIST MSG
 MAINMENU: -
  WRITE ****************************************
  WRITE * The following options are available:  *
  WRITE * 1 - Create a New File                  *
  WRITE * 2 - Delete an Existing File            *
  WRITE * 3 - List an Existing File              *
  WRITE * 4 - Rename an Existing File            *
  WRITE * 5 - Send a Message to Another User     *
  WRITE ****************************************
  WRITENR Please enter your choice (1-5 only):
  READ OPT
VALID_LOGIC: -
 SELECT (&OPT)
```

```
    WHEN (1) SET &DESCRIBE = CREATE
    WHEN (2) SET &DESCRIBE = DELETE
    WHEN (3) SET &DESCRIBE = LIST
    WHEN (4) SET &DESCRIBE = RENAME
    WHEN (5) SET &DESCRIBE = SEND
    OTHERWISE GOTO MAINMENU
  END
FILEGET: -
 IF &OPT GE 1 AND &OPT LE 4 THEN DO
    WRITE How Many Files to &DESCRIBE ? (1 or 2)
    READ FILENUM
    IF &FILENUM NE 1 AND &FILENUM NE 2 THEN GOTO +
    FILEGET
    DO &CNT = 1 TO &FILENUM
       SET &FILENAME =
       WRITE WHAT IS THE NAME OF FILE &CNT :
        READ FILENAME
        IF &CNT = 1 THEN SET &FILE1 = &FILENAME
         ELSE IF &CNT = 2 THEN SET &FILE2 = &FILENAME
    END
 END
 SELECT (&OPT)
  WHEN (1) GOTO ALLOC_IT
  WHEN (2:4) GOTO OTHER_IT
  WHEN (5) GOTO SEND_IT
  OTHERWISE GOTO EXIT
 END                                                          +
ALLOC_IT: -
 DO &CNT = 1 TO &FILENUM
    IF &CNT = 1 THEN SET &FN = &FILE1
       ELSE IF &CNT = 2 THEN SET &FN = &FILE2
    FREE F(FILE&CNT)
    WRITE *******&FN************************
    ALLOCATE F(FILE&CNT) DA(&FN) NEW TRACKS +
    SPACE (1,1) +
    RECFM(F B A) LRECL(255) BLKSIZE(25500) DSORG(PS)
    IF &LASTCC GT 0 THEN WRITE ALLOCATE FAILED.
 END
 GOTO EXIT
OTHER_IT: -
 DO &CNT = 1 TO &FILENUM
  SET &NEWFILE =
  IF &OPT = 4 THEN DO UNTIL &NEWFILE NE
```

```
          WRITE WHAT IS THE NEW FILENAME?
          READ NEWFILE
      END
      IF &CNT = 1 THEN SET &FNN = &FILE1
         ELSE IF &CNT = 2 THEN SET &FNN = &FILE2
      WRITE *******&FNN********************
      &DESCRIBE &FNN &NEWFILE
        IF &LASTCC GT 0 THEN WRITE &DESCRIBE FAILED
    END
    GOTO EXIT
   SEND_IT: -
    WRITE WHO WILL RECEIVE THIS MESSAGE?
    READ
    READDVAL USID
    WRITE WHAT IS YOUR MESSAGE?
    READ
    SET &NOTE = &STR('&SYSDVAL')
    IF &VERIFY = VERIFY THEN WRITE YOUR MESSAGE IS &NOTE
    WRITE MESSAGE IS BEING SENT
    SEND &NOTE U(&USID)
      IF &LASTCC GT 0 THEN WRITE MESSAGE FAILED
    GOTO EXIT
   EXIT: WRITE &DESCRIBE IS COMPLETED
```

TSO5COM Run (NOTRACE). User enters at the READY prompt:

```
Ex (TSO5COM)
```

Displayed, and user enters selection:

```
****************************************
* The following options are available:  *
* 1 - Create a New File                 *
* 2 - Delete an Existing File           *
* 3 - List an Existing File             *
* 4 - Rename an Existing File           *
* 5 - Send a Message to Another User    *
****************************************
Please enter your choice (1-5 only): 1
```

displayed:

```
How Many Files Do You Want to CREATE?
```

User enters:

```
1
```

displayed:

```
WHAT IS THE NAME OF FILE 1:
```

User enters:

```
HELP.TEXT
```

displayed:

```
*********HELP.TEXT*******************
CREATE IS COMPLETED
```

TSO5COM Explanation. TSO5COM is explained below by line number for all versions.

1. There are no positional (required) operands and two keyword operands. (You must enter VERIFY with a value.) Chapter 5 provides a version of the clist with comments.

2–3. The statements turn the trace facility on or off. A lengthy alternative for TSO/E Version 1 Release 4 and later is:

```
SELECT
  WHEN (&CTEST = CTEST) DO
       SET &SYSCONLIST = ON
       SET &SYSSYMLIST = ON
       SET &SYSLIST = ON
       SET &SYSMSG = ON
  END
  OTHERWISE SET &SYSMSG = ON
END
```

4–14. The MAINMENU section displays the menu and obtains the user's selection.

15–24. (15–23 TSO/E example) the VALID (VALID_LOGIC for TSO/E because longer labels are allowed) module validates user input by checking if the entered option is in the acceptable range. If it is not, reprompt the user. Based on the user's selection, assign a value to &DESCRIBE.

25–30. (24–28 TSO/E example) The FILEGET module uses a nested DO structure. If the selected option is not 5 (SEND a message), then prompt the user for how many files they will use (1 or 2). Creating this sequence using single-ampersand variables is difficult. Chapter 5 shows using double ampersands to prompt for a large number of file names.

31–39. (29–36 TSO/E example) A DO-WHILE structure (iterative DO in the TSO/E example) gets the correct number of file names. The DO-WHILE follows these steps.

a. If the counter variable &CNT is less than or equal to the total number of files selected, go to step *b*; otherwise, exit the DO-WHILE. At the end of step *d*, increment the counter value.

b. Assign &FILENAME a null value. This statement normally is not needed because null is the default value. Since &FILENAME temporarily holds the file name, you must clear it every iteration.

c. Prompt for the file name and assign it to &FILENAME.

d. Depending on the value of &CNT, assign the file name (stored in &FILENAME) to &FILE1 or &FILE2. (Chapters 5 and 6 shows validating a file name and its existence.)

40–43. (37–42 in TSO/E example.) If selecting a valid option, the clist goes to one of three labels where it performs the requested TSO operation.

44–56. (43–53 in TSO/E example.) The ALLOC_IT module performs the following steps:

a. If &CNT is less than or equal to the number of datasets requested, go to step *b*; otherwise, exit the DO-WHILE loop. At the end of step *d*, increment the counter value. Note additional ALLOCATE parameters (such as RECFM or LRECL and BLKSIZE) could be requested in a fully functional version.

b. The IF statement assigns variable &FN the correct file name stored in &FILE1 or &FILE2.

c. Free the dataset if previously allocated and then allocate it. Display on the screen the allocated dataset name. FILE&CNT translates to a value combining both a test string and a clist variable (i.e., FILE1 or FILE2).

d. Display ALLOCATE FAILED message if not succeeding.

57–72. (54–67 in TSO/E example.) The OTHER_IT section performs operations for the DELETE, RENAME and LIST commands. This section follows these steps:

a. If the counter variable &CNT is less than or equal to the total number of files selected, go to step *b*; otherwise exit the DO-WHILE. At the end of step *e*, increment the counter value. (Unless using a compound or iterative DO structure, reset the counter to 1.)

b. Set the temporary variable &NEWFILE to null. This can also be placed in the nested DO loop.

c. If selecting RENAME, then execute a nested DO structure. The DO prompts for a new file name—a good application for the DO-UNTIL structure.

d. Assign &FNN the filename stored in &FILE1 or &FILE2 depending on the counter value (&CNT).

e. Execute the TSO command:

(i) Display the name of the file to process.

(ii) Substitute &DESCRIBE with LIST, DELETE, or RENAME. (&FNN is the present file name and &NEWFILE the new filename for RENAME.)

(iii) If successful, no message displays. Otherwise. display &DESCRIBE FAILED.

73–84. (68–79 in TSO/E example) The SEND_MSG section is the same SENDMSG clist described earlier.

85. (80 in the TSO/E example) The EXIT section writes a message that the action requested (&DESCRIBE) is done. A more complete message would include the return code:

```
ALLOC_IT:
(other clist statements)
 ALLOC.....
  SET &RCD = &LASTCC
  (other clist statements)
  GOTO EXIT
EXIT: -
WRITE ALL ACTION IS COMPLETED
WRITE The Return Code for &DESCRIBE is &RCD
```

displayed:

```
ALL ACTION IS COMPLETED
The Return Code for CREATE is 0
```

EXCEPTION HANDLING

A needed feature in any language is dealing with unexpected results from user input or program execution by coding special (or exception) routines. The clist language has two such exception routines: ATTN for users pressing the PA1 or ATTN (Attention) keys and ERROR for TSO or clist statements with an abnormal (i.e., greater than zero) return code. Also included in this section is another special routine—those executed when exiting a clist.

Attention Routines (ATTN)

Some users try to "power out" of an executing clist by pressing the ATTENTION key repeatedly (usually the PA1 or ATTN keys). If not having an *attention routine* (a series of clist and TSO statements performed on pressing ATTENTION) your user may end up in worst trouble than before—a TSO "twilight zone"! An attention routine does two tasks:

1. Executes the clist and TSO statements in the routine
2. Either ends the clist or returns to the statement after the one invoking the attention routine. To create an attention routine, use the ATTN statement.

Table 4-8 shows some common formats of the ATTN statement:

ATTN Syntax. The following are guidelines for creating attention (ATTN) routines.

1. Use any of the statements in Table 4-9 in an ATTN routine. Always place the ATTN routine *before* the clist statements to be used with it—usually at the top of a clist or after a clist label. Three statements related to ATTN routines (EXIT, RETURN, and CONTROL MAIN) are discussed later in the chapter.
2. To override an ATTN routine, use ATTN OFF after an ATTN routine or invoke another ATTN routine.

Table 4-8. Common Formats of the ATTN Statement

Format	Example
Stop an ATTN routine	ATTN OFF (the default)
An ATTN routine with a series of statements	ATTN DO WRITE You pressed Attention END
An ATTN routine that exits the clist	ATTN DO EXIT END or ATTN EXIT
An ATTN routine that returns to the statement after the one invoking ATTN	ATTN DO RETURN END or ATTN RETURN (also use CONTROL MAIN or CONTROL NOFLUSH)

Table 4-9. Statements that Can Be Used in an ATTN Routine

Statement	Comments	What Happens
TSO command	1 per routine; no limit in rest of clist; ignores more than one command.	Executes command and exits ATTN routine. May call another clist; otherwise, executes the statement AFTER the one invoking ATTN.
Clist statement	No limit per routine	Executes statement then processes next command or statement in the ATTN routine.
Null line	1 per routine	Executes line and exits ATTN routine. Returns to the last statement executed before ATTN.
EXIT statement	EXIT or RETURN required if TSO command or null line not used.	Ends the ATTN routine and the clist.
RETURN statement	EXIT or RETURN required if TSO command or null line is not used	Ends the ATTN routine and executes the statement after the one invoking ATTN.

3. Use the Clist Attention Facility if your site is MVS/XA and uses programs to call a clist. The facility uses the IKJCAF service to process the attention routine and IKJCAFR to decide where the clist goes after ending the attention routine. Complete documentation on these services is in the *TSO Extensions Guide to Writing a Terminal Monitor Program or a Command Processor* for TSO/E Version 1 Release 3 and the *TSO Extensions Programming Services* for TSO/E Version 1 Release 4 and later.

4. A common practice is adding a WRITE statement notifying the user they are in an ATTN routine. Otherwise, a user continues to press the ATTN key causing a nested or multiple attention situation. (*Note:* The Clist Attention Facility for programs can ignore additional ATTN pressing.) The result of a nested routine is an ABEND (abnormal ending of the clist) or a blank screen that no longer recognizes user inputs (also called the "TSO/E twilight zone").

5. A bad practice is having a GOTO as part of the ATTN routine. Better alternatives are calling the same clist as part of your routine, returning to the last statement processed before invoking ATTN, or exiting the clist. The first alternative is shown below:

Bad	Better
ATTN DO	ATTN DO
WRITE BACK TO SOME_LABEL:	%SAMECLIST
GOTO SOME_LABEL	END
END	

6. When using multiple clists, a good practice is passing a unique condition code to the EXIT statement (such as 99 or 999) so that another clist easily identifies when ATTN was pressed. An example is the following:

```
ATTN DO
 WRITE YOU PRESSED ATTENTION. TIME TO EXIT THE CLIST.
 EXIT CODE(99)
END
```

7. Freeing any datasets that a clist allocated in the ATTN routine is another good coding habit. This prevents any DATASET CURRENTLY ALLOCATED problems from occurring when reexecuting the clist.

8. Unless using CONTROL MAIN or CONTROL NOFLUSH, previously entered commands and variable values are lost on entering an ATTN routine. So, without CONTROL MAIN, the following happens: (1) RETURN statements do not work, (2) ATTN is ignored after a READ statement, and much more. So, CONTROL MAIN or CONTROL NOFLUSH is a *must* in every clist before any ATTN routine.

9. Attention routines, unless executing under TSO/E Version 1 Release 4 and later and ISPF Version 2 Release 3 and later, incorrectly process under IPSF. However, there are still restrictions running under later releases:
   a. Attention routines will not work when using ISPF's TEST or TRACE routines.
   b. ISPF recognizes only a null line (and not EXIT, RETURN, or another clist) to end an ATTN routine.
   c. *Do not* call ISPF from an ATTN routine—the results are inconsistent.
   d. If ISPF displays more than one screen (or SPLIT SCREEN), the ATTN routine works only on the screen that it is called from.

   The *Interactive System Productivity Facility Dialog Management Guide* contains more information about this subject.

10. Attention routines do work correctly under TSO's Session Manager.

11. Some clist statements (such as a DO loop) ignore an ATTN routine. Beware!

An example of implementing ATTN routines in the TSO5COM clist is presented later.

Error Routines (ERROR)

Use *ERROR routines* to correct problems caused by the processing of a TSO command or clist statement. (Preventing the abnormal end of a clist.) ERROR routines are invoked when a return code greater than zero is given by a clist statement. (Appendix A lists common return codes.) The error routine does two tasks: (1) Executes the clist and TSO statements in the routine, and (2) either ends the clist or returns to the statement following the one invoking the routine. Table 4-10 compares error routines using IF &LASTCC ..THEN .. statements. The comparison shows that error routines are more powerful and offer more control than a SELECT or multiple IFs.

Table 4-11 lists some common formats of the ERROR statement. Three statements related to ATTN routines (EXIT, RETURN, and CONTROL MAIN) are discussed later.

Table 4-10. A Comparison of Error Routines and IF Statements

ERROR	IF &LASTCC = ...THEN ...
Applies to all TSO commands and clist statements it precedes.	Applies to only one TSO command or clist statement it follows.
May execute multiple TSO commands in a routine (including another clist).	Same
May list error message and the offending statement (ERROR) but does not end the clist.	List the error message and the offending statement—when there is no IF..&LASTCC and CONTROL MSG SYMLIST LIST statements.
Including a RETURN statement, the clist goes to the statement after the one invoking the error routine (With CONTROL MAIN/NOFLUSH.)	Can return to the statement invoking the IF with a nonzero return code but only if explicitly using labels and GOTOs (adding some lines of code.)

ERROR Syntax

The following are rules or guidelines to creating error routines with the ERROR statement. Table 4-12 compares ATTN and ERROR routines.

1. An ERROR statement used in or after an ERROR routine does the following: (a) Ends the ERROR routine, (b) displays the TSO command or clist statement causing the error, (c) displays the TSO (usually IKJ...) error message, and (4) executes the next statement after the one invoking the error routine.

Table 4-11. Common Formats of the ERROR Statement

Format	Example
Stop an ERROR routine and return to clist.	ERROR OFF
Stop an ERROR routine but list error message/and offending statement and return to clist.	ERROR (Only with EXEC clistname NOLIST and CONTROL MSG.)
An ERROR routine with a series of statements.	ERROR DO WRITE You had a major error (other clist statements) END
An ERROR routine that EXITs the clist.	ERROR DO EXIT END or ERROR EXIT
An ERROR routine that returns to the last statement before executing ERROR.	ERROR DO RETURN END or ERROR RETURN (Also uses CONTROL MAIN or CONTROL NOFLUSH.)

Table 4-12. Comparison of ATTN and ERROR Routines

ATTN	ERROR
One TSO statement per routine.	Multiple TSO statements per routine.
Place before the clist or TSO statements where it can be called.	Same
Once ending the routine, RETURN executes the statement after the one invoking the ATTN routine (same line if there is a null line in the routine).	Same
ATTN OFF or another ATTN routine overrides the current one.	ERROR OFF, ERROR, or another ERROR routine overrides the current one.
Use CONTROL MAIN or CONTROL NOFLUSH to retain previously entered commands and variable values. Put the CONTROL statement before the routine.	Same

2. Some good coding practices for ERROR routines are:

   a. If possible, reprocess the statement causing the error by reprompting for any missing or invalid information (dataset names, values, etc.). Also decide which return codes the routine processes or ignores (to continue processing the clist). The ERROR routine below, for TSO/E Version 1 Release and later, processes the WRITE statements only with a 100 or 200 return code. Otherwise, the routine ends and the clist continues processing.

```
ERROR DO
 SET &RCD = &LASTCC
 SELECT (&RCD)
  WHEN (100) THEN DO
    WRITE DATASET DOES NOT EXIST
    WRITE DO YOU WANT TO TRY AGAIN ? (Y/N)
     READ &CHOICE
    IF &CHOICE = Y THEN GOTO LABEL_1 ELSE RETURN
  END
  WHEN (200) THEN DO
    WRITE DATASET IS NOT PARTITIONED
    RETURN
  END
  OTHERWISE RETURN
 END
END
```

   b. Use WRITE messages to let the user know what is happening.

   c. If the routine EXITs the clist, consider putting the return code in the EXIT statement:

```
ERROR DO
 SET &RCD = &LASTCC
 WRITE An Error Has Occurred in the Clist
 WRITE The Return Code Was &RCD
 EXIT CODE(&RCD)
END
```

   d. Using ERROR OFF after or in an ERROR routine stops processing of an ERROR routine.

```
ERROR DO
 ERROR OFF
 WRITE A SERIOUS ERROR ...LEAVING CLIST
 GOTO EXIT
END
(some clist statements)
EXIT: EXIT
```

e. Consider logging an error message to a dataset. The following example takes the userid, date and time of the error message, and the return code and writes it out to a file. (The end of the chapter has the complete sequence and Chapter 5 presents control variables &SYSUID, &SYSDATE, and &SYSTIME.)

```
ERROR DO
 SET &RC = &LASTCC
 SET &LINE = &STR(ERROR OCCURRED BY &SYSUID ON -
  &SYSDATE -
 at &SYSTIME WITH A RETURN CODE OF &RC)
 (write out the line to a file)
END
```

3. ERROR routines do work correctly under Session Manager but not necessarily under ISPF (e.g., when accessing ISPF and returning to the READY prompt, an ERROR routine may still be resident even though the clist appears to have ended!)

EXIT Routines (EXIT and RETURN)

EXIT routines choose which statements execute after an ATTN or ERROR routine or subprocedure ends (see Chapter 8). EXIT ends the clist and returns to the READY prompt or the COMMAND===> line of ISPF/PDF. RETURN goes to the clist statement (or the one after it) where the routine or subprocedure was invoked. The TSO5COM clist presented at the end of the chapter has examples of both statements.

EXIT Statement

Use the EXIT statement to end a clist, a subprocedure, a multiple (nested) clist, or an ATTN or ERROR routine. The following are guidelines for using EXIT.

1. Using the CODE operand:
   a. When assigning no CODE operand, then &LASTCC stores the return code from EXIT.
   b. The code value may be an integer or a symbolic variable with an integer value.
   c. Use control variable &MAXCC to get the highest return code set when executing a clist or subprocedure. Also use &MAXCC in ATTN and ERROR routines. (Chapter 5 discusses &MAXCC.) *You can use EXIT as a label name without error.*

```
EXIT: EXIT CODE(&MAXCC)
```

Table 4-13. Major Uses of the RETURN Statement

Use	What Happens When Used
ATTN/ERROR	Once leaving the routine, executes the next statement after the one invoking the ATTN or ERROR routine.
SUBPROCEDURE (TSO/E Version 1 Release 4 and later.)	Returns to the next statement after the one that called the subprocedure (SYSCALL). A subprocedure may also issue a return code
Other cases	Ignored unless used in one of the above ways.

2. Use the QUIT operand with multiple (nested) clists to return to a previously invoked clist. (More specifically, the first clist found in a series with a CONTROL MAIN or CONTROL NOFLUSH.) If not using QUIT or no previously invoked clist contains a CONTROL MAIN or CONTROL NOFLUSH statement, then the clist returns to READY or the COMMAND ===> prompt in ISPF/PDF and the input stack is lost.

RETURN Statement

Since TSO/E Version 1 Release 4, the RETURN statement has an added importance with the ability to go back to a main clist from a *subprocedure* (part of a clist performing one or two tasks). (See Chapter 8 for subprocedures and multiple clists.) Table 4-13 summarizes the major uses of the RETURN statement and what happens when used.

RETURN Syntax

The following are guidelines for using RETURN.

1. Using the CODE operand (available in TSO/E Version 1 Release 4 or greater):
   a. When not using CODE, &LASTCC stores a null value.
   b. Typical uses for the CODE operand include:
      (i) Sending a return code from ATTN or ERROR to the clist (presents several ways).

```
ATTN DO                         ATTN DO
  SET &RCD = &LASTCC              RETURN CODE(&LASTCC)
  RETURN CODE(&RCD)             or
END                               RETURN CODE(&MAXCC)
                                  END
```

      (ii) Send a return code from a subprocedure to the "main" clist. (The subprocedure is part of the main clist—think of it as a label where the clist goes to and then returns.)

```
PROC 0
SYSCALL TIMER /* Calls subprocedure TIMER. */
 IF &LASTCC = 0 THEN WRITE SUBPROCEDURE WORKED!
TIMER: PROC 0
       WRITE THE TIME IS &SYSTIME
        SET &RCD = &LASTCC
       RETURN CODE(&RCD)
       END
```

c. Use control variable &MAXCC for getting the highest return code from a clist or subprocedure. (See Chapter 5 for &MAXCC.)

```
ERROR DO
 WRITE The highest return code encountered was -
 &MAXCC
 RETURN CODE(&MAXCC)
END
```

d. The CODE operand value can be a character string, integer, or a variable with a value of a character string or integer. The example below exits the clist when the return code has a value of A.

```
ERROR DO
 SET &RCD = &LASTCC
 IF &RCD = 332 THEN RETURN CODE(A)
 ELSE RETURN CODE(B)
END
(other clist statements)
OPENFILE
IF &LASTCC = A THEN DO
   WRITE SERIOUS ERROR...EXITING CLIST
   EXIT
END
ELSE GOTO LABEL_ONE
```

2. Without CONTROL MAIN, previously entered commands and variable values are lost when entering an ATTN/ERROR routine. So, CONTROL MAIN is a *must* in every clist before any ATTN/ERROR routine.

Input Stacks and the ATTN/ERROR Routines

The *input stack* stores TSO commands and clist statements in a ready-to-run (or EXECUTABLE) format using the "pushdown method" (the most recent statement on top of the stack, oldest statement on the bottom). When it reaches the first record, the stack is empty and the interpreter reads more input from the terminal. The input stack contains this information:

- TSO commands and clist statements processed
- Return, exit, and condition codes
- If attention and exit routines exist in a clist
- Dataset names
- Source of input (clist, command processor)
- The series of other clists (nested or multiple clists) previously invoked
- Symbolic variable values

If invoking an ATTN or EXIT routine and processing of the clist resumes after the routine ends, the default clist action is flushing (or erasing) the input stack. It is futile to continue processing a flushed clist. As mentioned earlier, this problem can be prevented by including a CONTROL NOFLUSH or CONTROL MAIN in your clist. A comparison of the two statements is given in Table 4-14. Once again, *always include a CONTROL MAIN or CONTROL NOFLUSH statement before an ERROR or ATTN routine with a RETURN statement*. See Chapter 11 for a comparison of the Clist and REXX stacks.

DATASET OPERATIONS

An important part of clist processing is adding and retrieving information from a small dataset—creating a JCL or COBOL program, log file, or a simple database. This dataset is either a partitioned dataset member or a physical sequential file. Both input and output clist dataset operations use the *queued sequential access method* or *QSAM*. QSAM is ideal for clists because:

1. It reads datasets sequentially, so *keys* (or unique record identifiers) are not needed. This is perfect for small sequential datasets and PDS members. However, a clist may have to read an entire dataset to retrieve a record, which is clearly inefficient for large datasets.
2. By being device- and mode-independent, QSAM runs in either interactive or batch TSO. This also means that QSAM is well suited for an interpreted language since it does not need compiling or recompiling.

Table 4-14. Comparison of CONTROL MAIN and CONTROL NOFLUSH

CONTROL MAIN	CONTROL NOFLUSH
Not the default (FLUSH)	Not the default (FLUSH)
Cannot flush this clist because of ERROR/ATTN (MAIN clist)	Cannot flush this clist because of ERROR/ATTN (one of a series of clists)
Overrides FLUSH	Overrides FLUSH for this clist (but not for previously invoked ones)

Table 4-15. Rough Benchmarks Using the Clist QSAM Facility

Records	Actual Time to Read All 1-byte Records	Actual Time To Read All 80-byte Records
1	Less than 1 second	Same
10	Less than 1 second	Same
100	Less than 1 second	Same
500	1 second	Same
1000	1 second	2 seconds
5000	6 seconds	8 seconds
10,000	15 seconds	17 seconds
50,000	1 minute, 15 seconds	1 minute, 26 seconds

To reinforce the point that the clist QSAM facility is ideal for small datasets, Table 4-15 shows some rough benchmarks using TSO/E Version 1 Release 3. The times given are how long it took to read to the end of the dataset. (With CONTROL CONLIST SYMLIST MSG LIST, these times are higher.)

A good rule of thumb for the clist QSAM facility is: *If more than 5000 records, send a message to the user that processing may take some time*. (Or use something else for dataset operations.) Table 4-16 gives skeletons of the clist statements used for most QSAM dataset operations. The following lists explain each statement, by number.

Table 4-16. Clist Statements Used for QSAM Dataset Operations

Read from Dataset	Write to Dataset
1. error routine	1. error routine
2. FREE F(ddn)	2. FREE F(ddn)
3. ALLOC F(ddn) DA(dsn) SHR	3. ALLOC F(ddn) DA(dsn) OLD
4. OPENFILE ddn INPUT	4A. OPENFILE ddn OUTPUT (Use with 5A.)
or	or
4. OPENFILE ddn	4B. OPENFILE ddn UPDATE (Use with 5B.)
5. GETFILE ddn	5A. Set &ddn = &symbolic
6. SET &symbolic = &ddn	or
7. CLOSFILE ddn	5B. GETFILE ddn
8 FREE F(ddn)	6. PUTFILE ddn
	7. CLOSFILE ddn
	8. FREE F(ddn)

READ FROM A DATASET

1. Error routines or IF &LASTCC = .. THEN .. statements are critical for the smoothly performing dataset operations. Failure to do this results in open datasets and unexpected termination. Some possible routines are: (a) Premature end of dataset found, (b) requested record not found, (c) unable to open or close a dataset, and (d) writing to a read-ready dataset or reading to a write-ready dataset.
2. Free a dataset if currently allocated. DDN is the ddname or file name of an allocated dataset used for clist QSAM operations.
3. Allocate the dataset with a disposition of SHR giving nonexclusive use.
4. The dataset opens after the OPENFILE statement. It is optional to use the operand of INPUT.
5. GETFILE reads a record and assigns it to symbolic variable with the same name as DDN. (So a GETFILE on a dataset with a ddname of FILEX uses symbolic variable &FILEX with a value of the last record read.) To read consecutive records, use a DO WHILE, DO-UNTIL (for later releases), or iterative DO (for later releases).

```
DO WHILE &FILEX NE &STR(HI THERE)
    GETFILE FILEX
END
```

   Reading records from a dataset can also simulate a LIST command displaying the contents of a dataset.

8. To "freeze" the current record, assign it to another symbolic variable or variables.

7–8. Close and free the dataset (delete a temporary dataset so it can be reused).

WRITE TO A DATASET

1. See the comments on error routines in the "read from a dataset" list.
2. Frees a dataset if allocated. DDN is the ddname or filename of the allocated dataset used for clist QSAM operations.
3. Allocate the dataset with a disposition of SHR for nonexclusive use, or use NEW or SHR or MOD (adds records at the end of the dataset).
4. Open the dataset after an OPENFILE. Choose either the OUTPUT (statement 4A adds a new dataset record) or UPDATE (statement 4B modifies an existing dataset record) operand.
5. To perform a PUTFILE (statement 6) on an OUTPUT dataset assign the value of the entered record to a symbolic variable with the same name as DDN (statement 5A.) Use the &STR function for retaining blanks. For an UPDATE, a GETFILE retrieves the record to be modified (statement

5B). To write consecutive records, use a DO-WHILE (for later releases) DO-UNTIL, or iterative DO.

6. The PUTFILE takes the value assigned to &DDN and writes it as the new record (OUTPUT) or modifies an existing record (UPDATE).

7–8. Close and then free the dataset.

Accessing a Dataset (OPENFILE, CLOSFILE)

Syntax and Guidelines

Most of the OPENFILE and CLOSFILE syntax was explained when reviewing the skeleton. Be aware of the following situations with OPENFILE—they could cause problems:

- Allocating a dataset without any RECFM, BLKSIZE, or DCB operands and then issuing an OPENFILE. Later releases of TSO/E provide default values for these operands.
- Concurrently writing a record (with PUTFILE) to two members of the same partitioned dataset. The clist could write the record to either member.
- Having the OPENFILE's logical record length (LRECL) being greater than 32,767 giving the message:

  ```
  IKJ79057I DATASETS WITH A LOGICAL RECORD LENGTH GREATER
  THAN 32767 ARE NOT SUPPORTED FOR CLIST I/O
  ```
- Trying to assign more than one dataset to an OPENFILE or CLOSFILE statement. This is invalid.

Common Problems

1. Getting an IKJ56541I message (NORMAL END OF FILE OCCURRED ON GETFILE (E400)). This message occurs when the GETFILE statement retrieves the last record in the dataset before the dataset is expected to close; 400 is the return code. (Return codes for the clist QSAM facility usually range from 336 to 416. Check Appendix B for a complete list.) *Suggestion:* Browse the dataset to see if any records match the DO-WHILE or DO-UNTIL criteria for the GETFILE symbolic variable. Change your criteria if they do not. Consider adding or modifying an error routine to handle this condition.
2. Getting an IKJ56545I message (TRIED TO OPEN A FILE THAT IS CURRENTLY OPEN). *Suggestion:* Put a CLOSFILE before another OPENFILE or remove the second OPENFILE. You may also have to log off to close the dataset and log on again to reuse it.

3. Getting an IKJ56549I message (PUTFILE ISSUED BEFORE ANY GETFILES—UPDATE MODE). *Suggestion:* Retrieve the record before updating it—place a GETFILE statement before the PUTFILE.
4. Being in the wrong "mode"—such as (a) using PUTFILE (instead of GETFILE) with OPENFILE &ddn INPUT, or (b) using GETFILE (instead of PUTFILE) with OPENFILE &ddn OUTPUT or OPENFILE &ddn UPDATE. *Suggestion:* Use the correct PUTFILE or GETFILE statement.
5. The CLIST ends before processing CLOSFILE. In rerunning the clist, the dataset does not reopen. *Suggestion:* Logging off closes the dataset and then log on again to reuse it.
6. A dataset processed by OPENFILE adds no ISPF statistics. *Suggestion:* Enter STATS ON at the Command ==> line once in the dataset to turn on statistics for all future editing.

Reading and Writing Records (GETFILE, PUTFILE)

Syntax and Guidelines

1. The following are limitations of GETFILE or PUTFILE:
   a. With GETFILE and concatenated datasets, no records or additional datasets are read if the first dataset in the concatenation is empty. (Even if the other datasets contain records.)
   b. For both GETFILE and PUTFILE, use the functions of &STR, &NRSTR, &SYSNSUB (see Chapter 6) to read special characters and JCL statements.
   c. GETFILE and PUTFILE can process all data characters from hexadecimal 40 to FF. Some additional characters such as Line Feed also are supported.
   d. GETFILE and PUTFILE text *always* converts to uppercase regardless of whether you are using CONTROL ASIS or CAPS. This is not yet documented in most versions of clist users' guides.
   e. Compare the following:

VALID (FILE1)	INVALID (&FILE1)
`alloc f(file1) da(..) old`	`alloc f(file1) da(..) old`
`SET &DATA1 = FILE1`	`SET &DATA1 = &FILE1`
`OPENFILE &DATA1`	`OPENFILE &DATA1`
`GETFILE &DATA1`	`GETFILE &DATA1`
`SET &TEST = &FILE1`	`SET &TEST = &FILE1`
`CLOSFILE &DATA1`	`CLOSFILE &DATA1`

The invalid example shows &DATA1 having the value of the record rather than the dataset name and the dataset does not open. The general rule is *use a symbolic variable in a GETFILE or PUTFILE statement, but only if it has a value used in reading or writing a record—not a file name*. Note usually the & is not used.

2. Use a DO loop for reading or writing multiple records in a sequential file or partitioned dataset member. The loop assigns each new record to another symbolic variable. Chapters 5 and 6 review double-ampersand variables. They also examine the built-in functions of &SYSNSUB, &STR, and &NRSTR which can be used to construct double-ampersand variables and control the number of symbolic substitution passes. Using built-in functions is a better way of assigning dataset records than the above method because you can easily store and recall one or more records.

   In the following examples, the contents of the first record is assigned to &FIRST, the third record to &MIDDLE, and the fifth record to &LAST. The second example has two GETFILE statements—although the counter increments by two, the record READ ONLY INCREMENTS BY ONE (because the file is read sequentially). Therefore, the second GETFILE allows the number of records read to catch up with the counter.

All Versions of TSO and TSO/E

```
alloc f (ex1) da(example.data) shr
OPENFILE EX1
SET &CNT = 1
DO WHILE &CNT LE 5
  GETFILE EX1
  IF &CNT = 1 THEN SET &FIRST = &EX1
    ELSE IF &CNT = 3 THEN SET &MIDDLE = &EX1
    ELSE IF &CNT = 5 THEN SET &LAST = &EX1
  SET &CNT = &CNT + 1
END
CLOSFILE EX1
FREE F (EX1)
```

TSO/E Version 1 Release 4 and Later

```
alloc f (ex1) da(example.data) shr
OPENFILE EX1
DO &CNT = 1 TO 5 BY 2
   GETFILE EX1
```

```
SELECT (&CNT)
 WHEN (1) SET &FIRST = &EX1
 WHEN (2) SET &MIDDLE = &EX1
 WHEN (3) SET &LAST = &EX1
 OTHERWISE EXIT
END
GETFILE EX1
END
CLOSFILE EX1
FREE F(EX1)
```

3. IFs nested in DO loops can perform special processing for selected records or read a range of records. The following assigns the value of the second record to &X. Otherwise, read the record without special processing and increment the counter.

```
alloc f(ex2) da(example.data) shr
OPENFILE EX2
SET &CNT = 1
DO WHILE &CNT LE 5
 IF &CNT = 2 THEN DO
    GETFILE EX2
    SET &X = &EX2
    WRITE X IS &X
    SET &CNT = &CNT + 1
 END
  ELSE DO
     GETFILE EX2
     SET &CNT = &CNT + 1
  END
END
CLOSFILE EX2
FREE F(EX2)
```

Common Errors

Most of the errors for GETFILES and PUTFILES previously have been listed. If the record is read in or written out incorrectly, a suggestion is to use the &STR function to retain blanks and process special characters. Check if the counter increment logic in the DO loop is correct (i.e., reading the right record). Check the value assigned by the SET or GETFILE before the PUTFILE.

Error Routines

Without ERROR and ATTN routines, a clist may abnormally end when using the QSAM file facility leaving an opened file. To use the file again, you must log off and log back on—an unfriendly situation for the unwary clist user. However, an ERROR routine solves most but not all problems. It is still possible for an error routine to loop and receive a message: IKJ56547I EXEC ERROR CODE ZZZZ HAS BEEN ISSUED RECURSIVELY. (ZZZZ is an abend or error code.) Early releases of TSO instead ask you to log on or log off!

A useful error routine is adding an end-of-file sequence. In the following example, if the record equals 9999 (last record), the file closes and the clist ends.

```
OPENFILE TESTME
  SET &CNT = 1
  DO WHILE &CNT LT 5
    GETFILE TESTME
    IF &TESTME = 9999 THEN DO
      WRITE RECORD NOT FOUND..END OF DATASET READ
      CLOSFILE TESTME
      FREE F(TESTME)
      EXIT
    END
    SET &CNT = &CNT + 1
END
CLOSFILE TESTME
FREE F(TESTME)
```

The following steps are usually part of an ERROR or ATTN routine used with the clist QSAM file facility:

1. For ERROR routines, capture the return code (&LASTCC).
2. Notify the user what happened and a probable cause of failure.
3. Choose an action based on the return code. These include: (a) If possible, close the dataset, if not, log off to close the dataset. (b) Free the dataset. (c) End the clist.

The following error routine shows common error conditions (or use a SELECT structure.) For example, if the clist ran out of records before matching the DO criterion, then it issues a return code of 400. The error routine displays the appropriate message for the return code.

```
ERROR DO
  SET &RC = &LASTCC
```

```
    IF &RC = 400 THEN WRITE NO RECORDS FOUND..END OF DATASET
      ELSE IF &RC = 404 THEN WRITE THIS IS A READ-ONLY +
      DATASET !
      ELSE WRITE UNKNOWN ERROR
    WRITE CLOSING FILE AND EXITING CLIST
    CLOSFILE TESTIT
    FREE F(TESTIT)
    EXIT
  END
  (Some clist statements)
  OPENFILE TESTIT
  (Some clist statements)
  PUTFILE TESTIT
```

TSO5COM with Exception Handling and File I/O

Here is the TSO5COM clist with ATTN and ERROR routines and the clist QSAM file facility. The new code is in bold.

```
PROC 0 CTEST VERIFY(NOVERIFY)
IF &CTEST = CTEST THEN -
 CONTROL SYMLIST CONLIST LIST MSG MAIN
   ELSE CONTROL NOSYMLIST NOCONLIST NOLIST MSG MAIN
ATT1: -
 ATTN DO
   WRITE YOU HAVE PRESSED THE ATTENTION KEY.
   WRITE DO YOU WISH TO EXIT THE CLIST? (Y/N)
     READ ANS
     IF &ANS EQ Y OR EQ   THEN DO
        EXIT CODE(99)
     END
       ELSE RETURN
 END
ERR1: -
 ERROR DO
   SET &RC = &LASTCC
   IF &RC = 360 THEN WRITE LOG file not currently -
OPENed
   ELSE IF &RC = 364 OR &RC = 368 THEN -
     WRITE LOG file never OPENed or not CLOSed
  ELSE DO
     WRITE Serious Problem with LOG File
     WRITE PLEASE contact Tom at Extension 3333
```

```
        WRITE Your return code is &RC
     END
     CLOSEFILE LOGIT
     FREE F(LOGIT)
    EXIT CODE(&RC)
    END
  MAINMENU: -
    WRITE ***************************************
    WRITE * The following options are available:  *
    WRITE * 1 - Create a New File                  *
    WRITE * 2 - Delete an Existing File            *
    WRITE * 3 - List an Existing File              *
    WRITE * 4 - Rename an Existing File            *
    WRITE * 5 - Send a Message to Another User     *
    WRITE ***************************************
  READ__LOG: -
    WRITENR Please enter your choice (1-5 only):
    READ OPT
    ALLOC F(LOFIT) DA(TSO5COM.USER.LOG) MOD
     OPENFILE LOGIT OUTPUT
      SET &LOGIT = &STR(&OPT &SYSUID &SYSTIME &SYSDATE)
      PUTFILE LOGIT
     CLOSFILE LOGIT
    FREE F(LOGIT)
  ERR2: -
    ERROR DO
     SET &RCD = &LASTCC
     WRITE An Error has been found
     WRITE Do you wish to exit the clist? (Y/N)
     READ &ANS2
     IF &ANS2 = Y OR &ANS EQ   THEN DO
        CLOSFILE LOGIT
        FREE DA(&FILE1,&FILE2,TSO5COM.USER.LOG)
        EXIT CODE(&RCD)
     END
     ELSE RETURN
    END
  VALID: -
    IF &OPT LT 1 AND &OPT GT 5 THEN GOTO MAINMENU
    IF &OPT NE 1 AND &OPT NE 2 AND &OPT NE 3 AND &OPT
    NE 4 -
    AND &OPT NE 5 THEN GOTO MAINMENU
```

```
IF &OPT = 1 THEN SET &DESCRIBE = CREATE
  ELSE IF &OPT = 2 THEN SET &DESCRIBE = DELETE
  ELSE IF &OPT = 3 THEN SET &DESCRIBE = LIST
  ELSE IF &OPT = 4 THEN SET &DESCRIBE = RENAME
  ELSE IF &OPT = 5 THEN SET &DESCRIBE = SEND
  ELSE GOTO MAINMENU
FILEGET: -
 IF &OPT GE 1 AND &OPT LE 4 THEN DO
    WRITE How Many Files to &DESCRIBE ? (1 or 2)
    READ &FILENUM
    IF &FILENUM NE 1 AND &FILENUM NE 2 THEN GOTO
    FILEGET
    SET &CNT = 1
    DO WHILE &CNT LE &FILENUM
       SET &FILENAME =
       WRITE WHAT IS THE NAME OF FILE &CNT :
          READ FILENAME
          IF &CNT = 1 THEN SET &FILE1 = &FILENAME
             ELSE IF &CNT = 2 THEN SET &FILE2 =
             &FILENAME
          SET &CNT = &CNT + 1
    END
 END
 IF &OPT EQ 1  THEN GOTO ALLOC_IT
  ELSE IF &OPT GE 2 AND &OPT LE 4 THEN GOTO OTHER_IT
  ELSE IF &OPT EQ 5 THEN GOTO SEND_IT
  ELSE GOTO EXIT
ALLOC_IT: -
 SET &CNT = 1
 DO WHILE &CNT LE &FILENUM
  IF &CNT = 1 THEN SET &FN = &FILE1
   ELSE IF &CNT = 2 THEN SET &FN = &FILE2
  FREE F(FILE&CNT)
  WRITE *****&FN**********************
  ALLOCATE F(FILE&CNT) DA(&FN) NEW TRACKS
  SPACE(1,1) +
   RECFM(F B A) LRECL(255) BLKSIZE(25500) DSORG(PS)
  IF &LASTCC GT 0 THEN WRITE ALLOCATE FAILED.
  SET &CNT = &CNT + 1
END
 GOTO EXIT
OTHER_IT: -
```

```
104.  SET &CNT = 1
105.  DO WHILE &CNT LE &FILENUM
106.  SET &NEWFILE =
107.  IF &OPT = 4 THEN DO
108.     WRITE WHAT IS THE NEW FILENAME?
109.     READ NEWFILE
110.   END
111.  IF &CNT = 1 THEN SET &FNN = &FILE1
112.     ELSE IF &CNT = 2 THEN SET &FNN = &FILE2
113.    WRITE ******&FNN*****************
114.    &DESCRIBE &FNN &NEWFILE
115.     IF &LASTCC GT 0 THEN WRITE &DESCRIBE FAILED
116.     SET &CNT = &CNT + 1
117.  END
118.  GOTO EXIT
119.  SEND_IT: -
120.   WRITE WHO WILL RECEIVE THIS MESSAGE?
121.   READ
122.   READDVAL USID
123.   WRITE WHAT IS YOUR MESSAGE?
124.   READ
125.   SET &NOTE = &STR('&SYSDVAL')
126.   IF &VERIFY = VERIFY THEN WRITE YOUR MESSAGE IS &NOTE
127.   WRITE MESSAGE IS BEING SENT
128.   SEND &NOTE U(&USID)
129.    IF &LASTCC GT 0 THEN WRITE MESSAGE FAILED
130.    GOTO EXIT
131. EXIT: WRITE &DESCRIBE IS COMPLETED
```

Explanation. The following is an explanation of the preceding clist by line number.

3–4. CONTROL MAIN guarantees RETURN statements in the ERROR and ATTN routines work correctly.

5–14. The entire clist uses this ATTN routine. It queries if the user wishes to exit the clist. If the answer is Y or blank, the clist ends and assigns a 99 return code. Otherwise, it returns to the statement *after* the one where the user pressed ATTENTION. (*Note:* If placing a CLOSFILE statement or FREE command (same as lines 55 and 56) in this routine before the file was opened or allocated, the clist accesses the ERROR routine resulting in a recursive error. Please be cautious in placing a CLOSFILE or FREE in an ATTN routine.

15–29. This is the error routine for lines 42–47. If issuing a nonzero return code after an OPENFILE, PUTFILE, or CLOSFILE, then the clist invokes the error routine. Appendix B lists possible return codes. If the return code is 360, 364, or 368, then display the appropriate error message. Otherwise, display a message saying whom to contact and the return code. The clist then ends.

42–47. Each time the clist executes, the result appends to a file called TSO5COM.USER.LOG. (If interested in only capturing abnormal terminations, add the following sequence to an ERROR or ATTN routine. Later, you can check the non-zero return code.)

```
SET &LOGIT = &STR(&OPT &SYSUID &SYSDATE
&SYSTIME &LASTCC)
```

A sample record could be:

1 UIC1 09:22:15 10/14/88 0

SET assigns &LOGIT a character string with the option used (&OPT), the user's TSO id (&SYSUID), the date (&SYSDATE), and time (&SYSTIME) the clist was used. (Chapter 5 discusses &SYS variables or CONTROL VARIABLES.) This LOG file then appends this string, closes it, and frees the file. (Remember, MOD appends records to an existing file.)

48–60. The ERROR routine for the remaining clist. (Similar to earlier ATTN routine.) It prompts the user if they wish to exit the clist. If the answer is Y or blank, then end the clist. Otherwise, return to the statement AFTER the one where the ERROR occurred. Then close the user log file, free datasets &FILE1 and &FILE2, and assign the return code to &RCD.

CONCLUSIONS

This chapter presents the important cornerstones for building a system with clists:

1. Reading and writing clist variables to a screen or from a file
2. Debugging concepts
3. Clist flow control structures
4. Exception handling

Our SENDMSG example grew into a powerful and lengthy TSO front-end. Yet there is much more left to cover. Chapter 5 touches on other parts of the clist language and miscellaneous topics helpful to intermediate and advanced SAS users. Chapter 6 reviews built-in functions for clists to process special strings and much more. For those needing more powerful file operations than the QSAM file facility, look at Chapters 7 and 10 and decide if TSO EDIT or PDF edit macros are best for you. Chapters 8 and 9 examine the final topics needed for building systems with clists—using multiple clists and ISPF. You are now on your way to taking full advantage of the power and flexibility of clists.

SUGGESTED READINGS

Braddock, Fred, 1983. Access Methods in *Encyclopedia of Computer Science and Engineering, Second Edition*. Anthony Ralston and Edwin D. Reilly Jr. (eds.). New York: Van Nostrand Reinhold, pp. 1444–1452.

Elston, Jay, 1982. Clist Esoterica—Advanced Examples. Techniques. *SHARE 59 Proceedings*, pp. 1857–1865.

Gehani, Narain, 1985. *C: An Advanced Introduction*. Rockville: Computer Science Press, pp. 81–91

Hoffman, Charles A., 1986. *Introduction to TSO Command Lists (Clists)*. Course Notes.

IBM Corporation, 1988. *INFO/SYSTEM Database*. Various Notes.

IBM Corporation, 1987. *Interactive System Productivity Facility: Dialog Management Guide MVS*. SC34-4112

IBM Corporation, 1987. *TSO Messages*. GC28-1310

IBM Corporation, 1987. *TSO/E Programming Guide*. SC28-1363

IBM Corporation, 1987. *TSO Extensions Clists*. SC28-1304

IBM Corporation, 1987. *TSO Extensions Programming Guide*. SC28-1363

IBM Corporation, 1987. *TSO Extensions Programming Services*. SC28-1364.

Kusnierz, Thomas E., 1986. Clist Tips and Techniques. *SHARE 67 Proceedings*. pp. 1–19 (handout).

Reilly, Edwin D. Jr., 1983. Structured Programming, in *Encyclopedia of Computer Science and Engineering, Second Edition*. Anthony Ralston and Edwin D. Reilly Jr. (eds.). New York: Van Nostrand Reinhold, pp. 1444–1452.

Williams, Gregg, 1985. Debugging Techniques. *Byte*. 10(6), pp. 279–290.

5

Clists: Advanced and Miscellaneous Topics

This chapter builds on Chapters 3 and 4 by examining advanced and miscellaneous clist subjects. These topics are included for the following reasons:

1. Most of these topics are touched on only briefly if at all during a clist course. Others, like double-ampersand symbolic vaiables, usually are not included because of their complexity.
2. Some topics are in the IBM user guides but are either not easy to find or briefly discussed.
3. Past IBM user groups meetings (e.g., SHARE or GUIDE) have reviewed a topic, but this information is not disseminated to most clist users.
4. Clist style and documentation standards have not appeared in a public document.

ADVANCED TOPICS

This section presents five important advanced topics: clist internals, double-ampersand symbolic variables, control variables, LISTDSI, and clist style. It first reviews each clist component and then shows its use. It then reinforces what you learned with our final look at the TSO5COM clist (see Chapter 4) with many of these features.

A Simplified Look at Clist Internals

The actual "behind-the-scenes" workings of clists are unknown to all but a minority of clist users. A general understanding of interpreter processing allows you to take advantage of the clist interpreter and debug programs faster.

Table 5-1. Phase 1 and 2 Checklist

Phase 1: Startup Tasks	
Exec:	Input
Does the exec dataset exist? Is it a REXX exec or clist? Is the EXEC implicitly or explicitly invoked? Are the EXEC operands valid? Are they in upper or lower case? (TSO/E Version 2)	Are there any TSO commands or clist statements to read? Is the syntax correct? Do all datasets to use exist?
Phase 2: Execute Clist	
Clist Processing	Execution
Are there any clist symbolic variables? Are any control variables or built-in functions requested?	Execute the clist and TSO commands. Get the return code.
Do both of these need scanning again to reach their final value? Are there any TSO commands to process?	Perform the ATTN or ERROR routine if an error occurs.

The EXEC interpreter invoking a clist processes in two distinct phases. Table 5-1 provides a checklist the interpreter goes through during processing. *This is based on "reverse engineering" rather than any restricted IBM documentation.* So, they may not be in the correct order.

In summary, phase 1 reads each clist statement and checks its syntax. Phase 2 performs the needed symbolic substitution and executes the clist. This is important to know when reviewing symbolic substitution and debugging clists.

Double-Ampersand Symbolic Variables

Double-ampersand symbolic variables are one of the hardest topics for clist users to understand. If not grasped correctly, the resulting clists contain unnecessary nested variables and unintelligible double-ampersand SET statements. This chapter tries to present double-ampersand variables in an easy-to-understand way.

Another Look at Symbolic Substitution

The clist interpreter performs symbolic substitution during phase 2. In other words, the symbolic variable name (i.e., &A) translates to a character or numeric value (i.e., 23). The interpreter considers the following factors when performing the substitution*:

- Symbolic naming conventions—an ampersand symbol and 252 or fewer alphabetical characters beginning with an alphabetic. (*Author's note:* See Chapter 4 for symbolic variable name/value syntax.)
- Optional omission of the leading ampersand on SET. READ, READDVAL, and file I/O statements (*Author's note:* Such as OPENFILE, CLOSEFILE, GETFILE, and PUTFILE; remember the ampersand is optional for these seven statements.)
- Line-by-line substitution order.
- Line scanning and substitution in left-to-right order.
- Nested variables required multiple line scans. (Nested variables are those represented in turn by variable names.) (*Author's note:* For example, SET &A = 10; SET &B = &A.)
- Line-scanning limit, as established as a value in the &SYSSCAN control variables—those strung together without intervening delimiters are substituted in scanning order. (*Author's note:* EXEC can scan a clist statement between 0 (no substitution) and $2^{31} - 1$ times.)
- Concatenation of variables to character strings (by the use of an intervening period to denote the concatenation) (*Author's note:* For example, SET &Y = &X.HAPPY).
- Substitution of a single ampersand for every pair encountered, prior to execution.
- If a built-in function is found. a module calls another module to evaluate the built-in expression. (*Author's note:* module names omitted.)
- The routine calls a module as necessary to evaluate expressions (*Author's note:* module names omitted.)

Another name for a scan is *level of symbolic substitution,* so one scan is the same as one level of symbolic substitution. Most single-ampersand variables (&) resolve symbolically in either the first or second scan, and most double-ampersand variables (&&) resolve symbolically in the second or third scan. Figure 5-1 and Table 5-2 list the values of single- and double-ampersand symbolic variables during each scan.

* The above factors are reprinted by permission from *OS/VS2 TSO Terminal Monitor Program and Service Routines Logic*, Copyright © 1984 by International Business Machines Corporation page 3-19 with additions noted.

Figure 5-1. The Clist Interpreter and Three Levels of Symbolic Substitution

Single Ampersand Variables
All Level 1
(Scan 1)

Simple SETs:
SET &X = 15.
After Scan 1. &X = 15

Simple concatenated expressions: SET &X = GOOD SET &Y = NIGHT SET &Z = &STR (&X &Y) *After Scan 1. &Z = GOOD NIGHT.*	Nested concatenated expressions: SET &X = GOOD SET &G = &X SET &Y = NIGHT SET &Z = &STR (&G &X) *After Scan 1. &Z = GOOD NIGHT.*
Nested values: SET &Y = 15 SET &X = &Y *After Scan 1. &X = 15.*	Double-nested symbolic variables: SET &G = 15 SET &Y = &G SET &X = &Y *After Scan 1. &X = 15.*
Combined expressions: SET &X = ABC SET &Y = &X.DEF *After Scan 1. &Y = ABCDEF.*	Nested combined expressions: SET &G = ABC SET &X = &G SET &Y = &X.DEF *After Scan 1. &Y = ABCDEF.*

Double Ampersand Variables

Level 2 (Scan 2)	Level 3 (Scan 3)
Simple SETs: SET &Y = 17 SET &X = &&Y *After Scan 2. &X = 17.*	
Simple concatenated expressions: SET &X = GOOD SET &Y = NIGHT SET &Z = &&X &&Y *After Scan 2. &Z = GOOD NIGHT.*	Triple-nested concatenated expressions: SET &X = GOOD SET &T = &X SET &G = &&T SET &Y = NIGHT SET &Z = &&G &&Y *After Scan 1. &Z = &G &Y.* *After Scan 2. &Z = &T NIGHT.* *After Scan 3. &Z = GOOD NIGHT*

Figure 5-1. *(continued)*

Simple nested values: SET &Y = 23 SET &X = &&Y *After Scan 2. &X = 23.*	Double-nested symbolic variables: SET &A = PBS SET &X = &&A SET &Z = &&X *After Scan 1. &Z = &X.* *After Scan 2. &Z = &A.* *After Scan 3. &Z = PBS.*
Combined expressions: SET &Y = 19 SET &X = &&Y.89 *After Scan 2. &X = 1989.*	Doubled-nested combined expressions: SET &X = SO SET &Y = TIRED SET &Z = &&X SET &Q = &&Y SET &FEEL = &&Z &&Q *After Scan 1. &FEEL = &Z &Q.* *After Scan 2. &FEEL = &X &Y.* *After Scan 3. &FEEL = SO TIRED.*

Double-Ampersand Syntax and Guidelines

Before learning how to build arrays, a review of double-ampersand variables is needed.

1. Think of the first ampersand in a double-ampersand variable as a dummy or "throw-away" value. So on the first scan, the clist interpreter substitutes a single ampersand on scanning a double-ampersand value. On later scans, the interpreter performs symbolic substitution if the single-ampersand variable is not assigned yet its final value. Or, after the first scan, the interpreter views &&S as &S and after later scans, as the value of &S. The following examples of nesting symbolic variables show this. In the first example, &A equals the value of &S after the first scan and 15 after the second. In the second example, &A equals &S after the first scan and blank on the second (i.e., &S has no value).

Example 1	Example 2
SET &S = 15 SET &A = &&S	SET &A = &&S

2. Create a double-ampersand variable with a SET assigning or nesting a value of variable name to another variable. Use these common methods in assigning double-ampersand symbolic variables.

Table 5-2. Values of Symbolic Variables during Three Levels of Symbolic Substitution

Symbolic Variable	Level 1 (Scan 1)	Level 2 (Scan 2)	Level 3 (Scan 3)
SET &X = 15	&X = 15	Same	Same
SET &X = 10 SET &Y = 10 SET &Z = &X + &Y	&X = 10 &Y = 10 &Z = 20	Same	Same
SET &X = X SET &CNT = 1 WRITE &X&CNT	&X&CNT = X1	Same	Same
SET &X=HI SET &Y=&X.HO	&Y = HIHO	Same	Same
SET &X = HI SET &Y = &X SET &Z = &Y.HO	&Z = HIHO	Same	Same
SET &Y = 10 SET &X = &&Y	&X = &Y	&X = 10	Same as Scan 2

SET &A = &STR (&&A)
SET &CNT = 1
DO WHILE &CNT LE 10
WRITE FILE &CNT:?
  READ &FNAM
  SET &A&CNT = &FNAM
  SET &CNT = &CNT + 1
END
	&A&CNT = value of &FNAM.	&A1 = value of &FNAM.	Same as Scan 2

Nesting a Double-Ampersand Variable

```
1. SET &A = &&Y
2. SET &A = &STR (&&Y)
3. SET &A = &NRSTR (&&Y)
```

You can assign a double-ampersand variable name as a value of another single- or double-ampersand variable. Use this (also called *nesting a symbolic variable*) for capturing a double-ampersand variable value and building arrays. After the first scan of statements 1 and 2, the interpreter assigns &A a value of &Y. Chapter 6 discusses &NRSTR, used in statement 3, which performs only one symbolic substitution scan and retains the single- or double-ampersand variable value. So, after the first scan, &A equals &&Y and &&Y retains the double-ampersand value. For TSO/E Version 1 Release 3 and later, try using the alternatives of &NRSTR or

&SYSNSUB. (Along with control variable &SYSSCAN specifying the number of symbolic substitution scans to perform.) (Chapter 6 has more on these built-in functions.)

Assigning to Single-Ampersand Variable

```
1. SET &Y = &&Y
2. SET &Y = &STR(&&Y)
3. SET &Y = &NRSTR(&&Y)
```

You may assign a double-ampersand variable to a single-ampersand variable with the same name. This is useful in controlling the symbolic substitution when building arrays. After the first scan of statements 1 and 2, the interpreter assigns &Y a value of &Y. I prefer using this approach because you enter uses less double ampersands in your program. *However, do place a comment next to the SET saying you are doing this*. For statement 3, after the first scan, &Y equals &&Y and &&Y retains the double-ampersand value.

3. You can assign a double-ampersand variable as a value to another or the same double-ampersand variable.

```
SET &E = &STR(&&E)
SET &E = &&D
```

After scan 1, &E equals &D. If instead using one SET statement, SET &&E = &&D, then the clist abruptly ends. The reason is &&E translates to & and the clist views this as an operator rather than a variable. (The exact error message is *IKJ56545I This statement has an expression with operators out of sequence*.)

4. Use three ampersands for assigning a double ampersand name as a value. TSO/E also does this with &NRSTR and &SYSNSUB built-in functions using double ampersands.

```
SET &X = &STR(&&X)
SET &B = &&&X
```

After Scan 1, &B equals &&X.

```
SET &X = &STR(&&X)
SET &C = &NRSTR(&&X)
```

After Scan 1, &C equals &&X.

```
SET &X = &STR(&&X)
SET &E = &STR(&&E)
SET &E = &&&X
```

After Scan 1, &E equals &&X.

Figure 5-2. A Clist Array

			The &A Array				
1	2	3	4	5	6	7	- Column
&A1	&A2	&A3	&A4	&A5	&A6	&A7	- Variable
A	22	HI	2+3	88	GO	Y	- Value

Clist Statements

```
SET &A1 = A
SET &A2 = 22
SET &A3 = HI
SET &A4 = &STR(2+3)
SET &A5 = 88
SET &A6 = GO
SET &A7 = Y
```

Building Arrays with Double-Ampersand Variables

Array Concepts. To have a clist process a series of related vlaues, assign them to symbolic variables with the same "root" name but a different number suffix (such as VAR1, VAR2, etc.). A group of similar data stored in a set of symbolic variables with nearly identical names is a *clist array*. Clist arrays usually are one-dimensional arrays. (If you are using a lot of two-dimensional or larger arrays in your clists, strongly consider programming in another language such as APL, C, FORTRAN, or PASCAL.) Figure 5-2 shows a representation of a clist array.

The "root" (i.e., &A) of an array symbolic variable name is the array name and the number suffix (i.e., 1–7) is the column or position number of the value. (So &A6 is located in "Column" 6 of the "&A array.") This representation makes the remainder of the discussion on clist arrays easier to understand and provides a tool to use when debugging clist arrays (e.g., drawing a box showing the array values after each symbolic scan). Now that you know what a clist array is, you are probably wondering how to use it. Some common applications of clist arrays are:

1. Processing multiple lines with the clist QSAM facility (see Chapter 4).
2. Processing a group of variables in an ISPF panel.
3. Processing a TSO command using similarly named datasets (i.e., ALLOCATE, LIST, DELETE, or CALL).

Syntax and Guidelines

1. Here is one way to create an array of TSO dataset names.

```
SET &CNT =1
SET &FILE = FILE
```

```
DO WHILE &CNT LE 3
  ALLOC F (&FILE&CNT) DA (DATA.A&CNT) SHR
  SET &CNT = &CNT + 1
END
```

The resulting ALLOCATE statements are:

ALLOC F (FILE1) DA (DATA.A1) SHR
ALLOC F (FILE2) DA (DATA.A2) SHR
ALLOC F (FILE3) DA (DATA.A3) SHR

2. To build an array of symbolic variable names as values:
   a. Use a DO-WHILE or iterative DO loop:
      (i) Once in the loop, set a symbolic variable equal to a array variable (e.g., SET &X = &&STATE&CNT) or symbolic variable (e.g., SET &&STATE&CNT = &X).
      (ii) Process additional TSO statements or clist commands.
      (iii) Increment the counter value and end the loop if reaching the end counter value or the condition is met. This example prompts for ten file names, storing them in &FILE1 through &FILE10.

```
SET &FILE = &STR(&&FILE)
SET &CNT = 1
DO WHILE &CNT LE 10
   WRITE WHAT IS THE NAME OF FILE &CNT ?
   READ FNAM
   SET &FILE&CNT = &FNAM
   SET &CNT = &CNT + 1
END
```

3. Use arrays to read or write multiple records with the clist QSAM facility. Using a DO-WHILE loop and arrays, the example adds five new records to a dataset. Use this approach for clists writing a program (in any language) out to a dataset. Clists allow last-minute substitutions—so &FILENAME translates to a file name based on a user's selection. Chapter 7 reviews creating JCL programs with this approach. The key is building an array containing the program statements that you want to have included (&CL1 to &CL10). Another approach that frees your clist of all the array definition statements (i.e., SET &CL1 = . . . , SET &CL2 = . . .) is using ISPF's file-tailoring facility. Chapter 9 looks at ISPF, including file tailoring.

```
SET &CL  = &STR(&&CL)
SET &CL1 = &STR(START OF NEW RECORDS)
SET &CL2 = &STR(100 KANSAS           316-555-8888)
SET &CL3 = &STR(200 CONNECTICUT      203-555-4523)
SET &CL4 = &STR(300 MASSACHUSETTS    508-555-8742)
SET &CL5 = &STR(END OF NEW RECORDS)
```

```
ALLOCATE F(IN) DA(CUSTOMER) SHR
OPENFILE IN OUTPUT
  SET &CNT = 1
  DO WHILE &CNT LE 5
    SET &IN = &STR(&CL&CNT)
    PUTFILE IN
    SET &CNT = &CNT + 1
  END
```

4. A second array can hold the values of the first one. This is helpful when the first array only temporarily holds the array variable value and the second array stores and uses the value for the rest of the clist run.

```
SET &ARRAY_ONE = &STR(&&ARRAY_ONE)
SET &ARRAY_TWO = &STR(&&ARRAY_TWO)
SET &CNT = 1
DO WHILE &CNT LE 10
   WRITE WHAT IS THE NAME OF FILE &CNT?
   READ FNAM
   SET &ARRAY_ONE&CNT = &FNAM
   SET &ARRAY_TWO&CNT = &ARRAY_ONE&CNT
   SET &CNT = &CNT + 1
END
```

Now use &ARRAY_ONE (after clearing) to hold values for another temporary array.

5. If using an array more than once in a clist, this sequence can clear it. *Remember this is not needed to initialize an array variable (because it has a default value of null).* A DO-WHILE loop clears an array of any size.

```
SET &A = &STR(&&A)
SET &CNT = 1
DO WHILE &CNT LE 50
  SET &A&CNT =
END
```

Control Variables (SYS)

In addition to creating your own symbolic variables, the clist language provides some predefined variables. These predefined variables, or *control variables*, contain current information about your site's computer system, your TSO session, and your clist's processing. Except &LASTCC and &MAXCC, control variables always start with &SYS, and some accept user-generated values. (Chapter 6 has some built-in functions also starting with &SYS.) With each new release of TSO/E, the number of control variables grows. Use control variables with the following clist components:

1. Built-in functions
2. Attention and error routines
3. Multiple clists and subroutines
4. Flow control structures
5. QSAM facility

Note the SYSVAR built-in function in REXX for TSO/E Version 2 also displays values for these variables.

Table 5-3 lists each control variable and other information.

What Software Is on My System?

If you start working at a new location with TSO or TSO/E and quickly want to learn about the new computer system, the following clist can help you get started:

NEWSITE CLIST

```
PROC 0
WRITE  ****************************************
WRITE * NAME: NEWSITE.CLIST                   *
WRITE * PURPOSE:  To provide information      *
WRITE *           about a computer system     *
WRITE *           and your current TSO        *
WRITE *           session.                    *
WRITE  ****************************************
WRITE
WRITE
WRITE My TSO/E Level is ....................&SYSTSOE
WRITE Is RACF on this System? ..............&SYSRACF
WRITE My Userid is .........................&SYSUID
WRITE My Dataset Name Prefix is ............&ASYSPREF
WRITE My Current LOGON Procedure is ........&SYSPROC
WRITE CPU Time for Session .................&SYSCPU
WRITE SRM Units for Session ................&SYSSRV
```

Table 5-3. Clist Control Variables

Variable Name	Variable Function	When First Available	Can User Change Variable Value?
	Computer System Control Variables		
&SYSCPU	CPU seconds for a session	TSO/E Version 2	No
&SYSHSM*	If hierarchical storage manager installed and level if it is.	TSO/E Version 3	No
&SYSLRACF*	Is RACF available?; level if it is.	TSO/E Version 3	No
&SYSRACF	Is RACF (resource access control facility) available?	TSO/E Version 2	No
&SYSSRV	SRM (system resource manager) service units for a session	TSO/E Version 2	No
&SYSTSOE	Level of TSO/E installed	TSO/E Version 3	No
&SYSLTERM†	Length of terminal screen	TSO/E Version 2	No
&SYSWTERM†	Width of terminal screen	TSO/E Version 2	No
	TSO Session Control Variables and Terminal Characteristics		
&SYSDATE‡	Current date as mm/dd/yy	TSO	No
&SYSJDATE‡	Current Julian date (yy.ddd)	TSO/E Version 2	No
&SYSPREF	User prefix	TSO	No
&SYSPROC	Log on procedure	TSO	No
&SYSSDATE‡	Current date as yy/mm/dd	TSO/E Version 2	No
&SYSSTIME‡	Current time as hh:mm	TSO/E Version 2	No
&SYSTIME‡	Current time as hh:mm:ss	TSO	No
&SYSUID	TSO userid	TSO	No
	Clist Processing: Return Codes, Input and Output, Statements Processed		
&LASTCC	Return code	TSO	Yes
&MAXCC	Highest return code	TSO	Yes
&SYSDLM‡	Character string to return to clist after TERMIN session	TSO	No

Table 5-3. (*continued*)

Variable Name	Variable Function	When First Available	Can User Change Variable Value?
Clist Processing: Return Codes, Input and Output, Statements Processed			
&SYSDVAL‡	User input from a TERMIN session, READ, and SET	TSO	Yes
&SYSENV	Clist in foreground or background Mode	TSO	No
&SYSICMD	Name used to implicitly invoke clist	TSO	No
&SYSISPF	Is the clist running from ISPF?	TSO/E Version 2	No
&SYSNEST	Multiple clists?	TSO	No
&SYSOUTLINE	Trapped output lines from TSO command	TSO/E Version 2	Yes
&SYSOUTTRAP	Maximum number of output lines allowed	TSO/E Version 2	Yes
&SYSPCMD	Last TSO command executed by clist	TSO	No
&SYSSCAN	Number of symbolic substitution scans allowed	TSO	Yes
&SYSSCMD	Last subcommand executed by clist	TSO	No
&SYSASIS#	Select CAPS or NOCAPS	TSO/E Version 4	Yes
&SYSCONLIST§	Select CONLIST or NOCONLIST	TSO/E Version 4	Yes
&SYSFLUSH§	Select FLUSH or NOFLUSH	TSO/E Version 4	Yes
&SYSLIST§	Select LIST or NOLIST	TSO/E Version 4	Yes
&SYSMSG§	Select MSG or NOMSG	TSO/E Version 4	Yes
&SYSPROMPT‡	Select PROMPT or NOPROMPT	TSO/E Version 4	Yes
&SYSSMLIST§	Select SYMLIST or NOSYMLIST	TSO/E Version 4	Yes

* Not discussed in this book.

† Discussed in Chapter 7 in Session Manager section.

‡ Discussed in the Miscellaneous Topics section of this chapter.

§ Discussed in Chapter 4.

User enters at READY prompt:

ex newsite

displayed:

```
*********************************************
* NAME:       NEWSITE.CLIST                 *
* PURPOSE:    To provide information        *
*             about a computer system       *
*             and your current TSO or TSO/E *
*             session.                      *
*********************************************

My TSO/E Level is ............... 1040
Is RACF on this System? ......... AVAILABLE
My Userid is .................... GR00
My Dataset Name Prefix is ....... GR00
My Current LOGON Procedure is ... LOGONA
CPU Time for Session ............ 23.10
SRM Units for Session ........... 100
```

An explanation by line number follows:

1. No position operands are required and no keyword operands are used by the clist.

2–8. The WRITE statements display an informational "flowerbox" on the screen with the name and purpose of the clist. Flowerboxes are discussed later.

9–10. Use blank lines to page a block of WRITE text correctly instead of writing to the middle of the block.

11. Level of TSO/E 1040 means Version 1, Release 04 (or 4), Modification 0. Chapter 4 discusses how this level number is useful for clist debugging.

12. RACF (resource access control facility) is the security system for this site.

13. GR00 is the userid for this TSO session. We first saw &SYSUID as part of the record written to the log file when the TSO5COM clist executed in Chapter 4.

14. GR00 is also the prefix to any dataset name not fully qualified (i.e., not in single quotes) for this session.

15. LOGONA is the log on procedure for this session. By knowing the log on procedure, you can find out what are the default session characteristics (such as profile characteristics, screen size, and if session manager is turned on).

16. 23.10; the CPU says 23 and 10 hundredths of a second have elapsed since the TSO session started.
17. 100 system resource manager (SRM) service units have been used by this TSO session. SRM units are one way to evaluate a clist's performance.

Syntax and Guidelines

Here are additional tips for using these control variables.

1. The PROFILE dataset stores your default dataset prefix—the prefix name of non-fully qualified dataset (i.e., datasets not in quotes). Your system's security softward (i.e., RACF, ACF2, TOP SECRET) or entering a PROFILE command with a PREFIX operand provides this value. Since this prefix can be either blank or a different value from your job userid, it is safer using &SYSUID or adding a sequence similar to the following:
```
IF &STR(&SYSPREF)¬= OR &STR(&SYSPREF) = &STR(&SYSUID) +
     THEN DO
     SET &D1 = '&SYSPREF..MAY.DATA'
END
allocate F(D1) da(&D1) shr
```
If &SYSPREF is not blank or &SYSUID has the same value as &SYSPREF, then assign &D1 a dataset name with &SYSPREF as the first qualifier. Remember. Use two periods to create a dataset name if a symbolic variable is concatenated to a character string. This sequence decides what a clist does if &SYSPREF is different from &SYSUID:
```
IF &STR(&SYSPREF) NE &STR(&SYSUID) THEN DO
  WRITE Your PREFIX is &SYSPREF
  WRITE and USERID is &SYSUID
CHOICE: WRITE Do you want to use PREFIX or US+
ERID (P or U):
  READ ANS
  IF &ANS NE P OR &ANS NE U THEN GOTO CHOICE
  IF &ANS EQ P THEN SET &PREFIX1 = &SYSPREF
    ELSE SET &PREFIX1 = &SYSUID
  END
allocate F(D1) da('&PREFIX1..MAY.DATA') shr
```
So, use either &SYSUID or &SYSPREF to assign a symbolic variable a value of a fully qualified dataset name (for the current user).
2. &SYSRACF is either *available* (when RACF is installed), *not available* (when RACF is installed but unavailable), or *not installed* (when RACF is not installed). The level of RACF is stored in &SYSLRACF (for TSO/E Release 1 Version 3 and later) and displays in a format identical to &SYSTSOE.

3. The following sequence lists how many SRM units were used to process a clist. (&SYSCPU can be used as well.)

   Near start of clist:
   ```
   SET &SRM_START = &SYSSRV
   ```

   Near end of clist:
   ```
   SET &SRM_END = &SYSSRV
   SET SRM_USED       = &SRM_START - &SRM_END
   WRITE SRM service units..............&SRM_USED
   ```
   Of course, the numbers generated include the SRM units it took to generate them! By using this unit of measurement, you can evaluate how resource- and time-efficient a clist is.

What Is My Clist Doing at the Moment?

Use these control variables to monitor the processing of a clist.

CGLANCE CLIST—CLIST AT A GLANCE

```
 1. PROC 0
 2. CONTROL MAIN
 3. ATTN DO
 4.  WRITE Here is the current status of +
     your CLIST
 5.  WRITE ISPF IS ........................ &SYSISPF
 6.  WRITE CLIST IS IN .................... &SYSENV
 7.  WRITE CLIST IS NESTED ................ &SYSNEST
 8.  WRITE NO. OF SYMBOLIC SCANS .......... &SYSSCAN
 9.  WRITE CLIST NAME (IMPLICIT ONLY) ..... &SYSICMD
10.  WRITE LAST TSO COMMAND EXECUTED ...... &SYSPCMD
11.  WRITE LAST TSO SUBCOMMAND EXECUTED .. &SYSSCMD
12.  WRITE LAST RETURN CODE ............... &LASTCC
13.  WRITE HIGHEST RETURN CODE ............ &MAXCC
14. END
    (rest of clist)
```
User enters at READY prompt:

```
ex cglance
(Presses Attention Once Clist Processes.)
```

displayed:

```
Here is the current status of your CLIST ...
ISPF IS ..................... NOT ACTIVE
CLIST IS IN ................. FORE
CLIST IS NESTED ............. NO
NO. OF SYMBOLIC SCANS ....... 16
CLIST NAME (IMPLICIT ONLY) ..
LAST TSO COMMAND EXECUTED ... EX
LAST TSO SUBCOMMAND EXE-
CUTED .......................
LAST RETURN CODE ............ 0
HIGHEST RETURN CODE ......... 0
```

An explanation by line number follows.

1. No positional operands are required and no keyword operands are used by the clist.

2–4. Once a clist processes, pressing ATTENTION invokes the clist monitor (really an ATTN routine.) CONTROL MAIN retains the input stack once, invoking the ATTN routine. This allows resuming clist processing once the routine successfully ends.

5. &SYSISPF tells if you invoked the clist from TSO's READY prompt, ISPF's COMMAND ===> line, or Option 6 (TSO Command Processor). A displayed value of NOT ACTIVE says the clist was issued from TSO while a value of ACTIVE says the clist was invoked from ISPF or ISPF/PDF. (ISPF may not be available on this system.)

6. Since this clist was invoked from the READY prompt, it is processed in foreground mode—so &SYSENV equals FORE.

7. NO indicates that the clist is not nested. (A nested clist is one clist invoking a second one.)

8. The maximum number of symbolic substitution passes allowed are 16. This is the default.

9. Since the clist was *explicitly* and not *implicitly* invoked, &SYSICMD is null. If CGLANCE is a partitioned dataset member name which is part of the SYSPROC concatenation, then CGLANCE displays. (Remember a clist is *implicitly* invoked when it is a partitioned dataset member part of a SYSPROC concatenation. Otherwise it is *explicitly* invoked.)

10. EX says the monitor routine was invoked shortly after the clist started processing. (The EXEC command.) Otherwise, the name of another TSO command is displayed instead.

11. Since EXEC does not have subcommands, the value of &SYSSCMD is null. (EDIT, OUTPUT, and TEST currently are the only TSO commands with subcommands.)

12–13. Both the clist's last and highest return code is zero, indicating normal processing.

Syntax and Guidelines

Here are additional tips on using the control variables discussed above:

1. The following are valid values for each variable:

&LASTCC	From 0–999, the same as clist return codes. Other values are Syyy and Uyyy where yyy is a three-digit number (i.e., system and user codes)
&MAXCC	Same as &LASTCC
&SYSENV	FORE (for foreground, from TSO or ISPF) or BACK (for background, from JCL job)
&SYSICMD	Any valid PDS clist member name part of the SYSPROC concatenation.
&SYSISPF	Active (if in ISPF) or nonactive (if ISPF not active or in TSO)
&SYSNEST	Yes (clist is nested) or no (clist is not nested)
&SYSPCMD	Any valid TSO command name. Initially depends how clist is invoked (i.e., EX for EXEC command from READY)
&SYSSCAN	A number from 0 to 2,147,483,647 (2^{31}) with 16 as a default. Zero performs no symbolic substitution.
&SYSSCMD	Any valid EDIT, OUTPUT, or TEST subcommand. If EXEC is used from READY, &SYSSCMD is null (because EXEC has no subcommands).

2. For a clist executing an ISPF application, using &SYSISPF in an IF-THEN-ELSE structure guarantees a clist correctly processing from TSO or ISPF. (Chapter 9 lists the complete structure.) If you are not in ISPF (&SYSISPF NE ACTIVE), the clist accesses ISPF and drops you into the application; otherwise it just drops you into the application.

```
IF &SYSISPF NE ACTIVE THEN DO
  access ISPF and invoke application
END
ELSE invoke application
```

3. If executing a clist under ISPF, &SYSPCMD shows correctly the last TSO command executed (in some releases, SPF is displayed instead).
4. &SYSPCMD and &SYSSCMD are related, so if &SYSSCMD displays a

subcommand (e.g., TABSET), &SYSPCMD has the value of the matching command (e.g., EDIT).

5. See Chapter 4 for using &MAXCC and &LASTCC in ATTN, ERROR, and EXIT routines; Chapter 7 on background processing; and Chapter 8 on nested clists.
6. Using &SYSNEST and &SYSENV determines the appropriate:
   a. ATTN, ERROR, and EXIT routine sequence
   b. Series of SET statements
   c. Record to write to a log dataset
   d. IF, DO, and SELECT structures

Input and Output Control Variables

There are four control variables for processing user input and trapping command output. Because &SYSDLM works with TERMIN, it is discussed in the Miscellaneous Topics part of this chapter. The remaining three control variables &SYSDVAL. &SYSOUTLINE, and &SYSOUTTRAP are mentioned here.

Input Control Variable (&SYSDVAL). In discussing the READ and READDVAL commands in Chapter 4, we already have looked at &SYSDVAL. It also played an important part in our first clist, SENDMSG. But if you have not read that chapter, here is a quick review:

1. &SYSDVAL contains user-supplied input assigned by (a) a READ statement with no variables, (b) a TERMIN session (see Miscellaneous Topics later in the chapter), and (c) a SET statement (i.e., SET &X = &SYSDVAL).
2. Like all clist variables, &SYSDVAL has a null initial value. You can also assign &SYSDVAL a null value by providing no input after a READ or TERMIN statement or by a SET statement assigning &SYSDVAL a null value.
3. If the values stored in &SYSDVAL are separated by delimiters (usually blanks or commas), READDVAL correctly retrieves the values and assigns them to one or more variables in order.
4. Use &SYSDVAL when processing records with the clist QSAM facility:

```
CONTROL MAIN
alloc f (sysdval) da(contacts.data) shr
(clist statements)
(error logic for end of file found)
(clist statements)
WRITE WHAT RECORD DO YOU WISH TO DISPLAY (ENTER-
NUMBER)?
READ RECNUM2
```

```
OPENFILE SYSDVAL
DO WHILE &RECNUM2 NE &RECNUM
  GETFILE SYSDVAL
  READDVAL RECNUM COMPANY CONTACT PHONE
  IF &RECNUM2 EQ &RECNUM THEN DO
  WRITE **** YOUR RECORD ****
  WRITE RECORD   = &RECNUM
  WRITE COMPANY  = &COMPANY
  WRITE CONTACT  = &CONTACT
  WRITE PHONE    = &PHONE
END
END
CLOSFILE SYSDVAL
free f (sysdval)
```

displayed:

```
**** YOUR RECORD ****
RECORD   = 234
COMPANY  = NEW_ENGLAND_WIDGITS
CONTACT  = TOMMY_TENSE
PHONE    = 202-555-8907
```

In the above example, the user must enter a record number for a customer's database. The clist then opens the database and sequentially checks each record until retrieving the one matching the user's selection. Every record is assigned to &SYSDVAL, and the READDVAL reassigns a part of the record to one of four positional symbolic variables (in other words, the record up to the first blank is assigned to the first READDVAL variable, etc.). If finding a matching record, it lists on the screen. Underscores instead of blanks are used to assign both the CONTACT and COMPANY values to only one symbolic variable.

Output Control Variables. For sites without Session Manager, using &SYSOUT-LINE and &SYSOUTTRAP provides a crude way of capturing output from a TSO command. &SYSOUTTRAP is the maximum allowed lines saved from a command and has *no effect* on the actual number of lines put out by a command. It is identical to the REXX OUTTRAP built-in function in TSO/E Version 2. &SYSOUTLINE is the actual number of lines saved. The following example of the two control variables in use gives a better sense of their function.

```
PROC 0
CONTROL MAIN
SET &SYSOUTTRAP = 500
SET &DSN = &STR(&&DSN)
LISTC LVL('HHG1.*.DATA')
```

```
SET &LINE_CNT = &SYSOUTLINE
SET &CNT = 1
DO WHILE &CNT LE &LINE_CNT
  SET &DSN&CNT = &&SYSOUTLINE&CNT
  SET &CNT = &CNT + 1
END
```

Notice the following in the above example:

1. When unsure how many lines a TSO command outputs, make &SYSOUTTRAP a large number. Remember, &SYSOUTTRAP has no effect on the number of lines put out by a command but decides the number of lines that &SYSOUTLINE actually saves.
2. &SYSOUTLINE saves each line put out from the command into a clist array variable called &&SYSOUTLINE&X, which symbolically translates to &SYSOUTLINE1, &SYSOUTLINE2, etc. The above example assigns the contents of the &SYSOUTLINE array variables to another set of array variables called &DSN1 . . &DSN100. Doing this allows reuse of &SYSOUTLINE to trap the output from another command in the same clist.

Here are some additional guidelines for using &SYSOUTTRAP and &SYSOUTLINE:

1. The value of &SYSOUTTRAP is important for trouble-free command trapping:
   a. Always set &SYSOUTTRAP larger than the actual number of lines that a TSO command can output. &SYSOUTTRAP and &SYSOUTLINE&X can be as large as 999999999999999999999 (21 digits) if your system lets you!
   b. There should be no &SYSOUTLINE array variable with a position number greater than the value of &SYSOUTTRAP—because this array variable would have invalid data (i.e., if &SYSOUTTRAP = 10, do not have &SYSOUTLINE11). A &SYSOUTLINE array variable with no associated trapped TSO command output has a null value.
   c. If not assigning &SYSOUTLINE values to another array (as in the above example), reset &SYSOUTTRAP to 0 to retain the present &SYSOUTLINE values.
2. &SYSOUTLINE tips:
   a. Running a clist with any of the trace facility control operands (i.e., CONTROL CONLIST LIST SYMLIST MSG) adds more output lines to &SYSOUTLINE. These additional lines may require a larger &SYS-

OUTTRAP to be trapped and need additional lines of code to weed them out.

b. If under ISPF, place &SYSOUTLINE and &SYSOUTTRAP in the clist after where invoking ISPF.

c. When using &SYSOUTLINE with nested clists; a nested clist is seen as a TSO command and all nested clist output (i.e., WRITE statements) is trapped in &SYSOUTLINE variables.

d. TSO uses the TPUT macro to display an output line to a terminal if line does not require insertion of text, use of secondary messages, and removal of message numbers. (Which instead uses the PUTLINE macro.) TPUT also displays some normal and error messages. *&SYSOUTLINE only captures information generated from the PUTLINE macro and not TPUT.*)

e. For programs, reset &SYSOUTLINE by invoking IKJCT441 (clist variable access routine). This routine also assigns or reassigns a value to a clist variable.

f. IF &SYSOUTTRAP is not equal to zero, &SYSOUTLINE resets to zero when the clist processes any additional TSO commands. This happens regardless if the clist sequence uses or not uses &SYSOUTLINE. If a clist executes a program with TSO commands, you, not the program, must reset &SYSOUTLINE to zero.

g. For a simple application of &SYSOUTLINE, a DO loop may not be needed. The following clist sequence stores the first three datasets starting with UIC1.MEMO in &SYSOUTLINE array variables and writes out the result.

```
SET &SYSOUTTRAP = 3
LISTC LVL ('UIC1.MEMO')
WRITE &SYSOUTLINE1 is . . . &SYSOUTLINE1
WRITE &SYSOUTLINE2 is . . . &SYSOUTLINE2
WRITE &SYSOUTLINE3 is . . . &SYSOUTLINE3
```

displayed:

```
&SYSOUTLINE1 is NONVSAM ------- UIC.MEMO.CURRENT
&SYSOUTLINE2 is IN-CAT ---- SYS1.ATOL.CATALOG
&SYSOUTLINE3 is NONVSAM -------UIC.MEMO.JUNK
```

LISTDSI (More Control Variables)

The LISTDSI statement was added to TSO/E Version 1 Release 3 allowing clists the means for capturing and storing information about a dataset into symbolic variables. LISTDSI stores the DCB (data control block), dataset dates, and directory block information in up to 25 LISTDSI control variables. An additional four variables store return codes and messages. Once this information is in a clist variable, it can be used by TSO statements (e.g., ALLOCATE) for creating new files or verifying some file attribute before performing an operation. A LISTDSI built-in function is also available for REXX under TSO/E Version 2. The typical format of the LISTDSI statement is simple:

```
LISTDSI datasetname DIRECTORY
                              or
                           NONDIRECTORY
```

Datasetname is the name of any valid TSO dataset (including VSAM but retrieving less information). With *NODIRECTORY* (the default), the PDS directory information is not retrieved. On the other hand, *DIRECTORY* retrieves this information but slows down processing. Table 5-4 lists 25 LISTDSI control variables and their common values.

The following example uses LISTDSI to supply the input parameters for creating a file (or use ALLOCATE's LIKE operand, which allocates a dataset with PROJ88.DATA's parameters). If the LISTDSI worked, &RCD is "recycled" to hold the return code of ALLOCATE.

```
LISTDSI PROJ88.DATA
   SET &RCD = &LASTCC
   IF &RCD = 0 THEN DO
     ALLOC F(PROJ88A) DA(PROJ88A) DSORG(&SYSDSORG) +
     DIR(10) +
       LRECL(&SYSLRECL) BLKSIZE(&SYSBLKSIZE) NEW +
       SPACE(&SYSPRIMARY,&SYSSECONDS) &SYSUNITS RECFM(V B)
       SET &RCD = &LASTCC
       IF &RCD = 0 THEN WRITE Dataset successfully+
       allocated
          ELSE WRITE ALLOCATE FAILED - Return Code &RCD
   END
   ELSE DO
    WRITE PROJ88.DATA does not exist or LISTDSI problem
    WRITE Return Code - &RCD
   END
```

Syntax and Guidelines

Here are some tips for using the LISTDSI statement:

1. Four control variables store LISTDSI messages and return code information (see Table 5-5).

Table 5-4. LISTDSI Special Control Variables

Variable Name	Function	Values
Allocation (Data Control Block)		
&SYSBLKSIZE	Block size	Any valid block size for record format
&SYSDSNAME	Dataset name	Any valid TSO dataset name
&SYSDSORG	Dataset organization	PS—Sequential PO—Partitioned VS—VSAM
&SYSKEYLEN	Key length	For DA (direct access) datasets only, otherwise 0
&SYSLRECL	Logical record length	Depends on record format and block size
&SYSRECFM	Record format	F—fixed length V—variable length A—control characters B—records blocked
&SYSUNIT	Unit name	Valid unit name
&SYSVOLUME	Volume serial number	Valid volume serial number
Space Information		
&SYSALLOC	Allocated units	Valid space unit
&SYSEXTENTS	Allocated extents	Valid extent number
&SYSPRIMARY	Allocated primary units	Valid space unit
&SYSSECONDS	Allocated secondary units	Valid space unit
&SYSTRKSCYL	Unit's tracks per cylinder	Valid number
&SYSUNITS	Space units	Block Cylinder Track
&SYSUSED	Used space units	Valid space unit
File Dates and Indicators		
&SYSCREATE	File creation date	Any valid date in yyyy/ddd format. yyyy = year; ddd = 0–365
&SYSEXDATE	File expiration date	Any valid date in yyyy/ddd format
&SYSREFDATE	Last referenced date	Any valid date in yyyy/ddd format
&SYSUPDATED	Update indicator	YES—Updated NO —Unmodified
Dataset Protection		
&SYSPASSWORD	Password protection indicator	NONE—No protection READ—password needed for read operations

Table 5-4. *(continued)*

Variable Name	Function	Values
	Dataset Protection	
&SYSRACFA	Is RACF available?	WRITE—password needed for write operations NONE—No GENERIC—Yes and dataset has generic protection DISCRETE—Yes and dataset has discrete protection.
	Directory/PDS Information (PDS Only)	
&SYSADIRBLK	Allocated directory blocks	Valid block number
&SYSBLKSTRK	Unit's directory blocks per track	Valid block number
&SYSMEMBERS	Number of PDS members	Valid member number
&SYSUDIRBLK	Used directory blocks	Valid block number

You can use these variables or just the control variables &LASTCC and &MAXCC. (For TSO/E Version 1 Release 3 and earlier sites, use multiple IF statements.)

```
LISTDSI TEMP.DATA
  SET &RCD = &LASTCC
  IF &SYSREASON GT 0 THEN DO
     WRITE LISTDSI FAILED
     WRITE Generic Return Code is &LASTCC
     WRITE Primary Error Message -- &SYSMSGLVL1
     WRITE Secondary Error Message -- &SYSMSGLVL2
END
  SELECT (&SYSREASON)
    WHEN (2) WRITE Dynamic Allocation Error
    WHEN (6) WRITE Bad Dataset Name
    WHEN (13) WRITE Cannot Open Dataset
    WHEN (17) WRITE System or User ABEND
    WHEN (18) WRITE Not all LISTDSI Variables Created
    WHEN (24) WRITE Dataset not found
    OTHERWISE WRITE See Clist Manual For Return Code+
    Meaning.
END
```

Why wasn't an ERROR routine used instead of the SELECT and IF statements? The answer is simple—ERROR routines do not recognize LISTDSI nonzero return codes.

Table 5-5. Control Variables that Store LISTDSI Messages

Name and Function	Common Values
&LASTCC (generic return code)	0 = Worked 4 = Partly worked (some LISTDSI variables not created) 16 = Failed, don't trust values of LISTDSI variables!
&SYSREASON (LISTDSI return code (Range 0–28))	0 = Worked 2 = Dynamic allocation error 6 = Bad dataset name? 13 = Cannot open dataset 17 = System or user ABEND 18 = Partly worked (not all LISTDSI variables created) 24 = Dataset not found
&SYSMSGLVL1 (primary error message)	
&SYSMSGLVL2 (secondary error message)	

2. Any information about a multivolume dataset stored by LISTDSI variables pertains only to the first volume.
3. Allocated space values stored in LISTDSI variable &SYSALLOC round up when &SYSUNITS equals CYLINDER (but the actual allocation is in tracks). The rounding usually occurs when space is released.
4. LISTDSI does not work with datasets on TAPE including generation datasets.
5. &SYSRECFM does not work in an ALLOCATE statement (no spaces between values—FB instead of F B).

Clist Style* (Good Practices, Self-documenting Clists)

Each clist programmer uses a unique ''handwriting'' for clists he or she creates. This ''handwriting'' is a good indicator of a person's clist knowledge and programming skills. Has the programmer written an efficient or inefficient program that is hard to follow; a ''bare'bones'' program that just does the task and nothing more; or one of those rare programs that efficiently does the task and is easy to follow?

Good writers use style books in creating a document. A style book lists common practices and helpful guidelines and provides a common framework for evaluating a document. Books on programming style have been available since the late seventies. Using and enforcing these practices throughout your department and company produces some minimum common elements in all clists.

* This section is partly based on the clists of and conversations with Al Buczynski and Chuck Hoffman of GTE Laboratories, Inc.

Part of the idea for this book grew from a desire of creating a clist style sheet and communicating the results to a larger audience. Please use this section as a starting point and add your and your company's conventions to this list.

Writing Clist Documentation that Works

I confess to being a strong advocate of clist documentation—especially after spending many hours pouring over long, undocumented, unstructured clists that I inherited from former employees. Because clists permit some bad programming practices and may produce sophisticated sequences, good documentation practices are essential. (See Chapter 4's DO loop section for some habits to avoid.) The following is my theory of clist documentation. (I also call this the "jump start" theory of documentation—because good documentation gets you up and running fast!)

Write as much documentation to allow you (after some time) or another person to understand quickly how the clist works.

The level of clist documentation written for other persons depends on the expertise of your co-workers and whoever else would support the clist. Assume the persons understand the function and syntax of most clist statements but need to comprehend what a particular statement does in your clist. Here are some guidelines in writing documentation in clists:

1. A *readable clist* is a good way for anyone to understand quickly its purpose. Here is a summary of ways to do this:
   a. In a word—*indent* (two to three spaces is adequate)
      A sequence of code under a label
      READs under WRITEs
      IF &LASTCC under a TSO command or clist statement
      Statements within a control logic structure (such as DO-WHILE, IF-THEN, and SELECT), and line up IFs, SELECTs, or DOs with ENDs. As stated earlier, when the DO is on the same line as the IF, it takes up less space. (It is also as readable.)

   Here is a clist sequence using these points:

```
MAINMENU: -
WRITE  ******************************
WRITE  *  Please Enter Your Choice  *
WRITE  *  1    ALLOCATE             *
WRITE  *  2    DELETE               *
WRITE  ******************************
```

```
WRITENR Choice (1 OR 2):
  READ CHOICE
    IF &CHOICE = 1 THEN GOTO ALL_LBL
        ELSE IF &CHOICE = 2 THEN GOTO DEL_LBL
        ELSE GOTO MAINMENU
ALL_LBL: -
  (some code)
  SET &RCD = &LASTCC
  IF &RCD GT 0 THEN DO
    WRITE ALLOCATE Failed
    WRITE Your Return Code is &LASTCC
  END
```

b. Use mixed-case and lowercase words as much as possible in a clist. This contrasts with the uppercase clist statements. The above WRITE statement used uppercase for emphasizing the command name (i.e., ALLOCATE or DELETE) and mixed-case for the remainder of the text. Another contrast is writing TSO commands in lowercase.

c. To increase readability and comprehension:

Use meaningful names for variables and labels.

Divide your clist into cohesive modules. Each module should perform no more than two functions. Start each module with a label.

Use another clist or command processor for performing general functions (i.e., file cleanup) instead of "cluttering" the main clist.

2. Adding comments to your clist is important and has no effect on the speed of clist processing. There are two general approaches to adding comments to clists:

a. Placing a comment after each *hard to understand statement*.

Advantage: Comment is next to the appropriate clist statement.

Disadvantage: Comments are not centralized. No understanding what a module does.

For example,

```
If &&OPT&CNT NE THEN DO /* If &OPT1 not blank,
delete file
```

b. Placing a comment *before* each *module* (label). Remember, a comment immediately after a label name stops the processing of a clist (and is hard to debug).

Advantage: It provides a good explanation of what a module does. Comments are centralized, creating an easier to read clist.

Disadvantage: There is no explanation of what a statement does. If done in detail (as below), it greatly increases the clist size.

For example,

```
/*************************************/
/* MAINMENU:                         */
/*    1. Displays menu of tasks      */
/*    2. User makes selection        */
/*    3. Selection is checked        */
/*    4. If valid, go to right module */
/*    5. If invalid, user reprompted  */
/*************************************/
MAINMENU: -
```

By combining the two approaches, you both centralize comments and provide a good explanation of what particular modules or statements do.

3. A file header or a "flowerbox of asterisks" at the start of your clist is a good "clist-at-a-glance" reference. Here is a skeleton of a sample flowerbox showing possible items to include:

```
/**********************************************/
/* Project Name: Customers Database           */
/* Program Name: USER.TEST.CLIST(MAINCLST)    */
/* Project Purpose: To allow employees at XYZ */
/*                  Widgets a database of their */
/*                  customer contacts         */
/* Created By: Cher Sululu, Mike Mansfield, and + */
               Lisa Rees                      */
/**********************************************/
/*                 OTHER DATASETS USED        */
/* Related Clists:                            */
/*    USER.TEST.CLIST(UPDATE) - updates customer +*/
/*    records                                 */
/*    SYS1.CLIST(CLEANUP) - deletes temporary +  */
/*    files                                   */
/* Datasets Used by Clist QSAM Facility       */
/* Test dataset: None                         */
/*    USER.CUSTOMER88.DATA - Customers Database  */
/* JCL Stored In:                             */
/*    USER.TEMP.CNTL(CUSTRUN) - Submit nightly +  */
/*    reports                                 */
/* ISPF Datasets:                             */
/*    Panels - INFO.PANEL.LIBRARY :           */
/*      PANEL01 - Opening Panel               */
/*    Skeletons - INFO.SKEL.LIBRARY :         */
/*      JCL1 - JCL Skeleton                   */
/*    (place other modules here)              */
/**********************************************/
```

```
/*                       Clist Info                    */
/* Characteristics: Foreground Only, Uses Nested       */
/* Files                                               */
/* Modules:                                            */
/*      MAINMENU - Choose Task and Send to Right       */
/*      Module                                         */
/*    (others go here)                                 */
/* Variables :                                         */
/*    &OPT - Menu Choice                               */
/*    &&ARRAY&CNT - &ARRAY1 -- &ARRAY10 holds          */
/*                  &SYSOUTLINE output                 */
/* Things to look out for:                             */
/* - Allowing only one symbolic subsitution pass-      */
/*   at module ARRAY_BUILD. (&SYSSCAN = 1)             */
/* - Using a compound DO (i.e. DO.TO.By with a         */
/* - WHILE and UNTIL statement.)                       */
/*******************************************************/
/*                 CLIST Modifications                 */
/* Name       Date        Change                       */
/* Lisa Rees  10/10/88    Changed clist                */
/*                        for TSO/E Ver 1, Rel 4       */
/*                        features:                    */
/*                        SELECT, Compound DO,         */
/*                        DO UNTIL                     */
/*******************************************************/
```

It is up to you how detailed your flowerbox is. Consider these factors when deciding the size of your flowerbox:

a. Size of clist (smaller clist may just need statement comments)
b. Complexity of clist
c. Knowledge of your clist support staff
d. Local clist documentation standards

Some of this information (such as variables) can be moved to an appropriate module comment or flowerbox.

4. Many projects allow only time at the end to document clists, and the result is no documentation. Clists should be documented *during the entire time of clist programming* and not just at the end. Documentation written during the creation of a clist is valuable input for the development process and better reflects what the clist does.

Clist Standards Considerations

In addition to good documentation and programming practices, a clist should conform to a set of guidelines or *standards*. Each site should have clist standards because (1) they provide some consistency across clists, (2) they help clist programmers develop good coding habits, and (3) they allow another person to understand the clist quickly. Implementing a standard at any site is not easy. Here are some tips for doing this:

1. Enforcing clist standards may not work at your site. It takes time and staff to review a clist before allowing public access. This slows down the time for public release and builds programmer resentment.
2. Implement only a few standards that make sense. A 300-page book of standards is ignored by nearly everyone.
3. The most practical way to implement standards is for your programmers to agree voluntarily to do them. Have their decision supported by (a) allowing extra time in coding a clist to add standards and documentation, and (b) have management recognize good programming habits.

The following outline lists possible areas for clist standards at your site:

1. Names
   a. Datasets
   b. Clists (public clists, computer center clists)
   c. Modules (clist labels, components)
   d. Variables
   e. Positional and keyword operands in a PROC statement.

2. Location of clists
   a. During testing and maintenance
   b. During public access

3. Procedures
   a. For clist development
   b. For putting a clist into a public area
   c. For modifying a public clist
   d. For monitoring clist usage
   e. For help documents

4. Resources
   a. In-house style sheets
   b. Public clists that can be called from other clists

5. Clists
   a. Documentation (flowerbox, user guides, comments)
   b. Supporting HELP screens (HELP clistname from READY)
   c. CONTROL MAIN PROMPT or CONTROL NOFLUSH PROMPT
   d. ATTN routines (free and close files)
   e. Error routines (common error conditions handled: end-of-file reached, too small region size)

f. Delete temporary files and free all others
g. Minimize global variables (see Chapter 8)
h. Sequence if invoked from TSO or ISPF (for ISPF applications.)
i. Sequence if nested clist
j. Error/informational messages—format, wording
k. Universal operand to turn on clist trace

```
PROC 0 TRACE
(some clist statements)
If &TRACE = TRACE THEN DO
    CONTROL CONLIST SYMLIST MSG LIST PROMPT MAIN
END
ELSE DO
  CONTROL NOCONLIST NOSYMLIST MSG NOLIST PROMPT MAIN
END
```

l. User menus (format, where to enter choice, letter or number selections, number menus and validations)
m. Create a test dataset to verify the correct execution of a clist (and mention in the main flowerbox)
n. If the clist allows the user to edit the dataset, give the user a choice of editors
o. Operands in clists (how many, when to have operands)
p. Use of TERMIN sessions (allowed at all?)

The Final Version of the TSO5COM Clist

This is our last look at the TSO5COM clist incorporating documentation, double-ampersand variables, control variables, and the LISTDSI statement. (You will need at least TSO/E Version 1 Release 3 to run TSO5COM.) Chapters 6,7, and 8 feature an example of building a simple customer database application.

```
PROC 0 CTEST VERIFY(NOVERIFY)
 /* ***********************************************/
 /* Name Of Clist:TSO5COM Clist                   */
 /* Clist Purpose: Clist Front-end to 5 TSO       */
 /* commands                                      */
 /* Clist Modules:                                */
 /*  ALLOC_IT - allocate requested files          */
 /*  ATT1 - generic attention routine             */
 /*  ERR1 - log file error routine                */
 /*  ERR2 - generic error routine                 */
```

```
/*  FILEGET - Get file names, go to right module  */
/*  MAINMENU - main menu of clist                 */
/*  OTHER_IT - delete, list, rename selected-     */
/*  files                                         */
/*  READ_LOG - write to log file                  */
/*  SEND_IT - send a message to a selected user   */
/*  VALID - validate menu choice, create proxy    */
/*          variable (&DESCRIBE)                  */
/* DATASET: TSO5COM.USER.LOG = transaction log    */
/* ***********************************************/
IF &CTEST = CTEST THEN -
 CONTROL SYMLIST CONLIST LIST MSG MAIN
    ELSE CONTROL NOSYMLIST NOCONLIST NOLIST MSG
    MAIN
/* ***********************************************/
/* ATT1: Generic Attention loop                   */
/* ***********************************************/
 ATT1: -
 ATTN DO
   WRITE YOU HAVE PRESSED THE ATTENTION KEY.
   WRITE DO YOU WISH TO EXIT THE CLIST? (Y/N)
     READ ANS
     IF &ANS EQ Y OR EQ THEN DO
        EXIT CODE(99) /* Return Code of 99 if yes
     END
       ELSE RETURN
 END
/* ***********************************************/
/* ERR1: Log File Error Routine                   */
/* &RC - 360 (File not Open), 364 (File Closed    */
/*       by System), 368 (File not Open)          */
/* ***********************************************/
ERR1: -
 ERROR DO
   SET &RC = &LASTCC
   IF &RC = 360 THEN WRITE LOG file not currently+
   OPENed
   ELSE IF &RC = 364 OR &RC = 368 THEN -
     WRITE LOG file never OPENed or not CLOSed
  ELSE DO
     WRITE Serious Problem with LOG File
     WRITE PLEASE contact Tom at Extension 3333
```

```
     WRITE Your return code is &RC
     WRITE Your highest return code is &MAXCC
     WRITE Your last TSO Command is &SYSPCMD
     WRITE Your last TSO Subcommand is &SYSSCMD
  END
  CLOSEFILE LOGIT
 FREE F(LOGIT)
 EXIT CODE(&RC)
 END
 /* ***********************************************/
 /* MAINMENU: main menu of clist (Choose 1-5)    */
 /* ***********************************************/
MAINMENU: -
 WRITE * *****************************************
 WRITE * The following options are available      *
 WRITE * 1 - Create a New File                    *
 WRITE * 2 - Delete an Existing File              *
 WRITE * 3 - List an Existing File                *
 WRITE * 4 - Rename an Existing File              *
 WRITE * 5 - Send a Message to Another User       *
 WRITE * *****************************************
 /* ***********************************************/
 /* READ_LOG: Write to Log File                  */
 /* Sample Record:                               */
 /*  2 HHG1 13:28 88/10/10                       */
 /* ***********************************************/
READ_LOG: -
 WRITENR Please enter your choice (1-5 only):
 READ OPT
 ALLOC F(LOGIT) DA(TSO5COM.USER.LOG) MOD
  OPENFILE LOGIT OUTPUT
   SET &LOGIT = &STR(&OPT &SYSUID &SYSSTIME +
   &SYSSDATE)
  PUTFILE LOGIT
  CLOSFILE LOGIT
 FREE F(LOGIT)
 /* ***********************************************/
 /* ERR2: Generic Error loop                     */
 /* ***********************************************/
ERR2: -
 ERROR DO
  SET &RCD = &LASTCC
  WRITE An Error has been found
```

```
    WRITE Do you wish to EXIT the clist? (Y/N)
    READ &ANS2
    IF &ANS2 = Y OR &ANS EQ THEN DO
       CLOSFILE LOGIT /* Close log dataset +
       free files*/
       FREE DA(&FILE1,&FILE2, TSO5COM.USER.LOG)
       WRITE Your return code is &RCD
       WRITE Your highest return code is &MAXCC
       Your last TSO Command is &SYSPCMD
       Write Your last TSO Subcommand is &SYSSCMD
       EXIT CODE(&RCD)
   END
   ELSE RETURN
  END
  /* ********************************************/
  /* VALID: Validate menu choice               */
  /* ********************************************/
 VALID: -
  IF &OPT LT 1 AND &OPT GT 5 THEN GOTO MAINMENU
  IF &OPT NE 1 AND &OPT NE 2 AND &OPT NE 3 AND +
  &OPT NE 4 -
  AND &OPT NE 5 THEN GOTO MAINMENU /*&DESCRIBE PROXY +
  VAR*/
  IF &OPT = 1 THEN SET &DESCRIBE = CREATE
    ELSE IF &OPT = 2 THEN SET &DESCRIBE = DELETE
    ELSE IF &OPT = 3 THEN SET &DESCRIBE = LIST
    ELSE IF &OPT = 4 THEN SET &DESCRIBE = RENAME
    ELSE IF &OPT = 5 THEN SET &DESCRIBE = SEND
    ELSE GOTO MAINMENU
  /* ********************************************/
  /* FILEGET: Get 1-100 Files                  */
  /* ********************************************/
 FILEGET: -
  IF &OPT GE 1 AND &OPT LE 4 THEN DO
     WRITE How Many Files to &DESCRIBE ? (Less Than +
     100)
     READ &FILENUM
     IF &FILENUM GT 100 THEN GOTO FILEGET
     SET &CNT = 1
     SET &FNN = &STR(&&FNN)
     DO WHILE &CNT LE &FILENUM
         SET &FILENAME =
         WRITE WHAT IS THE NAME OF FILE &CNT :
```

```
                READ FILENAME
                SET &FNN&CNT = &FILENAME /*SET
                &FNN1 = NAME*/
                SET &CNT = &CNT + 1
         END
  END
  IF &OPT EQ 1 THEN GOTO ALLOC_IT /* GO TO RIGHT +
  MODULE*/
   ELSE IF &OPT GE 2 AND &OPT LE 4 THEN GOTO OTHER
   _IT
   ELSE IF &OPT EQ 5 THEN GOTO SEND_IT
   ELSE GOTO EXIT
  /* ************************************************/
  /* ALLOC_IT: Allocate Files                       */
  /* ************************************************/
 ALLOC_IT: -
  SET &CNT = 1
  DO WHILE &CNT LE &FILENUM /* Allocate 1-100+
  Files */
    FREE F (FILE&CNT)
    WRITE*****&FNN&CNT**********************
    LISTDSI SAMPLE.DATA
    ALLOCATE F(FILE&CNT) DA(&FNN&CNT) NEW &SYSUNITS +
     SPACE(&SYSPRIMARY,&SYSSECONDS) RECFM(F B A) +
     LRECL(255) BLKSIZE(25500) DSORG(&SYSDSORG)
     DIR(1)
    IF &LASTCC GT 0 THEN WRITE &SYSPCMD FAILED.
    SET &CNT = &CNT + 1
  END
   GOTO EXIT
  /* ************************************************/
  /* OTHERIT: List, Delete, or Rename Files         */
  /* ************************************************/
  OTHER_IT: -
   SET &CNT = 1
   DO WHILE &CNT LE &FILENUM
   SET &NEWFILE =
   IF &OPT = 4 THEN DO /*RENAME only */
      WRITE WHAT IS THE NEW FILENAME?
       READ NEWFILE
    END
     WRITE ******&FNN&CNT*************
     &DESCRIBE &FNN&CNT &NEWFILE
```

```
168.        IF &LASTCC GT 0 THEN WRITE &SYSPCMD FAILED
169.        SET &CNT = &CNT + 1
170.      END
171.      GOTO EXIT
172.     /* ********************************************* /
173.     /* SEND_IT: Send a Message                        */
174.     /* ********************************************* /
175.      SEND_IT: -
176.        WRITE WHO WILL RECEIVE THIS MESSAGE?
177.         READ           /* Store in &SYSDVAL*/
178.         READDVAL USID
179.        WRITE WHAT IS YOUR MESSAGE?
180.         READ
181.        SET &NOTE = &STR('&SYSDVAL')
182.        IF &VERIFY = VERIFY THEN WRITE YOUR +
            MESSAGE IS &NOTE
183.        WRITE MESSAGE IS BEING SENT
184.        SEND &NOTE U(&USID)
185.        IF &LASTCC GT 0 THEN WRITE #SYSPCMD FAILED
186.        GOTO EXIT
187.     /* ********************************************* /
188.     /* EXIT: Exit Clist With Message                  */
189.     /* ********************************************* /
190.     EXIT: WRITE &SYSPCMD IS COMPLETED
```

Explanation. An explanation of new sections of TSO5COM (boldface in the clist), by line number, follows.

- 2–18. The file header or flowerbox lists the clist name, modules (labels), and the transaction log dataset.
- 22–24. A sample module flowerbox. Note in this clist the things to watch out for are in statement comments rather than here.
- 31. (Also lines 94, 110, 131, 135, 144, 162, and 177). Statement comments placed before or on the appropriate line. A more detailed explanation if needed can go in the module flowerbox.
- 35–39. This module flowerbox lists the meaning of three non-zero return codes. A fuller explanation can be placed here.
- 50–52. (Also lines 96–99) Display the highest return code given and the last TSO command and subcommand to help in debugging.
- 58–60. MAINMENU module flowerbox with valid selections listed.
- 70–74. READ_LOG module flowerbox has a handy sample record of the transaction log.
- 80. &SYSSTIME is used because seconds aren't needed and &SYSS-

DATE if sorting by date is needed. A deeper look at these control variables is found later under "Miscellaneous Topics."

84–86. (Also lines 104–106, 117–19, 139–41, 155–57, 172–74, 187–89) Standard module flowerboxes with module name and function.

122. You can now specify up to 100 files, but any upper limit can be used.

124. This statement reprompts the user if their upper limit is greater than 100.

126. Assigns &FNN a value of &&FNN to reduce the number of double ampersands appearing in the clist.

131. The double-ampersand value &&FNN&CNT (which symbolically translates to &FNN1..&FNN100) is recalled in statements 146, 148, 166, and 167.

146. Writes the user-specified filenames.

147–50. LISTDSI uses a model dataset (SAMPLE.DATA) providing space units, space allocations, and dataset organization. However, the clist uses a different logical record length, block size, number of directory blocks and record format than SAMPLE.DATA.

151. (Also lines 168, 185, 190) Use &SYSPCMD or &DESCRIBE for displaying the last TSO command executed.

166–67. Recall the array variables &FNN1..&FNN100 for listing, deleting, or renaming the selected datasets.

Other things you can do with TSO5COM:

- Place the OTHER_IT and ALLOC_IT into different clists so that they can be nested. For a TSO/E Version 4 and later, consider placing some modules as subprocedures.
- Add new options—display allocated files (LISTA) or members of a dataset (LISTDS). Use &SYSOUTLINE for trapping output from either command.
- Use built-in functions with &SYSUID or &SYSPREF for checking if a dataset exists and is fully qualified. (Chapter 6 shows how to do this.)
- Add sequence for returning to the main menu once the selected option is performed.
- Place the TSO commands in a file to be submitted as a batch job or later executed as a clist. You can also save this file for later use.

MISCELLANEOUS TOPICS

Most of the following information is briefly covered in hard-to-find places throughout the IBM TSO/E manuals. By placing them in one section, you may begin using these special but crucial concepts, statements, and commands. One topic, double-byte characters, is covered as part of the discussion of built-in functions in Chapter 6.

Clists and the Case of Text

Since TSO/E Version 1 Release 2, clist users can control whether part or all of a character string appears in upper-, lower-, or mixed-case letters. Use the following methods in Table 5-6 to do this.

If *all* of your text is in upper case, then method 1 is recommended because it automatically connects to uppercase and frees your clist from being cluttered with &SYSCAPS. Use method 2 if *some* or *nearly all* of your text is in uppercase. Chapter 6 shows an example of producing a mixed case character string and reviews both &SYSLC and &SYSCAPS.

The following are more tips on text case and clists:

1. TSO/E Version 1 Release 4 and later sites can also specify CONTROL CAPS or CONTROL NOCAPS by using the &SYSASIS control variable.

Statement	What Happens
SET &SYSASIS = ON	Same as CONTROL ASIS or CONTROL NOCAPS. Lowercase text does not convert to uppercase.
SET &SYSASIS = OFF	Same as CONTROL CAPS. Lowercase text is converted to uppercase.

Table 5-6. Two Methods to Control Case of Clist Text

Uppercase	Lower- or Mixed-Case
	Method 1
1. Have a CONTROL CAPS statement.	1. Have a CONTROL ASIS or a CONTROL NOCAPS statement.
2. Just enter text "as is." All text is automatically converted to uppercase.	2. Just enter text "as is"—lowercase is not converted to uppercase.
	3. Convert as-needed string to uppercase using the &SYSCAPS built-in function.
	4. Create as-needed mixed-case character strings by using a combination of the &SYSCAPS and &SYSLC functions.
	Method 2
1. Have a CONTROL NOCAPS or a CONTROL ASIS statement. Convert as-needed strings to uppercase using the &SYSCAPS built-in function	

2. &SYSCAPS or &SYSASIS does not convert the following:
   a. Special characters (hexadecimal codes 40–FF)
   b. Numbers (0–9)
   c. National characters (#, @, $)
   d. Double-byte characters (not true for TSO/E Version 1 Releases 2 and 3).
3. With the Clist QSAM facility, GETFILE and PUTFILE text is always converted to uppercase regardless if using CONTROL ASIS or CAPS. This is not documented in most versions of the *Clist Users' Guide*.
4. When working with input or data of unknown case, convert everything to uppercase by (a) using a CONTROL CAPS statement, (b) SET &SYSASIS = OFF, or (c) using a CONTROL ASIS or CONTROL NOCAPS statement and converting the string with a &SYSCAPS built-in function. This avoids the problem of IF &TDAY = MONDAY not executing because &TDAY is in lowercase (e.g., monday).
5. Use another CONTROL statement to overrride temporarily an existing one.

```
CONTROL CAPS
  SET &STRNG = &STR(THIS IS IN UPPERCASE)
  WRITE &STRNG /*OUTPUT: THIS IS IN UPPERCASE*/
CONTROL ASIS
  SET &STRNG = &STR(this is in lowercase)
  WRITE &STRNG /*OUTPUT: this is in lowercase*/
CONTROL CAPS /* Reset to uppercase*/
```

6. Using CONTROL ASIS retains the case of a user's input.

```
CONTROL ASIS
WRITE What is your street address?
READ
WRITE Your address is &STR(&SYSDVAL)
 /*OUTPUT: 10 Hale St.
```

7. Without CONTROL ASIS, READDVAL turns the contents of &SYSDVAL to uppercase.

Clist and Prompting

If you had a TSO command in a clist (e.g., ALLOCATE) and you forgot to include a positional operand (e.g., dataset name.), what would the clist do? Would you be prompted for the operand or would the clist display a message that the

Table 5-7. Conditions for Prompting and No Prompting

Prompting	No Prompting
1. The PROMPT operand is specified in your PROFILE dataset (default)	1. The NOPROMPT operand is specified in YOUR PROFILE dataset.
and	*or*
2. An EXEC clist PROMPT command has been entered	2. An EXEC clist NOPROMPT or EXEC clist command has been entered. (NOPROMPT is the default.)
or	*or*
A CONTROL PROMPT statement is in the clist.	A CONTROL NOPROMPT statement is in the clist.
or	*or*
A SET &SYSPROMPT = ON statement is in the clist. (TSO/E Version 1 Release 4 and later)	A SET &SYSPROMPT = OFF statement is in the clist. (TSO/E Version 1 Release 4 and later)

operand was missing and end the clist? The answer depends on your clist. (Unless otherwise stated, the following works for both TSO and TSO/E.) Table 5-7 lists the necessary conditions for both prompting or no prompting to occur.

The following is more information about prompting and clists:

1. Remember when using the EXEC command:
   a. NOPROMPT is the default.
   b. PROMPT only works when explicitly invoking a clist (e.g., EXEC datasetname) and specifying the PROMPT operand for your PROFILE dataset—the default.
   c. The PROMPT operand applies only to the first clist in a series of nested clists. To allow prompting, in all dis's use one of the above three ways in the remaining clists.
   d. A PROMPT operand sets LIST on (listing TSO commands and subcommands) unless the NOLIST operand is specified.
2. For TSO/E Version 1 Release 4 and later, also use the &SYSPROMPT control variable for specifying CONTROL PROMPT.

Statement	What Happens
SET &SYSPROMPT = ON	Same as CONTROL PROMPT—prompt the user for the missing operand.
SET &SYSPROMPT = OFF	Same as CONTROL NOPROMPT—give missing operand message and end clist.

3. Specifying control PROMPT can determine if your PROFILE dataset is

assigned the PROMPT operand. If the clist ends after executing the following sequence, your PROFILE dataset has a value of NOPROMPT. *Remember, the default value is PROMPT.*

```
CONTROL PROMPT
ALLOCATE
```

4. Use a control statement for overrriding the existing value for PROMPT.

```
CONTROL PROMPT
  ALLOCATE
CONTROL NOPROMPT
  DELETE /* Clist Ends */
```

Using the CALL and WHEN Commands

A clist uses the CALL statement for loading and executing a program in load module format. (Similar to the EXEC PGM= in JCL.) In addition, the WHEN command is similar to an IF or a SELECT structure by performing a command based on CALL's return code. The following is the syntax and guidelines when using these two commands:

CALL Statement Syntax

```
CALL datasetname 'parameters'
  or
CALL loadlibrary(membername) 'parameters'
```

loadlibrary = a valid sequential dataset or PDS member dataset name. The default name is TEMPNAME and the default file type is .LOAD. Fully qualified (i.e., with userid) datasets must be in quotes.

'parameters' = 1 to 100 parameters for a program separated by commas. For PL/I programs, start the parameters with a slash (/). For TSO/E Version 2, parameters can be in upper- or lowercase. Earlier releases support uppercase only.

Example

```
CALL DEMO(UTILPROG) 'NAME,RANK,PHONE'
```

The clist executes DEMO.LOAD(UTILPROG) and passes three parameters separated by commas to the load module before execution. If the load module unsuccessfully executes, TSO displays an error message. Chapter 9 includes a simple ISPF application that loads and executes a COBOL load module.

WHEN Command Syntax

```
CALL command. . .
WHEN SYSRC (operator number) commandname
```

SYSRC = Return code of CALL command.
operator = Relational operator in either symbolic (e.g., >) or character (e.g., GT) format. See Chapter 3 for a complete list of relational operators.
number = Usually 0 (program successfully executed) or 12 (program failed), although any nonzero return code can be given.
commandname = Any valid TSO command or clist that you are permitted to use.

Example

```
CALL 'HHG1.TEST.LOAD' '88'
  WHEN SYSRC (EQ 0) EXEC NEXTCALL
  WHEN SYSRC (GT 0) LIST ERROR.TEXT
```

The above example executes and loads the load module 'HHG1.TEST.LOAD' and sends a parameter of 88. If the CALL succeeds, the NEXTCALL clist executes. Otherwise, list the error log (ERROR.TEXT.). In either case, the clist ends and performs the command specified by the matched condition.

You can also use a SEND command as the equivalent of WRITE statement for displaying a return code:

```
call 'public.proglib(plotxy)'
WHEN SYSRC (GT 0) SEND 'MAXCC = &MAXCC' U(&SYSUID)
```

You can use a WHEN command in a select structure (which has a when statement). To do this, the WHEN command must be in a DO-END block:

```
SELECT (&OPT)
  WHEN (3) DO /* WHEN statement*/
    call'rps.utillib(erascrn)'
    WHEN SYSRC (GT 0) LIST ERROR.TEXT /*WHEN command*/
  END
END
```

Using the TERMIN Statement

The TERMIN command passes control to the user for creating input. After entering the desired input, the user enters a string or word to return to the clist. If this sounds like a potential source of serious problems, you are right. I do not recommend TERMIN because users may not remember the desired exit word and try to "power their way out" by pressing ATTENTION. The result is opened datasets (including the clist) and one frustrated user. Instead, have the user choose among specific options. But for those TSO+TSO/E clist coders who *must* have a TERMIN statement in their clists, here are the syntax and guidelines for using the statement.

1. TERMIN acts as an EXIT statement under ISPF and ends a clist. So you can use it as an implied EXIT statement.
2. The TERMIN statement takes one of three forms:
   a. TERMIN—Entering a null line returns control to the clist.
   b. TERMIN ,ADIOS,RUN—Allows a null line as a valid exit word and specifies more exit words. With multiple exit words, the null line must always be the first one in the TERMIN statement.
   c. TERMIN A,B,C, – Three exit words and none is a null line.
3. Two control variables are used during a TERMIN session. &SYSDVAL is the input entered by the user while in TERMIN and &SYSDLM is the position of the exit word selected by the user. (For example, if a clist has a TERMIN ABORT, EXIT, RETRY statement, and the user enters EXIT, then &SYSDLM has a value of 2, since EXIT is the second exit word in the TERMIN statement.)
4. TERMIN works correctly under Session Manager.

Example

Here are two examples of prompting for three dataset names. One example uses TERMIN and the other does not. In the first example, the user enters DLIST and the three dataset names. They are listed and control returns to the clist. A null ELSE (for &SYSDLM any value except 1) immediately returns control to the clist. In the second example, fewer statements obtain the same information without a termin session.

Example 1—With TERMIN

```
WRITE  Enter the name of THREE Datasets that you want to +
list
WRITE   Place the word DLIST and a blank in front of the
```

```
WRITE    datasets SEPARATED BY COMMAS.
WRITE  Enter BYEBYE to quit processing
READ
READDVAL DA1 DA2 DA3 /* NAME OF THREE DATASETS */
TERMIN DLIST,BYEBYE /* EXIT WORDS OF DLIST AND BYEBYE */
IF &SYSDLM EQ 1 THEN DO /* IF DLIST IS ENTERED */
   LIST &DA1
   LIST &DA2
   LIST &DA3
END
/* A Null ELSE implies end the TERMIN session when +
BYEBYE is +
entered*/
```

Example 2—Without TERMIN

```
WRITE  Enter the Name of Three Datasets
WRITE  Separate the Dataset Names by COMMAS
  READ
  READDVAL DA1 DA2 DA3
LIST &DA1
LIST &DA2
LIST &DA3
```

Authorized Environments (TSOEXEC)

One area confusing to many TSO/E users is authorized commands and authorized environments. By not understanding these concepts, users never know when it is proper to use the TSOEXEC command.

An *authorized command* is simply a TSO command that your computer center must give special permission so that users can access it. If you do not have permission, you cannot use the command. During TSO installation, your installer may add to the following list of authorized commands and programs:

IEBCOPY (authorized program)
LISTB
LISTBC
RACONVERT
RECEIVE
SE
SEND
SYNC
TRANSMIT
XMIT

In addition, you may not be allowed to use certain TSO commands in batch (background). An *authorized environment* is a permitted state where one can successfully access and execute an authorized command. For those sites having TSO/E Version 1 Release 2 and later, use the TSOEXEC command or the TSO Service Facility (IKJEFTSR or TSOLNK module documented in *TSO/E Programming Services*) for executing authorized commands in both authorized and unauthorized environments. In other words, if allowed to use a command, you can execute anywhere under TSO + TSO/E because there is no need to worry if the environment is authorized or not. TSO/E Version 2 includes table lookup features to verify if a command is authorized and if a command can be used in background (hatch) mode.

For ISPF sites with Version 2 Release 2 and later, the TSO Service Facility can automatically be invoked for authorized commands and programs. (Without this, the command execution fails because ISPF is an unauthorized environment.) The rest of this topic discusses the syntax and guidelines of the TSOEXEC command.

TSOEXEC

1. The command syntax is simple:
   TSOEXEC command
   command = Any valid TSO command including authorized commands (see above list) or clist.
2. You can use four control variables with TSOEXEC, as listed in Table 5-8.

Table 5-8. TSOEXEC Control Variables

Variable and Function	Common Return Codes
&LASTCC (TSOEXEC's return code; if greater than zero, display error message)	0 = Command worked 4 = Command has a nonzero return code stored in &SYSCMDRC and processing ended 8 = You pressed Attention 12 = Processing failed; results in &SYSABNCD (ABEND code) and &SYSCMDRC (return code) 24 = Failed abruptly 28 = Not a TSO/E command
&SYSABCND (TSOEXEC's ABEND code)	Not available
&SYSABNRC (TSOEXEC's ABEND reason code)	Not available
&SYSCMDRC (Return code from TSO command executed by TSOEXEC)	Not available

Use these control variables in your clist processing:

```
TSOEXEC EXEC 'Hi Mom' US(MOM1)
 SET &RCD = &LASTCC
   IF &RCD GT 0 THEN DO
    WRITE TSOEXEC processing partially or not +
    successful
    WRITE TSOEXEC Return Code        is &RCD
    WRITE TSOEXEC ABEND Code         is &SYSABNCD
    WRITE TSOEXEC ABEND Reason Code is &SYSABNRC
    WRITE TSO/E Command Reason Code is &SYSCMDRC
   END
```

displayed:

```
TSOEXEC processing partially or not successful.
TSOEXEC Return Code       is 4
TSOEXEC ABEND Code        is
TSOEXEC ABEND Reason Code is 0
TSO/E Command Reason Code is 12
```

The above used EXEC instead of SEND. The return code of 4 indicates that the EXEC command failed. The other three control variables can provide additional information in debugging a problem.

Working with Time and Date Values in Clists

This section shows how to obtain the current date or time in several different formats. It then examines what you can do with these obtained date and time values.

Date and Time Control Variables

Table 5-9 lists the control variables with the current date or time as values.

Table 5-9. Date and Time Control Variables

Variable	Function	Sample
&SYSDATE	Current date in mm/dd/yy format	12/01/88
&SYSJDATE*	Current date in Julian (yy/ddd) format	88.335
&SYSSDATE*	Current date in yy/mm/dd format	88/12/01
&SYSSTIME*	Current time in hh : mm format	13 : 11
&SYSTIME	Current time in hh : mm : ss format	13 : 11 : 43

* TSO/E Version 1 Release 2 and later. (*Note:* Time is in a 24-hour format, so 13 : 11 instead of 1 p.m.)

Having so few functions causes the following limitations:

1. Presently, there is no easy way for changing a date or time into a different format. (This can be done by writing a clist using built-in functions.)
2. There are no month, day, year, hour, minute, second, yymmdd (without slashes), or mmddyy (without slashes) control variables; instead create a substring from one of the existing variables. This is shown a little later.
3. You must perform your own date and time calculations, although time in a 24-hour format and &SYSSDATE makes this easier.
4. There is no a.m. or p.m. function. You need to write a clist sequence similar to the following:

   ```
   SET &HOUR = &SUBSTR(1:2,&SYSTIME) /* Get the current
   hour
   IF &HOUR GE 12 AND &HOUR LE 24 THEN SET &TOD = P.M.
      ELSE SET &TOD = A.M.
   ```

   An alternative may be using a Rexxexec with a time built-in function. Notice that it is easier to create a nested variable (&HOUR) instead of taking a substring every time. A similar sequence can create morning, afternoon, and evening values.
5. Use the &STR function for date and time control variables in all clist statements (except WRITE). This is because date and time variables contain slashes, colons, and periods.

   ```
   IF (&SYSTIME) = &STR(15:18:20) THEN WRITE &SYSTIME
   ```

Using Clists with Date and Time Values

Here are some things you can do with date and time values in clists:

1. Use the SUBSTR built-in function to extract the desired date or time part. Table 5-10 is a handy look-up chart of the SUBSTR values of all five control variables. The format is

   ```
           SET &X = &SUBSTR(b:e,&z)
   where &x = any symbolic variable
            b = beginning position of desired substring
            e = ending position of desired substring
           &z = the date/time control variable or any con-
                trol variable
   ```
2. Once extracted, the time part can be used as a normal clist variable. Robert Virgile, an independent trainer and consultant in the Boston area, has the following in his menu and large clists:

   ```
   SET &SECONDS = &SUBSTR(7:8,&SYSTIME)
   SET &CNT = 1
   ```

```
DO WHILE &CNT LE 5000
  SET &CNT = &CNT + 1
END
IF &SECONDS LE 6 WRITE Look who's doing some work!
  ELSE IF &SECONDS LE &STR(12) THEN +
    WRITE Putting your nose to the grindstone?
  ELSE IF &SECONDS LE &STR(18) THEN +
    WRITE Coffee Break must finally be over!
ELSE IF &SECONDS LE &STR(24) THEN +
    WRITE Don't Strain Yourself!
  ELSE IF &SECONDS LE &STR(30) THEN +
    WRITE Nothing like work to break up the monotony!
  ELSE IF &SECONDS LE &STR(36) THEN +
    WRITE Your Annual Review coming so soon?
  ELSE IF &SECONDS LE &STR(42) THEN +
    WRITE Who woke you up?
  ELSE IF &SECONDS LE &STR(48) THEN +
    WRITE Even two hour lunches have to end some time!
  ELSE IF &SECONDS LE &STR(54) THEN +
    WRITE Are you working for a change?
  ELSE WRITE Its about time you did some work!
```

Table 5-10. SUBSTR Control Variable Values Look-up Chart

Part	Beginning Position (b)	Ending Position (e)	
	&SYSDATE (&z)		
Month	1	2	
Day	4	5	
Year	7	8	
	&SYSJDATE (&z)		
Year	1	2	
Day_of_Year	4	6	
	&SYSSDATE (&z)		
Month	7	8	
Day	4	5	
Year	1	2	
	&SYSSTIME and &SYSTIME (&z)		
Hour	1	2	
Minute	4	5	
Second	7	8	(&SYSTIME only)

Bob points out that the user thinks that the messages are random since it is different almost every time. (I added a null DO loop that takes long enough to give different messages if you use this clist twice in a row. Null DO loops are useful when you want to slow down clist processing.) You could vary the number of messages from 1 to 60 (a different one every second!) A similar sort of program can be done for time of day or day of the week.

3. To calculate the difference between two dates in yy/mm/dd format you will have to remove the slashes. The following sequence calculates the difference between today's date and a user-specified date (TSO/E Version 1 Release 2 and later):

```
WRITE Enter Todays Julian Date (YYDDD):
READ DATE2
SET &CUR_Year = &SUBSTR(1:2,&SYSJDATE)
SET &USER_YR = &SUBSTR(1:2,&DATE2)
SET &CUR_DY = &SUBSTR(4:6,&SYSJDATE)
SET &USER_DY = &SUBSTR(3:5,&DATE2)
SET &DIFF1 = &USER_YR - &CUR_YR
SET &DIFF2 = &USER_DY - &CUR_DY
IF &DIFF1 > 0 THEN SET &DIFF_VERB EQ GREATER
  ELSE SET &DIFF_VERB EQ LESS_THAN
WRITE Your date is &DIFF_VERB than &SYSDATE by +
roughly +
WRITE &DIFF1 Years and &DIFF2 Days
```

displayed:

Your date is GREATER than 12/02/88 by roughly 1 Years and 28

If you are using TSO or TSO/E Version 1, use the following sequence to place your date in yymmdd format.

```
SET &DATE1 = &STR(&SYSDATE) /*date in mm/dd/yy format
SET &PART1 = &SUBSTR(7:8,&DATE1) /*extract year
SET &PART2 = &SUBSTR(4:5,&DATE1) /*extract month
SET &PART3 = &SUBSTR(1:2,&DATE1) /*extract day
SET &NEWDAY = &STR(&PART1./&PART2./&PART3) /*with +
slashes
SET &NEWDAY2 = &PART1&PART2&PART3 /*without slashes
```

This can also be done in one statement but is harder to understand and debug.

4. To calculate the difference between two times, use the a sequence similar to the following. This clist tells the difference between the present time and 3:30 P.M.

```
SET &HR = &SUBSTR(1:2,&SYSSTIME) /*hour variable
SET &MN = &SUBSTR(4:5,&SYSSTIME) /*second variable
```

```
IF &HR GE 15 and &MN GE 30 THEN WRITE Time to Leave!
If &MN LE 30 THEN DO
  SET &DIFF_MN = 30 - &MN
  SET &DIFF_HR = 15 - &HR
END
ELSE DO
  SET &DIFF_MN = (60-(&MN - 30))
  SET &DIFF_HR = (15 - &HR) - 1
END
WRITE &DIFF_HR Hours and &DIFF_MN to GO!
```

5. There are all sorts of routines available in other languages that you can use in clists:
   a. Regular date to 24-hour format and vice versa.
   b. Regular date to Julian format and vice versa.
   c. Add two times together.

Date algorithms are available from the Association of Computing Machinery to convert dates between formats. A good concise article on the subject is R. W., Bemer, 1979, "Time and the Computer," *Interface Age,* February, pp. 74–79.

Working with Money Values in Clists

Since clist values cannot be decimals or fractions, any sequence to work with money values is rather long. In the back of the *OS/VS2 TSO Terminal User's Guide* is such an example called PIZZA.CLIST. About 30 lines are given just to round an amount to the nearest nickel. Since this pushes clists far beyond what they were designed to do, no examples are given here. Rather than reinventing the wheel, use a language like BASIC, C, FORTRAN, PASCAL, and REXX (see Chapter 11) which works well with decimal values.

Clearing a Screen

Clearing a screen from a clist makes for a nicer application. However, there is no one TSO command that does this—but there are at least two ways this can be done:

1. Using Session Manager (if installed)—use a DELETE.WINDOW or /CHANGE.STREAM CLEAR/ command to erase or delete the current screen (more on Session Manager in Chapter 7).
2. Creating an assembly language module with a STLINEO LINE=1 macro (for 3270-type terminals only). The macro erases the screen and starts the next display on line 1. The macros are documented in the "Using Terminal

Control Macro Instructions'' section of *TSO/E Programming Services* and the ''Writing a Full-Screen Command Processor'' of *TSO/E Programming Guide*. Sites with TSO or pre-TSO/E Version 1 Release 4 can find this information in the *TSO Extensions Guide to Writing a Terminal Monitor Program or a Command Processor*.

Calling Clists from a Program (IKJCT441)

This section briefly examines what the Clist Variable Access Module or IKJCT441 does. A more detailed description is found in *TSO/E Programming Services*, *TSO/E Programming Guide*, and *TSO Extensions Guide to Writing a Terminal Monitor Program or a Command Processor*. IKJCT441 allow programs written in other languages to use CLIST or REXX (TSO/E Version 2 only) variables. Some functions of IKJCT441 are:

1. Create a clist/REXX variable (if not existing).
2. Assign a value to a clist/REXX variable.
3. Return the value of a clist/REXX variable.
4. Show all working clist variables and their assigned values. See Chapter 11 for additional programming facilities for REXX.

Some additional information about IKJCT441:

1. This module becomes more efficient and powerful with each new release of TSO/E. Check your manual for the latest features.
2. You must reset &SYSOUTLINE to 0 after every TSO command executed. Programs called within clists can use &SYSOUTLINE.
3. Use this module to perform complex processing and return the results to the clist or REXX exec. This module also accepts input (active variables and values) from clists and REXX execs.
4. There is a set of return codes for each clist action between 0 and 76.
5. For TSO/E Version 2, this can be used in TSO/E area only (not in the non-TSO/E area of MVS).

Where Can I Find More Examples of Clists and TSO Commands?

Clists

There are many places that one can look for other useful clists. Some of these are the following:

- Other clist programmers in your department
- Clist programmers or programs used by your computer center

- Clist programmers at other sites
- Borrowing ideas from programs in other languages
- Contacting the MVS Group of the Operating Systems Support (for TSO) and the ISPF Group of the Graphics and Integrated Systems Division of SHARE Inc. The general address for SHARE is 111 East Wacker Drive, Chicago, IL 60601; telephone 312-822-0932. Or contact the other group of GUIDE Inc. The general address for GUIDE is 111 East Wacker Drive, Chicago, IL 60601; telephone 312-644-6610.

  For Europe, the Middle East, and Africa, the address of Share Europe Association (SEAS) is 17, rue Pierres dulviton, 1207 Geneve, Switzerland; telephone: (41) 22-35-40-66

*Commands**

Even though you have TSO/E and ISPF/PDF installed on your system, you may find that you have a need for other TSO commands, such as stand-alone COPY or LIST commands, which can be executed from a clist. There are several vendors who also supply such utilities.

Additionally, there many TSO commands in the public domain, usually available for the cost of postage and the tape to send them to you on. Such commands include:

FREEALL	For freeing patterns of DSNAMEs
SYSIN/INSTREAM	For doing what "DD *" does in JCL
VTOC	For reading or editing VTOCs
FREESP	For expanding/trimming file space
JSTATUS	For looking at JES2 queues
PDS	Does *everything* for a PDS

There are many, many others. They are written in assembly language and are easy to install. (Generally, you do not have to be an assembly language programmer to install these commands.) The author's names and telephone numbers are in the source.

Some sources of public domain TSO commands are given in Table 5-11.

Your Local Clist Environment

In addition to the built-in functions and clist statements that TSO and TSO/E provide, your site may have locally written functions and clist statements. Here is some information about them.

* This section was written by Charles Hoffman of GTE Laboratories, Inc.

Table 5-11. Sources of TSO Commands in the Public Domain*

TSO Commands	*CBT Mods*
Bill Smith SYNTEX (U.S.A.) Inc. 3401 Hillview Avenue P.O.B. 10850 Palo Alto, CA 94303	Arnold Casinghino Connecticut Bank and Trust Co. Technical Support Section F04L 99 Founders Plaza East Hartford, CT 06108-3292 Send 2400-ft reel (6250 bpi) or 3820 cartridge and $30.
Air Force: TSO Commands	*SHARE: MVS or JES2 Mods*
Jim Marshall, Capt Department of Defense Y421 9800 Savage Road Ft. Meade, MD 20755-6000	Share Program Library Agency Triangle Universities Computation Center P.O. Box 12076 2 Davis Drive Research Triangle Park, NC 27709 $50, includes price of tape.
JES3 Mods	
Alan C. Field Watterau Inc. 345 Dunn Rd. Florissant, MO 67031-7995	

* The following reference may also be useful. It discusses the SHARE mods tape and the most important modules: Jurgansen, J., and Moinil P., 1986. The SHARE Mods Tape. *Proceedings of the SEAS Spring Meeting 1986*, pp. 85–86.

1. A local built-in function begins with &SYSX and may be up to 248 additional characters. They follow the standard naming conventions described in Chapter 4.
2. Use a local built-in function to create control variables and perform text or mathematical tasks.
3. Return codes for a local built-in functions include:

0 or 4	Successfully worked with a value produced. Clist resumes processing.
8	Undefined local built-in function with a null value produced. Clist resumes processing.
12	Unable to process function. Writes an error message, assigns a reason code of 604, and gives a return code to the control variable &SYSREASON.

16 Same as 12 but *no* error message is given; you must add one to your function.

4. Local clist statements also can be created and used. They also must follow standard clist statement conventions but have no required prefix.
5. Local clist statements may give the following return codes:

0	*Not* a local statement, so instead treated as a TSO command.
4	Statement successfully worked.
12	Unable to process statement. Writes an error message, assigns a reason code of 608, and gives a return code to the control variable &SYSREASON.
16	Same as 12 but gives *no* error message; you must add one to your statement.

How to create a local built-in function or clist statement is documented in IBM's *TSO/E Customization Guide*.

CONCLUSIONS

Your knowledge of the clist language and what you can do with it has grown. With arrays, control variables, and special TSO commands, you now know how to take full advantage of the clist language. You know where to obtain more TSO clists and commands are also available to you. Yet, there are still important areas left to cover. Chapters 6 through 8 continue the remainder of advanced and miscellaneous clist topics such as built-in functions for string processing, clists with line editors and batch processing, and multiple clists/clist subprocedures. Chapters 9 and 10 will more than get you started with ISPF and edit macros. (With a few advanced tips thrown in too.) Chapter 11 looks at the future direction of clists by reviewing REXX.

SUGGESTED READINGS

Beebe, Caroline, 1988. Developing Screen Design Standards. *Proceedings of the Digital Equipment Computer Users Society USA Spring 1988*. pp. 77–84.

Buczynski, Al, 1986. *Public Clist Standards*. In-house document, GTE Laboratories.

Elston, Jay, 1982. Clist Esoterica—Advanced Examples. *SHARE 59 Proceedings*. pp. 1857–1865.

German, Hallett, 1987. *Clist Standards Outline*. Unpublished document, GTE Laboratories.

German, Hallett, 1987. *Clist Tips*. Unpublished document, GTE Laboratories.

Hoffman, Charles A., 1986. *Introduction to TSO Command Lists (Clists)*. Course notes.

IBM Corporation, 1986. *OS/VS2 TSO Terminal Monitor Program and Service Routines Logic*. SY28–0650.

IBM Corporation, 1988. *INFO/SYSTEM Database*. Various notes.

IBM Corporation, 1987. *TSO/E Programming Guide*. SC28–1363.

IBM Corporation, 1987. *TSO Extensions Clists*. SC28–1304.

IBM Corporation, 1987. *TSO Extensions Customization*. SC28–1380.

IBM Corporation, 1984. *TSO Extensions (TSO/E) General Information Manual*. GC28–1061.

IBM Corporation, 1987. *TSO Extensions Guide to Writing a Terminal Monitor Program or a Command Processor*. SC28–1136.

IBM Corporation, 1987. *TSO Extensions Programming Guide*. SC28–1363.

IBM Corporation, 1987. *TSO Extensions Programming Services*. SC28–1364.

Kusnierz, Thomas E., 1986. Clist Tips and Techniques. *SHARE 67 Proceedings*. pp. 1–19 (handout).

Northeast Utilities, 1982. *TSO-User Introductory Guide*. Unpublished in-house user's guide. pp. 28–24.

Zwass, Vladimir, 1981. *Programming in FORTRAN*. pp. 75–88. New York: Barnes and Noble Books.

6

Clists: Built-In Functions

WHY HAVE BUILT-IN FUNCTIONS?

Clists cannot directly read character strings (including ampersands), JCL statements, and double-byte characters. However, enclosing these characters in *built-in functions* provides a means for processing them and returning a result. Built-in functions also can return a clist variable's value type and determine if a dataset or member exists.

From a more technical view, built-in function processing occurs during the interpreter's second phase. If using a function, then invoke the load module that returns the result of function processing. A built-in function also performs any needed symbolic substitution for returning the result. Then built-in functions are special environments allowing clists to process special characters and perform other tasks they otherwise would be unable to do.

Like control variables, the number of built-in functions grows with each new release (there are 5 functions in TSO and 15 in TSO/E Version 1, Release 4). Table 6-1 lists each function and its purpose. An *argument* is a character string, double-byte character string, JCL statement, symbolic variable, or expression that the built-in function evaluates.

Your site may also use local built-in functions, which always start with &SYSX. The "Local Clist Environment" section of Chapter 5 has further information on this topic. Built-in functions are easy to recognize because they use the following format:

&functioname(argument,[argument, argument])

The following list summarizes function syntax:

1. An *argument* is any valid user-supplied character string, double-byte character string, JCL statement, symbolic variable, or expression.
2. The user supplies at least one and up to three arguments enclosed in parentheses. The parentheses set the "boundaries" of the argument. (Brackets

Table 6-1. Overview of Built-in Functions

Function	Purpose	When First Available
&DATATYPE	To tell if a value is character or numeric	TSO
&EVAL	Mathematical result of an argument	TSO
&LENGTH	Number of characters in an argument	TSO
&NRSTR	Prevents symbolic substitution of double ampersands	TSO/E Version 1 Release 1
&STR	Converts argument to a character string	TSO
&SUBSTR	Extracts part of a character string	TSO
&SYSCAPS	Converts argument to uppercase	TSO/E Version 1 Release 2
&SYSCLENGTH	Number of characters in an argument with double-byte characters	TSO/E Version 1 Release 4
&SYSCSUBSTR	Extracts part of a double-byte string	TSO Version 1 Release 4
&SYSDSN	Verifies if a dataset or member exists	TSO/E Version 1 Release 2
&SYSINDEX	Finds the position of a character in an argument	TSO/E Version 1 Release 3
&SYSLC	Converts argument to lowercase	TSO/E Version 1 Release 2
&SYSNSUB	Controls symbolic substitution level	TSO/E Version 1 Release 3
&SYSONEBYTE	Converts double-byte characters to a character string	TSO/E Version 1 Release 4
&SYSTWOBYTE	Converts a character string to double-byte characters	TSO/E Version 1 Release 4

indicate the second and third arguments which may be optional for a function.)

3. Use commas for separating arguments.
4. The second argument of &SUBSTR and &SYSCSUBSTR always begins with a colon (e.g., :2.)
5. *There are no blank spaces between the function name and the parentheses enclosing the argument(s) or the parenthesis and an argument*. However, an argument may have blank spaces between clist operators. (i.e., 4+5 and 4 + 5 are both valid.)

All built-in functions fall into two types: string operation functions and other (nonstring) operation functions. The rest of the chapter discusses both function

Figure 6-1. Symbolic Substitution Control Hierarchy for String Operation Functions

Highest Level	&SYSNSUB (Total control of symbolic substitution scans, TSO/E Version 1 Release 3)
	↑
Middle Level	&NRSTR (Some control of symbolic substitution scans, TSO/E Version 1 Release 1)
	↑
Lowest Level	&EVAL/&STR (Limited control of symbolic substitution scans, TSO and TSO/E)

types and uses them in the CUSTOMER clist. This clist, which performs transactions on a customer's database, is used to reinforce concepts covered in Chapters 6 through 8.

String Operations

One way to think about string operation built-in functions is that they help "beat the system." In other words, built-in functions create a desired result by controlling the number of symbolic substitution scans and other aspects of clist variable processing. A result with double ampersands or blank spaces may be contrary to normal clist processing, thus beating the system! String operation functions are divided into four categories: (1) controlling the number of symbolic substitution scans, (2) string manipulation, (3) case operations, and (4) double-byte characters. Each of these functions is reviewed.

Controlling Symbolic Substitution (&NRSTR, &STR, &SYSNSUB)

Each new release of TSO/E increases user control over the number of symbolic substitution scans performed on an argument. Figure 6-1 shows the symbolic substitution control hierarchy for string operation functions. The following summarizes the syntax, results, and error messages of &NRSTR, &STR, and &SYSNSUB.

&NRSTR

First Available: TSO/E Version 1 Release 1

Function: Allows only one symbolic substitution scan and creates a nonrescannable character string. Thus, single-ampersand variables do not convert to a value (e.g., &CITY remains &CITY and does not become CHICAGO), and double-ampersand variables do not become single-ampersand variables (e.g., &&ZIPCODE remains &&ZIPCODE and does not become &ZIPCODE). &NRSTR is a weaker version of &SYSNSUB because it provides limited control over symbolic substitution.

Syntax: &NRSTR(argument)

Example: `WRITE &NRSTR(&&X)`

displayed:

&&X

*Argument:*Any mix of numeric, alphanumeric, national (@,$,#), special (i.e., hexadecimal 25 for line feed), clist operators, or double-byte characters. This includes JCL statements.

Returned Value: A nonrescannable argument after one scan of symbolic substitution.

Special Nonzero Return Codes: None

Common Error Messages: IKJ56545I A MISSING BUILT-IN FUNCTION OPERAND.

Solution: Add a parenthesis or remove the space between the parenthesis and the function name.

Commonly Used With: &SYSCAPS converts a result to uppercase or &SYSLC to lowercase.

&STR

First Available: TSO

Function: Converts an argument to a character string retaining blanks. &STR is kind of the opposite of &EVAL, which performs mathematical operations on an argument.

Syntax: &STR(argument)

Example: `WRITE &STR(3*4)`

displayed

```
3*4 /*Retains leading blank and does not*/
    /*perform a mathematical operation.*/
```

Argument: Any mix of numeric, alphanumeric, national (@,$,#), special (i.e., hexadecimal 25 for line feed), clist operators, or double byte characters. This includes nested variables.

Returned Value: The argument as a character string.

Special Nonzero Return Codes: None

Common Error Messages: IKJ56545I—A MISSING BUILT-IN FUNCTION OPERAND.

Solution: Add a parenthesis or remove the space between the parenthesis and the function name.

Commonly Used With: &LENGTH gets the length of an argument with blanks.

&SYSNSUB

First Available: TSO/E Version 1 Release 3

Function: Performs as many symbolic substitution scans as requested by the user—a more powerful version of &NRSTR and &STR.

Syntax: *&SYSNSUB(np,str)*

np = Number of symbolic substitution scans.
str = String to control symbolic substitution.

Example: `SET &SYSSCAN = 3`
Example: `SET &OLD_VAR = HI`
Example: `SET &NEW_VAR = &&OLD_VAR`
Example: `WRITE LEVEL 0 &SYSNSUB(0,&NEWVAR)`
Example: `WRITE LEVEL 1 &SYSNSUB(1,&NEWVAR)`
Example: `WRITE LEVEL 2 &SYSNSUB(2,&NEWVAR)`

Example: displayed

```
LEVEL 1 &NEWVAR     (no substitution)
LEVEL 2 &OLDVAR     (one ampersand disappears)
LEVEL 3 HI          (final symbolic value)
```

Argument: STR is any mix of numeric, alphanumeric, national (@,$,#), special characters (i.e., hexadecimal 25 for line feed), or clist operators. It usually is a clist symbolic variable. NP has a value from 0 to 99. 0 means perform no symbolic substitution. NP is always less than or equal to the value of &SYSSCAN.

Returned Value: The argument after *np* scans of symbolic substitution.

Special NonZero Return Codes:

716—Invalid number of symbolic scans specified
Solution: Give np a value from 0 to 99.

720—Missing one or more arguments.
Solution: Add missing argument (*np* or *str*).

724—Using a built-in function in the *np* argument.
Solution: Assign the function's result to a variable or use a value for np.

Common Error Messages:

IKJ56545I—A MISSING BUILT-IN FUNCTION OPERAND.

Solution: Add a parenthesis or remove the space between the parenthesis and the function name.

IKJ79004I—THIS STATEMENT HAS AN INVALID &SYSNSUB LEVEL PARAMETER: THE LEVEL PARAMETER IS A NUMBER 0–99.

Solution: Make np between 0 and 99.

IKJ79005I—THIS STATEMENT HAS A MISSING &SYSNSUB LEVEL PARAMETER AND/OR EXPRESSION PARAMETER.

Solution: Make np between 0 and 99 and *use* a valid argument for *str*.

IKJ79006I—THIS STATEMENT HAS A &SYSNSUB LEVEL PARAMETER THAT HAS USED A BUILT-IN FUNCTION AS A SYMBOLIC VARIABLE.

Solution: Assign the function's result to a variable or use a value in *np* operand.

Commonly Used With: The np operand of &SYSNSUB cannot use results from other functions.

Tips, Tricks, and Traps

1. The following are some tips on using for &NRSTR, &STR, and &SYSNSUB:
   a. Use &NRSTR or &SYSNSUB (level 0 for no substitution) for processing JCL statements with ampersands, such as DD statements for temporary datasets and statements with symbolic parameters. Try &STR for processing JCL statements not containing ampersands. Using these functions guarantees that SET and clist QSAM facility statements retain their current values and no unexpected symbolic substitution occurs. Chapter 7 reviews clist processing of JCL statements.
   b. Use &SYSCAPS (uppercase) or &SYSLC (lowercase) for converting the result of &NRSTR to a different case. The following statement converts a variable to uppercase (i.e., &&A) and retains the double ampersand:

   ```
   SET &STRNG = &NRSTR(&SYSCAPS(&&a))
   ```

   See later in the chapter in the "Case Operators Text" section for more on &SYSCAPS and &SYSLC.
   c. &STR and Blanks (Processing of Blank Strings)
      (i) You do not need statements like SET &VAR_ONE = or SET &VAR_ONE = &STR( ) because clist variables have initially a null value.
      (ii) Use statements like SET &VAR_ONE = &STR ( ) for assigning a variable a value of one or more blanks.

(iii) For removing trailing blanks, set a variable equal to itself. SET &VAR_ONE = &VAR_ONE

(iv) Either of these approaches keeps leading/trailing blanks or leading zeros in a numeric argument.

Approach 1

```
SET &BK = &STR(                    )
SET &CITY = TAOS
SET &CITY = &STR(&CITY&BK)
SET &CITY = &SUBSTR(1:20,&CITY)
```

The first statement creates a variable equal to 20 blanks. The third statement takes the value of &CITY (TAOS) and adds these blanks at the end of the value. The fourth statement extracts the first 20 characters of &CITY—guaranteeing that &CITY always has a length of 20. Note you can combine the last two statements:

```
SET &CITY = &SUBSTR(1:20,&STR(&CITY&BK))
```

Approach 2

```
SET &BK = &STR(                    )
SET &CITY = TAOS
SET &CITY = &STR(&CITY&SUBSTR(1:20-&LENGTH+
  (&CITY),&BK))
```

or &VALUE is any symbolic variable to pad blanks onto.

```
SET &BLANK = &STR(                    )
SET &STOP = &LENGTH(&STR(&BLANK))
SET &VALUE = &STR(&VALUE&SUBSTR(&LENGTH+
  (&VALUE+1:&STOP,&BLANK)) *
```

The key to the second approach is the last statement, which forms a string always 20 characters long. To do this, the following occurs:

(*a*) Extract the needed number of blanks for &CITY to be 20 characters (i.e., 20–4 or 16 blanks plus TAOS)

(*b*) Concatenate the value of &CITY and the string of blanks.

The approach you use depends on your clist style. The first approach has more statements but is easier to follow and debug. In contrast, the second approach is more efficient but harder to debug. If you are a novice to creating multiple built-in function statements, try doing it first by using one function per statement and then later combining

* Reprinted by permission from Thomas Kusinerz Share 67 presentation copyright © 1986 by International Business Machines Corporation.

statements. Going the opposite way helps in debugging statements with multiple built-in functions.

d. Other uses of &STR:

(i) Processing values entered in ISPF panels, processing a READ statement, or anytime you have little control over user input. The following example assigns the entire user input to &NAME.

```
WRITE What is your NAME?
READ
SET &NAME = &STR(&SYSDVAL)
```

(ii) Processing JCL statements without ampersands. Instead, use &SYSNSUB or &NRSTR.

(iii) Clist statements other than WRITE using any date or time control variables.

```
SET &TODAY = &STR(&SYSDATE)
```

(iv) Use &STR not to evaluate a string mathematically.

```
WRITE &STR(8*8)
```

displayed:

```
8*8
```

(v) Use &STR for distinguishing local clist statements from IBM's or the SELECT statement from RACF's SELECT subcommand (e.g., &STR(TERMIN ABCD) when TERMIN is a local statement).

e. Uses of &SYSNSUB:

(i) Like &NRSTR, keeps single or double ampersand values (with np operand = 0).

(ii) Array processing:

Old Way

```
SET &VAR = &NRSTR(&&VAR)
SET &CNT = 1
DO WHILE &CNT LE 10
  SET &L = &VAR&CNT /*Sets &L = &VAR1*/
  SET &CNT = &CNT + 1
END
```

New Way

```
SET &VAR = &NRSTR(&&VAR)
SET &CNT = 1
DO WHILE &CNT LE 10
  SET &L = &SYSNSUB(2,&VAR&CNT) /*Sets &L = &VAR1 */
  SET &CNT = &CNT + 1
END
```

The advantage of the new way is that you, and not the interpreter, controls the number of symbolic substitution scans on single- and double-ampersand variables.

2. Avoid these common traps for &NRSTR, &STR, and &SYSNSUB:
   a. Thinking that &NRSTR permanently converts a variable:

```
SET &VAR_ONE = &NRSTR(&&VAR_TWO)
WRITE VAR_ONE = &VAR_ONE
```

displayed:

```
VAR_ONE = &VAR_TWO /* Once out of &NRSTR, loses the*/
                   /* double ampersand. */
```

   b. If &SYSSCAN is 0, then do no symbolic substitution scans for any built-in function. Since the default value of &SYSSCAN is 16, this is rarely changed (or use &SYSNSUB). However, if you alter &SYSSCAN, assign a value of one or higher when using &NRSTR or a value greater or equal to the *np* value of &SYSNSUB.
   c. Using &NRSTR for complete control over symbolic substitution; use &SYSNSUB instead. Another trap is not realizing that &SYSNSUB with one symbolic substitution scan is identical to &NRSTR.
   d. Using &STR instead of &NRSTR or &SYSNSUB(0,str) for processing JCL statements with ampersands. This includes SET and clist QSAM facility statements.
   e. Before TSO/E Version 1 Release 4 Modification 2, &NRSTR incorrectly translates double-byte characters.
   f. Using &STR for preventing symbolic substitution of single- and double-ampersand values; try &NRSTR or &SYSNSUB instead.
   g. Creating statements for initially assigning a value of null—they are not needed. SET &X = &STR( )
   h. Do not place these operators at the end of a variable value unless processed with &STR, &NRSTR, or &SUBSTR (Read below on using parentheses.): + (plus operator), − (minus operator), * (asterisk), / (slash), ** (two asterisks), // (two slashes), ((left parenthesis), and) (right parenthesis).

The + and − fail because they are line continuation characters. The rest fail because the interpreter thinks they are mathematical operators—which cannot be preceded by character data. However, you can place most operators at the start or middle of a variable value when using &NRSTR, &STR, and &SUBSTR (e.g., SET &WILL_WORK = X&STR(*)Y correctly translates to X*Y.) The following example adds left and right parentheses to a character string. A built-in function still processes correctly if not using a right parenthesis. Note the technique for doing this: assign the parenthesis as a value to a symbolic variable, then use the variable enclosed by a built-in function.

```
SET &LEFT = &STR((
SET &RIGHT = ) or SET &RIGHT = &STR())
SET &PAREN1 = X&STR(&LEFT)
SET &PAREN2 = Y&STR(&RIGHT)
WRITE &PAREN1 &PAREN2
```

displayed:

```
X( )Y
```

An exception is that a left or right parenthesis at the beginning or middle of a character string does not need a built-in function (e.g., SET &WILLWORK = X(Y correctly translates to X(Y!) For further information, chack entery E207625 in the IBM Information System database.

i. Using a built-in function for suppling the *np* operand value of &SYSNSUB. This is not supported.

String Manipulation (&EVAL, &LENGTH, &SUBSTR, &SYSINDEX)

Use any of these four built-in functions for manipulating a character string to a desired result.

&EVAL

First Available: TSO

Function: Converts a string argument to numeric and then does the requested mathematical operation—a kind of opposite to &STR.

Syntax: &EVAL(argument)

Example: `WRITE &EVAL(1+1)`

displayed:

2

Argument: A mix of valid numeric characters and mathematical operators. Multiple operations and additional parentheses for controlling that operation are allowed. You may place blanks between numeric characters and mathematical operators. *Double-byte characters are not valid.*

Returned Value: Mathematical result of argument.

Special Nonzero Return Codes: Usually, a 8xx return code (evaluation error). However, you get a 0 return code even when using character arguments and invalid operators!
820—Operators out of order
Solution: Supply missing operator or numeric character.

832—The result of mathematical operation is outside valid range.
Solution: Use smaller numbers or another language.

852,856,860,864—character data
Solution: Make a character item numeric. The interpreter views decimal and fraction values as character data.

Common Error Messages:

IKJ56545I—A MISSING BUILT-IN FUNCTION OPERAND.
Solution: Add a parenthesis or remove the space between the parenthesis and a function name.

IKJ56545I—EXCEEDED THE MAXIMUM NUMBER DURING EVALUATION
Solution: Use smaller numbers or another language.

IKJ56545I—THIS STATEMENT HAS AN EXPRESSION WITH MISSING OPERATORS.
Solution: Supply missing operator(s).

IKJ56545I—AN EXPRESSION WITH OPERATORS OUT OF SEQUENCE.
Solution: Supply missing operator or numeric character.

IKJ56545I—AN EXPRESSION WITH A CHARACTER DATA ITEM USED NUMERICALLY.
Solution: Change a character item to numeric. (The interpreter views decimal and fraction values as character data.)

Commonly Used with: None

&LENGTH

First Available: TSO

Function: Returns the length (number of bytes or characters) present in an argument. Performs any needed symbolic substitution or mathematical operations to do this.

Syntax: &LENGTH(argument)

Example:
```
SET &LEN = &LENGTH(2*10)
WRITE The Length of &LEN IS . . . &LEN
```
displayed:
```
The Length of &LEN IS . . . 2 /* 20 is two -
characters*/
```

Argument: A mix of numeric, alphanumeric, national (@,$,#), special (i.e. hexadecimal 25 for line feed), clist operators, or double-byte characters.

Returned Value: Number of characters in argument. &LENGTH returns a value of 0 if an argument is a null value.

Special Nonzero Return Codes: None

Common Error Messages:

IKJ56545I A MISSING BUILT-IN FUNCTION OPERAND.

Solution: Add a parenthesis or remove the space between the parenthesis and the function name.

Commonly Used with:

&STR: Not performing mathematical operations and keeping blanks.

&SYSNSUB, &EVAL, &NRSTR, &STR: Use results from these functions as arguments for &LENGTH, &STR, &NRSTR, and &SYSNSUB also control the symbolic substitution of an argument.

&SUBSTR: Marks the range of a substring.

SUBSTR

First Available: TSO

Function: Extracts part of a selected string argument with a specified range.

Syntax: *&SUBSTR(s:[e],str)*

s = Starting position of an extract.

e = Ending position of an extract. *This is optional.*

str = String to extract from.

Example:

```
SET &FISH = &STR(TUNA FISH)
SET &TODAYS_FISH = &SUBSTR(1:4,&FISH)
WRITE Todays Fish is . . . &TODAYS_FISH
```

displayed:

```
Todays Fish is . . . TUNA
```

Argument: Any mix of numeric, alphanumeric, national (@,$,#), special (i.e. hexadecimal 25 for line feed), double-byte characters, or clist operators.

Returned Values: The specified substring

Special Nonzero Return Codes:

912—Invalid range of &SUBSTR

Solution: Use a valid range to extract the desired substring.

916—Invalid start or end position value

Solution: Use a numeric, not character, start or end position value.

920—Zero or negative start position value.

Solution: Use positive numbers for position values.

924—Invalid substring syntax

Solution: Check if a colon is missing.

932 - &SUBSTR outside of range or string argument.
Solution: Check the start and the end position values—are they too large?

Common Error Messages:

IKJ56545I—A MISSING BUILT-IN FUNCTION OPERAND.
Solution: Add a parenthesis or remove the space between the parenthesis and the function name.

IKJ56545I—AN INVALID &SUBSTR RANGE OR EXIT CODE EXPRESSION
Solution: Check if the start and the end position values are too large or are character values.

Commonly Used with: &STR for concatenations, &LENGTH for length of substring with blanks, &SYSLC or &SYSCAPS changes the case of a substring, and &NRSTR or &SYSNSUB controls the symbolic substitution of a substring.

&SYSINDEX

First Available: TSO/E Version 1 Release 3

Function: Finds a specified character or characters in a substring and returns its position in a string.

Syntax: &SYSINDEX(ts,ss,[s])
ts = Target string (what to search for)
ss = Search string (where to search for it)
s = starting position in search string (*optional*)

Example:

```
SET &STRNG = &STR(X SEE THE X NOW)
SET &FINDX = &SYSINDEX(X,&STRNG,2)
WRITE X Found in position &FINDEX
```

displayed:

```
X Found in position 11
```

The above example looks for a X starting in position 2 of the &FINDX string (bypassing the first X in position 1). If the starting position is 12, then &FINDX is 0 (target string not found).

Argument: Any mix of numeric, alphanumeric, national (@,$,#), special (i.e., hexadecimal 25 for line feed), double-byte characters, or clist operators. *Starting position* must be a positive number.

Returned Value:
0 — Target string not found in the search string.
>0 — Usually the starting position of the target string in the specified string.
708 — Invalid &SYSINDEX argument.

Solution: Check &SYSINDEX argument—is the target/search string invalid?

712—Invalid &SYSINDEX starting position. Must be a positive number (not zero).

Solution: Change starting position to a positive number.

Special Nonzero Return Codes:

IKJ56545I—A MISSING BUILT-IN FUNCTION OPERAND.

Solution: Add a parenthesis or remove the space between the parenthesis and the function name.

IKJ79002I—THIS STATEMENT HAS AN INVALID &SYSINDEX START PARAMETER. START PARAMETER MUST BE A NONNEGATIVE WHOLE NUMBER.

Solution: Change starting position to a positive number.

IKJ79003I— THIS STATEMENT HAS AN INVALID &SYSINDEX EXPRESSION.

Solution: Check &SYSINDEX argument. Is the search/target string invalid?

Tips, Tricks, and Traps

1. The following are tips on using &EVAL, &LENGTH, &SUBSTR, and &SYSINDEX:
   a. &EVAL shows mathematical operations in a WRITE. All other clist statements do not need &EVAL to do this.
   b. &LENGTH with &STR gives the length of a string with blanks and leading zeros.
   ```
   WRITE &LENGTH(&STR( N Y))
   ```
   displayed:
   ```
   4 /* NY with two spaces. */
   ```
   c. Use results from other built-in functions as arguments for &LENGTH (i.e., &SYSNSUB, &EVAL, &NRSTR)
   ```
   WRITE &LENGTH(&EVAL(2+2))
   ```
   displayed:
   ```
   1 /*Since 4 has a length of 1.*/
   ```
   d. Use the result of &LENGTH in mathematical operations.
   ```
   SET &STATE_LEN = 2 + &LENGTH(&STR)( N Y))
   WRITE STATE_LEN is &STATE_LEN
   ```
   displayed:
   ```
   STATE_LEN is 6 /* 2 + 4   value of &LENGTH(&STATE) */
   ```
   e. &LENGTH can mark the start or end of a substring or use &SYSINDEX.
   ```
   SET &STATE = &STR(NEW MEXICO)
   ```

```
SET &STATE_ABB = &SUBSTR(1:&LENGTH(&STATE) +
5,&STATE)
WRITE STATE_ABB is &STATE_ABB
```
displayed:

*STATE_ABB is NEW M /*Characters 1-5 of NEW MEXICO*/*

f. The end position operand is optional if extracting only the first character.

```
SET &STRNG = &STR(ONE CHARACTER)
SET &FIRST = &STR(1,&STRNG) or SET &FIRST =
WRITE &FIRST
&STR(1:1,&STRNG)
```
displayed:

O /* First character of ONE CHARACTER string.*/

g. Use &SUBSTR with other built-in functions:

(i) &STR for concatenations.

```
SET &STRNG1 = &STR(RIGHT)
SET &STRNG2 = &STR(AWAY IS MY LOVE)
SET &STRNG3 = &STR(&STRNG1 &SUBSTR(1:4,&STRNG2))
WRITE &STRNG3
```
displayed:

RIGHT AWAY

(ii) &LENGTH for length of substring with blanks.

```
SET &STRNG1 = &STR(A STRING WITH BLANKS)
SET &STRNG2 = &LENGTH(&SUBSTR(1:9,&STRNG1))
WRITE Length of STRNG2 . . . &STRNG2
```
displayed:

Length of STRNG2 . . . 9 / Extracted -- A +*
*/*STRING.*/*

(iii) &SYSLC or &SYSCAPS controls case of substrings.

```
  CONTROL ASIS
  SET &S = &STR(hi)
WRITE &SYSCAPS(&SUBSTR(1,&S))&SYSLC
  (&SUBSTR(2,&S))
```
displayed:

Hi / Extract ''h'' and set to uppercase, and* extract ''i'' and set to lowercase. */

(iv) &NRSTR or &SYSNSUB controls the number of symbolic substitution scans of a substring.

```
SET &STRNG1 = &SUBSTR(1:2,&SYSNSUB(0,&&X))
WRITE &STRNG1
```
displayed:

&& / No symbolic substitution occurs.*/*

(v) Specify the position or search string using clist variable values or results from other functions. &STR is used for specifying the search string position.

```
SET &S = &STR(A STRING WITH BLANKS AND  )
SET &T = &STR(&SUBSTR(&LENGTH(&STR(&S)) +
11:&LENGTH(&S)-,&S))
WRITE &T
```

displayed

```
BLANKS AND /* Extract positions 14 through 25.*/
```

h. Some useful guidelines for &SYSINDEX:

(i) Blanks may be in the search and target strings. If putting a blank in the search string, it counts in finding the starting position of the target string. Use &STR, &NRSTR, or &SYSNSUB when the search or target string contains blanks, commas, ampersands, or other special characters.

```
SET &STRNG_ONE = &STR(A STRING WITH A ,COMMA)
SET &TARG_STRNG = &SYSINDEX(&NRSTR(,),&STRNG +
  _ONE,1)
WRITE &TARG_STRG
```

displayed:

```
17 /* Includes four blanks.*/
```

(ii) Like &LENGTH, you may use results from other built-in functions for a start or end position value. The following example looks for "TEST" starting in position 12 (or 1 multiplied by 12.)

```
SET &STRG_ONE=&STR(THIS IS A TEST . . ONLY A-
  TEST)
SET &SP = 1
SET &TARG_STRG = &STR(TEST,&STRG_ONE,&SP*12)
WRITE &TARG_STRG
```

displayed:

```
25 /* Start of Second TEST string.*/
```

(iii) Use &SYSINDEX in DO loops and IF statements with character searches such as looking for selected records with the clist QSAM facility. In some cases, you may not need a DO loop.

Old Way—IF

```
SET &STRNG = &STR(1988----)
IF &SUBSTR(5,&STRNG) = &STR(-) THEN DO
```

New Way—IF

```
SET &STRNG = &STR(1988----)
IF &SYSINDEX(&STR(-),&STRNG,5) NE 0 THEN DO
```

Old Way—DO

```
SET &CNT = 1
SET &TXT = &STR(&&TXT)
DO WHILE &STR(&TEMP) NE &STR(#)
   SET &TEMP =
   WRITENR NAME OF VARIABLE ? (# TO END)
    READ &TEMP
     SET &TXT&CNT = &TEMP /*&TXT1 =. .
     &TXT99=. .*/
     SET &CNT = &CNT + 1
END
```

New Way - DO

```
SET &CNT = 1
SET &TXT = &STR(&&TXT)
DO WHILE &SYSINDEX(&STR(#),&TEMP) EQ 0
  SET &TEMP =
   WRITENR NAME OF VARIABLE ? (# TO END)
     READ &TEMP
   SET &TXT&CNT = &TEMP /*& TXT1 =. .+
   &TXT99=. .*/
  SET &CNT = &CNT + 1
END
```

2. Avoid these common traps for &EVAL, &LENGTH, &SUBSTR, and &SYSINDEX:
   a. Using fractions or decimals in an argument for &EVAL. These are seen as character values! Also, all numeric values must be in the range of -2^{31} to 2^{31}.
   b. For &SYSINDEX, having a target string in uppercase and a search string in lowercase, or the reverse. The result is 0—string not found because &SYSINDEX is case-sensitive. If in doubt, &SYSCAPS converts both the search and target string to uppercase.

String Parsing

String parsing is the decomposing of a character string into several parts which are assigned to symbolic variables. No one built-in function performs this task; instead, use the following method.

STEP 1 If many clists use a parsing sequence, consider writing a program in another language and passing the result to a clist or use the REXX language available for TSO/E Version 2. For further information, read *TSO/E Extensions Programming Services*.

STEP 2 If writing a parsing sequence with clists, then use *at least* TSO/E Version 1 Release 3. This release has the &SYSINDEX built-in function, which allows a faster and more efficient parsing sequence.

STEP 3 (*For clist parsing sequence only*.) Examine the character strings to parse. Is there a character marking where each string part begins or ends? (i.e., quotation mark, period, comma, blank) If these characters always occur in the same place, then one or more &SUBSTR statements may be enough. However, if these characters do not have a fixed position, do the remaining steps (e.g., periods in dataset names).

STEP 4 Write the first pass of the parsing routine testing for a "simple to moderate" case.

a. For sites before the TSO/E Version 1 Release 3, use a DO-WHILE loop, reading each character of the string to parse. If finding a parse delimiter, then assign the location to a variable. Otherwise, continue reading the string until the end of the string occurs.

b. For sites with TSO/E Version 1 Release 3 and later, &SYSINDEX finds the location of a parse delimiter. When found, then execute a IF-THEN-DO-END sequence or assign the delimiter location to a variable.

Note: Creating a table like Table 6-2 makes it easier to parse a variable. In the table, &DLM1 is the location of first delimiter, &DLM2 is the location of the second delimiter, and &TEXT is the string to parse.

Table 6-2. String Parsing Variables

Variable	Start	End
		Two-Variable Parse
1	Position 1	Up to the first delimiter (e.g., &DLM1-1)
2	Past the first delimiter (e.g., &DLM1+1)	End of string (e.g., &LENGTH(&STR(&TEXT))
		Three-Variable Parse
1	Position 1	Up to the first delimiter (e.g., &DLM1-1)
2	Past the first delimiter (e.g., &DLM1+1)	Up to the second delimiter (e.g., &DLM2-1)
3	Past the second delimiter (e.g., &DLM2+1)	End of string (e.g., &LENGTH(&STR(&TEXT)))

STEP 5 Once the parse sequence works, test with "worst cases" and make any needed changes.

To make these points clearer, let's build a simple parse routine. The routine parses a character value into first, middle (if available), and last name. We make the following assumption:

1. &NAME has a name as a value.
2. This value has two formats:
   FIRST NAME LASTNAME
   FIRSTNAME MIDDLENAME LASTNAME

All Releases. (Lines 7 to 10 are based on a sequence developed by Tom Buonomo of SCA Corporation.)

```
 1. SET &NAME = (JOHN EDWARD SMITH)
 2. SET &NLEN = &LENGTH(&STR(&NAME))
 3. SET &NCNT = 1
 4. SET &CNT = 1
 5. SET &BLANK = &STR(&&BLANK)
 6. DO WHILE &CNT LE &NLEN
 7.    IF &SUBSTR(&CNT,&NAME) EQ THEN DO
 8.       SET &BLANK&NCNT = &CNT
 9.       SET &NCNT = &NCNT + 1
10.    END
11.    SET &CNT = &CNT + 1
12. END
13. SET &FNAME = &SUBSTR(1:&BLANK1-1,&NAME)
14. IF &BLANK2 EQ THEN DO
15.   SET &LNAME = &SUBSTR(&BLANK1+1:&NLEN,&NAME)
16.   WRITE &FNAME &LNAME
17. END
18. ELSE DO
19.    SET &MNAME = &SUBSTR(&BLANK1+1:&BLANK2-1,&NAME)
20.    SET &LNAME = &SUBSTR(&BLANK2+1:&NLEN,&NAME)
21.    WRITE &FNAME &MNAME &LNAME
22. END
```

Explanation. Following is an explanation of the preceding routine by statement number.

1. You could also use a READ statement for getting a name.
2. Assigns to &NLEN the length of &NAME. &STR correctly processes blanks and other special characters. By creating &NLEN, the &SUBSTR statements are easier to type and understand.

3–4. Sets the counter variables &CNT and &NCNT. &CNT decides the current position of the NAME value. &NCNT helps create array variables &BLANK1 and &BLANK2.

5. Creates the array variable "root" &BLANK, which results in &BLANK1 and &BLANK2.

6. The DO loop continues checking if each character of &NAME is a blank until reaching the end of the &NAME value.

7–10. The nested DO loop does the following:
   a. Checks if each character of &NAME is blank.
   b. If the character is blank:
      (i) Assign the value of &CNT to &BLANK1 or &BLANK2.
      (ii) Increment the &NCNT counter value by 1—so the next array variable is &BLANK2.
      (iii) End the nested loop.

11–12. Whatever character &NAME is, increment the &CNT counter value by 1.

13. Parse &NAME and assign the value up to the first blank (i.e., &BLANK1-1) to &FNAME. This is the person's first name.

14–17. If no second blank, then assign everything past the first blank (i.e., &BLANK1+1) to the end of &NAME to &LNAME. This is the person's last name. Write the complete name to the screen.

18–22. Otherwise, assign everything past the first blank (i.e., &BLANK1+1) until the second blank (i.e., &BLANK2−1) to &MNAME. This is the person's middle name. To get just the middle initial, substitute for statement 19.

```
SET &MNAME = &SUBSTR(&BLANK1+1,&NAME)
```

Assign all characters from the second blank (i.e., &BLANK2+1) to the end of the &NAME value to &LNAME. This is the person's last name. The complete name writes to the screen.

TSO/E Version 1 Release 3 and Later

```
1. SET &NAME = (JOHN EDWARD SMITH)
2. SET &BLANK1 = &SYSINDEX(&STR( ),&NAME)
3. SET &FNAME = &SUBSTR(1:&BLANK1-1,&NAME)
4. SET &BLANK2 = &SYSINDEX(&STR( ),&NAME,&BLANK1+1)
5. SET &NLEN = &LENGTH(&STR(&NAME))
6. IF &BLANK2 EQ 0 THEN DO
7.   SET &LNAME = &SUBSTR(&BLANK1+1:&NLEN,&NAME)
```

```
 8.    WRITE &FNAME &LNAME
 9.  END
10.  ELSE DO
11.      SET &MNAME = &SUBSTR(&BLANK1+1:&BLANK2-1,&NAME)
12.      SET &LNAME = &SUBSTR(&BLANK2+1:&NLEN,&NAME)
13.      WRITE &FNAME &MNAME &LNAME
14.  END
```

Explanation. Following is an explanation of the above routine by statement number.

1. You could also use a READ statement for getting the name.
2. Finds the first blank character in &NAME and assigns the position to &BLANK1. Notice there is no DO loop to get this!
3. Parse &NAME and assign the value up to the first blank (i.e., &BLANK1−1) to &FNAME. This is the person's first name.
4. &SYSINDEX searches for a second blank character from one character after the first blank (i.e., &BLANK1+1) to the end of &NAME. If found, then assign it to &BLANK2.
5. Creates proxy variable &NLEN with a value of the length of the &NAME, &STR correctly processes blanks and other special characters. By creating &NLEN, the &SUBSTR statements are easier to type and understand.

6–9. If there is no second blank, then assign everything past the first blank (i.e., &BLANK1+1) to the end of the &NAME to &LNAME. This is the person's last name. The complete name writes to the screen.

10–14. Assign everything past the first blank (i.e., &BLANK1+1) up to the second blank (i.e., &BLANK2−1) to &MNAME. This is the person's middle name. To get just the middle initial, substitute for statement 11.

```
SET &MNAME = &SUBSTR(&BLANK1+1,&NAME)
```

Assign all characters from the second blank (i.e., &BLANK2+1) to the end of &NAME to &LNAME. This is the person's last name. The complete name writes to the screen. The execution of the second method was slightly faster. As a rough benchmark, it takes 2 actual seconds to parse a 1000-character string with two blanks. The "Other Operations" section of this chapter presents a more complicated sequence to parse datasets.

Case Operations (&SYSCAPS,&SYSLC)

Please review the section on "Clists and the Case of Text" in Chapter 5 before reading this. The emphasis here is on mixed-case operations with &SYSCAPS and &SYSLC.

&SYSCAPS

First Available: TSO/E Version 1 Release 2

Function: Converts an argument to uppercase. (If CONTROL CAPS or &SYSASIS-OFF is active.)

Syntax: &SYSCAPS (argument)

Example:
```
CONTROL CAPS
SET &NAME=&STR(tom)
WRITE name in uppercase . . . &SYSCAPS(&NAME)
```
displayed:

name in uppercase . . . TOM

Argument: Any mix of numeric, alphanumeric, national (@,$,#), special (i.e., hex 25 for line feed), double-byte characters, or clist operators.

Returned Value: Argument in uppercase. &SYSCAPS does not change: (1) numbers, (2) national characters (@,$,#), (3) special characters, and (4) double-byte characters (TSO/E Version 1 Release 4 and later).

Special Nonzero Return Codes: None

Common Error Message:
IKJ56545I—A MISSING BUILT-IN FUNCTION OPERAND.
Solution: Add a parenthesis or remove the space between the parenthesis and the function name.

Commonly Used with: &STR, &NRSTR, &SUBSTR, &SYSINDEX, &SYSNSUB controls the case of a string or substring.

&SYSLC

First Available: TSO/E Version 1 Release 2

Function: Converts an argument to lower case. (If CONTROL ASIS or CONTROL NOCAPS or &SYSASIS-ON is active.)

Syntax: &SYSLC (argument)

Example:
```
CONTROL ASIS
SET &NAME=&STR(TOM)
WRITE name in lowercase . . . &SYSLC(&NAME)
```
displayed:

name in lowercase . . . tom

Argument: Any mix of numeric, alphanumeric, national (@,$,#), special (i.e., hex 25 for line feed), double-byte character, or clist operators.

Returned Value: Argument in lower case. &SYSLC does not change:

(1) numbers, (2) national characters (@,$,#), (3) special characters, and (4) double-byte characters (TSO/E Version 1 Release 4 and later).

Special NonZero Return Codes: None

Common Error Message:

IKJ56545I—A MISSING BUILT-IN FUNCTION OPERAND.

Solution: Add a parenthesis or remove the space between the parenthesis and the function name.

Commonly Used with: &STR, &NRSTR, &SUBSTR, &SYSINDEX, &SYSNSUB controls the case of a string or substring.

Tips, Tricks, and Traps

1. The following are some tips for using &SYSLC and &SYSCAPS. See Chapter 5 for more uses on &SYSLC and &SYSCAPS.
   a. When using both &SYSLC or &SYSCAPS with another function, *always* have them enclose the other function. Otherwise, you may not get the desired result. The following example has &SYSLC correctly enclosing &SUBSTR.

```
CONTROL ASIS
WRITE &SYSLC(&SUBSTR(1:2,MESS))
```

   displayed:

```
me
```

2. Avoid these common traps when using &SYSLC and &SYSCAPS.
   a. &SYSASIS = OFF or CONTROL CAPS with &SYSLC.
   b. &SYSASIS = ON or CONTROL NOCAPS or CONTROL ASIS with &SYSCAPS
   c. &SYSCAPS or &SYSLC with double-byte characters. Before TSO/E Version 1 Release 4, they changed their case.
   d. Some versions of TSO/E have invalid results if using &SYSLC with &SUBSTR or &SYSCAPS with &NRSTR.

Parsing and Changing Case of a String

An extremely powerful sequence is changing the case of a substring. The following is a revised version of the parse sequence that does this:

TSO/E Version 1 Release 3 or Higher Clist Parsing and Case Operation Sequence. This is an alternative to an example from the *TSO/E Extensions Clist* guide and is for TSO/E Version 1 Release 3 or Higher. We make the following assumptions:

1. &NAME has a name as a value.
2. This value takes on one of two formats:

FIRSTNAME LASTNAME
FIRSTNAME MIDDLENAME LASTNAME
The result is

```
Dee Taylor or Dee R. Taylor
```

Capitalize only the first letters of the parsed first, middle, and last name. Convert the rest to lowercase. If including a middle name, then extract only the first letter and place a period after it. Statements in boldface type are discussed in the explanation that follows this routine.

```
 1. CONTROL ASIS
 2. SET &NAME = &STR(DEE ROSE TAYLOR)
 3. SET &BLANK1 = &SYSINDEX(&STR( ), &NAME)
 4. SET &FNAME = &SYSCAPS(&SUBSTR(1,&NAME))+
 5.               &SYSLC(&SUBSTR(2:&BLANK1-1,&NAME))
 6. SET &BLANK2 = &SYSINDEX(&STR( ), &NAME, &BLANK1+1)
 7. SET &NLEN   = &LENGTH(&STR(&NAME))
 8. IF &BLANK2 EQ 0 THEN DO
 9.   SET &LNAME = &SYSCAPS(&SUBSTR(&BLANK1+1,&NAME))+
10.                &SYSLC(&SUBSTR(&BLANK1+2:&NLEN,&NAME))
11.   WRITE &FNAME &LNAME
12. END
13. ELSE DO
14.     SET &MINIT = &SUBSTR(&BLANK1+1,&NAME)&STR(.)
15.     SET &LNAME = &SYSCAPS(&SUBSTR(&BLANK2+1,&NAME))+
16.                  &SYSLC(&SUBSTR(&BLANK2+2:&NLEN,&NAME))
17.     WRITE &FNAME &MINIT &LNAME
18. END
```

Explanation. An explanation, by statement, of the boldface lines in the preceding routine follows:

4–5. Concatenate the following strings and assign the result to &FNAME. This is a person's first name.
  a. Capitalize the first character of &NAME (the uparsed name).
  b. Set in lowercase all the remaining characters before the first blank—i.e., &BLANK–1.
  Note: The continuation character on statements 4, 9, and 15 is a plus sign, thus ignoring leading blanks on lines 5, 10, and 16.

9–10. If no middle name, then concatenate the following strings and assign the result to &LNAME. This is a person's last name.

a. Capitalize the first character past the first blank in &NAME—i.e., &BLANK1+1.
b. Set in lowercase all of the remaining characters in &NAME—i.e., &LENGTH(&STR(&NAME))

11. Write out the complete name (i.e., first and last name) capitalizing the first letter of each part of the name.

14. Otherwise if there is a middle name (2 blanks), extract and capitalize the first character past the first blank—&BLANK1+1. Concatenate a period at the end of the character and then assign the result to &MINIT. This is the person's middle initial.

15–16. Concatenate the following strings and assign the result to &LNAME. This is a person's last name.
a. Capitalize the first character past the second blank—& BLANK2+1.
b. Set in lowercase all of the remaining characters in &NAME—i.e., &LENGTH(&STR(&NAME)).

17. Write out the complete name (i.e., first, middle, and last name) capitalizing the first letter of each part of the name.

Double-Byte Characters (&SYSCLENGTH, &SYSCSUBSTR, &SYSONEBYTE, &SYSTWOBYTE)

Until quite recently, clists and ISPF did not recognize or process mixed and double-byte character strings. TSO/E Version 1 Release 4 and ISPF Version 2 fully resolves that problem. (*Double-byte characters process only under MVS/XA.*) This section discusses:

1. What double-byte characters are and why are they used.
2. How each built-in function processes double-byte characters.
3. Common error messages when using double-byte characters.
4. Four built-in functions available in TSO/E Version 1 Release 4 for processing double-byte characters.

A single-byte character string has up to 256 different characters. This is adequate for most national languages except Japanese (Kanji), Korean, and Chinese. For processing these languages, the *double-byte,* or *two-byte,* character set (or DBCS) was devised (i.e., character strings taking up two bytes of data). Double-byte characters are or soon will be available in all IBM operating systems (including OS/2). Taking full advantage of double-byte characters requires a special terminal.

Figure 6-2. A Double-Byte Character String

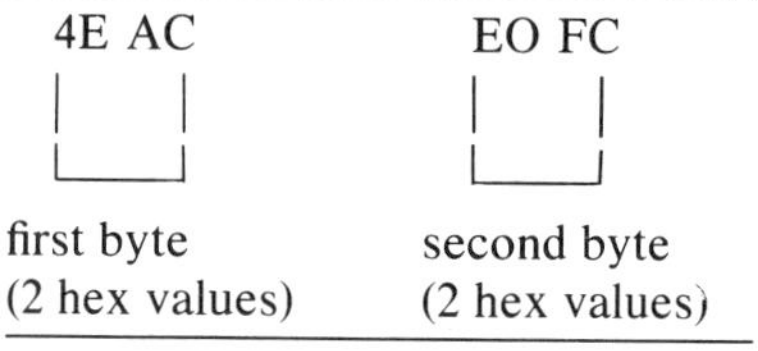

Four hexadecimal values from 41 to FE or 4040 (blank) compose a double-byte character. Hexadecimal value 4195 replaces any invalid characters found. Figure 6-2 shows an example of double-byte character string. Placing an X before a string and enclosing it in single quotes is the format TSO/E and ISPF uses for recognizing a hexadecimal string. The previous double-byte character string is shown with this notation:

```
X'4E' X'AC' X'EO' X'FC'
```

Since this is hard to follow, double-byte characters are represented as shown

```
db1 db2
```

Where *db1, db2,* are two different double-byte characters (each representing four hexadecimal values). *Hexadecimal values X'OE'* (or SHIFT-OUT) and *X'OF* (or SHIFT-IN) *always* enclose double-byte characters. *SHIFT-OUT* marks a change from EBCDIC (i.e., "normal" characters) to double-byte characters, and *SHIFT-IN* marks a change from double-byte characters to EBCDIC. < and > will represent the shift characters. One, two or four double-byte characters usually make up a double-byte character string. So, the following represents a typical double-byte character string displayed in this section.

```
<db1 db2 db3 db4
↓                   ↓
 SHIFT-OUT           SHIFT-IN
 X'OE'               X'OF'
```

Note: A blank space is placed between all examples of double-byte characters for clarity but must not be included when calculating the length or extracting a substring of a double-byte character string.

Even with the four new built-in functions of TSO/E Version 1 Release 4, there still are limitations for using double-byte character strings:

1. Only use double-byte character strings as symbolic variable *values* or in *comment* statements. They are not valid for symbolic variables, clist variables, quoted datasets, and quoted passwords for datasets or TSO/E userids.
2. Double-byte character strings *are not numeric* and cannot be used by &EVAL or clist statements performing mathematical operations.
3. In addition to using special terminals to create and process double-byte character strings, a certain level of VTAM (MVS/XA only) must be installed at your site. If interested, have your computer center staff check into this. (VTAM stands for Virtual Telecommunications Access Method, a system controlling the data flow between your terminal and the application software you are using.)
4. &SYSCAPS and &SYSLC do not change the case of double-byte character strings. (For TSO/E Version 1 Release 4 Modification 2, &NRSTR translates double-byte character strings to lowercase unless applying PTF UY13022.)
5. Place double-byte character strings on multiple lines only if enclosed in shift characters. The clist regards the entire string as a double-byte character string and removes the second pair of shift characters!

```
SET &TWOLINES = <db1 db2> +
  <db3 db4>
```

Clist processes &TWOLINES as: <db1 db2 db3 db4> *—one complete double-byte character!*

Note: Although TSO/E Version 1 Release 3 can process double-byte character strings, there are *many* problems doing this. Only TSO/E Version 1 Release 4 and later will correctly process double-byte character strings.

Using Double-Byte Character Strings with Other Functions

How each built-in function (except &SYSCLENGTH, &SYSCSUBSTR, &SYSONEBYTE, and &SYSTWOBYTE) uses double-byte character strings is shown.

&DATATYPE

Reads double-byte characters: Yes

Reads mixed (EBCDIC and double-byte) character strings: Yes

Output from double-byte characters: Returns DBCS if a double-byte character string has the format <db1 . . dbx> or <> and *MIXED* for other formats with double-byte characters. DB1 and dbx are any valid double-byte characters.

Additional guidelines: Using *more than one* set of shift characters returns MIXED.

Example

```
SET &ONE_SET = &DATATYPE(<db1 db2 db3 db4>)
```

Result: DBCS—*Correctly sees as a double-byte character string.*

```
SET &TWO_SET = &DATATYPE(<db1 db2><db3 db4>)
```

Result: MIXED—*Although there are two complete double-byte character strings!*

&EVAL

Reads double-byte characters: No—not numeric.
Reads mixed (EBCDIC and double-byte) character strings: No
Output from double-byte characters: None
Additional guidelines: *Cannot use &EVAL* and double-byte character strings together.

&LENGTH

Reads double-byte characters: Yes
Reads mixed (EBCDIC and double-byte) character strings: Yes
Output from double-byte character (i.e., db1) as *two* characters and each shift character as *one* character. This also is valid for mixed character strings.

Example

```
SET &DBCS_STRG = &LENGTH(<db1 db2 db3 db4>)
```

Result: 10—*(4 double-byte characters × 2 each) + 2 shift characters*

```
SET &MIXED_STRG = &LENGTH(<db1 db2 db3 db4>GOOD)
```

Additional guidelines: When calculating a double-byte character string's length, if you want each double-byte character (i.e., db1) to count as *one* character and *not to include* the shift characters, then use &SYSCLENGTH. &SYSCLENGTH is *character-based,* not *byte-based.*

&NRSTR

Reads double-byte characters: Yes
Reads mixed (EBCDIC and double-byte) character strings: Yes

Output from double-byte characters: Retains the current value of a double-byte character string and performs no symbolic substitution. Remember &NRSTR defines a nonrescannable character string.

Example

```
SET &STRNG = &NRSTR(<db1 db2>)
```

Result: <db1 db2>—*unchanged.*

Additional guidelines: For TSO/E Version 1 Release 4 Modification 2, &NRSTR converts double-byte character strings to lowercase unless applying PTF UY13022.

&STR

Reads double-byte characters: Yes
Reads mixed (EBCDIC and double-byte) character strings: Yes
Output from double-byte characters:
Like &NRSTR, prevents the clist from further evaluating a double-byte character string, keeping its current value.

Example

```
SET &STRNG = &STR(<db1 db2>)
```

Result: <db1 db2>—*unchanged.*
Additional guidelines: You must use shift characters for identifying the start and end of a double-byte character string.

&SUBSTR

Reads double-byte characters: Yes
Reads mixed (EBCDIC and double-byte) character strings: Yes
Output from double-byte characters: Counts each double-byte character (i.e., db1) as *two* characters and each shift character as *one* character. Usually the result is shift characters enclosing the desired substring of double-byte characters. However, because &SUBSTR may truncate or adjust a double-byte character, generally use &SYSCSUBSTR instead.

Adjustment Rules

1. If a substring *starts* or *ends* on a *shift* character, replace the character with a 1-byte blank.

&BLANK = &SUBSTR(6, <db1 db2>)
Result: *A 1-byte blank for a shift-in character.*

2. If a substring *starts* on the *second* byte or *ends* on the *first* byte of a DBCS character string, then replace the byte with a *shift-in* (for ending first byte) or *shift-out* (for starting second byte) character.
   &SHIFT = &SUBSTR(4, <db1 db2>)
   Result <—*Shift-out character for starting second byte.*
3. If a substring *starts* on the *first* byte or *ends* on the *second* byte of a double-byte character string, then replace the byte with a *1-byte* blank.
4. In addition, if the substring *starts* on the *first byte,* then replace the next byte to the right with a *shift-out* character. Or the substring *ends* on the *second byte,* then replace the next byte to the left with a *shift-in* character.
   SET &BLK_SHIFT = &SUBSTR(2, <db1 db2>)
   Result: b<—*a 1-byte blank and shift-out character.*
4. If a substring has an *invalid double-byte character* or *two adjacent shift characters,* then replace the character with a *1-byte* blank.
5. &SUBSTR keeps intact adjacent sets of shift characters.

Additional guidelines: If you want each double-byte character (i.e., db1) to count as *one* character and *not include* shift characters, then use &SYSCSUBSTR instead. &SYSCSUBSTR is CHARACTER-BASED not BYTE-BASED.

&SYSCAPS

Reads double-byte characters: Yes
Reads mixed (EBCDIC and double-byte) character strings: Yes
Output from double-byte characters: Retains the current case of a double-byte character string.

Example

SET &UNCHANGE = &SYSCAPS(<db1 db2 db3 db4>)
Result: <db1 db2 db3 db4>—*case unchanged.*
Additional guidelines: None

&SYSDSN

Reads double-byte characters: No, invalid for dataset name
Reads mixed (EBCDIC and double-byte) character strings: No
Output from double-byte characters: None
Additional guidelines: Cannot use &SYSDSN and double-byte character strings together

The next section has more information about &SYSDSN.

&SYSINDEX

Reads double-byte characters: Yes
Reads mixed (EBCDIC and double-byte) character strings: Yes
Output from double-byte characters:

1. The starting location of the EBCDIC, double-byte or mixed target string in the search string.
2. In finding the location, *shift characters do not count* and double-byte characters (i.e., db1) count as *one* character.

Example

SET &D = &SYSINDEX(<db1>,<db1 db2>)
Result: 1—*Shift character is ignored.*
Additional guidelines:

1. Search and target strings may be EBCDIC, double-byte, or mixed characters.
2. You must enclose a double-byte search or target string in shift characters.
3. An EBCDIC search string cannot find a double-byte target string with the same hexadecimal value.

Example

SET &STRNG = &SYSINDEX(FE,<db1 db3 db3 db4>)
Result: 0—*Target string not found even if db2 has a hex value of FE!*

4. If using two or more pairs of shift characters in a target string, then the matching string *must* include the shift characters.

Example

SET &COMPLEX = &SYSINDEX(<db1><db2>,<db1><db2><d3>)
Result: 1—*position of string <db1><db2>*
0—*if search string is <db1 db2>, then it is not found in the target string.*

5. If using a pair of shift characters with no hex values in the target string, then the result is position of the first character after the shift characters (and shift characters count as one character).

SET &PAIR = YSYSINDEX(<>,<db1 db2><><db3 db4>)
Result: 4—*the position of db3 (db1 and db2 = 2 characters, <> = 1 character)*

6. There is currently no built-in function counting double-byte characters as *two* characters or *includes shift characters* in the target string.

&SYSLC

Reads double-byte characters: Yes
Reads mixed (EBCDIC and double-byte) character strings: Yes
Output from double-byte characters: Retains the current case of a double-byte character string

Example

Set &UNCHANGE = &SYSLC(<db1 db2 db3 db4>)
Result: <db1 db2 db3 db4>—*case unchanged.*
Additional guidelines: None

&SYSNSUB

Reads double-byte characters: Unknown
Reads mixed (EBCDIC and double-byte) character strings: Unknown
Output from double-byte characters: Unknown
Additional guidelines: Unknown

Common Error Messages for Double-Byte Characters

Some of the common error messages and return codes encountered when using double-byte characters strings are listed below:

1. No message
   Example: SET &STRNG = &STR(<&DBL_1 &DBL_2)
   If &DBL_1 and &DBL_2 are double-byte character values, then the clist may perform incorrect symbolic substitution.
   Solution: This problem is fixed in later releases.
2. Return Code 588—Invalid hex value. Value outside valid range for double-byte characters (X'41' - X'FE and X'4040).
   or
   IKJ56725I OUT-OF-RANGE DBCS CHARACTER IN INPUT WAS REPLACED.
   or
   IKJ79039I OTHER THAN DBCS CHARACTERS FOUND IN A DBCS STRING.
   or
   IKJ79043I STMT XX OTHER THAN DBCS CHARACTERS—

FOUND IN A DBCS STRING. (xx = statement number)
Solution: Use a hexadecimal value in the valid range.

3. Return Code 592—Incomplete double-byte character string.
   or
   IKJ56724I ODD (LAST) BYTE DROPPED FROM DOUBLE-BYTE-CHARACTER STRING
   or
   IKJ79040I ODD NUMBER OF BYTES FOUND IN A DBCS STRING.
   or
   IKJ79044I STMT XX ODD NUMBER OF BYTES FOUND IN A-DBCS STRING. (xx = statement number)
   Solution: Add missing hexadecimal value(s) to make up an even number of bytes.
4. Return Code 596—Missing shift-in character
   or
   IKJ56723I FALSE SHIFT-OUT CHARACTER IN INPUT WAS IGNORED
   or
   IKJ7904I UNABLE TO FIND THE END OF A DBCS STRING.
   Solution: If a double-byte character string, add shift-in character; otherwise remove shift-out character.
5. Return Code 600—Missing shift-in character between two adjacent shift-out characters.
   or
   IKJ79042I SECOND SHIFT-OUT FOUND BEFORE FINDING A SHIFT-IN
   Solution: Adding missing shift-out character at correct location.

The following summarizes the syntax, valid arguments, and error messages of &SYSCLENGTH, &SYSCSUBSTR, &SYSONEBYTE, and &SYSTWOBYTE:

&SYSCLENGTH

First Available: TSO/E Release 4

Function: Returns number of characters in double-byte or mixed character argument.

Syntax: &SYSCLENGTH(argument)

Example: SET &LEN = &SYSCLENGTH(<db1 db2>)
displayed:
2—*db1 and db2 are one character each.*

Argument: Any valid mix of double-byte or EBCDIC (alphanumeric, numeric, and national) character strings and clist operators.

Returned Value: The result is similar to &LENGTH but is *character-based,* not *byte-based.* This means shift characters *do not* count and each double-byte characters (i.e., db1) has a length of one character—both for double-byte and mixed character strings.

Special Nonzero Return Codes: None

Common Error Messages: See previous section.

Commonly Used with: None

&SYSCSUBSTR

First Available: TSO/E Version 1 Release 4

Function: Extracts a substring from a double-byte character string.

Syntax: *&SYSCSUBSTR(s:[e],str)*

s—starting position of an extract.
e—ending position of an extract. *This is optional.*
str—string to extract from.

Example: SET &PART = &SYSCSUBSTR(3:4,<db1 db2 db3 db4>)
Result: <db3 db4>—third and fourth characters.

Argument: Any valid mix of double-byte or EBCDIC (alphanumeric, numeric, and national) character strings, and clist operators.

Returned Value: The result is similar to &SUBSTR but is *character-based,* not *byte-based.* This means shift characters do *not* count and each double-byte character (i.e., db1) has a length of one character—both for double-byte and mixed character strings. &SYSCSUBSTR does not truncate double-byte character strings. However, the result adds shift characters to the result for double-byte character strings.

Special Nonzero Return Codes: None

Common Error Messages: See the previous section.

Commonly Used with: None

&SYSONEBYTE

First Available: TSO/E Release 4

Function: Converts from a double-byte character string to an EBCDIC character string.

Syntax: *&SYSONEBYTE(argument)*

Example: SET &CONVERT = &SYSONEBYTE(<db1 db2 db3 db4>)
Result: *FEBA—complete conversion.* See argument on what is needed for a successful complete conversion.

Argument: A double-byte or mixed character string. For &SYSONEBYTE to convert a double-byte character string completely, a double-byte character must start with a value of X'40' (blank) or X'42'. &SYSONEBYTE strips the value from the string and performs the EBCDIC conversion. The remaining double-byte characters must have values in the range of X'41' to X'FE' or X'4040' (blank).

Returned Value:

1. The EBCDIC equivalents of db1 and db2 if db1 starts with a value of X'40' or X'42'.
2. If not meeting the above condition or the double-byte character has no EBCDIC equivalent, then &SYSONEBYTE places shift characters around the untranslated character string.

Special Nonzero Return Codes: None

Common Error Messages: See previous section.

Commonly Used with: None

&SYSTWOBYTE

First Available: TSO/E Release 4

Function: Converts from an EBCDIC character string to a double-byte character string.

Syntax: &SYSTWOBYTE(argument)

Example: SET &CONVERT = &SYSTWOBYTE(FEFE)
Result: <db1 db2 db3 db4>—*Complete double-byte conversion.*

Argument: One or more hex values with each value in the range of X'41' - X'FE' or X'40'. Any hex value outside of this range gives a 620 return code.

Returned Value: If giving a valid argument, then returns a double-byte character string with the first byte starting with a X'42' value. The exception is a blank value (X'40') for first byte of a double-byte character string. It is unclear what happens if the argument has two sets of shift characters!

Special Nonzero Return Codes:

620—Not a valid EBCDIC value (between X'41' - X'FE' or X'40'.) Corrrect the hex value to be in this range.

or

IKJ79061I—EBCDIC DATA FOR &SYSTWOBYTE IS OUTSIDE VALID DBCS RANGE.

Solution: Not between X'41' and X'FE' or X'40'. Correct the hex value to be in this range.

Commonly Used with: None

OTHER OPERATIONS

Two nonstring built-in operations are now available for clist processing. &SYSDSN verifies the existence of a dataset or the member of a dataset. &DATATYPE confirms the category of a symbolic variable value. Both of these functions are different from the ones previously shown because their result is a preset character string (i.e., a kind of "text return code"). Part of the discussion on &SYSDSN includes a parsing dataset name sequence.

Argument Type (&DATATYPE)

&DATATYPE is a useful built-in function when validating user input such as after a READ. The following summarizes its syntax, valid arguments, and error messages.

&DATATYPE

First Available: TSO

Function: Confirms if argument is character, numeric, mixed, or double-byte string.

Syntax: &DATATYPE(argument)

Example:

```
NAME: WRITE What is your FIRST name?:
READ FNAME
IF &DATATYPE(&FNAME) NE CHAR THEN GOTO NAME
```

Result: *Reprompts user if input is numeric, mixed, or double-byte character string.*

Argument: Any valid mix of double-byte or EBCDIC (alphanumeric, numeric, and national) character strings, and clist operators.

Returned Value:

CHAR—No double-byte characters and at least one alphabetic (A–Z) or national (#,@,$) character.
NUM—All numeric characters (0–9).
DBCS—A double-byte character string (<db1 db2 . . . dbx>) (TSO/E Version 1 Release 4 and later)
MIXED—A String with both EBCDIC (CHAR and NUM) types. Also includes two adjacent DBCS strings. (TSO/E Version 1 Release 4 and later)

Special Nonzero Return Codes: None.

Common Error Messages: See previous section.

Commonly Used with: None

Tips, Tricks, and Traps

Here are some additional guidelines for using &DATATYPE:

1. A set of shift characters enclosing a double-byte character string returns "DBCS." Using *more than one* set of shift characters returns "MIXED."
   SET &ONE_SET = &DATATYPE(<db1 db2 db3 db4>)
   Result: DBCS—*Correctly sees as a double-byte character string.*
   SET &TWO_SET = &DATATYPE(<db1 db2><db3 db4>)
   Result: MIXED—*Although there are two double-byte character strings!*
2. Numerical character strings with numeric operators return a NUM not CHAR result.
   SET &NUMERIC = &DATATYPE(1+1*2/4)
   Result: NUM—*A numeric not character string.*
3. Character strings with decimals return a CHAR result.
   SET &CHARACTER = &DATATYPE(3.68)
   Result: CHAR—*Decimals always are characters and not numeric.*
4. Use &SUBSTR to return only a C, D, M, or N.
   IF &SUBSTR(1,&DATATYPE(&AGE)) NE N THEN GOTO REPROMPT
5. Use &DATATYPE when a value is an unknown data type or with user input. This includes READ, processing ISPF panel variables, and all clist flow control statements such as IF-THEN-ELSE, DO-WHILE and other DOs, and SELECT.

Existence of a Dataset (&SYSDSN)

For avoiding abnormal termination, a good clist program checks if a dataset exists before performing any operation. Since TSO/E Version 1 Release 2, you can easily do this with &SYSDSN. &SYSDSN returns a character string describing the status of the dataset or member. This section also includes a description on parsing a dataset name into two or more parts.

&SYSDSN

First Available: TSO/E Version 1 Release 2

Function: Confirms if a dataset or a member of a partitioned dataset exists.

Syntax: &DATATYPE(datatasetname[membername])

Example: IF &SYSDSN('USR.TEST.DATA') = OK THEN -
DELETE 'USR.TEST.DATA'
Result: IF 'USR.TEST.DATA' exists, then delete it.

Argument: Any valid fully qualified (i.e., in quotes with user prefix) or unqualified (i.e., no quotes and no user prefix) dataset name with an optional member name. A symbolic variable may be used to specify a data set or member name.

Returned Value: There are 10 possible returned values that fall into three categories:

1. Dataset found
   a. OK—Dataset Found
2. Name, Dataset Type, and Archived/Missing Dataset Problems
   a. Member specified but dataset not partitioned.
   Solution: Drop the member name from the statement or specify partitioned dataset with that member.
   b. Member not found.
   Solution: Drop the member name from that statement, specify another partitioned dataset with that member, or specify another member name.
   c. Dataset not found.
   Solution: Check the spelling of the dataset name or specify another dataset.
   d. Invalid dataset name, *datasetname*
   Solution: Check the spelling, length, and use of invalid characters in the *datasetname*
   e. Missing dataset name
   Solution: Put a dataset name in the parentheses after &SYSDSN.
   f. Volume not on system
   Solution: Check with your computer center staff if the dataset is archived or on another volume.
3. Other problems
   a. Error processing requested dataset.
   Solution: Check with your computer center staff.
   b. Protected dataset.
   Solution: Your security system protects the dataset and member. Contact your Computer Center staff on getting access to the dataset.
   c. Unavailable dataset.
   Solution: Another user is editing the dataset. There may be a command procesor (such as WHOHAS) installed at your site listing all users using a dataset. If there is, you can contact the person to see how much longer they will be using the dataset. If not, try again in a few minutes to see if the dataset is in use. If so, contact your computer center staff for finding out who is using it.

Special Nonzero Return Codes:
332—Invalid file name syntax
Solution: Check the spelling, length, and invalid characters in the dataset name

Common Error Messages: None

Commonly Used with: None

Tips, Tricks, and Traps

Here are some additional guidelines for using &SYSDSN:

1. Fully qualified (i.e., with userid prefix) *must* be in single quotes. Note that you do not need to use fully qualified names.

   ```
   SET &DATA_STATUS = &SYSDSN('AGG6.DATA.Y1988')
   ```
   Result: *Fully qualified dataset name*

   ```
   SET &DATA_STATUS = &SYSDSN(DATA.Y1988)
   ```
   Result: *If userid is AGG6, same result as fully qualified dataset name.*
2. Dataset names may be in any case including mixed.

   ```
   SET &DATA_STATUS = &SYSDSN(DATA.y1988)
   ```
   Result: *Same result whether in uppercase, lowercase, or mixed-case letters.*
3. Use &SYSDSN with any flow control statement such as IF-THEN-ELSE, DO-WHILE and other DOs, and SELECT for performing an action only if a dataset exists. The following sequence lists the members of a partitioned dataset if a dataset exists. Otherwise display the return character string and reprompt the user for a dataset name.

   ```
   LBL_ONE: -
     WRITE List Members Program
     WRITE What is the Dataset NAME (Userid NOT needed)?
     WRITE DO NOT USE QUOTES!!!!!!!
       READ DSET
       IF &SYSDSN(&DSET) = OK THEN listds &DSET members
         ELSE DO
           WRITE Dataset Status -- &SYSDSN(&DSET)
           WRITE Please REENTER your dataset NAME.
           GOTO LBL_ONE
         END
   ```
4. Double-byte characters are invalid for dataset names.
5. For TSO/E sites before Release 1 Version 4, you may get a 913 return code (an invalid return code) when opening a dataset. This is common when using

a non-IBM secutiry package and accessing an unprotected dataset. In earlier releases, you are requested to log off. Version 4 and later returns you to the READY prompt.

Parsing a Dataset Name

Dataset name parsing is similar to the name parsing example presented earlier. If you have TSO/E Version 1 Release 3 and later, you easily can create a sequence with &SYSINDEX. Otherwise, you need a more complicated clist. Examples of both versions are presented using an identical approach:

1. Decide if a unique delimiter exists and assign its position to a symbolic variable. Delimiters include a period, quote, or right parenthesis.
2. Parse the string using the symbolic value of the delimiter position.
3. Assign the result to a symbolic variable.

To make the program easier to understand, neither clist has validations for a second period, parenthesis, or quote.

For All Releases of TSO and TSO/E

```
PROC 1 DS
/**************************************************/
/* Name of Clist:  DSPARSE                         */
/* Clist Purpose:  To parse a dataset into second  */
/*                 qualifier and type              */
/* Clist Modules:  QUOTES - Strip Quote Marks      */
/*                 M_PARSE - Parse Member Name     */
/*                 D_PARSE - Parse Remainder       */
/**************************************************/
  SET &LEN = &LENGTH(&STR(&DS))
/**************************************************/
/* QUOTES - Removes quotes from &DS                */
/**************************************************/
QUOTES: -
  IF &SUBSTR(1,&DS) = &STR(') THEN DO
     SET &DATA_SET = &SUBSTR(2:&LEN-1,&DS)
  END
  ELSE SET &DATA_SET = &STR(&DS)
  SET &LEN2 = &LENGTH(&DATA_SET)
/**************************************************/
/* M_PARSE Assigns MEMBER NAME to &MEM             */
/**************************************************/
```

```
23.  M_PARSE: -
24.    IF &SUBSTR(&LEN2,&STR(&DATA_SET)) = &STR()) THEN DO
25.      SET &LS = 1
26.      DO WHILE &SUBSTR(&LS,&STR(&DATA_SET)) NE &STR((
27.        SET &LS = &LS + 1
28.      END                                                  */
29.      SET &MEM = &SUBSTR(&LS+1:&LEN2-1,&DATA_SET)
30.      SET &DATA_SET = &SUBSTR(1:&LS-1,&DATA_SET)
31.      SET &LEN2 = &LENGTH(&DATA_SET)
32.    END
33.    ELSE SET &MEM =
34.  /*************************************************/
35.  /* D_PARSE - Parses remainder of DATASET NAME    */
36.  /*            INTO &FULL, Second qualifier to    */
37.  /*            &SECOND, and dataset type to       */
38.  /*            &TYPE.                             */
39.  /* EXAMPLE: MEMO.DATA &FULL=MEMO.DATA, SECOND=MEMO */
40.  /*          &TYPE=DATA                           */
41.  /*************************************************/
42.    D_PARSE: -
43.    SET &LS2 = 1
44.      DO WHILE &SUBSTR(&LS2,&DATA_SET) NE &STR(.) AND -
45.        &LS2 LE &LEN2
46.          SET &LS2 = &LS2 + 1
47.      END
48.      SET &LS3 = LS2 + 1
49.      DO WHILE &SUBSTR(&LS3,&DATA_SET) NE &STR(.) AND -
50.        &LS3 LE &LEN2
51.          SET &LS3 = &LS3 + 1
52.      END
53.      SET &FIRST = &SUBSTR(1:&LS2-1,&DATA_SET)
54.      SET &SECOND = &SUBSTR(&LS2+1:&LS3-1,&DATA_SET)
55.      SET &TYPE = &SUBSTR(&LS3+1:&LEN2,&DATA_SET)
56.      SET &FULL = &SUBSTR(1:&LEN2,&DATA_SET)
57.      WRITE FULL = &FULL SECOND = &SECOND TYPE = &TYPE
58.      WRITE MEMBER = &MEM FIRST = &FIRST
```

Explanation. An explanation of the preceding clist, by statement number, follows.

1. One positional parameter is required when invoking the clist:

```
READY
EX DSPARSE 'CT32.YEAR.DATA'
```

For passing the parsed variables to another clist, the next statement is GLOBAL SECOND FULL TYPE MEM. Chapter 8 discusses multiple clist processing.

2–9. Documentation flowerbox with clist purpose and modules.

10. Assign &LEN the length of &DS. This helps to locate the positions of substrings.

11–13. Also lines 20–22, 34–41. Label flowerboxes make it easy to see where a module begins. Note the D_PARSE flowerbox has a sample result.

14–17. If the dataset name is quoted, then remove the quotes and assign this value to &DATA_SET. (Or the dataset name from one character past the quote mark to the last character before the second quote mark.) For example,

```
&DS = 'GROO.GOOD.DATA(SAM1)'
```
The result is
```
&DATA_SET = GROO.GOOD.DATA(SAM1)
```

18–19. If the dataset is unquoted, the assign &DATA_SET the value of &DS. (&DATA_SET is used from now on instead of &DS.) &LEN2 is the length of &DATA_SET regardless of whether the dataset was quoted or not.

23–28. If &DATA_SET has a member name, then execute a DO-WHILE loop determining the position of the left parenthesis (&LS). (A member name exists when the clist finds a right parenthesis in the last position.) Remember the right parenthesis is optional when using &STR with a left parenthesis value.

29–33. Assign &MEM the member name. (Or the characters from one character past the left parenthesis to one character before the right parenthesis.) Assign the remainder of the dataset name (all characters before the left parenthesis) to &DATA_SET and the new length of &DATA_SET to &LEN2. If &DATA_SET has no member name, then assign &MEM a blank value. For example,

```
&DATA_SET = GROO.GOOD.DATA(SAM1)
```
The result is
```
&MEM = SAM1
&DATA_SET = GROO.GOOD.DATA
```

42–47. Execute another DO-WHILE loop locating the first period in &DATA_SET. Assign the position to &LS2. THE DO-WHILE executes until finding the end of string or a period.

48–52. Execute a third DO-WHILE loop locating the second period in &DATA_SET. Assign the result to &LS3. The search starts from one character past the first period (&LS2+1).

53–58. Assign &FIRST the first qualifier (all characters before the first period). If &FIRST and &SYSPREF are the same, this is not needed. Give &SECOND the second qualifier value. (One character past the first period until the second period.) Assign &TYPE the dataset type. (One character past the second period until the end of &DATA_SET.) Assign &FULL the dataset name without quotes. Then display the results. For example,

```
&DATA_SET = GROO.GOOD.DATA
```

The result is

```
&FULL = GROO.GOOD.DATA
&FIRST = GROO
&SECOND = GOOD
&TYPE = DATA
```

TSO/E Version 1 Release 3 and Later

```
PROC 1 DS
/**************************************************/
/* Name of Clist: DSPARSE                         */
/* Clist Purpose: To Parse a dataset into second  */
/*                qualifier and type              */
/* Clist modules: QUOTES - Strip Quote Marks      */
/*                M_PARSE - Parses MemberName     */
/*                D_PARSE - Parses Remainder      */
/**************************************************/
SET &LEN = &LENGTH(&STR(&DS))
/**************************************************/
/* QUOTES - Removes quotes from &DS               */
/**************************************************/
QUOTES: -
  IF &SYSINDEX(&STR('),&DS) GT 0 THEN DO
    SET &SQ = &SYSINDEX(&STR('),&DS,2)
    SET &DATA_SET = &SUBSTR(2:&SQ-1,&DS)
  END
  ELSE SET &DATA_SET = &STR(&DS)
  SET &LEN2 = &LENGTH(&DATA_SET)
/**************************************************/
/* M_PARSE Assigns MEMBER NAME to &MEM            */
/**************************************************/
M_PARSE: -
SET &RIGHT = &STR())
SET &LEFT = &STR((
  IF &SYSINDEX(&STR(&RIGHT),&DATA_SET) GT 0 THEN DO
```

```
28.        SET &LS = &SYSINDEX(&STR(&LEFT),&DATA_SET)
29.        SET &MEM = &SUBSTR(&LS+1:&LEN2-1,&DATA_SET)
30.        SET &DATA_SET = &SUBSTR(1:&LS-1,&DATA_SET)
31.        SET &LEN2 = &LENGTH(&DATA_SET)
32.      END
33.        ELSE SET &MEM =
34.    /**********************************************************/
35.    /* D_PARSE - Parses remainder of DATASET NAME             */
36.    /*           INTO &FULL, Second qualifier to              */
37.    /*           &SECOND, and dataset type to                 */
38.    /*           &TYPE.                                       */
39.    /* EXAMPLE: MEMO.DATA &FULL=MEMO.DATA, &SECOND=MEMO       */
40.    /*          &TYPE=DATA                                    */
41.    /**********************************************************/
42.      D_PARSE: -
43.        SET &LS2 = &SYSINDEX(&STR(.),&DATA_SET)
44.        SET &LS3 = &SYSINDEX(&STR(.),&DATA_SET,&LS2+1)
45.        SET &FIRST = &SUBSTR(1:&LS2-1,&DATA_SET)
46.        SET &SECOND = &SUBSTR(&LS2+1:&LS3-1,&DATA_SET)
47.        SET &TYPE = &SUBSTR(&LS3+1:&LEN2,&DATA_SET)
48.        SET &FULL = &SUBSTR(1:&LEN2,&DATA_SET)
49.        WRITE FULL = &FULL SECOND = &SECOND TYPE = &TYPE
50.        WRITE MEMBER = &MEM FIRST = &FIRST
```

Explanation. Following is an explanation of the boldface portions of the preceding clist.

15–17. If &DS is quoted, then assign the position of the second quote to &SQ. &DATASET uses &SQ for creating the unquoted dataset name value.

25–28. If finding a right parenthesis, then assign &LS the position of the left parenthesis. It is easier to read lines 27 and 28 because a proxy symbolic variable is used for representing the parenthesis.

43–44. Assign &LS2 the position of the first and &LS3 of the second period.

The second program is slightly but not significantly faster. Either approach takes roughly 1 second for processing a 30-character name.

CUSTOMER CLIST

The examples in Chapter 6 through 8 use a Customer QSAM file for reviewing major concepts. In the following example, the QSAM facility creates a dataset with customer information. However, the integrity of the data is unknown. The clist listed below does the following:

1. Checks if the CUSTOMER file exists.
2. Reads the records in the dataset and assigns them to array variables.
3. Capitalizes the first letters of the first and last name and sets the rest of the name in lowercase.
4. Reformats phone number by putting dashes in the correct places.

The clist does not include attention and error routines.

CUST1 Clist (TSO/E only)

```
    PROC 0 TRACE
/*********************************************************/
/* Name of Clist:  CUST1                                 */
/* Clist Purpose:  To clean up the CUSTOMER dataset      */
/* Clist Modules:  CHEK_ALL  - Check and Allocate        */
/*                             CUSTOMER file             */
/*                 ERR_ONE   - Error message for         */
/*                             bad record                */
/*                 OPEN_IT   - Open file and set         */
/*                             array variables           */
/*                 PHONE_CK  - Add dashes to PHONE       */
/*                 READ_IT   - Read record and put       */
/*                             name in mixed case        */
/*                 WRITE_IT  - Places modified           */
/*                             records in array          */
/*                             variables                 */
/* QSAM File:  Customer.DATA                             */
/* Sample Record                                         */
/* FNAME    LNAME     COMPANY     PHONE                  */
/* THOMAS   JACKSON   WORK_INC.   5555551212             */
/*********************************************************/
  CONTROL ASIS MSG
  IF &TRACE = TRACE THEN CONTROL CONLIST LIST MSG ASIS
/*********************************************************/
/* CHEK_ALL - Check if the dataset exists and            */
/*            allocate it if does.                       */
/*********************************************************/
CHEK_ALL -
 IF &SYSDSN(CUSTOMER.DATA) NE OK THEN DO
   WRITE Dataset Status -- &SYSDSN(CUSTOMER.DATA)
```

```
    WRITE Contact Ananda Jones at extension 7766
    EXIT
  END
/*************************************************/
/* OPEN_IT - Open dataset and initialize array   */
/*      array variables                          */
/*************************************************/
  OPENIT: -
  ALLOCATE F(SYSDVAL) DA(CUSTOMER.DATA) SHR
  OPENFILE SYSDVAL
    SET &CNT = 1
    SET &RECNUM = &STR(&&RECNUM)
    SET &FNAME = &STR(&&FNAME)
    SET &LNAME = &STR(&&LNAME)
    SET &COMPANY = &STR(&&COMPANY)
    SET &PHONE = &STR(&&PHONE)
/*************************************************/
/* READ_IT - Read record and put name in mixed
*/ case.                                          */
/*************************************************/
  READ_IT: -
  DO WHILE &CNT LE 1000
     GETFILE SYSDVAL
     READDVAL RECNUM FNAME LNAME COMPANY PHONE
  IF &DATATYPE(&FNAME)     = CHAR AND -
     &DATATYPE(&LNAME)     = CHAR AND -
     &DATATYPE(&PHONE)     = CHAR AND -
     &DATATYPE(&COMPANY) = CHAR THEN DO
        SET &FNAME = &SYSCAPS(&SUBSTR(1,&FNAME))+
         &SYSLC(&SUBSTR(2:&LENGTH(&FNAME),&FNAME))
        SET &LNAME = &SYSCAPS(&SUBSTR(1,&LNAME))+
         &SYSLC(&SUBSTR(2:&LENGTH(&LNAME),&LNAME))
/*************************************************/
/* PHONE_CK Adds dashes for both 7 and 10 digit  */
/*          numbers in correct place.            */
/*************************************************/
  PHONE_CK: -
          IF &LENGTH(&STR(&PHONE))= 7 THEN DO
             SET &PHONE = &SUBSTR(1:3,&PHONE)&STR(-)+
                &SUBSTR(4:7,&PHONE)
         END
         IF &LENGTH(&STR(&PHONE)= 10 THEN DO
```

```
72.            SET &PHONE = &SUBSTR(1:3,&PHONE)&STR(-)+
73.              &SUBSTR(4:6,&PHONE)&STR(-)&SUBSTR(7:10,&PHONE)
74.          END
75.   /***************************************************/
76.   /* WRITE_IT Assigns modified values to array       */
77.   /*           variables                              */
78.   /***************************************************/
79.     WRITE_IT: -
80.          SET &RECNUM&CNT = &SYSNSUB(1,&RECNUM)
81.          SET &FNAME&CNT = &SYSNSUB(1,&FNAME)
82.          SET &LNAME&CNT = &SYSNSUB(1,&LNAME)
83.          SET &COMPANY&CNT = &SUSNSUB(1,&COMPANY)
84.          SET &PHONE&CNT = &SYSNSUB(1,&PHONE)
85.        END /*Ends IF &DATATYPE ... THEN DO loop*/
86.   /***************************************************/
87.   /* ERR_ONE Error Message if invalid data           */
88.   /*          numbers in correct place.               */
89.   /***************************************************/
90.     ERR_ONE: -
91.       ELSE DO
92.         WRITE INVALID DATA IN RECORD &RECNUM
93.         WRITE RECORD CONTENTS &STR(&SYSDVAL)
94.       END
95.     SET &CNT = &CNT + 1
96.     END /*Ends DO-WHILE LOOP */
97.     CLOSFILE SYSDVAL
98.     FREE F(SYSDVAL)
```

Explanation. Following is an explanation, by statement number, of the customer clist.

1. Also lines 22–23. &TRACE is a keyword operand turning CONLIST and LIST on. Use ASIS for reading &FNAME and &LNAME in mixed case.

2–21. Documentation flowerbox with clist purpose, modules, and a sample record.

24–27. Also lines 34–37, 47–49, 62–65, 75–78, and 86–89. Module flowerboxes describing their function.

28–33. Write an error message and exit the clist if the CUSTOMER file doesn't exist.

38–46. Allocate the CUSTOMER file with a filename of SYSDVAL. Use SYSDVAL and READDVAL together for putting a record into more than one variable. Initialize the array variables holding the values of each record and the counter variable.

50–61. Creates a DO-WHILE loop (ends statement 96) reading the first 1000 records (usually finds an end-of-file before &CNT = 1000 and the right error routine executes). If finding a valid record (i.e., a character name, company, and phone number), then execute the PHONE and FNAME/LNAME sequences. The NAME routines capitalize the first letter of &FNAME and &LNAME and set the rest of the name to lowercase (because of CONTROL ASIS). Remember the plus continuation character eliminates leading blanks, allowing the indentation of the second line of SET &FNAME and &LNAME.

66–74. This is a good example of decomposing and re-creating a character string. The sequence adds dashes in the correct places for both seven- and ten-digit numbers. Normally, you add the dashes when creating the records.

79–85. Assigns values of the new &FNAME, &LNAME, and &PHONE plus the unchanged &COMPANY and &RECNUM to array variables. Using &SYSNSUB with one level of symbolic substitution results in a value of &FNAME1 . . . &FNAME1000 and for the other variables as well. The IF &DATATYPE . . . THEN DO loop ends.

90–94. Writes an error message and record contents for invalid records.

95–98. Increments the DO_WHILE loop after completing all processing and reads the next record. If the DO-WHILE loop completes, then close and free the CUSTOMER file.

This chapter gives an overview of a major intermediate clist topic—built-in functions. In the process of doing this, the chapter also examines advanced areas such as parsing a string and double-byte characters. Other than processing multiple clists, using editors, running in batch mode, and creating full-screen applications, there is very little that you cannot do with the clist information presented so far. The next chapter increases the efficiency of your editing operations by running clists in batch mode and using line editors such as TSO EDIT. It also gives a look at Session Manager and clists.

SUGGESTED READING

Elston, Jay, 1982. Clist Esoterica—Advanced Examples. *SHARE 59 Proceedings*. pp. 1857–1865.

German, Hallett, 1987. *Clist Tips*. Unpublished document. GTE Laboratories.

Hoffman, Charles A., 1986. *Introduction to TSO Command Lists (Clists)*. Course Notes.

IBM Corporation, 1988. *INFO/SYSTEM Database*. Various notes.

IBM Corporation, 1980. *OS/VS2 TSO Command Language Reference*. GC28-0646.

IBM Corporation, 1980. *OS/VS2 TSO Terminal User's Guide*. GC28-0645.

IBM Corporation, 1987. *TSO/E Programming Guide*. SC28-1363.

IBM Corporation, 1987. *TSO Extensions Clists*. SC28-1304.

IBM Corporation, 1984. *TSO Extensions (TSO/E) General Information Manual*. GC28-1061.

IBM Corporation, 1987. *TSO Extensions Guide to Writing a Terminal Monitor Program or a Command Processor*. SC28-1136.

IBM Corporation, 1987. *TSO Extensions Programming Guide*. SC28-1363.

IBM Corporation, 1987. *TSO Extensions Programming Services*. SC28-1364.

Kusnierz, Thomas E., 1986. Clist Tips and Techniques. *SHARE 67 Proceedings*. 1–19 (Handout)

7

Clists: Using Session Managers, Line Editors, and Background Processing

SPECIAL ENVIRONMENTS

An important point mentioned early in this book is that TSO (and clists) provides flexibility in building applications *because of ties to many languages and products*. This chapter talks about those ties by reviewing TSO line editors, session managers, and background processing, and how clists interface with each. Because each of these topics deserves its own chapter, an approach is needed for presenting these areas in a useful format for all programming levels. The approach used for this chapter includes the following:

1. Providing an overview of each special environment.
2. Reviewing the needed commands to get you up and running in the environment.
3. Revealing tips, tricks, and traps for the environment, including interfacing with clists.
4. Listing a documented clist used in the environment.

Later chapters review ISPF and PDF edit macros interfaces with clists.

SPECIAL PROCESSING: DATA-ENDDATA, DATA PROMPT-ENDDATA, AND CONTROL END

Three clist statements not yet discussed are the cornerstone for processing special environments: DATA-ENDDATA, DATA PROMPT-ENDDATA (TSO/E), and

CONTROL END. The following summarizes the syntax, valid arguments, and error messages for each statement:

Syntax and Guidelines

1. DATA starts and ENDDATA ends a structure containing TSO commands and subcommands. Once placed in a DATA-ENDDATA structure, TSO, not the clist, processes commands and subcommands. A TSO END subcommand (used by ACF2, EDIT, QED, SESSION MANAGER, TEST, and OUTPUT), marking the end of command operation, correctly processes. The result is the clist not processing an END subcommand as part of a DO-END structure. (The CONTROL END statement does a similar function.) In the following example, the END subcommand of EDIT correctly processes because it is placed in a DATA-ENDDATA structure. (See later in the chapter an EDIT.)

```
LBL_ONE: -
WRITE What is the name of the DATASET you wish to-
LIST?
READ DSET
IF &DSET NE THEN DO
  DATA
    EDIT &DSET DATA OLD
      UNNUM
      TOP
      LIST
    END NOSAVE    /* END terminates EDIT not DO-
    processing */
  ENDDATA
END    /* END terminates DO structure processing */
ELSE GOTO LBL_ONE
```

2. DATA-PROMPT starts and ENDDATA ends immediately before a structure with replies to prompts from TSO commands and subcommands (TSO/E only.) The interpreter gives a 968 (DATA PROMPT-ENDDATA without prompts) return code or IKJ56545I message (SUPPLIED AN UNREQUESTED PROMPT REPLY) if no TSO command or subcommand appears right before the DATA-ENDDATA structure. Common uses of DATA PROMPT-ENDDATA are to allow a clist to process a TSO command or subcommand "nonstop" instead of pausing the clist, manually entering the answer to the command prompts, and restarting the clist (or having a TERMIN session); and so that clists running in background can process

TSO commands and subcommands with prompts. The following example gives answers to the prompt for CALL:

```
CONTROL PROMPT
call
DATA PROMPT
  'gr32.good.load(lo1)'
ENDDATA
```

3. CONTROL END(endname) is an alternative to DATA-ENDDATA. *Endname* is one to four characters and is used instead of END for marking the finish of a control flow structure or subprocedure (see Chapter 8). Common names for endname are FINI and ENDO. The above example now uses CONTROL-END instead of DATA-ENDDATA.

```
CONTROL END(FINI)
LBL_ONE: -
WRITE What is the name of the DATASET you wish to-
LIST?
READ DSET
IF &DSET NE THEN DO
  EDIT &DSET DATA OLD
    UNNUM
    TOP
    LIST
  END NOSAVE    /* Terminates EDIT not DO processing.*/
FINI    /* Note no DATA-ENDDATA structure.          */
ELSE GOTO LBL_ONE
```

4. Other information about DATA-ENDDATA, DATA PROMPT-ENDDATA, and CONTROL END follows.

DATA-ENDDATA

a. Clist statements in a DATA-ENDDATA structure are processed as TSO commands causing "unknown TSO command" error messages.

b. A DATA statement may have a clist label but not ENDDATA.

c. All symbolic substitution (usually dataset names or text strings) for DATA-ENDDATA or DATA PROMPT-ENDDATA occurs before the TSO command/subcommand or prompt reply executes.

d. Use DATA-ENDDATA or CONTROL END in ATTN/ERROR routines for ending normal command or subcommand processing when unexpected events occur. The following example lists the contents of HHG1.MEMO.TEXT:

```
ATTN DO
  DATA
    END NO SAVE    /* Ends EDIT.*/
```

```
  ENDDATA
END
DATA
  EDIT 'HHG1.MEMO' TEXT
    UNNUM
    TOP
    LIST
  END NOSAVE
ENDDATA
```

e. If using no END statements in a clist, then you do not need DATA-ENDDATA or CONTROL END.

```
edit rr data
  UNNUM
  TOP
  LIST
END NOSAVE
WRITE rr dataset LISTED.
```

DATA PROMPT-ENDDATA

a. For DATA PROMPT to work, the clist must permit prompting. (Use the right combination of EXEC PROFILE, CONTROL PROMPT and PROFILE PROMPT—See the clist and prompting section of Chapter 5 for more information.)

b. The replies in a DATA PROMPT-ENDDATA structure must be in the same order and number as the command or subcommand prompts. Otherwise the command may abnormally end or process incorrectly.

USING SESSION MANAGER

Session Manager, both in TSO and TSO/E, significantly enhances IBM 3270-type terminal usage. The Session Manager retains an entire session and uses both multitasking and multiwindow displays. Flexibility and ease of customization also are attributes of this product. The following summarizes the major features of Session Manager:

1. *Find, reexecute, or print commands entered in your session to date.* (How often have you said, "If only I could recall the command entered two commands back and make one small change to it?" Note ISPF Version 2 Release 3 has a recall key that does the task.) Session Manager capabilities are available for your entire TSO session.
2. *Customize many aspects of your session,* such as number of windows displayed, size and other aspects of windows, when and how long to lock the keyboard, what each PF key does, terminal characteristics, cursor location and much more.

3. *Run all TSO commands and full-screen programs without changes*. Session Manager can be used as the TSO Command Processor in ISPF option 6. (The screen then reads "Enter Session Manager Y/N?".) Entering a null line returns to ISPF.

So, the advantages of Session Manager are:

1. Easy creation of a customized session environment fully compatible with TSO commands and other full-screen software. (A *session environment* is the current definition of screens, windows, and PF keys.)
2. Easy recall of all previously entered commands for printing, reusing, and manipulating. Without Session Manager, a command is gone once entered and no session history is maintained.
3. Enhancement of TSO commands (which are line-oriented) by using them in a full-screen environment.

Those looking for a good examination of Session Manager internals, refer to the McCrossin (1978) reference. The power and capabilities of Session Manager will become clearer when we next look at the concepts behind the product.

Concepts

Understanding the major concepts behind Session Manager is needed for taking advantage of the product. If you have not used Session Manager before, many of these concepts will be unfamiliar.

Streams

A *stream* stores session input (what you enter) and output (the results from TSO commands and subcommands). It is a buffer with your TSO input or output that you can retrieve from or add to. Streams use a "bottom-up" format, so the latest command is always on bottom and the oldest command is on the top. Once a stream is full, it discards the oldest line, moves up the next oldest line to the top, and adds the latest line to the bottom. This is called *wrapping around*. If your stream is usable to wrap around, then you may get an ADF025I message "STREAM streamname is full." You can make as many Session Manager streams as needed. (This depends on your LOGON region size, hardware storage/memory capabilities, and other factors.)

There are three types of streams: *input* (the TSO commands and other input entered), *output* (the results from TSO commands, program execution, and messages), and *extra* (miscellaneous information such as how to set up the display screen, and information you copied into it). Extra is used often as a temporary stream.

The default Session Manager display module is ADFMDFLT. It contains nine default streams; two commonly used for TSO/E input and output (also called the TSO/E function) are

TSOIN—Entered TSO commands and other TSO input. Commands are highlighted while executing.

TSOOUT—All output from TSO commands and programs, error and other messages, and your complete TSO session or *session journal*. (Output and highlighted input similar to TSOIN.) Maintaining your entire TSO session is called *journaling*.

Two commonly used for Session Manager input and output (also called the SESSION MANAGER FUNCTION) are

SMIN—Entered Session Manager commands.

SMOUT–Session Manager messages, output, and your complete Session Manager session (usually not displayed).

Each stream name is no longer than eight characters. Table 7-1 gives more information about each stream. For example, TSOIN allows a maximum of 300 lines or 8192 bytes to be entered. Holding this information uses another 488 bytes of overhead. A displayed stream starts with a header (contained in the HEADER stream) between 26 to 34 characters. The following are the headers for each stream:

```
TSOIN -- *** THIS IS THE TSOIN STREAM ***
TSOOUT -- *** TSO SESSION OUTPUT ***
SMIN -- *** THIS IS THE SMIN STREAM ***
SMOUT -- *** THIS IS THE SMOUT STREAM ***
```

Here is a quick overview of stream performance. Each stream uses index descriptor blocks (IDBs) for finding previously entered lines. The default number of lines assigned to an IDB is 5. Changing this number has an impact on wrapping efficiency and search time for previous commands. (Usually a lower number means faster search time but more overhead and more IDBs. Having a

Table 7-1. Default Session Manager Stream Characteristics

Stream	Maximum Number of Usable Lines	Maximum Number of Usable Bytes	Overhead in Bytes
TSOIN	300	8192	488
TSOOUT	4000	147456	6408
SMIN	300	8192	488
SMOUT	150	4096	248

higher number of lines per IDB means the opposite.) Using AMASPZAP modifies ADFMDFLT (the default Session Manager display module) and changes this number. The "Customizing Session Manager" section of the *TSO/E Customization Guide* documents this.

Windows

A *window* is one or more unique physical areas on the display screen tied to a certain stream. (A *screen* is what you see on your terminal.) However, the presence or absence of a window does not impact stream input or output. Window size has two limitations: (1) It cannot be larger than the physical screen used, and (2) it cannot physically overlap another window.

Pressing selected PF keys or entering Session Manager commands shifts a window in a desired direction by a specified number of scroll units. *Scrolling* is the process of shifting in a specified manner over a stream. This allows you to see any or all of the current contents of the stream.

Related to scrolling is the concept of *scroll locking*. A *locked window* keeps the selected lines on the screen and does not scroll to display new input or output. (However, new lines can still be placed in a stream.) An *unlocked window* scrolls to display the next input or output. The UNLOCK command of Session Manager easily unlocks a window.

Later in the chapter we discuss the specific windows used by the Session Manager default display screen and window operations.

Customizing Session Manager

You site may have a customized version of Session Manager. The following lists areas of Session Manager that can be customized:

1. Modifying all aspects of the default environment—running AMASPZAP changes ADFMDFLT. (ADFMDFLT is the default Session Manager display module.)
2. Providing more than one default environment.
3. Having Session Manager appear in ISPF Option 6 (TSO Command Processor).
4. Accessing the Session Manager exits for monitoring and logging Session Manager usage. This includes saving a user's session journal, and analyzing the performance of a TSO or Session Manager command/subcommand. The three Session Manager-supplied exits are:
   a. ADFEXIT1 (initialization): Specifies the streams for monitoring. Locking is not recognized.

b. ADFEXIT2 (stream monitoring): Monitors the stream and performs the needed processing to do this. Locking is part of this process.
c. ADFEXIT3 (termination): Performs "cleanup" processing before Session Manager or TSO ends.

The "Customizing Session Manager" section of the *TSO/E Customization Guide* gives more information.

Getting Started With Session Manager

This section reviews basic and intermediate operations of Session Manager.

Invoking Session Manager

Usually, you just log on to access Session Manager. (If the default Session Manager environment is installed on your system.) What you see is similar to Figure 7-1. You may not realize, it but this display screen actually has ten windows, although only six are commonly used. The letters A through F on the above screen list the location of these windows. Table 7-2 is a list of Session Manager window names and locations and their functions.

Entering and Processing Commands in Session Manager

So how do you enter TSO or Session Manager commands on the default screen?

TSO Command (placing commands in the TSOIN stream)

1. Type the TSO command/subcommand at the ENTRY window (i.e. ⇒) and press the ENTER Key, or

Figure 7-1. Sample Session Manager Screen

```
***TSO SESSION OUTPUT***
READY

                              D

------.------1------.------2------.------3------.------4------.------5------.------6------.------7------.------
***TSO SESSION OUTPUT***      A                  F SCROLL ⇒ HALF
READY                        ]                   C MAIN ⇒ UNLOCKED
⇒ _B
                                  | E
```

Reprinted by permission from *TSO Extensions Session Manager Terminal User's Guide* © 1984 by International Business Machines Corporation page 7 Figure 3.

Table 7-2. Six Commonly Used Session Manager Windows

Window Name	Location	Function
CURRENT	A	Initially is the last two lines of TSOOUT but then displays the last two TSO commands or subcommands entered (TSOIN).
ENTRY	B	Where you enter TSO commands or subcommands. This provides input for TSOIN.
LVALUE	C	Displays if the MAIN window is locked or unlocked. This is part of the HEADER stream (not discussed.)
MAIN	D	Displays all TSO input and output—your Session Journal. This is the TSOOUT stream.
PASSWD or PASSWORD	E	Displays error messages. This is the SMOUT stream.
SVALUE	F	Displays the scroll amount with a default value of HALF for scrolling a half-screen This is an EXTRA stream (not discussed).

2. Type the clist name at the ENTRY window and press the ENTER key.

Session Manager Commands (placing commands in the SMIN stream)

1. Pressing the CLEAR key temporarily clears the display and enters a Session Manager command(s). Pressing ENTER returns to the default Session Manager display, *or*
2. Type the clist name at the ENTRY window and press the ENTER key.

The following are some important points when processing TSO and Session Manager commands under Session Manager:

1. With SMPUT, you can enter multiple (or "stacking") Session Manager commands by putting a semicolon between each command. A maximum of 512 characters can be entered for the SMIN stream and 32,768 for other streams. TSO commands cannot be stacked with SMPUT.
2. Assign PF keys to execute TSO or Session Manager commands. Some later examples show this.
3. Session Manager executes commands from the top to bottom and left to right of the screen (regardless of the order entered.) So anything in the LVALUE window processes *before* the ENTRY window.
4. To reexecute a TSO or Session Manager command, just retype one character in the command and press ENTER.
5. For obtaining a desired output, add any needed text from a previously entered command and press ENTER. For example, LISTDS MEMBERS lists the member names. Simply type del, add the rest of the dataset name to the member, press ENTER to delete it.

PF and Other Keys under Session Manager

In addition to entering commands, PF and other keys play an important role in Session Manager. Table 7-3 lists the default PF keys frequently used by Session Manager. Figure 7-2 summarizes the keys' functions. Note PF 5 and PF 7 to 12 work on whatever the default window is. (It does not have to be MAIN.) CHANGE.TERMINAL resets the default window.

Table 7-3. Session Manager Default PF Keys

Key	Function
PF 1/13	Print the EXTRA stream that contains "snapshots" of your session (from pressing PF 4) on the default printer. After printing, clear the stream contents. (TSO only)
	Not defined but the *TSO/E Users Guide* gives the code for simulating this. A "PF1 NOT DEFINED" message appears in the PASSWD window (TSO/E only)
PF 2/24	Change the scroll value and scroll the window by the desired amount. The window briefly locks to do this. Once processed, any scrolling key (PF 7-8, and 10-11) uses this value.
PF 3/15	Enter Session Manager commands in the SMIN stream. The CLEAR key replaces this in TSO/E. (TSO)
	Not defined. A "PF 3 NOT DEFINED" message appears in the PASSWD window. (TSO/E Only)
PF 4/16	Take a screen "snapshot" and place in the EXTRA stream (six snapshots maximum.) (TSO)
	Not defined. A "PF4 NOT DEFINED" message appears in the PASSWD window. (TSO/E Only)
PF 5/17	Scroll Backward (moving up) the MAIN window searching for a specified text string. Once found, pressing PF 5/17 continues searching for the text string until reaching the top line of the stream. The window temporarily locks during the searching.
PF 6/18	Toggle between displaying the last two lines of the TSOOUT (at initialization) or TSOIN stream for the current window.
PF 7/19	Scroll *back* half a page (moving up) and lock the MAIN window.
PF 8/20	Scroll *forward* half a page (moving down) and lock the MAIN window.
PF 9/21	Scroll to *top* of the stream and lock the MAIN window.
PF 10/22	Scroll *left* half a page and lock the MAIN window.
PF 11/23	Scroll *right* half a page and lock the MAIN window.
PF 12/24	Scroll to *bottom* of the stream and unlock the MAIN window.

Figure 7-2. PF Key Functions

PF 1/13 Print Snapshot Stream (TSO) ------ Undefined (TSO/E)	PF 2/14 Assign Scroll Quantity	PF 3/15 Enter Session Manager Commands (TSO) ------ Undefined (TSO/E)	PF 4/16 Take a Screen "Snapshot" (TSO) ------ Undefined (TSO/E)	PF 5/17 Search or Repeat Search of Session Journal
PF 6/18 Toggle Current Window to TSOIN or TSOOUT.	PF 7/19 Scroll Back Half a Page (Moving UP)	PF 8/20 Scroll MAIN Window Forward (Moving DOWN)	PF 9/21 Scroll MAIN Window TOP (Oldest Lines)	PF10/22 Scroll Window Half a Page Left
PF 11/23 Scroll Window Half a Page Right	PF 12/24 Scroll MAIN Window BOTTOM (Newest Lines)	CLEAR Enter Session Manager Command (TSO/E)	ENTER Process TSO Command or Subcommand	

Command Syntax and Overview

Before reviewing the major Session Manager commands, it is helpful to look at the command syntax. The following are some guidelines in creating Session Manager commands:

1. The structure of a Session Manager command is
   `Command.Descriptor Positional Operand Keyword Operand`
   Command is a common verg, such as CHANGE, DEFINE, DELETE.
   Descriptor describes in more detail the command action such as FUNCTION in CHANGE.FUNCTION. Note that a period separates the command and descriptor and not all commands have descriptors.
   Operand is a specific "object" such as stream name or window name for performing an action. Operands are *positional* (must enter them in order) or *keyword* (may enter them in any order.) Keyword operands *operand values* of keyword operands are enclosed in parentheses. POSITIONAL OPERANDS need their values enclosed by single quotes to retain lowercase.

(Without CONTROL ASIS, a clist also converts values to uppercase, regardless of the presence of quotes.) Use blanks for separating commands or descriptors from operands and operands from each other.
2. Like TSO commands, Session Manager commands have default values. Commands, descriptors, and keyword operands also may use uniquely identifying abbreviations.
3. With many commands, the default window (MAIN) does not need to be specified. The exception is DELETE.WINDOW.
4. Remember to separate multiple Session Manager commands by semicolons.

Table 7-4 lists the Session Manager commands to be discussed.

Table 7-4. Session Manager Commands

Command	Function
	General Operations
CHANGE.PFK	Resets PF key command assignment.
CHANGE.TERMINAL	Resets time locking a keyboard.
QUERY.PFKS	Lists current PF key assignments.
	Stream and Session Operations
CHANGE.STREAM	Changes stream attributes.
QUERY.FUNCTION	Lists streams and their attributes.
SCROLL	Scrolls a stream in a specified direction and amount.
SMCOPY	TSO command that copies a stream to another stream or dataset.
SMFIND	TSO command that finds the line number of a text string in a stream.
SMPUT	Places a text string in a stream.
SNAPSHOT	Captures current screen.
	Window Operations
CHANGE.CURSOR	Puts a marker at a cursor location.
CHANGE.TERMINAL	Changes default window.
CHANGE.WINDOW	Changes window attributes.
DEFINE.WINDOW	Creates a window.
QUERY.TERMINAL	Lists window attributes.
QUERY.WINDOWS	Lists window size and positions.
RESET	Recalls the default environment.
RESTORE.SCREEN	Recalls a saved screen.
RESTORE.WINDOW	Recalls a saved window.

General Operations Commands

Here are guidelines when setting terminal attributes and PF key values.

1. The CHANGE.TERMINAL command:
   a. Settings stay in effect until overridden by another CHANGE.TERMINAL or RESTORE.WINDOW command.
   b. Session Manager must lock your keyboard for processing TSO or Session Manager commands and updating the screen. (TSO also locks the keyboard when processing commands.) This means it recognizes no keyboard input. However, CHANGE.TERMINAL resets the number of seconds for keeping a terminal locked. To do this, use the CONTROL operand and specify a value in seconds (between 0 and 999):
      (i) CHANGE.TERMINAL CONTROL(0) By using a low value for CONTROL (0 to 9 seconds), your keyboard unlocks when the screen is redrawn. You can then enter more commands even while your previous command is processing. However, *only* pressing ENTER displays the output from a TSO/Session Manager command or subcommand. Note that the CONTROL value is the maximum time that a keyboard stays locked; it is possible it may unlock faster than this value.
      (ii) C T C(15) This is a valid abbreviation for CHANGE.TERMINAL CONTROL(15). If used in a clist without comments, it may be too concise and hard to follow. However, it saves keystrokes when entering long commands, allows more commands to be entered in a SMPUT string, and takes up fewer lines in a clist. This is the initial value for the default window (MAIN). Usually, a CONTROL value between 10 and 25 is satisfactory for both unlocking the keyboard and updating the screen. Use a CONTROL value between 26 and 70 for processing large programs or commands with large output. The screen rewrites only when all processing is done and all output produced.
      (iii) CHANGE.TERMINAL CONTROL (999) A very high CONTROL value (200 to 999) ends all processing and displays all output before you can enter the next TSO/Session Manager command or subcommand.
      (iv) CHANGE.TERMINAL CONTROL(LAST) Uses the last greater-than-zero CONTROL value you entered. If not entering a CONTROL value before, then assign a default value.
2. The CHANGE.PFK command:
   a. We saw that Session Manager provides default settings for PF keys. However, you can use any defined or undefined PF key (PF 1/13, PF 3/15,

PF 4/16—TSO/E only) for processing one or more TSO commands, TSO subcommands (useful for TEST, OUTPUT, and EDIT), and Session Manager commands. CHANGE.PFK also provides the powerful capability of symbolic substitution. To save your PF key definitions (for later recall by RESTORE.PFKS), use SAVE.PFKS.

b. CHANGE.PFK ' 1 CHANGE.TERMINAL CONTROL(0)' SMIN

PF Key	One or more Session Manager or TSO (one only) commands. Use quotes for including special characters.	Stream Name (Usually SMIN or TSOIN.)

Pressing PF 1 in the above example executes the CHANGE.TERMINAL CONTROL(0) command of Session Manager (in the SMIN stream).

c. CHANGE.PFK 3 'LIST A.DATA' TSOIN Allows PF 3 to execute a TSO command. Separate by commas multiple Session Manager commands.

d. CHANGE.PFK 3 'LIST ˜1' TSOIN SUBSTITUTE (˜) The SUBSTITUTE operand enables symbolic substitution. The default symbolic substitution character is ampersand (&), although any character besides blank or comma is valid. Session Manager symbolic variables use this character plus an integer (e.g., &1). The above example uses a tilde (˜) as a symbolic variable character. Changing the Session Manager symbolic substitution character is recommended for clists for avoiding confusion with clist symbolic variables. For specifying the symbolic variable character as part of a text string, type it in twice (e.g.,˜˜ makes ˜). Also, entering two adjacent quotes makes one in a TSO or Session Manager command. To process the above example, enter the name of the dataset to list and press PF 3. Then the specified dataset lists.

e. CHANGE.PFK 5 '' TSOIN Assigns PF 5 a null value.

3. The QUERY.PFKS command:
   a. Entering QUERY.PFKS displays the current PF key definitions.
   b. QUERY.PFKS places the output from this command in the TSOOUT stream by default. Here is a sample output listing:

```
PFK NO   STREAM   ID DELIM   TEXT
1        TSOIN    +          'LIST + 1'
2        SMIN                'CHANGE. TERMINAL-
                             CONTROL (0) '
```

The listing tells the symbolic variable identifier (+ for PF 1) and TSO/ Session Manager command(s) for each PF key.

4. Using the clist control variables &SYSLTERM and &SYSWTERM.
   a. Since TSO/E Version 1 Release 2, clist users can obtain the length (e.g., number of lines) and width of a screen. This is useful for clists with Session Manager commands.
   SET &WIDTH = &SYSWTERM /* *Width of Screen* */
   SET &LEN = SYSLTERM /* *Length of Screen* */
   (Session manager commands using these values.) A later example uses these clist control variables.

Stream and Session Commands

Here are guidelines for using stream and session manipulation commands.

1. Three useful TSO commands are available for stream operations:
   a. SMCOPY copies portions or a complete stream to another stream or dataset.
      (i) SMCOPY TODATASET(STREAM.TEXT) copies the entire session journal (in TSOOUT) to a dataset called stream.text. Session Manager allocates a dataset if one does not exist with that name. Dataset DCB values are a VB record format, a logical record length of 255, and a block size of 3120.
      (ii) SMCOPY FROMSTREAM(SMIN) PRINT ASIS copies the entire SMIN stream to a SYSOUT dataset for printing in mixed case (ASIS) on the default printer. (Using a default SYSOUT class of A.) Note that entering just SMCOPY prints the entire session log to the default printer.
      (iii) SMCOPY FS(SMIN) TS(SMOUT) LINE(2:18) copies from the second through eighteenth lines of the SMIN stream to the SMOUT stream. Valid operand abbreviations are FS (FROMSTREAM), TS (TOSTREAM), FDS (FROMDATASET), and TDS (TODATASET.) Use SMFIND for retrieving the line number(s) of a specified text string.
   b. SMFIND gets the line number of a text string in a specified stream. Use SMFIND instead of FIND in a clist because &LASTCC contains the line number of the text string (if found).
      (i) SMFIND 'GR00' ANY looks in the TSOOUT stream (default) for the first previous (both defaults) appearance of GR00 in any case. (ASIS is the default.) When found, list the line with the string. If using SMFIND in a clist, &LASTCC contains the line number of the found text string.

(ii) SMFIND 'Change' STREAM(SMIN) looks in the SMIN stream for any appearance of change in the same exact case.

c. SMPUT inserts a string in a specified stream.

(i) SMPUT 'CHANGE.TERMINAL CONTROL(0)' SMIN INTENSITY(0) places the Session Manager command CHANGE.TERMINAL CONTROL(0) in the SMIN stream (the default). Because the intensity value is zero, the command is not displayed. The default intensity is 1.

2. Changing and querying functions
   a. For changing the alarm (i.e., beeps on entering input or displaying output), intensity setting, or which is a TSO or Session manager input/output stream, use CHANGE.FUNCTION. Since this is not commonly done, it is not discussed.
   b. QUERY.FUNCTION gives a display like the following.

FUNCTION NAME	INPUT STREAM	ALARM	OUTPUT STREAM	ALARM	INT
TSO	TSOIN	N	TSOOUT	N	1
SM	SMIN	N	SMOUT	Y	2

This displays the TSO and Session Manager functions and their matching input/output streams. The command also displays the intensity (1 normal, 2 highlighted) and alarm setting.

3. Changing and querying streams.
   a. CHANGE.STREAM TSOOUT CLEAR this clears your entire session journal but the stream still exists.
   b. To find out information about the current streams, use the QUERY-.STREAMS command. Here is the default listing from QUERY-.STREAMS for TSO streams:

STREAM NAME	LINE LOW	RANGE HIGH	MAX LINES	SIZE BYTES	USED LINES	BYTES	TYPE	ALARM
TSOIN	1	4	305	8192	4	82	INPUT	N
TSOOUT	1	47	4005	147456	47	4677	OUTPUT	N

This shows starting and ending line number, largest stream size in both bytes and lines, number of bytes and lines used, type of each stream, and alarm setting.

4. SNAPSHOT "captures" the current display.
   a. You can easily assign SNAPSHOT to a PF key during any Session Manager session. The *TSO/E User's Guide* shows how.
```
SNAPSHOT SMIN  /* Captures the current SMIN window */
SMCOPY FS(SMIN)  /*And then prints it.*/
```

5. The SCROLL command scrolls in a specified direction and amount. Here are some common examples:
   a. SCROLL.BACKWARD scrolls toward the top of a stream.
   b. SCROLL.FORWARD scrolls toward the bottom of a stream.
   c. SCROLL.FORWARD AMOUNT(MAX) - MAX scrolls to the top or bottom depending on command used. Other values for AMOUNT are HALF (half a page), PAGE (a full page), or a number.
   d. SCROLL.NEWEST scrolls to the bottom of a stream and SCROLL.OLDEST to the top.
   e. SCROLL.LEFT and SCROLL.RIGHT provide horizontal scrolling in a specified direction.

Window Operations Commands

The following are guidelines on using window operation commands.

1. Defining a window with DEFINE.WINDOW.
   a. Window Concepts:
      (i) DEFINE.WINDOW creates a new window and CHANGE.WINDOW modifies most all window characteristics. (And overrides a DEFINE.WINDOW.)
      (ii) Window size is determined by setting the following:
         (a) STARTING ROW (top line) of the window.
         (b) STARTING COLUMN of the window.
         (c) NUMBER OF LINES (rows) in the window.
         (d) WIDTH (number of columns) in the window.
      (iii) The following is other information about window sizes:
         (a) None of these operands has a default value.
         (b) A window usually is no larger than the physical screen. (By using line 1 and WRAP for width in TSO/E or line 1 starting column 1 for TSO, a window is considered logically wider than the actual physical screen. More on this later in the chapter.)
         (c) Also a window cannot overlap a previously defined window. (But can overlap itself while scrolling a stream.)

b. Examples and Syntax:

(a) DEFINE.WINDOW NEWONE 1 1 15 80

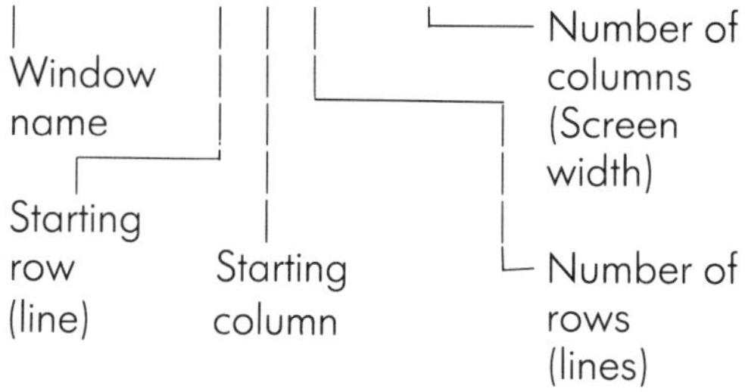

Define window NEWONE starting in the first column and row with 15 rows and 80 columns. It looks like Figure 7-3.

Assign default settings to the remaining window attributes: shut off the alarm (ALARM OFF), do not hold the screen when scrolling forward (HOLD(0)), permit input in the window (PROTECT NO), use the TSOIN stream for processing window input (TARGET TSOIN), display latest output in the "bottom-up, wrapping around" mode (UPDATE LINE), always keep the last line when scrolling between windows (OVERLAP(1)), and place the output in the TSOOUT stream (VIEW (TSOOUT)).

(b) DEFINE.WINDOW NEWTWO −10 −5 MAX MAX-ALARM(YES) UPDATE(PAGE) TARGET(SMIN) VIEW (SMOUT) From the previous example, you know the above statement defines a window named NEWTWO using input from the SMIN stream and displaying output in the SMOUT stream. A beep (alarm) sounds when scrolling input or output. However, the negative, numbers, MAX, and PAGE values are different. Let us look at each of these.

Figure 7-3. Window NEWONE

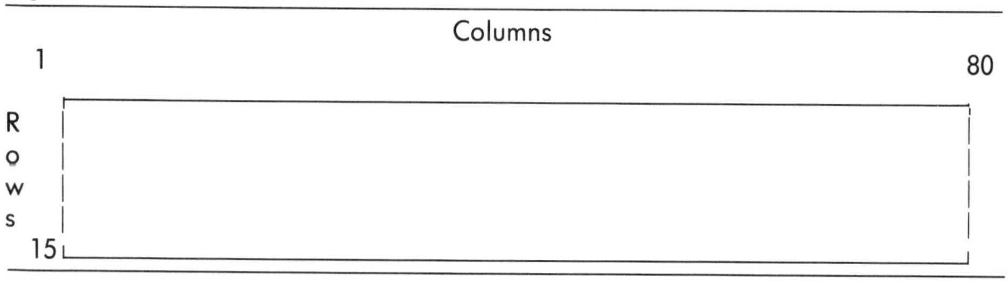

One of the strengths of the DEFINE.WINDOW command is using relative positioning. *Relative positioning* decides the value of a row or column by moving back a specified number of rows or columns (i.e., −10, −5) from the actual last row or column. This avoids using a set value for the starting row and column which may be wrong for a user's screen or coding a long IF–THEN sequence with many conditional fixed values. The specified value, whether positive or negative, cannot be larger than the actual number of rows and columns. So if a screen had 24 rows and 80 columns, the NEWTWO window starts in row 15 (10 back from 24 rows) and column 76 (5 back from 80 columns). A diagram of NEWTWO later in the chapter shows this.

The numbers of rows and columns are numeric or character values. Valid numeric values range from 1 to the last row or column and valid character values are MAX (for both number of rows and columns) and WRAP (only for number of columns). MAX means the size of the window is between the starting row or column and the last row or column (or the starting row or column of another window). Assuming a screen of 24 rows and 80 columns, the window is the area between rows 15 through 24 and columns 76 and 80. Since this is hard to visualize, Figure 7-4 provides the layout of the NEWTWO window.

MAX is also a relative positioning value because the computer decides the window area based on the size of the screen and other windows. This avoids many headaches and having a longer program. The next example discusses WRAP. A clist with &SYSLTERM and &SYSWTERM can also do this:

```
SET &SROW = SYSLTERM - 9  /* Same as -10.  */
SET &SCOL  = &SYSLTERM - 4 /* Same as -5.  */
SMPUT /DEFINE WINDOW NEWTWO &SROW &SCOL +
         &SYSLTERM &SYSWTERM ALARM(YES) +
         UPDATE(PAGE) TARGET(SMIN) VIEW(SMOUT)/
```

Clists use SMPUT for placing a block of Session Manager commands in the SMIN stream. (A unique delimiter like slashes mark the start and end of the Session Manager command block.) This is a "coming attraction"—more on clists and Session Manager later in the chapter.

It was mentioned earlier that the default value of the UPDATE operand was LINE (continuous wrapping and display of the latest lines in the stream). Other valid values are NEWEST (scrolls forward to the bottom of stream with the latest lines) and PAGE (scrolls

Figure 7-4. Layout of NEWTWO Window

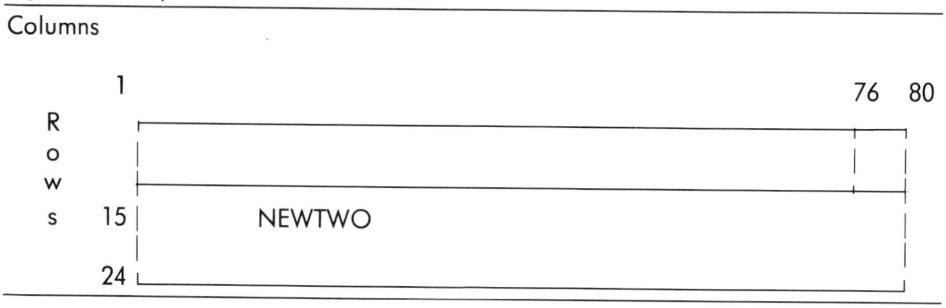

forward with the latest lines when the stream is large enough to fill up the window.)

(c) DEFINE.WINDOW LONGWIN 10 15 1 WRAP Because the command specifies the number of lines as 1 and a WRAP value for the number of columns, Session Manager views the window area (from row 10 column 15 to the window's last row and column) as one logical line. This is helpful for windows used for entering long lines of text. (You have already seen an example of this—the ENTRY window on the default Session Manager screen.) For TSO sites, the alternative is defining a window with starting in column 1 and having 1 line. The window cannot take up the entire screen.

2. Performing other window operations.
   a. Once defining a window, CHANGE.WINDOW overrides any of the window's attributes (except name and size). If you are unsure of what the current window attributes are, use the QUERY.WINDOW command. The following example changes the window attributes of NEWTWO, which an earlier example created:

```
CHANGE.WINDOW NEWTWO ALARM(NO) UPDATE(NEWEST) +
  OVERLAP(5) TARGET(TSOIN) VIEW(TSOOUT)
```

   This changes the input stream from SMIN to TSOIN and the output stream from SMOUT to TSOOUT, screen scrolling from PAGE to NEWEST, alarm from YES to NO, and line overlap from 1 (the default) to 5.

   b. DELETE.WINDOW clears one or more windows.

```
DELETE.WINDOW OLDONE /* Deletes the oldone window. */
DELETE.WINDOW *      /* Deletes ALL windows. Press*/
                     /* CLEAR before entering     */
                     /* input.                    */
```

   Then use DEFINE.WINDOW for placing a new window in a deleted area or RESET for restoring the Session Manager default window.

   c. CHANGE.TERMINAL specifies the default window. If a command such as CHANGE.WINDOW specifies no window, then perform the operation on the default window. The next example changes the default window to ENTRY:

```
CHANGE.TERMINAL DEFAULT(ENTRY)
```

d. RESET restores the default Session Manager environment (including the default screen) without logging off. However, this command also erases any PF key, screen, or window definitions stored by SAVE.PFKS, SAVE.SCREEN, or SAVE.WINDOW command. RESET cannot be on the same line as another command because the other command executes first.

e. A handy feature is setting an interim or permanent marker for a cursor location in a window by using CHANGE.CURSOR. The permanent marker is where the cursor goes to when pressing a key. (It includes all PF, ENTER, CLEAR, PA1, and PA2 keys.) The interim marker locates where the cursor resides until the next line of input. Session Manager uses the permanent marker until another CHANGE.CURSOR command with an old or new interim marker.

```
CHANGE.CURSOR ENTRY /* Changes permanent marker to*/
                    /* row 1, column 1 for ENTRY  */
                    /* window.                    */
                    /* Note: This is default lo-  */
                    /* cation.                    */
CHANGE.CURSOR 3 10  /* Changes permanent          */
                    /* marker in the              */
                    /* default window to row 3,   */
                    /* column 10.                 */
CHANGE.CURSOR 5 1 MAIN TEMPORARY /* Changes       */
                                 /* interim       */
                                 /* marker to     */
                                 /* row 5,        */
                                 /* column 1 in
                                 MAIN.            */
CHANGE.CURSOR TEMPORARY /* Uses a previously      */
                        /* defined interim        */
                        /* marker.                */
```

f. SAVE.SCREEN and SAVE.WINDOWS store screen and window attributes. RESTORE.SCREEN and RESTORE.WINDOW recall the stored attributes.

(i) SAVE.SCRÉEN stores the screen size, cursor location, locked terminal time value, and window definitions (everything in SAVE. WINDOWS).

(ii) SAVE.WINDOW stores window definitions including the window's last stream position and locked/unlocked status but not the starting and ending positions. (See DEFINE.WINDOW for valid operands.)

You may enter more than one SAVE.SCREEN or SAVE.WINDOW command.

```
SAVE.WINDOW     /* Saves window attributes      */
                /* of DEFAULT window            */
SAVE.WINDOW ENTRY   /* Saves window attri-      */
                    /* butes of                 */
                    /* ENTRY window.            */
```

(iii) RESTORE.SCREEN recalls screen and window definitions. (Each SAVE.SCREEN is in a stack with the most recent one on top and the oldest on bottom—a "push-down" strategy. To recall the oldest SAVE.SCREEN, you obtain newer screen definitions which "pushes up" the oldest definition to the top of the stack.) If there were five SAVE.SCREENs, then use five RESTORE.SCREENs for recalling the first one entered.

(iv) RESTORE.WINDOW recalls just the window definitions. Like RESTORE.SCREEN, enter as many RESTORE.WINDOWs as needed for recalling the desired window definitions.

```
RESTORE.WINDOW   /* Recall attributes for       */
                 /* DEFAULT                     */
                 /* window.                     */
RESTORE.WINDOW ENTRY  /* Recall attributes      */
                      /* for ENTRY.             */
```

g. QUERY.TERMINAL and QUERY.WINDOWS display current screen and window values:

(i) Here is sample output from QUERY.TERMINAL. This displays each window and matching attributes. (See DEFINE.TERMINAL for more information.)

```
WINDOWS      CURRENT #     MAXIMUM #      DEFAULT      CURSOR POSITION
                15             25           MAIN          ENTRY  1  1
NAME     VIEW      LOCKED    PROT    TARGET    ALARM    HOLD    OVERLAP
ENTRY    HEADER      Y        N      TSOIN       N       0         0
MAIN     TSOOUT      N        N      TSOIN       N       1         9
```

(ii) The output of QUERY.WINDOWS displays the window size, window starting position, and the last lines used both for displaying a locked window and the newest lines in the stream. This is a sample output from QUERY.WINDOWS (note the width of ENTRY due to wrapping):

```
                                                        PRESENT
                                            VIEWING    TOP    BOTTOM
WINDOW    ROW    COL    LINES    WIDTH      STREAM     LINE   LINE
ENTRY      24     6       1       120       HEADER      7       7
MAIN        1     1      22        80       TSOOUT      1      22
```

Using Clists with Session Manager

The following are guidelines for using Session Manager with clists:

1. The following clist components are extremely useful when in Session Manager:
   a. Control variables &SYSLTERM and &SYSWTERM performs arithmetic operations determining cursor, screen, and window positions.
   b. Control variable &LASTCC obtains the line number of a string in a specified stream.
   c. Control variable &SYSOUTLINE captures output from TSO commands to be used later by the clist.
   d. PROC statement passes fixed and user-entered values to Session Manager commands.
   e. WRITENR statement returns the cursor to the permanent marker location and not the end of the text string entered by WRITENR, so it should be used sparingly.
   f. Clist labcls and comments separate blocks of code.

2. Use the TSO SMPUT command for entering Session Manager commands. Include unique delimiters for marking a block of Session Manager commands. If entered in the SMIN stream, the block size may be up to 512 characters, otherwise large as 32,768 characters. (Both numbers do not include the delimiters.) Use plus signs for continuing statements and ignoring leading blanks.

3. Here is a possible skeleton for a clist using Session Manager:

```
PROC 0        /* Operands supplying values for Session     */
               /* Manager commands.                         */
/*********************************************************/
/* SAVE_DEF:                                              */
/*            Save screen, PF keys, and as many windows  */
/*            as needed                                   */
/*********************************************************/
SAVE_DEF: -
SMPUT 'SAVE.SCREEN;SAVE.PFK;SAVE.WINDOW MAIN' SMIN
/*********************************************************/
/* DEL_DEF:                                               */
/*          Delete as many windows as needed.            */
/*********************************************************/
DEL_DEF: -
SMPUT 'DELETE.WINDOW MAIN' SMIN
/*********************************************************/
```

```
/* CHG_PF:                                                  */
/*         Change as many PF key definitions as             */
/*         needed.                                          */
/*         Use the code below to clear a screen and         */
/*         clear a stream.                                  */
/**********************************************************/

SMPUT /CHANGE.PF 4 'CHANGE.STREAM SMIN CLEAR'/ SMIN
/**********************************************************/
/* DEF_WIN:                                                 */
/*         Define as many new windows as needed.            */
/*         Use the code below to clear a screen and         */
/*         create a long, narrow window.                    */
/**********************************************************/
DEF_WIN: -
SMPUT 'DEFINE.WINDOW MAIN 10 1 1 80' SMIN
/**********************************************************/
/* OTH_OP:                                                  */
/*         Place as many blocks as needed of other          */
/*         operations.                                      */
/**********************************************************/
OTH_OP: -
. . .
```

Although this may mean having more SMPUTs, which are larger, a modular format is easier to maintain and to follow.

4. Place your comments before the SMPUT for enhancing readability.
5. Clists are not recommended for modifying the default environment because they are unable to change screen size and the clist ends if a user enters a RESET during processing.

Clist Example

Both the *TSO Session Manager's User's Guide* and the *TSO/E Session Manager Program Reference* have good examples. In TSO/E Version 1 Release 4, the *TSO/E Command Reference* and *User's Guide* include Session Manager. Instead, let us look at an interesting example from Mark Scherfling of GTE Laboratories, which recalls and reexecutes previously entered TSO commands:

X CLIST

```
1.  PROC 1 STRING FORWARD CTEST
2.  /**********************************************************/
```

```
/* Author: Mark Scherfling                                */
/* Function: A clist like UNIX's history mechanism        */
/*           that easily executes a command               */
/*           previously entered. Executes Session         */
/*           Manager commands for performing an           */
/*           operation. UNIX is a trademark of AT&T       */
/*********************************************************/
/* Operands:                                              */
/* STRING - string to search for in TSOIN stream          */
/* FORWARD - changes the search to FORWARD.               */
/*********************************************************/
IF &CTEST = CTEST THEN CONTROL SYMLIST LIST CONLIST
ELSE CONTROL NOSYMLIST NOLIST NOCONLIST
/*********************************************************/
/*SET_MRK: -                                              */
/*     Sets marker (***) used for finding line            */
/*********************************************************/
SET_MRK: -
SET &SYSOUTTRAP = 1 /* Trap line returned by SMFIND. */
                    /* Copy stream and set a marker  */
                    /* to stop an endless loop.      */
SMPUT 'CHANGE.STREAM EXTRA1 CLEAR' SMIN
SMCOPY TOSTREAM(EXTRA1) FROMSTREAM(TSOIN)
SMPUT '***' EXTRA1
/*********************************************************/
/*LOOK_MRK -                                              */
/*     Finds marker (***) and then looks for string       */
/*********************************************************/
LOOK_MRK: -
  SMFIND '***' S(EXTRA1) /* Locate the line of marker */
    SET &MARK = &LASTCC
      IF &MARK = 2 THEN GOTO NOTFOUND
        ELSE SET &MARK = &MARK-2
/*********************************************************/
/* Search for the STRING before the clist line           */
/*********************************************************/
SMF /&STRING/ STREAM(EXTRA1) ANY &FORWARD
LINE(1:&MARK)
  SET &LINE = &LASTCC
  SET &SYSOUTTRAP = 0    /* Make ALL lines PRINT
    IF &LINE NE 0 THEN DO    /*STRING found reexecute
      smc tos(tsoin) froms(extra1) asis line(&line)
```

```
44.        EXIT
45.      END
46.      ELSE GOTO NOTFOUND
47. NOTFOUND: - /*STRING not found logic.
48.   WRITE '&STRING' not FOUND
49.   EXIT
```

Explanation. Following is an explanation of the X Clist by statement number.

1. If this clist is named yourid.X.CLIST (yourid is your userid), then enter:
   EXEC X 'COPY'
   This finds the last instance of COPY. An optional operand is FORWARD, which searches toward the most recent command entered. (The default is BACKWARD—toward the oldest command.)

2–13. Clist comment flowerbox.

14–15. "Standard" turn on trace logic. Note there is no CONTROL ASIS.

16–19. Also lines 27–30, and 36–38. label flowerboxes.

20–26. SET_MRK performs the following sequence:
- *a.* &SYSOUTTRAP captures one line of output from SMFIND and does not display it. (Because it produces more output, use a larger &SYSOUTTRAP with the clist trace facility.)
- *b.* Place a CHANGE.STREAM command in the SMIN stream to erase but not delete the EXTRA1 stream.
- *c.* Copy the contents of the TSOIN stream to EXTRA1.
- *d.* Place a unique marker (***) at the bottom of the stream. This stops going past the marker when searching for previously entered commands. However, it is possible to loop with this program if part of your string is the name of this clist!

31–46. LOOK_MRK performs the following sequence:
- *a.* Finds the marker at the bottom of the stream.
- *b.* Assigns the location of the marker to &MARK.
- *c.* If &MARK's value is 2 or less, then no other command has been entered and go to the NOTFOUND module. (The two lines are the marker and EXEC command invoking the clist.) Otherwise, subtract two from marker so that it won't reinvoke the clist.
- *d.* Search for the string from the marker to the top of the stream (the oldest command entered). If using the FORWARD operand, it searches toward the bottom of the stream (latest command entered). Assign &LINE the string location if found by SMFIND.

e. If found (i.e., &LINE greater than 0), then copy the one line from the EXTRA1 stream into TSOIN for execution (and exit the clist). Otherwise, go to the NOTFOUND module.

47–49. The NOTFOUND module prints a "not finding the string" message and exits the clist.

USING EDIT

What Is a Line Editor?

Two types of editors are available for TSO users: line and full-screen. Users of *line editors* (e.g., EDIT and QED) enter a command or subcommand (needed for most operations) on a single line. The editor then does the operation on a line or a block of lines. *Full-screen editors* (e.g., ISPF) display a full screen of text. You can then modify a record by overtyping desired text. You can do operations on a line, screen, or the entire dataset. Line editors were very popular when mainframe systems used little memory. Today EDIT is used only in clist processing and not day-to-day dataset editing. Paans (1986) is a good resource on the performance aspects of EDIT, QED, and ISPF.

EDIT is one way for creating and modifying datasets. If a clist uses EDIT in either foreground or background, then it performs edit operations without intervention from the user ("cruise control editing"). The major problem with this is that most subcommands do not give return codes, making it impossible to use error routines. The following is a brief look at some EDIT concepts.

EDIT accesses most types of datasets (both partitioned and sequential.) EDIT predefines certain kinds of datasets (12 in TSO, 14 in TSO/E), including DCB attributes. You will commonly use three of these: (1) CLIST for clists (a logical record length of 255 bytes), (2) CNTL for JCL (batch programs with a logical record length of 80 bytes), and (3) DATA for clist dataset operations (a logical record length of 255 bytes). All three datasets are in uppercase (but DATA can be in mixed case) and have 8-byte line numbers at the start or end of a line.

There are two modes in EDIT—INPUT (or IMODE) and EDIT (or EMODE.) INPUT creates a new dataset and adds records to it. EDIT prompts for adding as many new lines as needed to the file. EDIT sees any entered subcommand as data, not something to execute. Each line becomes a record in the dataset with a line number. Pressing RETURN or ENTER on an empty line leaves INPUT MODE and goes into EDIT MODE (pressing again switches back). Once in EDIT MODE, EDIT executes subcommands for a specified line or string of text. EDIT mode is for edit operations on existing datasets. It is easy to tell which mode you are in because the screen displays EDIT or INPUT. Later will be more on these modes.

Customizing EDIT

It is possible that the EDIT command at your site has been modified for local use. Some possible areas of customization are:

- Purchase of optional IBM products for formatting and merging datasets while in EDIT.
- Defining more kinds of datasets or changing the DCB attributes of the predefined datasets.
- Creating a syntax checker for datatypes besides FORT (FORTRAN).
- Modifying line numbering performance.
- Adding more EDIT subcommands.

The "Customizing the EDIT Command" chapter of *TSO/E Customization* guide tells how to do this.

Command Overview

This section discusses these EDIT subcommands. Enter them in either upper- or lowercase. Table 7-5 lists EDIT subcommands.

Getting Started with EDIT

Starting EDIT

Enter the following to access a dataset with EDIT.

```
EDIT datasetname type disp
```

or

```
E   datasetname type disp
```

datasetname= Name of new or existing dataset
type= Type of dataset (e.g., CLIST, CNTL, DATA)
disp= File disposition (e.g., NEW or OLD—the default)

Here are examples of starting an EDIT session. (Enter them at READY.)

```
edit or tempfile data new
```

or

```
e tempfile d n
```

Table 7-5. EDIT Subcommands

Command	Function
	Moving around a Dataset
BOTTOM	Goes to the end of a dataset.
DOWN	Moves pointer to the end of the dataset.
TOP	Goes to the start of a dataset.
UP	Moves pointer to the start of the dataset.
	Adding and Checking Data
END	Ends EDIT and saves a dataset.
HELP	EDIT Subcommand HELP
INPUT	Switches to INPUT mode.
LIST	List records at specified location.
	Modifying Data
CHANGE	Modifies one or more lines.
COPY	Copies lines between locations in a dataset.
DELETE	Erases records.
FIND	Searches for string in dataset.
INSERT	Adds a line between two lines.
MOVE	Moves lines between locations in dataset.
RENUM	Renumbers dataset.
UNNUM	Unnumbers dataset.
VERIFY	Shows result of EDIT operation.
	TSO Operations
ALLOCATE	Allocate a dataset.
ATTRIB	Assign dataset attributes.
EXEC	Run a clist.
FREE	Free a dataset.
RUN	Compile, link, and run a program.
SEND	Send a message.
SUBMIT	Submit a background job.

Edits a new sequential dataset named yourid.TEMPFILE (yourid is your userid) of type DATA. If TEMPFILE exists, a message displays when saving the file. Otherwise, it saves the file. This is also true for partitioned datasets (i.e., EDIT TEMPFILE(TEMP) DATA NEW). Entering EDIT displays similar to the following:

```
INPUT —Mode of EDIT
00010 —The first line of the dataset (10 = 1, 20 =
       2, 30 = 3, etc.)
```

Enter as many lines as needed (remember INPUT does not recognize subcommands) until pressing ENTER or RETURN going back to edit mode.

```
EDIT CUST.DATA(DATA1) DATA ASIS
```

Edits an existing partitioned dataset and supports mixed case (i.e., ASIS, not the default CAPS). If the dataset does not exist, EDIT creates it. EDIT also says if you left out a member name for a partitioned dataset (TEMPNAME is the default) or gave a member name for a sequential dataset. Entering EDIT gives a display similar to the following:

```
EDIT    —EDIT mode indicator
        —Cursor position
```

The cursor is right below the EDIT mode indicator. You may now press ENTER for accessing input mode or entering EDIT subcommands for changing the dataset.

If the inevitable happens—you are editing a dataset while your system goes down, then use the RECOVER operand (i.e., EDIT . . . RECOVER). If a backup file does not exist, then an error message displays.

Moving Around a Dataset

Before learning the EDIT subcommands for moving around a dataset, it is important to understand pointers. This includes what a pointer is, how EDIT subcommands can find the current line position, and which EDIT subcommands may modify pointer position. The *pointer* is either the current or last line you performed an EDIT operation on. Rather than using a line number to reference the pointer, use the symbol *. The EDIT subcommands BOTTOM, CHANGE, COPY, DELETE, DOWN, INPUT, FIND, INSERT, LIST, MOVE, TOP, and UP all can use the pointer symbol (*). Beware of using the pointer symbol alone—this deletes the current line! Also, a pointer value of 0 shows the pointer is before the first line. Most EDIT subcommands change the pointer position. Some of these are shown in Table 7-6.

In the discussion of EDIT subcommands that move around a dataset, we will use this five-line dataset:

```
EDIT                                      —EDIT Mode Indicator
00010  First Line (Top)────┐
00020  Second Line         │
00030  Third Line          │ Records (lines of data)
00040  Fourth Line         │
00050  Fifth Line (Bottom)─┘
```

Table 7-6. Changes in Pointer Positions with EDIT Subcommands

Subcommand	Pointer location after processing
BOTTOM	End of the dataset
CHANGE	Latest line changed
COPY	Latest line copied
DELETE	Line before deleted line (which may be before first line)
DOWN	The specified number of lines after the previous current line
FIND	Line with found string else the current line
INPUT/INSERT	Latest line added
LIST	Latest line listed
MOVE	Latest line moved
TOP	Before the first line
UP	The specified number of lines before the previous current line

Enter the following below the EDIT mode indicator:

1. BOTTOM or B
   Function: Moves pointer to the bottom of the dataset.
   Current or next line: 00050 Fifth Line (Bottom)
   Pointer: Last line of dataset.
   Comments: Setting the dataset pointer to BOTTOM is useful for an EDIT operation at the end of the dataset. (Such as adding lines with INPUT.) With UNNUM, TOP and BOTTOM are the only way for finding pointer position in a dataset.

2. DOWN n or D n
   Function: Moves forward a specified number of lines. n is the number of lines to move after the current line toward the end of the dataset. The default amount is 1.
   Example:
   ```
   EDIT  ─  Edit line indicators
   top
   EDIT        You enter subcommands
   down 2
   ```
   Current or next line: 00030 Third Line.
   Pointer: The third line of the dataset.
   Comments: Use with numbered or unnumbered datasets.

3. TOP
   Function: Moves pointer to the top of the dataset.
   Current or next line: 00010 First Line (Top)
   Pointer: Before the first line (value of 0).
   Comments: Setting the dataset pointer to TOP is useful for an EDIT opera-

tion on the entire dataset. (Such as searching for a string.) With UNNUM, TOP and BOTTOM are the only way for finding pointer position in a dataset.

4. UP n
   Function: To move the pointer up a specified number of lines. n is the number of lines to move before the current line (a default of 1) toward the dataset's start.
   Example:
   EDIT — Edit line indicators
   bottom — You enter subcommands
   EDIT
   up 2
   Current or next line: 00030 Third Line.
   Pointer: The third line of the dataset.
   Comments: Use with numbered or unnumbered datasets.

Adding and Checking Lines

Here are some basic EDIT subcommands.

1. HELP
   Function: Display help text on an EDIT subcommand.
   Current or next line: Current Line (Unchanged).
   Pointer: Current Line (Unchanged).
   Example: Listing the available help in EDIT.
   EDIT
   help
   SUBCOMMANDS -
   ALLOCATE, BOTTOM, CHANGE, COPY, DELETE, (partial listing)
   FOR MORE INFORMATION ENTER HELP SUBCOMMANDNAME OR HELP HELP.
   Comments: Entering HELP and the subcommand name (e.g., HELP DELETE) displays information on the subcommand.

2. INPUT or I line increment mode pnp
   line—Starting line number of input. * (current line) is a valid value. The default is the end of the dataset.
   increment—Amount to increase line numbers with a default of 10. Use no value with * (current line). Previous use of INPUT and RENUM changes the increment value.
   mode—I (insert new lines) or R (replace existing lines). Replace mode requires a line number.

pnp—PROMPT (displays line numbers or prompt) or NOPROMPT (displays no prompt).

Function: To add or replace lines in a dataset.

Current line/pointer: Latest line added or line past current line.

Example: Start at line 5 and increment by 5 while prompting the user.

```
EDIT  ---------+
               |   EDIT mode indicator
input  5 5 I prompt
INPUT ---------+
00005  This is line 5 _    <---- Start adding lines here
00010  This is line 10
(Press ENTER)
EDIT
```

Comments: Like INSERT but defaults to adding lines at the bottom of the dataset instead of after the current line pointer.

3. LIST start end nsum *or* LIST * number nsum
   - L = Valid abbreviation for list.
   - Start = Starting line of list.
   - End = Ending line of list.
   - * = Current line.
   - number = (only if using *) number of lines to display.
   - nsum = NUM (display lines and line numbers. This is the default). or SNUM (lines only).

   Function: Display part or entire dataset.

   Current line/pointer: Latest line listed.

   Example: List the next 10 lines from the current line (line 110 with a line number increment of 10).

```
EDIT
list * 10 or list 110 200
00110  I shot an arrow in the sky
00120  it landed in a field nearby
(partial listing)
00200  and that the way my story goes
```

   Comments: LIST and no operands displays the entire dataset. Pressing PA1 returns to the EDIT mode indicator—but pressing twice ends EDIT without saving your dataset!

4. END SAVE or END NOSAVE
   - Save = Saves your changes.
   - Nosave = Dataset saved without changes.

   Function: Finishes the EDIT session and saves/not saves your dataset.

   Current line/pointer: Current line (unchanged)

Example: End and save an EDIT session.

```
EDIT       EDIT mode indicator.
end save   end EDIT session and save dataset.
READY      Returns to TSO and saves dataset.
```

Comment: If specifying no operand, EDIT prompts for one: NOTHING SAVED. ENTER SAVE OR NOSAVE. To save a dataset but not end an EDIT session, just enter SAVE at the EDIT/INPUT prompt. SAVE also allows renumbering or removing line numbers of a dataset, and saving them to a different dataset.

Modifying Lines

Here are EDIT commands that modify existing records and perform other functions.

1. CHANGE start end number1 from to (ALL) number2

C	=	valid abbreviation for CHANGE.
start	=	Starting line number to change. The current line pointer (*) is a valid number.
end	=	Last line number to change.
number1	=	(only for *) Number of lines to change.
from	=	From string (string to change). String is in quotes or a delimiter precedes it.
to	=	To string (string to change it with). String is in quotes or a delimiter precedes it. When finding a record and having no *to* string, then display the line up to the string and prompt to complete the line.
ALL	=	Display all appearances of string 1.

Function: to modify part of or an entire line.

Current line/pointer: latest line changed.

Examples:

a. Change HAPPY to SAPPY at line 100 and check the change with the LIST subcommand.

```
EDIT
change 100 'happy' 'sappy'
EDIT
list 100
00100 Things looked so sappy today.
EDIT
```

b. Remove all appearances of EMPTY (replace empty with blank). Note the / before and after EMPTY instead of single quotes and no space between the second and third slash signifying a null string. Only two slashes are needed if not using the ALL operand.

EDIT
change 1 999/EMPTY// all

c. Line 1 is "He said after dinner all would be fine." Display the line up to "after" and manually change it. Use LIST to verify the replacement.

```
EDIT
change 1 /after    Display line 1 up to ''after.''
HE SAID-    Note after is not included.
before lunch life is tough.    Type in new text.
EDIT
list 1    List if making a replacement.
00001  He said before lunch life is tough.
```

Comments: An easy way to replace an entire line is: * *newline* (current line) or *number newline* (specified line) with newline being the replacing line of text.

2. COPY start end to
   CO = valid abbreviation for COPY
   start = Starting line number of line/of block to copy
   end = Ending line number of block to copy
   to = Line number where to copy line/block

Function: Copies one or more lines to a different place in the dataset.
Current line/pointer: Last line copied.
Example: Copy line 30 after 10.

Before		After	
00010	First line	00010	First line
00020	Second line	00020	Third line <--pointer
00030	Third line	00021	Second line
00040	Fourth line	00030	Third line
		00040	Fifth Line

EDIT
copy 30 10

Comments: Other capabilities of COPY are (1) changing the line number increment of copied lines (the default is 1), (2) copying a line before or after itself, and (3) single-line copying (COPY 1 5—copies line 1 after line 5).

3. DELETE start end
   DEL = Valid abbreviation for DELETE.
   start = Starting line number of line/block to delete.
   end = Ending line number of block to delete.

Function: Removes one or more lines.
Current line/pointer: Line before deleted line.
Example: Delete the eighth through tenth lines.
EDIT
del 8 10
Comments: Specifying just * (current line) or a line number (specific line) also deletes a line. Only DELETE removes more than one lines.

4. FIND 'string' column
   F = valid abbreviation for FIND.
   string = String to search for.
   column = Column in line to start search from.

   Function: Search for a string and display the line where it is found.
   Current line/pointer: If finding a search string, line with string. Else the current line.
   Example: Finds "test" in any case. Issue TOP to start from the beginning of the dataset.
   EDIT
   find 'test'
   00090 Test the dataset - 10/10/90 Test in mixed case
   Comments: FIND without operands displays the next line. If finding no matching lines, then display IKJ52506I TEXT not found message.

5. INSERT newline
   IN = Valid abbreviation for INSERT.
   newline = New line to be added to dataset.

   Function: Add a new line after the current line.
   Current line/pointer: The latest line added.
   Example: Add a new line after line 66. Note the TOP and DOWN commands.
   EDIT
   top top of data
   EDIT
   down 66 go down to line 66
   EDIT
   INSERT * 'New line of text' add a line of text
   Comments: With no operands, then INSERT goes into INPUT mode. Or just specify a new line number and the text string (e.g., 88 new text) for inserting a line.

6. MOVE start end to
   MO = Valid abbreviation of MOVE.

start = Starting line number of line/block to move.
end = Ending line number of block to move.
to = Line number where to move line/block to. The default is the current line.

Function: Move one or more lines to a specified location.
Current line/pointer: Last line moved.
Example: Move line 40 after 10

```
                 Before                          After
00010        First line          00010 First line
00020        Second line         00020 Fourth line <--pointer
00030        Third line          00021 Second line
00040        Fourth line         00030 Third line
00050        Fifth line          00040 Fifth line
             EDIT
             move 40 10
```

Comments: Similar to COPY but moves lines instead of inserting them. The default increment is 1.

7. RENUM new increment start end
   REN = Valid abbreviation for RENUM.
   new = Starting value of new line numbers.
   increment = Increment of renumbering.
   start = Starting line number/block to renumber.
   end = Ending line number/block to renumber. If not specified, the default is the end of the dataset.

   Function: Add line numbers to an unnumbered dataset or renumber a numbered dataset.
   Current line/pointer: Same line after renumbering.
   Example: Renumbers lines 100 through 200 in increments of 20. The first line number of the renumbered lines is line 30.

   ```
   EDIT
   ren 30 20 100 200
   EDIT
   ```

   Comments: Use RENUM to add line numbers to an unnumbered dataset and to renumber the dataset after MOVE, COPY, DELETE, and INSERT. RENUM and no operand renumbers the entire dataset in increments of 10.

8. UNNUM or UNN
   Function: Removes line numbers from a dataset.
   Current line/pointer: Same line after unnumbering.
   Example: To unnumber a dataset.

   ```
   EDIT
   unnum
   ```

Comments: Commonly used by clists to perform edit operations. Renumbering an unnumbered dataset may cause loss of records.

9. VERIFY ON or VERIFY (the default) and VERIFY OFF
   ON or no operand displays current line.
   OFF does not display current line.

   Function: Invaluable command displaying the current line. This is very helpful in checking the results of a CHANGE, COPY, or MOVE command.

   Example: Check if a CHANGE was made.

```
EDIT
verify on                    Turn verify on.
EDIT
top                          Go to the top line.
00010 The top line           Verify displays the line.
EDIT
change * /top/changed/       Change the top line.
00010 The changed line.      The line with the change.
```

TSO Operations

EDIT allows selected TSO commands to be issued during an editing session. Here is a brief look at them. Except for RUN, these are the same as entered from READY. See Chapter 2 for further information.

ALLOCATE Allocates a dataset needed by a program or clist.

ATTRIB Gives the file attributes needed to allocate a dataset needed by a program or clist. (TSO/E only)

EXEC Executes a clist during an EDIT session.

FREE Frees the files needed by a program or clist. (TSO/E Only)

RUN Compiles, links, and executes a source program in the edited dataset. Use FREE, ALLOCATE, and ATTRIB subcommands in allocating datasets. Do not use RUN with a DATA dataset type. For example, to run an assembly language subroutine stored in TEST.LOAD. If not specifying a LIB operand, the subroutine is in the edited dataset.

```
EDIT
run '77,scream' lib(test.load)
```

SEND Sends a message to another user. Unless disabled by the PROFILE command, you will receive messages while in EDIT.

SUBMIT datasetname (another dataset) or SUBMIT * (a CNTL dataset being edited) Submits a dataset with JCL commands and data as a background job. SUBMIT can generate a JOB card.

Tips, Tricks, and Traps using EDIT with clists

The following are additional guidelines for EDIT.

Using EDIT with Clists

As mentioned before, clists can do EDIT operations. These are not trouble-free since EDIT subcommands usually do not give return codes. On finding a problem, you are "dropped" to the EDIT prompt and processing of the clist ends. EDIT is not recommended for creating CLIST source programs but is a good way to perform simple database operations. (It does not support double-byte characters and is sometimes unforgiving with comments and continuation symbols.) Use a DATA-ENDDATA structure or CONTROL END so that EDIT subcommands do not process as clist statements (i.e., the END subcommand). UNNUM eases processing, and using TOP at the end returns the pointer to the beginning of the dataset. Here are some EDIT skeletons for basic database operations:

Add to bottom of an existing dataset.

```
DATA
  edit somedata data
  unnum
  bottom
  insert &STRNG  Insert a symbolic
                 variable value.
  top            Return pointer to
                 top.
  end save       End the EDIT session.
ENDDATA
```

Update an existing dataset.

```
DATA
  edit somedata data
  unnum
  top
  find &STRNG                         Searches for a string
                                      from the top.
  change * /&STRNG/&STRNG2/ all       Replaces all
                                      appearances of
                                      string with new value.
  top                                 Return pointer to top.
  end save                            End the EDIT session.
ENDDATA
```

Delete an existing dataset.

```
DATA
  edit somedata data
  unnum
  top
  find &STRNG Find a symbolic variable value.
  delete *    Delete current line—could be trouble!
  top         Return pointer to top.
  end save    End EDIT session.
ENDDATA
```

Use clist statements in an EDIT session if not in a DATA–ENDDATA structure. The next example has an IF statement in an EDIT session:

```
WRITE Enter the SEARCH string:
  READ
SET &STRNG - &STR(&SYSDVAL)
    edit cust data
      UNNUM
      TOP
      FIND &STRNG
      IF &STRNG NE THEN WRITE listed &STRNG
      LIST *
      TOP
      END NOSAVE
```

Using EDIT in a Background Job

A background EDIT session performs nearly the same as it does when entered from the READY prompt with one small (and annoying) difference. Blanks lines are seen as null lines that switch unannounced from INPUT to EDIT mode. There are a couple of ways around this. (1) Use a unique proxy character and then enter a CHANGE subcommand to switch the null lines to blanks before ending the session; or (2) use the EMODE operand on entering EDIT, forcing the adding of line numbers.

The JCL skeleton for submitting EDIT (or any TSO or clist command) in background is provided in the "Running Clists in Background" section later in the chapter.

Using EDIT with Session Manager

If using EDIT as a general-purpose editor, then I recommend running it under Session Manager. Additional features are (1) prompting on operand omission, (2) entering MULTIPLE lines at once in INPUT mode (without line numbers unless specifying the Input R subcommand), (3) changing on-screen any desired lines—more use of keyboard and less of EDIT subcommands. *OS/VS2 MVS TSO 3270 Extended Display Support Session Manager User's Guide and Reference* has an annotated EDIT session.

EDIT and Large Datasets

It is common to run out of space when editing a large dataset. If this happens, consider breaking the dataset into smaller ones or using another editor. Even if EDIT can read a large dataset, it takes time to process (because EDIT reads lines sequentially) whether in a clist, foreground, or background. This problem is also true for ISPF/PDF Edit Macros (see Chapter 10).

CUSTOMER Database Example

The following example uses EDIT for performing database operations on the CUSTOMER file. The CUSTPROG program can add, change, query, or delete a record. Chapter 8 breaks this program into different clists.

CUSTPROG Clist

```
PROC 0 TRACE
/*************************************************/
/*Name of Clist: CUSTPROG                         */
/*Function: Performs database operation on        */
/*CUSTOMER.                                       */
/*Clist Modules:                                  */
/*  MENU_100: - Main Menu                         */
/*  ADD_200:  - Add a Record                      */
/*  UPD_210:  - Update a Record                   */
/*  QRY_220:  - Query a Record                    */
/*  DEL_230:  - Delete a Record                   */
/*  EXIT_300: - Exit Clist                        */
/*Customer File: CUSTOMER.DATA                    */
/*A Sample Record:                                */
/*FNAME    LNAME    COMPANY    PHONE              */
/*Thomas  Jackson  WORK_INC  555-555-1212         */
/*************************************************/
CONTROL ASIS MSG CAPS
IF &TRACE = TRACE THEN CONTROL CONLIST LIST MSG
CAPS
/*************************************************/
```

```
/*MENU_100 - Select Database Operation                         */
/***************************************************************/
MENU_100: -
 WRITE **********************************************
 WRITE *              CUSTOMER DATABASE               *
 WRITE *                                              *
 WRITE * Please select ONE of the following           *
 WRITE *                                              *
 WRITE * 1 - Add a Record                             *
 WRITE * 2 - Update a Record (Selected Fields)        *
 WRITE * 3 - Query a Record                           *
 WRITE * 4 - Delete a Record                          *
 WRITE **********************************************
 WRITENR Your Selection:
  READ OPT
    IF &DATATYPE(&OPT) NE NUM THEN GOTO MENU_100
    IF &OPT LT 0 OR &OPT GT 4 THEN GOTO MENU_100
    IF &OPT = 1 THEN GOTO ADD_200
    IF &OPT = 2 THEN GOTO UPD_210
    IF &OPT = 3 THEN GOTO QRY_220
    IF &OPT = 4 THEN GOTO DEL_230
/ ************************************************************/
/*ADD_200 - Add a Record to Database                           */
/ ************************************************************/
ADD_200: -
  WRITE How many records do you wish to ADD?
  READ RECNUM
    SET &REC = &STR(&&REC)
    SET &CNT = 1
DO WHILE &CNT LE &RECNUM
    NAME1:WRITENR FIRST name?
        READ FNAME
          IF &DATATYPE(&FNAME) NE CHAR THEN GOTO NAME1
    NAME2:WRITENR LAST name?
      READ LNAME
        IF &DATATYPE(&LNAME) NE CHAR THEN GOTO NAME2
    COMP3:WRITENR COMPANY? (Put underscores -
    between words)
      READ COMPANY
      IF &DATATYPE(&COMPANY) NE CHAR THEN GOTO COMP3
    PHON4:WRITENR PHONE? (Use dashes --617-555-1212)
      READ PHONE
        IF &DATATYPE(&PHONE) NE CHAR THEN GOTO PHON4
```

```
      SET &REC = &STR(&FNAME &LNAME &COMPANY &PHONE)
      SET &REC&CNT = SYSNSUB(1,&REC)
    DATA
      EDIT CUSTOMER DATA
        unnum
        top
        insert &REC&CNT
        top
      END SAVE
    ENDDATA
    SET &CNT = &CNT + 1
  END /* End DO-WHILE. */
  WRITE &EVAL(&CNT -1)Records Added
  GOTO EXIT_300
  /*************************************************/
  /*UPD_210 - Update a Record to Database.          */
  /*************************************************/
  UPD_210: -
   WRITENR Enter OLD company name or phone number:
   READ OLD_STR
   WRITENR Enter NEW company name or phone number:
   READ NEW_STR
   DATA
     EDIT CUSTOMER DATA
       unnum
       top
       find '&OLD_STR'
       change * /&OLD_STR/&NEW_STR/
       top
    END SAVE
  ENDDATA
  WRITE Record Updated
  GOTO EXIT_300
  /*************************************************/
  / *QRY_220 - Query a Record in the Database.       */
  /*************************************************/
  QRY_220: -
   WRITENR Enter a string unique to the record:
     READ &STRG
  DATA
   EDIT CUSTOMER DATA
     unnum
     top
```

```
105.     find "&STRG'
106.     list*
107.     top
108.   END SAVE
109.   ENDDATA
110. WRITE Record listed.
111. GOTO EXIT_300
112. /***********************************************/
113. /*DEL_230 - Delete a Record in the Database.   */
114. /***********************************************/
115. DEL_230: -
116.   WRITE This record will be DELETED forever.
117.   WRITE Enter a string unique to the record.
118.   WRITE Enter EXIT to leave the Clist.
119.     READ &STRG
120.   IF &STRG = EXIT THEN GOTO EXIT_300
121. DATA
122.   EDIT CUSTOMER.DATA DATA
123.     unnum
124.     top
125.     find '&STRG'
126.     del *
127.     top
128.   END SAVE
129. ENDDATA
130. WRITE Record deleted
131. GOTO EXIT_300
132. /***********************************************/
133. /* EXIT_300 - Exit the Clist                   */
134. /***********************************************/
135. EXIT_300: -
136. EXIT
```

Explanation. Following is an explanation of the preceding clist by statement number.

1–18. Something new in this example are the label names. Label names are three to four characters followed by an underscore and a module number. Numbers with a 100 are menus, 200 are processing modules, and 300 are exit modules. New modules increment by 10, but use any scheme that makes sense. This approach eases creating a system with multiple clists or many modules. Note use of CONTROL CAPS avoids matching problems.

19–40. MENU_100 (for TSO/E Version 1 Release 4 and later, use SELECT instead.)

41–63. ADD_200 The DO-WHILE structure adds the required number of new records after the top of a dataset. The clist prompts for each field with simple validations. Note that each data validation label has a single number. (Again, use your own scheme.) The SET concatenates field values (separated by spaces) and assigns them to &REC. Then assign them to array variable &REC&CNT. (Which translates as &REC1, &REC2.)

64–75. ADD-200 The EDIT part. This takes the record and adds it to the top of the dataset. The pointer resets to top and EDIT saves the dataset. Repeat the DO-WHILE until adding the required number of records. If your site has a SORT command for TSO, you may also want to sort the database. On accessing the dataset you may get the message: *IKJ523381 DATASET NOT LINE NUMBERED using NONUM*. Control NOMSG turns off the informational messages from EDIT.

76–94. UPD_210 Because first and last names are not unique, a complex sequence must be written to update them (or have a unique record key [not shown]). But company and phone number usually are unique and can be updated without trouble. The clist first obtains the old and new company name or telephone number. Then it finds the old value and replaces it with the new one. Again, all validations normally included are inoperable under EDIT.

95–111. QRY_230 This module searches the database for a record with a unique string and then displays it. You can add a sequence for multiple searches.

112–131. DEL_230 This module has potential for trouble! It finds the first record with a specific and I hope unique string. If found, then it deletes it. But suppose it was the second record matching the string the user wanted! The need for return code and adding conditional logic becomes apparent. Chapter 10 on ISPF/PDF edit macros shows this capability. Because the dataset is unnumbered, there is no need to number the dataset after the delete. Note you may enter EXIT to leave the clist before deleting a record.

132–136. EXIT_300 Exit clist after completing the module.

USING QUICK EDITOR (QED)

Instead of EDIT, some sites use Quick Editor (QED) from Triangle Universities Computing Center (TUCC). This section presents a brief look at QED and how it differs from TSO EDIT.

The following are the major differences between QED and TSO EDIT:

- QED uses virtual storage instead of temporary datasets for editing data. This is usually faster than EDIT, but the trade-off is a smaller maximum dataset size. That can be a major problem if your dataset runs out of space before saving it. (Usually the AUTOSAVE feature of QED is more than adequate for backup.)
- On entering the dataset type, QED appends the type to the end of the dataset name. (So a dataset called TEST with a data type of CLIST becomes automatically TEST.CLIST!)
- You can use almost all TSO commands in a QED edit session except LOGOFF and TEST.
- QSET can assign a clist variable a line, record, or string location in a dataset (QED Release 4).
- QED has 10 (Release 3) and 18 (Release 4) subcommands not in EDIT. More valid operands and abbreviations for EDIT subcommands also exist.

Getting Started with QED

The syntax for invoking QED is similar to EDIT:

QED datasetname type disp
or
qed `datasetname type disp`

Either case like EDIT.

datasetname	=	Name of new or existing dataset. QED automatically assigns the kind of dataset as the last qualifier.
type	=	Type of dataset (e.g., CLIST, CNTL, DATA).
disp	=	File disposition (e.g., NEW or OLD—the default).

For example, to edit a dataset called userid.CUSTOMER.DATA in mixed case.

```
QED CUSTOMER DATA ASIS
```

As with EDIT, each data type has a default set of DCB default values. For new datasets, you will be in INPUT mode (still indicated by INPUT) and EDIT mode (QED not EDIT appears on the screen). Pressing RETURN on a blank line switches between modes (like TSO EDIT). You may enter any valid QED subcommand under the QED prompt. Datasets are numbered or unnumbered.

QED has some additional valid abbreviations for EDIT subcommands. Table

7-7 lists some of them. The *TUCC TSO Editor QED Guide* provides a complete list. Here are some useful subcommands unique to QED:

1. CLP line (Release 4 and later) Moves the current line pointer to a given location. CLP 15 moves either to line 15 (numbered datasets) or 15 lines down from the current line pointer.
2. INCLUDE datasetname start end (Release 3 and later) Copies part (Start and end operands specify the range of lines.) or the entire dataset (with the datasetname operand) to another edited dataset. Or use the to operand for setting where to move a copied dataset.
3. REPEAT number or REPEAT * (Release 3 and later) Stores a block of QED subcommands (200 characters maximum) until issuing a GO subcommand. The number operand specifies the number of iterations of the subcommand block. The * operand means the block continues to execute until the dataset end or an error, or pressing the ATTENTION key. (This is the default.) This is the same as a clist for processing a QED edit session.
4. RLN (Release 3 and later) Displays the relative line number. This is important for finding records in an unnumbered dataset after a COPY, MOVE, or DELETE.
5. STACK (Release 4 and later) Same as an EXEC command and immediately executes the edited dataset.
6. WHERE (Release 4 and later) Lists the positions of all instances of a string in a line.

A more complete QED command reference is in the *TUCC TSO Editor QED Guide*.

FSE—Full-Screen Interface to QED

An invaluable product not found at many QED sites is the FSE (full-screen edit) interface to QED and TSO EDIT sold by Applied Software Inc. To access the product, enter the FSE subcommand at the QED (EDIT mode indicator) prompt. A full-screen display of your dataset is shown. You may use the FSE commands or

Table 7-7. QED Abbreviations for EDIT Subcommands

Abbreviation	QED/TSO EDIT Command
+	DOWN
−	UP
/	LIST
FT	TOP and FIND together

PF keys that are assigned FSE commands) to manipulate the dataset. To return to QED, enter T at the subcommand line (i.e., line with "PF"). The *TSO QED Full-Screen Edit User's Guide* has more on FSE.

Tips, Tricks, and Traps (Using QED with Clists)

Here are some guidelines for using QED with clists:

1. QED in a clist does not require DATA-ENDDATA.
2. A common way for invoking QED in a clist is:
   `QED datasetname NEW EMODE`
   By using EMODE (edit mode), you can enter QED subcommands and then return to INPUT mode despite this being a new dataset.
3. Use the following to submit a batch job from a temporary dataset (Release 4

```
QED TEMP CNTL NEW EM+   Edit temporary dataset.
ODE
in (JCL statement:      Add as many JCL statements as-
add more if needed)     needed.
submit                  Submit job in edit session.
end nosave              Delete dataset.
```

   An important difference between QED and TSO EDIT is that QED requires JCL job card statements but EDIT does not.
4. If not in a DATA-ENDDATA block, mix clist statements with QED subcommands.
5. The QSET subcommand (Release 4 and later) assigns QED session settings to symbolic variables. Here is an example of a QED session monitor. (Do not use an ampersand for a symbolic variable in a QSET.)

```
QED OLD DATA
   QSET CONTENTS LINE(*)        Assign the text of
                                the current line to
                                &CONTENTS.
   QSET LNUM NUMBER             Assign the current
                                line number to &LNUM
                                (if numbered dataset.)
   QSET RNUM RLN                Assign the current
                                relative line
                                number to &RNUM.
   QSET DTYPE+                  Assign the dataset
   ATTRIBUTES(TYPE)             type to &DTYPE.
```

```
    QSET STRNG WHERE * 'INPUT'   Assign the starting
                                 location of
                                 'INPUT' on the
                                 current line--like
                                 &SYSINDEX.
WRITE QED SESSION MONITOR
WRITE The current line for numbered datasets is -
&LNUM
WRITE The current line for unnumbered datasets is -
&RNUM
WRITE The contents of the current line - &CONTENTS
WRITE The dataset type is - &DTYPE
WRITE The location of 'INPUT' on current line - &STRNG
END SAVE
```

Displayed:

The current line for numbered datasets is - 0000001
The current line for unnumbered datasets is - 0000001
The contents of the current line - Text on line 1
The dataset type is - DATA
The location of 'INPUT' on the current line - 0000010

RUNNING CLISTS IN BACKGROUND

Why Run Clists in Background or Use Them for Generating JCL Statements?

The last special environment discussed is background processing. This includes clists creating JCL programs that you submit for background processing or clists/ TSO commands running in background. Why should you use clists to perform either of these tasks?

1. Clists can create a customized, ready-to-run JCL program based on user selections.
2. Clists or TSO commands running in background free your terminal to execute other jobs (simultaneous allocation of the same dataset for a foreground and background job spells disaster for one of the jobs).
3. Clists or TSO commands that take some time to process can be submitted overnight and be ready when you come in the next day.
4. Using background processing may give more information to help debug a clist. However, as said in earlier chapters, background processing is not for trial-and-error coding.

Remember, SUBMIT is an authorized command—you may not have permission to use it. The strengths and capabilities of clists and background processing will become clearer when reading this section.

Generating JCL Statements

The following are guidelines for using clists to generate JCL programs:

1. There are three different ways to create JCL programs with clists:
   a. Entering a SUBMIT * END(endvalue) Specifies to process the JCL statements immediately after SUBMIT. This continues until finding the string specified by the END operand. The endvalue must be one or two characters. This way no temporary datasets to submit the job are created.
   ```
   submit * end(by) notify
   //AG1703A JOB AG8,CLASS=A
   //STEP1    EXEC PGM=TESTIT
   (JCL statements)
   by
   ```
   b. Using EDIT or QED:
   ```
   edit temp.cntl cntl new emode
     IN //STEP1    EXEC PGM = TESTIT
     (JCL statements)
     qed temp cntl emode
     submit * jobchar(a) notify
   end nosave
   ```

   The advantage of this approach is that a job card is not needed (true for EDIT not QED) and a dataset is not saved. The JOBCHAR operand specifies a job name of your userid and the character A is used. This relieves you from being prompted for a character.
   c. Using the clist QSAM facility with a preallocated dataset:
   ```
   delete temp.cntl
   SET &LINE1 = &STR(//AG1703A JOB AG8,CLASS = A)
   SET &LINE2 = &STR(//STEP1 EXEC PGM=TESTIT)
   (More SET statements.)
   alloc f(in) da(temp.cntl) shr
   OPENFILE IN OUTPUT
   SET &CNT = 1
   DO WHILE &CNT LE 4
     SET &JCL = &STR(&&LINE&CNT)
     SET &IN = &STR(&JCL)
     PUTFILE IN
   ```

```
  SET &CNT = &CNT + 1
END
CLOSFILE IN
free f(in)
submit temp.cntl notify
```

There are serious disadvantages to using this approach: (1) Processing can be slow for a large JCL program, and (2) a temporary dataset exists until the next time the program is run.

2. Some useful tips for creating JCL programs with clists:
   a. Use &SYSUID to create your jobname.

```
SET &ID =&SYSUID.A

//&ID       JOB G08,&SYSUID,CLASS=A,NOTIFY=&SYSUID
```

   b. Use clist symbolic variables to create your JCL statements:
      (i) Changing the job class based on current time. If the time is after 2 p.m., then submit the job to process overnight. Otherwise, submit to process now.

```
IF &SUBSTR(1:2,&SYSTIME) GT 14 THEN SET -
&CLASS = 0
  ELSE SET &CLASS = A
```

      (ii) The PROC statement (1) assigns default values and (2) allows the user to override these values. The next example overrides the default class variable, gives an account number and submits the job. In Clist: PROC 1 ACCOUNT CLASS(A), the user enters at READY:
      EXEC BATCHJ GT67 CLASS(B)
   c. Use clist functions when creating JCL programs. Otherwise, unexpected results occur.
      (i) &STR for most JCL statements with special characters (such as blanks and JCL comments). This is notably true when running a clist in background creating a JCL program. The following has a comment with special characters:

```
&STR(//* THIS IS A COMMENT WITH # @ $ %)
```

      (ii) &NRSTR or &SYSNSUB(0, . .) not to perform symbolic substitution on JCL statements with ampersand such as temporary datasets or symbolic parameters:

Temporary Dataset

```
// TEMP1     DD DSN=&&TEMP1(TEMP)...
```

<u>In Clist</u>

```
// TEMP1     DD DSN=SYSNSUB(0,&&TEMP1(TEMP))
```

&&TEMP1(TEMP)—Name of a temporary partitioned dataset.

Symbolic Parameter

```
// DATA1     DD DSN = &A. . .
```

In Clist

```
// DATA     DD DSN = &NRSTR(&A).
```

&A -- Symbolic parameter having the value of a dataset name.

Robert Virgile, an independent consultant in the Boston area, uses the following clist to submit background jobs. He assumes many people are using a clist that does database additions and updates on a transaction file. These transactions are added to the master database by running an overnight job. (This assumes there is an overnight job class, which is common at most sites.) If performing no transactions that day (i.e., not executing the clist that day), then the overnight job does not submit. The interesting part is how the clist "decides" when to submit the overnight job. If the date in another file (date.job.lastrun) is not today's date (&LASTDATE NE &SYSDATE), then submit the overnight job. Otherwise, the batch job is already submitted. Here is the sequence to do this:

```
ERROR OFF  /* Stops any existing ERROR routines. */
free f(lastdate)
alloc f(lastdate) da(date.job.lastrun) shr
OPENFILE LASTDATE UPDATE
 ERROR GOTO GETOUT /* Close file on any error. */
 GETFILE LASTDATE
 /*Execute if overnight job not submitted yet today. */
 IF &STR(&LASTDATE) NE &STR(&SYSDATE) THEN DO
   submit overnite.cntl(update) /* Submit overnight       */
   job. */
   SET LASTDATE = &STR(&SYSDATE)
   PUTFILE LASTDATE /* Update with today's date. */
 END
GETOUT: -
  CLOSFILE LASTDATE
  FREE F(LASTDATE)
```

Further examples of clists generating JCL programs are found in *TSO Extensions Clists* or OS/VS2 Terminal User's Guide. (This uses a different approach by having another dataset pass operand values. The use of global variables and TSO EDIT are also noteworthy. Chapter 8 reviews using global variables.)

Running Clists and TSO Commands in Background

The rest of this section presents: (1) the JCL used to submit clists and TSO commands in background, (2) TSO and clist differences while running in background, and (3) a clist creating a JCL program submitting another clist for background processing. See Chapter 11 for running REXX programs in batch.

JCL Skeleton

The following is the skeleton of a JCL program which processes a TSO command or clist in background.

```
1.  //(jobcard)
2.  //STEP1  EXEC PGM=IKJEFT01,DYNAMNBR = 30
3.  //SYSTSPRT DD SYSOUT=A    Sends to printer.
    or
3.  //SYSTSPRT DD DSN=dataset, DISP=OLD    Writes to an
                                          existing
                                          dataset.
4.  //SYSTSIN DD *    TSO commands or clist immediately
                     follows this statement.
5.  (Clist or TSO commands)
    or
4.  //SYSTSIN DD DSN = dataset, DISP = SHR    TSO commands
                                              or clist
                                              in another
                                              dataset.
6.  //SYSUDUMP DD SYSOUT = A
```

Explanation. Following is an explanation of the preceding clist by statement number.

1. Job card marks the start of the job and provides the required processing information. See your computer center staff on setting this up correctly.
2. EXEC statement uses the IKJEFT01 program. (The terminal monitor program which goes between you and TSO.) If giving a nonzero return code, the next step (block of JCL statements with another EXEC statement) immediately executes. (Note in TSO/E Version 1 Release 2 and earlier, IJKEFT01 you can only use in single-step programs.) You can also use PGM=IKJEFT1A to end this step before executing the next one. DYNAMNBR specifies (between 1 and 1635) the maximum number of dynamic dataset allocations allowed for the job step. PARM= may also be used for passing

parameters (such as positional operand values for a clist) to a clist or TSO command.

3. SYSTSPRT sends the output from the clist or TSO command to a printer, a hold queue for later viewing, or a new or existing dataset.
4. SYSTSIN reads TSO command or a clist placed immediately after this command or in another dataset (which is not concatenated).
5. TSO Commands or Clist. Each command or subcommand must be on its own line. Further restrictions and guidelines are discussed later in the chapter.
6. A good habit is including a SYSUDUMP DD statement so that a dump of user areas occurs if an error takes place. (The job ends after the dump outputs.)

TSO Commands in Background

The following are guidelines on how some TSO commands perform in a background job:

1. If the CALL command calls a program using a SYSIN dataset, then issue an ALLOCATE statement before the CALL:
```
//STEP1  EXEC PGM = IJKEFT1A, DYNAMNBR = 50
//SYSTPRT DD SYSOUT = H
//SYSTSIN DD *
  allocate f(sysin) da(old.program) old
  call test(run1) /* Calls test.load(run1). */
```
2. As previously mentioned, blank lines cannot directly be added to a dataset during an EDIT session. Some indirect ways to do this are in the "Tips, Tricks, and Traps" part of the EDIT section. The RECOVER operand is invalid for background processing.
3. LOGOFF ends both your TSO interactive session and the batch job it is in.
4. OPERATOR and TERMINAL do not work in background.
5. The USER(*) operand of SEND only works if RACF is installed. Explicitly specifying a userid does work.
6. SUBMIT * will not generate a NOTIFY message and you must specify a USER operand and value for the job for processing normally (with RACF you need no user operand).

Clist Statements in Background

Use these guidelines for creating clists to run in background:

1. READ, READDVAL and TERMIN do not operate in a batch environment.
2. Control variables under background:

a. &SYSPROC returns the id of the started task (INIT for INITIATOR). Earlier TSO/E manuals mistakenly state &SYSPROC returns a null value in background.

b. However, &SYSUID does have a null value in background regardless of the security system used.

c. &SYSPREF has a null value unless RACF is installed or a PROFILE command was previously issued with a PREFIX operand and value. Therefore all dataset names *must* be fully qualified (i.e., in quotes starting with your userid).

d. &SYSDLM and &SYSDVAL do not work in batch.

e. Writing &LASTCC after certain commands provides useful information in debugging a clist and monitoring the execution of a TSO command or statement.

```
LIST TEMP.DATA
WRITE LIST action: &STR(&LASTCC)
```

f. Using &SYSENV = BATCH for conditionally executing a certain sequence for batch processing.

g. &SYSOUTTRAP and &SYSOUTLINE provide a good way for capturing and manipulating TSO command output.

h. &SYSLTERM has a value of 0 and &SYSWTERM has a value of 132. Please change your programs accordingly.

i. &SYSPCMD uses EXEC in background and EX in foreground signifying the initial TSO command.

3. Use &NRSTR and &STR to create JCL statements in a batch environment. Also use &STR for included program statements (after a //SYSIN DD *) with blanks, special characters, or anything that can be confused for a clist statement.

4. Include a DATA PROMPT-ENDDATA structure if a TSO command provides prompts. The syntax of this statement is shown earlier in the chapter.

5. If executing ISPF Version 2 Release 2 or earlier in a non-MVS/XA environment, you cannot call a clist from a previously running program. This can be done only in a MVS/XA environment with ISPF Version 2 Release 3 and later.

Sample Clist. Let's look at a clist that creates and submits a background job for another clist.

NEWJCL

```
1. PROC 0 CLASS(A) OCLASS(H) TIME(5) CTEST
2. /****************************************************/
```

```
/* Name of Clist: NEWJCL                                    */
/* Function: to create the JCL for running                  */
/*           another clist in background                    */
/* Clist Modules:                                           */
/* JCL100 - creates JCL statements and submits              */
/*          it to batch                                     */
/* EXIT200 - exit the clist and write message               */
/ ********************************************************/
IF &CTEST = CTEST THEN CONTROL CONLIST LIST MSG
  ELSE NOCONLIST NOLIST NOMSG
/ ********************************************************/
/*  JCL100 - create and submit JCL                          */
/ ********************************************************/
JCL100: -
free da(xsubmit.cntl)
delete xsubmit.cntl
CONTROL MSG
edit xsubmit cntl new emode
IN //&SYSUID.A   JOB 'account', 'CLIST RUN',TIME=
&TIME,
IN//     CLASS=&CLASS,&MSGCLASS=&OCLASS,NOTIFY=
&SYSUID
IN // ***********************************************
IN //*  STEP1 - run HHG1.CLIST(IN) in batch.            *
IN // ***********************************************
IN //STEP1      EXEC PGM=IKJEFT01,DYNAMNBR=50
IN //SYSTSPRT    DD SYSOUT=H
IN //SYSUDUMP    DD SYSOUT=H
IN //SYSTSIN    DD*
IN exec 'hhg1.clist(in)'
/*
SUBMIT
END SAVE
/ ********************************************************/
/* EXIT200 - Send message to the user and exit.          */
/ ********************************************************/
EXIT200: -
WRITE ********************************************
WRITE * Your job is submitted for execution.          *
WRITE ********************************************
EXIT
```

IN CLIST

```
1. WRITE Batch processing with clists is fun!
```

BATCH OUTPUT(ABBREVIATED)

```
1. J E S 2  J O B  L O G
   (job execution statistics)
2. //HHG1A   JOB 88A, 'CLIST RUN',TIME = 5,
   (rest of JCL statements, allocation, and condition
   codes)
3. READY
4. Batch processing with clists is fun!
5. READY
6. END
```

Explanation. Following is an explanation of selected statements.

(NEWJCL CLIST)

1. The clist uses default values for the job class, message class, and job time. A user can override these.

16–17. Delete the JCL dataset if it previously exists.

18–19. Start inserting JCL statements into xsubmit.cntl. Clist variables provide all that is needed for the job card except the accounting information. CONTROL MSG permits displaying the message that the job is submitted.

26–27. Places both the output and any dump in the hold queue rather than printing something you may not want.

29. Execute the clist using a fully qualified name. /* marks the end of the input stream.

(IN CLIST)

1. The clist to run in background looks like any foreground clist.
2. In batch output the job log shows what the clist symbolic variables translate to. This is shown for &SYSUID and &TIME.
3. In batch output the processing of the clist is shown. Note the two READYs and the END statement.

CONCLUSIONS

This chapter takes the knowledge you have gained about clists so far and applies it to three different environments: Session Manager, TSO line editors, and background processing. By doing this, the projects you can now do with the clist language have greatly increased. The next chapter presents the final advanced clist topic of multiple clists and subroutines. Chapters 9 and 10 will introduce you to the ISPF/PDF environment and edit macros, which are far more powerful than TSO EDIT or QED. Chapter 11 gives a glimpse of the future for clists by discussing REXX. In Version 2 and later, REXX programs (called execs) can coexist with clists (and eventually will replace them). Your appreciation of the power and flexibility of clists should dramatically grow after reading these chapters.

SUGGESTED READINGS

Applied Software, 1979. *TSO QED Full-Screen Edit (FSE)*. Coral Gables, Fla.: Applied Software.

Elston, Jay, 1982. Clist Estoterica—Advanced Examples. *SHARE 59 Proceedings*, pp. 1857–1865.

German, Hallett, 1987. *Clist Tips*. Unpublished Document. GTE Laboratories.

Hoffman, Charles A., 1983. *TSO Fundamentals for Applications Programmers*. Course notes.

IBM Corporation, 1988. *INFO/SYSTEM Database*. Various notes.

IBM Corporation, 1987. *MVS/Extended Architecture JCL Reference*. GC28-1352.

IBM Corporation, 1977. *OS/VS2 MVS TSO 3270 Extended Display Support - Session Manager User's Guide and Reference*. SC28-0912.

IBM Corporation, 1980. *OS/VS2 TSO Command Language Reference*. GC28-0646.

IBM Corporation, 1980. *OS/VS2 TSO Terminal User's Guide*. GC28-0645.

IBM Corporation, 1987. *TSO/E Programming Guide*. SC28-1363.

IBM Corporation, 1987. *TSO Extensions Clists*. SC28-1304.

IBM Corporation, 1986. *TSO Extensions Command Language Reference*. SC28-1307.

IBM Corporation, 1987. *TSO Extensions Customization*. SC28-1380.

IBM Corporation, 1984. *TSO Extensions (TSO/E) General Information Manual. GC28-1061.*

IBM Corporation, 1987. TSO Extensions Guide to Writing a Terminal Monitor Program or a Command Processor. SC28-1136.

IBM Corporation, 1987. *TSO Extensions Programming Guide*.SC28-1363.

IBM Corporation, 1987. *TSO Extensions Programming Services*. SC28-1364.

IBM Corporation, 1984. *TSO Extensions Session Manager Terminal User's Guide*. SC28-1305.

IBM Corporation, 1987. *TSO Extensions User's Guide*. SC28-1333.

Kusnierz, Thomas E., 1986. Clist Tips and Techniques. *SHARE 67 Proceedings*, pp. 1–19 (handout).

McCrossin, J. M., R. P. O'Hara, and L. R. Koster, 1978. A Time-sharing Display Terminal Session Manager. *IBM Systems Journal*. 17(3):260–275.

Ott, James A., 1977. *TUCC TSO Editor QED Release 3*. Research Park: Triangle Universities Computation Center.

Paans, Ronald, 1986. *A Close Look at MVS Systems: Mechanisms, Performance, and Security*. Amsterdam: Elsevier Science Publishing Company.

Rohrbach, Chris F., TSO Session Manager—A Product Update. *SHARE 60 Proceedings*, pp. 368–373.

Sonstrom, Janet, James D. Oleksiw, and Donald M. Lawyer, 1979. *Computer Terminal Introductory Operations Guide*. Northeast Utilities. In-house user guide.

Townsend, Clarence A., 1984. *TUCC QED Editor Release 4*. Research Park: Triangle Universities Computation Center.

Van Dam, A., and N. Meyerowitz, 1983. Text Editing Systems, in *Encyclopedia of Computer Science and Engineering*, Anthony Ralston and Edwin D. Reilly, Jr. (eds.) New York: Van Nostrand Reinhold, p. 1507.

8

Clists: Multiple Clist Operations

Earlier chapters discussed *modular programming*, with each clist label referring to a set of clist statements doing one or two functions. Using this approach allows quick conversion of a module to another clist or subprocedure. This chapter reveals the hows and whys of doing this by reviewing two advanced clist areas—nested clists and subprocedures (TSO Version 1 Release 4 and later). Because using nested clists and subprocedures pushes clists to their limits, consider using another language for developing sophisticated applications.

NESTED CLISTS

Any clist (from now on called the "main" clist) may execute another clist, including itself. This is called *nesting clists*. (A *nested clist* is any clist executed within another clist.) The following is some basic information about nested clists:

1. All processing in the main clist stops until the second clist finishes. Also called asynchronous processing.
2. The number of levels of nested clists is virtually unlimited (i.e., a nested clist may execute another clist).
3. Processing always starts with the first statement in the nested clist. On return to the main clist, the statement after the one calling the nested clist executes.
4. A nested clist operates only at the current command level. For example, if the main clist is at the EDIT, OUTPUT, or TEST subcommand level, then a nested clist can only issue valid subcommands until returning to the command level with an END subcommand.

5. CONTROL and other clist statements (i.e., ATTN, ERROR) are active only for the current clist and are ignored by main and other nested clists. If you want the clist trace facility on for all nested clists, then assign a global variable in each nested clist to do this (a later example does this).

The section focuses on the rationale for nested clists, how multiple clists "communicate" with each other, and other guidelines for using nested clists.

Why Nest Clists?

Nested clists offers these advantages:

- If a nested clist performs a common task, you only need one copy, and nesting clists also reduces the number of statements in the main clist.
- An application broken down into multiple clists placed in a partitioned dataset is easier to debug and maintain. Nested clists allow building of clist systems and utility clists.

Nested clists do have their limitations. Concurrent (or synchronous) processing is not possible, so a main clist cannot execute in parallel with a nested clist. This increases the execution time if you have a long main clist. Unlike FORTRAN, you cannot specify which statement in the nested clist executes first or which statement in the main clist to return to. Note these shortcomings are also valid for sub-procedures.

Communicating between Clists (GLOBAL and EXIT)

GLOBAL and EXIT statements in a nested clist pass symbolic variable values and return codes between the main and nested clists and vice versa. Since clist programmers often abuse and misunderstand global variables, this area deserves special attention. Both statements exist for TSO and TSO/E.

Passing Values between Clists

Placing a GLOBAL statement in both the main (Defines the global variables available to all nested clists.) and one or more nested clists (Specifies the available global variables.) allows clists to pass variable values to each other. The syntax of the GLOBAL statement is simple:

```
GLOBAL var1 var2. . . varn
```

Var1 through varn are a specified number of global variables. (There is no limit.) The clist permits use of any valid clist name not taken by another global or clist variable. You can use similar or different names for global variables appearing in the main and nested clists. Before mentioning some guidelines for creating and using global variables, let's review three common misconceptions about them.

One confusing point not understood by many clist users is that *the position and not the symbolic name decides the value of a global variable*! The first variable of a nested clist's GLOBAL statement gets the value of the first variable of the main clist's GLOBAL statement and so forth. So if the main clist has a GLOBAL A B statement and a nested clist has a GLOBAL B A statement, then the symbolic variable B in the nested clist has the value of variable A in the main clist! Therefore, keeping track of the position of a variable in a GLOBAL statement is extremely important.

Another potential problem area is the maximum and minimum number of global variables for a nested clist. Use these rules when creating nested variables:

1. The maximum number of variables in a nested clist's GLOBAL statement is the number of global variables used by the main clist's GLOBAL statement. So, if the main clist has GLOBAL A B C D, there can be no more than four variables in the nested clist's GLOBAL statement.
2. When using global variables in a nested clist, the minimum is the number of variables up to and including the desired variable in a main clist's GLOBAL statement. For example, if the main clist has GLOBAL A B C D E and the nested clist uses the value of D, then a GLOBAL statement in the nested clist has four variables. Failure to follow these rules results in the error message *IKJ56535I NESTED GLOBAL PARMS SPECIFIED EXCEEDS THE MAX DEFINED BY THE FIRST-LEVEL CLIST* or you have too many variables in the nested clist's GLOBAL statement.

The last misconception is not understanding that GLOBAL variables are cumulative. For example, if the main clist has a GLOBAL A B C D E and the nested clist has GLOBAL F G, then seven global variables (five from main and two from a nested clist) are available for your use.

Use these guidelines when processing global variables:

1. Do not declare any more global variables than needed—usually three to five variables. Strongly consider rewriting your clist or use another language when having ten or more global variables. Carefully plan where and how many global variables an application uses, especially in the main clist.
2. Place a global variables "scorecard" similar to the following in your clist header flowerbox:

```
/* GLOBALS
/*
/* Clist     Pos1     Pos2     Pos3     Pos4
   -----     ----     ----     ----     ----
```

```
/* MAIN100   DATASET   CTEST   BATCH
/* NEST200   DS        CTEST
```

3. Consider standardizing global variable usage if nested clists with global variables interface with clists created by other programmers.
4. Placing the most heavily used global variables first or second reduces the number of global variables to define. This includes a CTEST or something similar, which turns on the clist trace facility for all clists used.
5. Incorrect use of the GLOBAL statement for both TSO and TSO/E gives a return code of 312.
6. Do not use a GLOBAL variable name already included in a PROC statement. Otherwise you get the message: *IKJ56530I VAR IS A MULTIPLY DEFINED SYMBOLIC PARM.*

Later is an example of global variables.

Passing Return Codes between Clists

Specifying EXIT without operands passes the return code to the main clist, storing it in control variable &LASTCC. To pass your own return code to the main clist, use EXIT with a CODE operand and value. This stores the return code in &LASTCC. The CODE value can also be &MAXCC, which is the highest return code given when processing a nested clist. The following example shows this:

MAIN CLIST

```
%NEST100
SET &RCD = &LASTCC
IF &RCD = 0 THEN WRITE Nested Clist WORKED!
  ELSE WRITE Nested Clist FAILED!
```

NEST100 CLIST

```
(Clist Statements)
EXIT CODE(%MAXCC)
```

For both TSO and TSO/E, EXIT with an wrong CODE operand value gives a return code of 964.

Other Considerations

The following are more guidelines for multiple clists:

1. GOTOs are only valid for the current clist and do not move to a label in another clist. This is also true for subprocedures.

2. Use control variable &SYSNEST for executing a sequence only in nested clists. &SYSNEST returns NO for a single clist and YES for a nested clist. The next example gives a different return code for a nested clist.

```
IF &SYSNEST EQ YES THEN EXIT(21)
  ELSE EXIT(0)
```

3. Including CONTROL MAIN or CONTROL NOFLUSH is extremely important for nested clists. This preserves the input stack with the sequential order of nested clists when finding an error or pressing ATTN. (Chapter 4 has more on the input stack, attention, and error sequences.) Then INTERPRETER begins processing of a nested clist's ATTN or ERROR sequence. INTERPRETER can pass a return code to the main clist through the CODE operand of EXIT (with or without the QUIT operand). Not using CONTROL MAIN returns the clist to TSO or ISPF with opened datasets and an incomplete clist.
4. Other releases of TSO/E prompt, executing a nested clist with CONTROL NOPROMPT and without operand values gives an error message. Other prompt regardless if using CONTROL PROMPT or CONTROL NOPROMPT.
5. An ATTN routine in the main clist may call another clist. This allows processing of more than one TSO command or subcommand per ATTN routine. The clist returns to the statement in the main clist after the one invoking the error or attention routine.

MAIN CLIST

```
ATTN
%NEST100
END
```

NEST100 CLIST

```
WRITE You pressed Attention
(TSO Commands)
```

CUSTOMER Database Example

Here is the CUSTOMER database application from chapter 7 as a multiple clist with global variables and exit codes.

MENU10C CLIST (MAIN)

```
1. PROC 0 CTEST
2. GLOBAL TRACE REC_ACT
```

```
CONTROL MAIN MSG CAPS
/*************************************************/
/*Name of Clist: MENU_100                         */
/*Function: Coordinate Customer Application       */
/*Globals:                                        */
/* Clist    Pos1   Pos2                           */
/* MENU10C  TRACE  REC_ACT                        */
/* ADD20C   TRACE                                 */
/* UPD22C   TRACE                                 */



/*************************************************/
IF &TRACE EQ TRACE OR &CTEST = CTEST THEN -
   CONTROL MAIN CONLIST LIST CAPS
IF &CTEST = CTEST THEN SET &TRACE = TRACE /*NEST+
TRACE*/
/*************************************************/
/*MENU_100: Select Database Operation             */
/*************************************************/
MENU_100: -
  WRITE  *****************************************
  WRITE *            CUSTOMER DATABASE            *
  WRITE *                                         *
  WRITE * Please select ONE of the following:     *
  WRITE *                                         *
  WRITE * 1   Add a record                        *
  WRITE * 2   Update a record (selected fields)   *
  WRITE * 3   Query a record                      *
  WRITE * 4   Delete a record                     *
  WRITE  *****************************************
  WRITENR Your Selection:
    READ OPT
    IF &DATATYPE(&OPT) NE NUM THEN GOTO MENU_100
    IF &OPT LT 0 OR &OPT GT 4 THEN GOTO MENU_100
    IF &OPT = 1 THEN DO
      SET &OPTION = ADD
      %ADD20C
    END
    IF &OPT = 2 THEN DO
      SET &OPTION = UPDATE
  &UPD22C
```

```
    END
    IF &OPT = 3 OR &OPT = 4 THEN DO
      WRITENR Give a string unique to the record:
      READ REC_ACT
    END
    IF &OPT = 3 THEN DO
      SET &OPTION = LIST
      %QRY24C
    END
    IF &OPT = 4 THEN DO
      SET &OPTION = DELETE
      %DEL26C
    END
/**************************************************/
/* EXIT_300    Exit Clist with Status Report.      */
/**************************************************/
EXIT_300:
  SET &RCD = &LASTCC
   IF &RCD = 0 THEN WRITE &OPTION SUCCEEDED
        ELSE IF &RCD = 20 and &OPT = 4 THEN DO
              WRITE RECORD NOT DELETED
      END
      ELSE WRITE &OPTION FAILED   CHECK THE RECORD
```

UPD22C CLIST (NESTED)

```
PROC 0 CTEST
GLOBAL TRACE
CONTROL MAIN MSG CAPS
/**************************************************/
/* Name of Clist: UPD22C                           */
/* Function: Update a record in CUSTOMER database. */
/**************************************************/
IF &TRACE = TRACE OR &CTEST = CTEST -
  THEN CONTROL MAIN CONLIST LIST MSG CAPS
/**************************************************/
/* UPD_210    Update a Record to Database.         */
/**************************************************/
UPD_210: -
  WRITENR ENter OLD company name or phone number:
  READ OLD_STR
  WRITENR Enter NEW company name or phone number:
```

```
    READ NEW_STR
    DATA
      EDIT CUSTOMER DATA
        unnum
        top
      find '&OLD_STR'
      change * /&OLD_STR/&NEW_STR/
      top
    END SAVE
ENDDATA
EXIT QUIT
```

QRY24C CLIST (NESTED)

```
PROC 0 CTEST REC
GLOBAL TRACE QRY_REC
CONTROL MAIN MSG CAPS
/*********************************************************/
/* Name of Clist: QRY24C                                 */
/* Function: Query a record in CUSTOMER database.        */
/*********************************************************/
IF &TRACE = TRACE OR &CTEST = CTEST -
  THEN CONTROL MAIN CONLIST LIST MSG CAPS
/*********************************************************/
/* QRY_220 - Query a Record in the Database.             */
/*********************************************************/
QRY_220: -
  IF &REC = AND &QRY_REC = THEN DO
      WRITENR Enter a string unique to the record:
        READ &QRY_REC
  END
  ELSE IF &QRY_REC = AND &REC NE THEN SET &QRY_REC =+
& REC
DATA
  EDIT CUSTOMER DATA
    unnum
    top
    find '&QRY_REC'
    list *
    top
  END SAVE
ENDDATA
EXIT QUIT
```

DEL26C CLIST (NESTED)

```
 1. PROC 0 TRACE REC
 2. GLOBAL TRACE QRY_REC
 3. CONTROL MAIN MSG CAPS
 4. /*************************************************/
 5. /* Name of Clist: DEL26C                         */
 6. /* Function: Delete a record in CUSTOMER database */
 7. /*************************************************/
 8. IF &TRACE = TRACE OR &CTEST = CTEST -
 9. THEN CONTROL MAIN CONLIST LIST MSG CAPS
10. /*************************************************/
11. /* DEL_230 - Delete a Record in the Database.    */
12. /*************************************************/
13. DEL_230: -
14.   IF &REC = AND &DEL_REC = THEN DO
15.     WRITE This record will be DELETED forever.
16.     WRITE Enter a string unique to the record.
17.     WRITE Enter EXIT to leave the Clist.
18.       READ DEL_REC
19.   END
20.   ELSE IF &DEL_REC = AND &REC NE THEN SET &DEL_REC =+
    & REC
21.     IF &SYSCAPS(&DEL_REC) = EXIT THEN EXIT CODE(20) QUIT
22.   DATA
23.   EDIT CUSTOMER.DATA DATA
24.     unnum
25.     top
26.     find '&DEL_REC'
27.     del *
28.     top
29.   END SAVE
30.   ENDDATA
31.   EXIT QUIT
```

Explanation. Following are explanations, by statement number, of the preceding clists.

MENU10C

1–2. The next two chapters focus on ISPF applications. If storing both ISPF panels and clists in the same partitioned dataset, they can be hard to tell apart. Using a naming scheme with a C suffix for clist and a P for panel, one can quickly grasp which members are which. However, the name of the main clist the user executes should be easy to type in.

Each clist uses one or two global variables. (With a total of four defined.) &TRACE turns on the clist trace facility for all clist and &REC_ACT provides the record to list (in the nested clist as &QRY_REC) or delete (in the nested clist as &DEL_REC).

3–15. Place the usual clist information here and a handy global variable "scorecard." You can also list the nested clists' names and functions. CONTROL MAIN enables proper handling of error and ATTN routines.

18. Specifying the CTEST operand in the main clist turns on the trace facility for all nested clists by setting &TRACE equal to TRACE.

37–56. Process each nested clist and then return to the main clist with a status code. The main clist then issues a status message and the operation name. A centralized location is easier to maintain and slightly reduces the number of lines in the nested clist. Note selecting the query or delete option prompts the user for a unique string identifying a record. This becomes the value to global variable &REC_ACT.

UPD22C (ADD20C (not shown) has similar changes.)

1–9. This is identical to changes in the other nested clients. You can use a different name for &TRACE.

27. Using the QUIT operand of EXIT leaves the nested clist and returns to the first clist in the series with a CONTROL MAIN or CONTROL NOFLUSH statement (in this case MENU10C). This is also true when invoking an error or attention sequence.

QRY24C

2. Accesses the second defined global variable (&REC_ACT) as &QRY_REC.

14-18. If not supplying &QRY_REC, then prompt for it. When specifying only &REC, then assign &REC as the value of &QRY_REC. (&REC is passed when invoking QRY24C as the main clist.)

23. Uses &QRY_REC instead of &STRG.

DEL26C

2. Accesses the second defined global variable (&REC_ACT) and renames it &DEL_REC.

14-19. If not supplying &DEL_REC, then prompt for it. When specifying only

&REC, then assign &REC as the value of &DEL_REC. (&REC is passed on invoking DEL26C as the main clist.)

21. Entering EXIT returns to the main clist a code of 20. The record is not deleted.
26. Use &DEL_REC instead of &STRG.

SUBPROCEDURES

TSO/E sites with Version 1 Release 4 and later can use subprocedures. A *subprocedure* (called subroutine in other languages) is a sequence residing in the main clist used one more or times by the clist when performing a task. Coding this routine only once reduces program development time and the overall program size. Because a subprocedure is tied to one label and performs one or two tasks, it is consistent with modular programming. Like nested clists, subprocedures can pass or receive values/return codes from the main clist. The earlier mentioned limitations for multiple clists—being unable to choose its entry point or its return point in the main clist—also apply. Subprocedures also do not support parallel processing with the main clist. The rest of this section presents an overview of subprocedures, some guidelines for their use, and an example.

Subprocedure Overview

Here is a skeleton of a subprocedure:

MAIN CLIST

```
1. CONTROL MAIN MSG
   /* If using NGLOBAL, do not need a SYSREF statement or */
   /* operands with a SYSCALL statement.                  */
2. NGLOBAL GLOB1, GLOB2, GLOB3
3. SET &D = 2
4. SET &Q = 4
5. SYSCALL SUB1 HAPPY D &Q
6.   IF &LASTCC = 0 THEN WRITE SUBPROCEDURE WORKED
```

SUBPROCEDURE

```
1. SUB1: PROC 3 VALUE1 VALUE2 VALUE3
2. SYSREF VALUE2
3. WRITE &VALUE1 &EVAL(&VALUE2 + &VALUE3) /*Writes-
   HAPPY 6*/
4. RETURN CODE(0)
5. END
```

Explanation

MAIN CLIST

1. CONTROL MAIN permits normal processing of a clist during an error or attention routine.
2. NGLOBAL shares variables between different subprocedures. Using an NGLOBAL statement avoids defining variables in the main clist's SYSCALL statement (which invokes the subprocedure) and the subprocedure's PROC statement (which defines the operands passed to a subprocedure). NGLOBAL does not have some of GLOBAL's limitations: (a) A subprocedure does not require a NGLOBAL statement, and (b) variable *name*, not position, defines NGLOBAL variables. Here is an example of a NGLOBAL statement:

```
CONTROL MAIN MSG
NGLOBAL D
SET &D = 2
SYSCALL SUB1 /* No Operands */
       IF &LASTCC = 0 THEN WRITE SUBPROCEDURE WORKED
SUB1:  PROC 0 /* REQURED */
       WRITE &EVAL(2 + &D)  /* 4 */
       RETURN
END
```

3–4. Sets the value of two variables before being passed to subprocedure.
5. The SYSCALL statement can be confusing for a new user. It is how the main clist invokes the subprocedure. The first and required operand is the subprocedure name. Additional operands are the variable names and values passed to the subprocedure. These operands take several forms: a variable *name* (such as D—do not use ampersands) or a variable *value*, (such as &Q [the value of &Q] and HAPPY).

   SYSREF in the subprocedure tells the interpreter that an operand (e.g., D) is a variable name and also may modify a variable's value (not name) in the main clist. Use SYSCALL in subprocedures to invoke itself, other subprocedures (you may nest subprocedures), or the main clist.
6. A RETURN in the subprocedure passes a return code to the main clist. &LASTCC stores this value for later use in a IF &LASTCC . . . statement.

SUBPROCEDURE

1. The label before PROC is the name of the subprocedure. (It cannot be on its own line.) Any SYSCALL invoking the subprocedure must use this name. The remaining operands define variable names available to the subprocedure

which are either keyword or positional. One area for confusion is having a subprocedure change the value of a variable in the main clist. Here is one way to do this.

```
CONTROL MAIN MSG CAPS
MAIN_100: -
SET &ST1 = &STR(IDAHO)
SYSCALL STATE ST1 OTH2
  IF &LASTCC = 0 THEN WRITE SUBPROCEDURE WORKED
  WRITE &ST1 /
/* What is entered in STATE subprocedure.*/
STATE: PROC 2 VALUE1 VALUE2
       SYSREF &VALUE1 /* Allows modifying &ST1. */
       WRITENR WHERE DO YOU LIVE?
       READ
       SET &VALUE1 = &STR(&SYSDVAL)
       RETURN CODE(0)
END
```

The above example goes through the following sequence:

a. Set &ST1 with a default value in the MAIN clist.
b. Call the STATE subprocedure passing the variable name ST1.
c. The subprocedure assigns the variable name of &ST1 to &VALUE1. SYSREF passes a variable value (not the variable name) changed by the subprocedure back to the main clist. Therefore, SYSREF variables are potentially GLOBAL in scope—beware!
d. Reset the value of &ST1 to the user's choice.
e. Return to the main clist and write the new value of &ST1.

Keep these points in mind when doing this:

- The subprocedure often uses a different variable than the main clist for holding a main clist's variable name.
- Using ampersands in a SYSCALL statement means passing the value, not the name, of the variable.
- Subprocedure variables are not accessible by the main or nested clists unless using GLOBAL or NGLOBAL.

2. See the above discussion on PROC for more on SYSREF.

3. A WRITE or SET statement uses the passed operand values.

4. Using the CODE operand of RETURN stores the subprocedure's return code in the control variable &LASTCC.

5. END marks the end of the subprocedure and returns to the main clist. Else, display the message *END OF FILE ON CLIST INPUT OCCURRED BEFORE ALL PROC STATEMENTS WERE CLOSED.*

Other Considerations

These are additional guidelines for creating subprocedures:

1. The following are nonzero return codes given when using subprocedures:
   508—Cannot find subprocedure (check the label).
   512—RETURN has invalid operand.
   572 or 576—Cannot find variable used in SYSREF statement (check SYSCALL operands).
2. Do not use GOTOs in a subprocedure for branching to another clist or subprocedure.
3. ATTN or ERROR sequences in subprocedures follow the same syntax and rules as sequences in a main clist with these exceptions:

   - Do not nest ATTN or ERROR sequences.
   - An error or attention sequence in the main clist may invoke a subprocedure. A subprocedure used this way must have only one TSO statement. Once completing the TSO command, processing begins with the next statement in the main clist after the one where ATTN was pressed. In any case, the attention or error sequence "sleeps" until the subprocedure ends, regardless if the subprocedure uses an error or attention sequence.
   - ERROR routines must use a RETURN statement for exiting to the statement following the error in the main clist.

Here is an example of ATTN routine invoking a subprocedure:

```
CONTROL MSG MAIN
ATTN DO
  SYSCALL BAD
END
MAIN100: -
SET &ST1 = &STR(IDAHO)
SYSCALL STATE ST1 OTH2
  IF &LASTCC = 0 THEN WRITE SUBPROCEDURE WORKED
STATE: PROC 2 VALUE1 VALUE2
        SYSREF &VALUE1
        WRITE WHERE DO YOU LIVE?
        READ /* IF Press ATTN here, then BAD executes. */
        /* Next statement (SET) executes after BAD */
        /* if pressing ATTN during READ. */
        SET &VALUE1 = &STR(&SYSDVAL)
        RETURN CODE(0)
```

```
END
 BAD:  PROC 0
       WRITE GOT HERE
       LISTC
       LISTDS MEMO.TEXT MEMBERS /* NEVER
       EXECUTES*/
END
```

4. Main clist CONTROL statements also "sleep" while processing a subprocedure. Subprocedures may use CONTROL statements that are in effect while they are processing.

5. To pass a subprocedure a variable with blanks, enclose the variable with the &STR function. &STR can also retain other special characters.

```
MAIN_100: -
SET &ST1 = &STR(NEW YORK)     /*String with blank.*/
SYSCALL STATE &STR(ST1) OTH2    /*Retain blank.*/
  IF &LASTCC = 0 THEN WRITE SUBPROCEDURE WORKED
  WRITE &ST1
STATE: PROC 2 VALUE1 VALUE2
       SYSREF &VALUE1
       WRITENR WHERE DO YOU LIVE?
       READ
       SET &VALUE1 = &STR(&SYSDVAL)
       RETURN CODE(0)
END
```

6. Keep track of subprocedure variables with a variable "scorecard." The next example uses one.

Example

This example shows a smaller version of the TSO5COM clist from earlier chapters now with a subprocedure.

(SUB1 C CLIST)

```
PROC 0 CTEST
/*****************************************************/
/* Name of Clist: SUB_1C                              */
/* Function: List or delete a file using subprocedure*/
/*****************************************************/
IF &CTEST = CTEST THEN CONTROL CONLIST LIST SYMLIST-
MSG
```

```
  ELSE CONTROL NOCONLIST NOSYMLIST NOCONLIST NOLIST MSG
/************************************************/
/* MAIN_100: - Main Menu - prompts user for selection*/
/************************************************/
MAIN_100: -
  WRITE  *****************************************
  WRITE * The following options are available:        *
  WRITE * 1 - List an Existing File                    *
  WRITE * 2 - Delete an Existing File                  *
  WRITE  *****************************************
  WRITENR Please Enter your choice (1-2 only):
/************************************************/
/* VALID_110: Validate Choices and obtain dataset    */
/*            name.                                  */
/************************************************/
VALID_110: -
  READ OPT
    IF &OPT LT 1 and &OPT GT 2 THEN GOTO MAIN_100
    IF &DATATYPE(&OPT) NE NUM THEN GOTO MAIN_100
    IF &OPT = 1 THEN SET &PARAM1 = LIST
    ELSE IF &OPT = 2 THEN SET &PARAM1 = DELETE
  WRITE Quotes are NOT needed for your datasets.
  WRITE Enter the name of the dataset to &PARAM1.
    READ
      SET &DSET = &STR(&SYSDVAL)
/************************************************/
/* CALL_200: - calls subprocedure if dataset exists  */
/************************************************/
CALL_200: -
  IF &SYSDSN(&DSET) = OK THEN DO
     SYSCALL SUB1 &STR(&DSET) PARAM1 COMMENT /*SUB+
     PROCEDURE*/
      SET &RCD = &LASTCC
        IF &RCD = 0 THEN WRITE &PARAM1 SUCCESSFUL
             ELSE WRITE UNABLE TO &PARAM1
  END
  ELSE WRITE &SYSDSN(&DSET)
  EXIT
/************************************************/
/* SUB1:  The subprocedure that lists or deletes a   */
/*        dataset.                                   */
/*        Dataset Name  Option                       */
/* Main:  &DSET         &PARAM1                      */
```

```
50. /* SUB1:   &DS              &OPE1                         */
51. /*********************************************************/
52. SUB1: PROC 2 DS OPE1
53.         SYSREF OPE1
54.         &OPE1 &DS
55.         SET &RC = &LASTCC
56.       RETURN CODE(&RC)
57. END
```

Explanation. An explanation by line number follows.

37–44. If the dataset exists, then call subprocedure SUB1 passing the name of the dataset and TSO command. Write a status message based on the subprocedure's return code (from the RETURN statement.) If the dataset does not exist, then list the message from control variable &SYSDSN.

45–51. This is an example of a subprocedure variable "scorecard," which I strongly recommend.

52–57. Subprocedure SUB1 does a TSO operation on a specific dataset and gives a return code to the main clist.

This ends the clist overview started in Chapter 3. The concepts presented in this chapter: nested clists, global variables, and subprocedures are the keys to building powerful clist systems. Chapter 9 shows how to build full-screen applications with the more sophisticated data validation capabilities of ISPF (Interactive System Productivity Facility).

SUGGESTED READINGS

Elston, Jay, 1982. Clist Esoterica—Advanced Examples. *SHARE 59 Proceedings*, pp. 1857–65.

Gehani, Narain, 1985. *C: An Advanced Introduction*. Rockville, Md.: Computer Science Press.

IBM Corporation, 1988. *INFO/SYSTEM Database*. Various notes.

IBM Corporation, 1980. *OS/VS2 TSO Command Language Reference*. GC28-0646.

IBM Corporation, 1980. *OS/VS2 TSO Terminal User's Guide*. GC28-0645.

IBM Corporation, 1987. *TSO Extensions Clists*. SC28-1304.

Lee, J. A. N., and A. Ralston, 1983. Subroutine, in *Encyclopedia of Computer Science and Engineering*. Anthony Ralston and Edwin D. Reilly Jr. (eds.) New York: Van Nostrand Reinhold, pp. 1454–1455.

9

Building Applications with ISPF

MVS, VM, and VSE programmers can take advantage of the Interactive System Productivity Facility, or ISPF. (From 1974 to 1980 called Structured Program Facility and from 1980 to 1982 System Productivity Facility. Both products are also called SPF.) This product allows programmers to easily and quickly develop interactive applications. Features include data entry validation, help screens, tutorials, dynamic program creation, and simple database transactions. The chapter emphasizes developing ISPF applications with clists rather than programs in COBOL or other languages. It reviews important ISPF concepts and then builds a sample application. Howard Fosdick's *Using IBM's ISPF Dialog Manager Under MVS, VM, and VSE,* published by Van Nostrand Reinhold, is a more complete review of ISPF. All discussed commands and user guides are for ISPF Version 2 Release 3. (The system variable ZENVIR's value tells the ISPF version at your site.)

WHAT IS ISPF?

ISPF offers the following features:

- A consistent interface across various operating systems. Developing your dialogs with REXX or compiled programs provides some degree of portability.
- Saving user- or dialog-generated variable and table values for future dialog sessions or other dialogs.
- Device-independent panel design with displayed panels adapting automatically to terminal size.
- Services (such as Library Access) for easily performing system utility tasks using dialogs.

Other capabilities will become clear with the following review of ISPF services. The clist language is a good match for building ISPF applications. Taking advantage of this requires a good understanding of available ISPF services and the parts of an ISPF application. To build full-screen applications or DIALOGS requires using ISPF Dialog Manager services. These include:

- *Display services* oversees the input/output processing on full-screen *panels*.
- *Table services* coordinates the adding, modifying, deleting and saving of data into a two-dimensional array or *table*.
- *Variable services* manages user-generated and system variables between and within dialogs.
- *File Tailoring (skeleton) services* generates programs used for foreground or background (batch) processing.
- *Message* and other services controls the dialog's help and tutorial panels and also processes any dialog messages.

In addition to Dialog Manager services, ISPF has a sample dialog called *Program Development Facility*, or PDF. PDF provides most of the capabilities of TSO commands and JCL utilities but in a full-screen format. This includes editing/browsing data, foreground compiling and testing of programs, and other dataset operations. Chapter 10 takes a closer look of PDF.

Components

This part examines the components of an ISPF dialog.

Dialog

A *dialog* (or application from now on) is a full-screen interactive application using programs or clists for managing a set of panels processed in a certain order. It also provides continuous two-way communications between the user and the computer during the dialog's run. Let us later return to what is a dialog after reviewing its components. Tables, messages, and file tailoring (skeletons) do not need to be present in an application (dialog).

Function

A *function* is a clist or program managing an ISPF dialog by selecting which panels and other ISPF services to process. Using a program or REXX (starting with ISPF Version 3) means good application portability to another operating system using ISPF.

Panels

Each panel an application uses needs a *panel definition*. Panel definitions include how to display or process a panel and do not need recompiling. Use your favorite editor to change easily a panel definition. Once defined, any ISPF dialog can use a panel. A menu selection or other user input decides which panels and ISPF dialog manager services to invoke. These are five different types of panels:

- *Selection or menu panels*—Executes a specified dialog, clist, or program based on the user's menu selection.
- *Data entry panels*—Captures and processes user input (such as userid or name of dataset).
- *Data display panels*—Lists information that users cannot change. (Such as a screen verifying a report selection.) This category often includes tutorial or help panels.
- *Table display panels*—Lists the contents of a selected table.
- *Tutorial or help panels*—Provides both context-sensitive information on a chosen feature and a complete tutorial on an application. They are often considered a special type of data display panel: this is a read-only panel.

Variables

Temporary (just for the current dialog session) or permanent (saved for future ISPF sessions) variables allow customization of dialog processing and pass information between dialog components.

An ISPF session places variables into a *pool*, which is a group of related variables. ISPF searches these pools when processing variables in a panel or another dialog component. There are three types of pools available to a dialog:

1. *Function pool*. Stores *function variables*, which a dialog function such as a clist or a program uses. (Clist variables are automatically available as dialog [function] variables while program variables must be explicitly defined.) Other functions cannot access these variables unless put in a shared pool. Do not use global or clist control variables in a dialog—instead work with the equivalent ISPF system variable.
2. *Shared pool*. Stores *shared variables* that are available to dialogs using the same application id (of one to four characters). The "Invoking a Dialog" part of the chapter further explains application ids. Variables in a menu (selection) panel are available to other dialog functions because a shared or profile pool stores them.
3. *Application or profile pool*. Permanently stores *profile variables* available for future ISPF sessions. Automatically places saved variables in a user's

profile dataset at the end of an ISPF session. At the start of the next session for that dialog, ISPF recalls the stored values.

ISPF dialog variables are one of two types—*user-generated* and *system-generated* (Z variables.) Variable names are up to eight characters (for TSO/E Version 1 Release 4 and later) with variable values up to 32,767 bytes. Variable names starting with an ampersand says perform symbolic substitution while those starting with a Z are *system variables* (so, do not start your dialog variables with Z). More on system or Z variables later.

Messages

ISPF offers a variety of informational, warning, and error messages that you can specify their content (message text including symbolic substitution), frequency of appearance (such as on getting errors, pressing a PF key, or filling a field), and display location (location in a panel, which panels). *Message defintions* are the means for doing this.

Tables

As mentioned earlier, tables are two-dimensional arrays holding related data. Once created, a table may exist just for the current session (temporary) or future ISPF sessions (permanent). Like panels, other dialogs can use an existing table. Tables often provide the most headaches for beginning ISPF users.

File Tailoring (Skeletons)

A *file-tailoring skeleton* (also called just *skeleton*) is a dataset containing a template of a clist, program, or JCL. User input decides which statements the final version includes and supplies the values for dynamic symbolic substitution, then saves the generated program, clist, or JCL into a temporary or permanent dataset for either foreground or background processing. Skeletons are an underutilized feature of ISPF Dialog Manager.

Now back to the question "what is a dialog?" A dialog is a hierarchical structure containing at least a function and a panel. Figure 9-1 shows a possible design for the CUSTOMER database presented in earlier chapters. This is identical to the design of the CUSTOMER database application of Chapter 8, that was a main clist invoking one of four other nested clists for processing and then returning for displaying a confirmation message. Additional features are a HELP panel accessible from the MENU panel, using full-screen panels for reading required operand values (with associated data validations) and listing the queried record on

Figure 9-1. Hierarchical Design for CUSTOMER Database

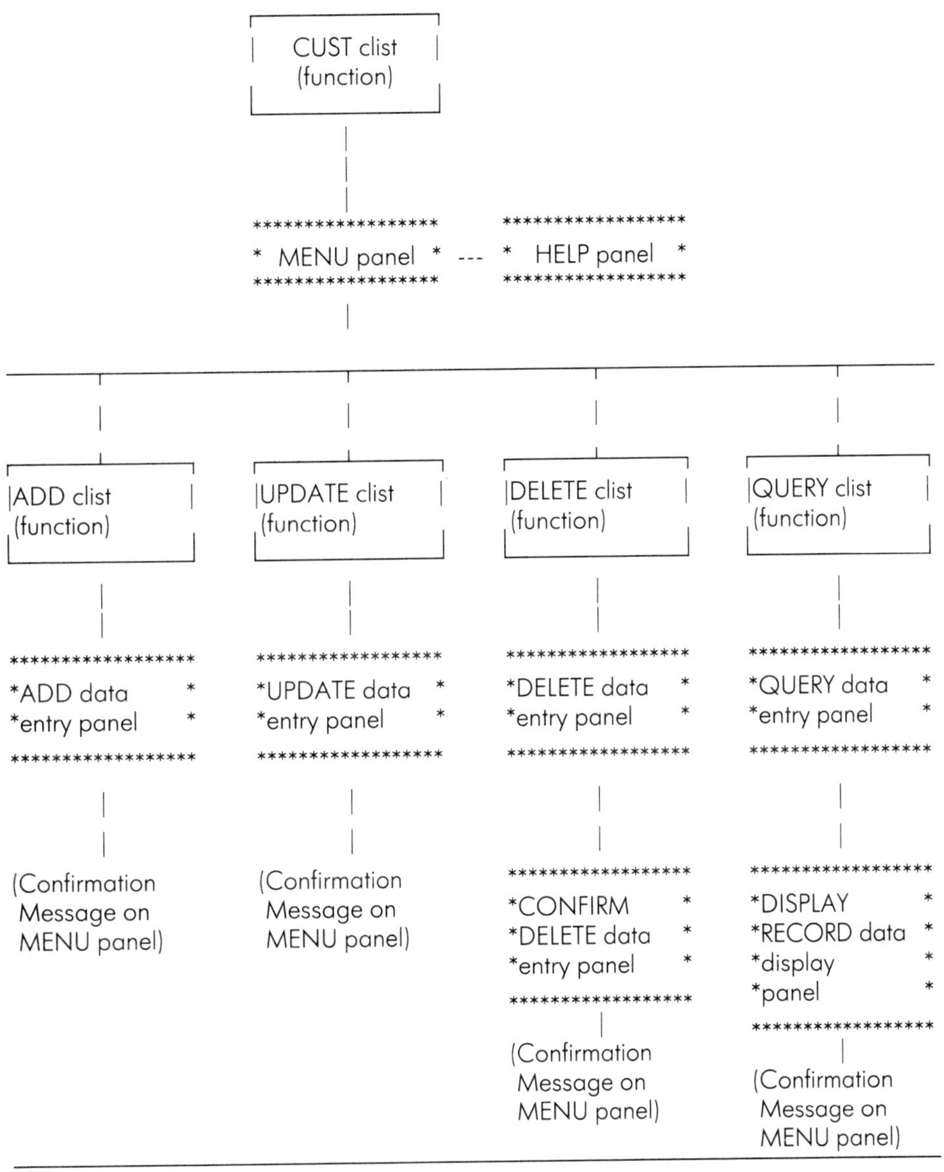

a data display (read only) panel. Optional features could be using ISPF table services instead of TSO EDIT, and adding more messages or HELP panels.

Consider these guidelines when developing an ISPF dialog:

1. If your company has a standard name and numbering scheme for Dialog Manager components, then use it. Otherwise, create one, such as three or four letters signifying the application id followed by component number and the first letter of the component type. In MXY100P, 100 is the first panel (P) in the MXY application. Other areas for standardization are panel design, message format, skeleton use, invoking an application, error handling, use of help panels, table use, variable names, and enabling of split screens in the dialogs.

2. This is one strategy for creating ISPF applications:
   a. *Application (dialog) planning/design*
      - Develop application specifications. (What does each component do? List data validations, associated messages, related components, and sample format.) This can be as formal as needed. If the application is for end-users, then having user input throughout the entire development cycle is important.
      - Develop application design (flow diagram including a name/numbering scheme).
   b. *Develop the application*
      - Create fully working versions of all application components such as functions, panels, and messages.
      - Develop in-program documentation and a first draft of user's guide.
      - The result is an application ready for testing.
   c. *Test the application*
      - Programmers test application from TSO or ISPF, or using the ISPF Dialog Test Facility (option 7 in PDF).
      - Peers test application (i.e., response time, error handling, efficiency, CPU utilization).
      - Users test application (i.e., needed features, panel format, response time, adequacy of help and application tutorial).
   d. *Modify the application*
      - Add necessary fixes and enhancements to an application resulting from test period comments. Have a demo for testers to show the removal of bugs or the adding of enhancements. Use a shorter test period if necessary.
      - Complete user's guide and in-program documentation.
   e. *Implement the application*
      - Move into production libraries.

- Notify users of availability. Also distribute the user's guide and (if possible) provide training.

f. Maintain the application

- Review after installing new ISPF releases to see which new features (if any) future versions of the application can take advantage of. For ISPF Version 3 and later sites, consider converting the application of CUA (Common User Access) interface.
- Periodically meet with key users for their reaction to the application and to plan scheduling of future enhancements.
- Consider porting the application to other operating systems.

STARTING TO BUILD ISPF APPLICATIONS

This section supplies the information needed for building sound intermediate-level ISPF applications (dialogs). It includes reviewing the statements used for creating and changing each dialog component.

Invoking an Application

This subsection reviews the three steps for successfully invoking and processing an ISPF application (dialog):

- Allocating application and system libraries.
- Invoking ISPF and the application.
- Executing the remaining application by having a function (clist) invoke other ISPF services.

Also examined are the CONTROL service and ISPF system variables.

Allocations

Chapter 3 used a TSO ALLOCATE command for concatenating personal and system clist datasets to a preassigned ddname or filename or SYSPROC. This same concept also applies when allocating the datasets needed to run an application (dialog). The following is a sample allocation. (Your application may not need all of these.)

SAMPLE ALLOCATION

```
1. FREE F(SYSPROC ISPPLIB ISPMLIB ISPSLIB ISPTLIB -
   ISPPROF -
```

```
 2.  ISPSFILE ISPTABL ISPLLIB)
 3.  ALLOC F(SYSPROC) DA('PROD1.MYLIB.CLIST' -
 4.                     'SYS1.SYSTEM.CLIST') SHR REUSE
 5.  ALLOC F(ISPPLIB) DA('PROD1.APP1.ISPPLIB') SHR REUSE
 6.  ALLOC F(ISPMLIB) DA('PROD1.APP1.ISPMLIB' -
 7.                     'SYS1.ISPMLIB') SHR REUSE
 8.  ALLOC F(ISPSLIB) DA('PROD1.APP1.ISPSLIB') SHR REUSE
 9.  ALLOC F(ISPTLIB) DA('PROD1.APP1.ISPTLIB') SHR REUSE
10.  ALLOC F(ISPPROF) DA('PROD1.APP1.PROFILE') SHR REUSE
11.  ALLOC F(ISPFILE) DA('PROD1.APP1.ISPFILE') SHR REUSE
12.  ALLOC F(ISPTABL) DA('PROD1.APP1.ISPTABL') SHR REUSE
13.  ALLOC F(ISPLLIB) DA('PROD1.APP1.ISPLLIB') SHR REUSE
```

Explanation. An explanation of the above sample allocation by statement number follows.

1–2. Frees files if now allocated. You can place any of these statements in the startup clist that executes when you log on to the computer or in a separate clist that also invokes the application.

3–4. Allocates clists (functions) used by ISPF. As in any ISPF library concatenation, place the application library before a system library. (Usually there are many system libraries allocated.)

5. Allocates the panel *library* (dataset) used by the application. Usually many system panel libraries are also allocated.

6–7. Allocate the application and system message libraries.

8. Allocates the skeleton input library if the application uses ISPF file-tailoring skeleton services.

9. Allocate the table input library if the application uses ISPF table services. System, not application tables, usually use this library. You can also use it for table output.

10. Allocate the user's ISPF profile dataset for storing the permanent ISPF variable pools recalled by later ISPF sessions.

11. Because ISPF automatically allocates a temporary file-tailoring output library when using file-tailoring services, this statement is not required. However, you may also specify a temporary or permanent library.

12. Allocate the table output dataset. It also can be allocated dynamically and used for table input. Application rather than system tables are more likely to use this.

13. Allocate a load library.

These are additional guidelines in creating ISPF dataset allocations:

1. You may have noted the common practice of the filename being the same as the last qualifier in the library name. This is usually true for system libraries as well.
2. A common beginner's problem is library concatenations. A concatenated library usually has a default block size of 3120 (or a multiple of 80), a fixed-block record format, and a logical record length of 80. However, panel and skeleton output libraries can have larger record lengths. Always place first in the concatenation the library with the largest block size.

   A common problem is having libraries of different block sizes in the same concatenation. This usually results in a message about "I/O error in retrieving panel." Possible solutions are using variable-length record libraries and the BLKSIZE operand specifying the maximum block size lengths for libraries in a concatenation.
3. Do not use concatenated libraries with ISPTABL and ISPFILE.
4. Since ISPF Version 2 Release 3, the LIBDEF command is available for dynamically allocating application libraries and guarantees to search them before system libraries. You must process a LIBDEF before invoking ISPF. LIBDEF searches either for *datasets* (with the DATASET or EXCLDATA operand) or *ddnames* (with the LIBRARY or EXCLLIBR operand—this is not discussed further). A LIBDEF allocation exists only for an ISPF session unless overriden by another LIBDEF. Note entering just LIBDEF (no operands) removes an application allocation.

LIBDEF with the DATASET Operand. Using LIBDEF and the DATASET operand eliminates ALLOCATE statements (except uncataloged libraries) and may improve library search time. Here is the above allocation example using LIBDEF.

```
1.  ISPEXEC LIBDEF ISPPLIB DATASET ID('PROD1.APP1.ISPPLIB')
2.  ISPEXEC LIBDEF ISPMLIB DATASET ID('PROD1.APP1.ISPMLIB')
3.  ISPEXEC LIBDEF ISPSLIB DATASET ID('PROD1.APP1.ISPSLIB')
4.  ISPEXEC LIBDEF ISPTLIB DATASET ID('PROD1.APP1.ISPTLIB')
5.  ISPEXEC LIBDEF ISPFILE DATASET ID('PROD1.APP1.ISPFILE')
6.  ISPEXEC LIBDEF ISPTABL DATASET ID('PROD1.APP1.ISPTABL')
```

However, ALLOCATEs are still needed for the application function (tied to the SYSPROC concatenation), the user profile dataset (ISPROF), and system and other application libraries (more on this later). Here are the components of the above statements:

1. ISPEXEC This denotes an ISPF, not a TSO command. (Programs use instead CALL ISPLINK; this is the only way for accessing some ISPF statements.) ISPEXEC precedes all ISPF statements used by a clist in this chapter.

2. LIBDEF The ISPF service used.

3. ISPPLIB, etc. The library type of the allocated dataset.

4. DATASET ID is a library name not a ddname.

5. ID(libraryname) The application library to allocate. You can also allocate (concatenate) up to fifteen libraries. Once allocated, you can retrieve any specified panel in that library.

6. Other operands:
   a. COND Allocates an application library only if another one of the same type is not now allocated. The default is UNCOND, which allocates an application library even if another one is now allocated.
   b. EXCLDATA Allocates only cataloged application link libraries (i.e., those with a ddname of ISPLLIB) and eliminates using an ALLOCATE statement.

7. If using the following ddnames, YOU CAN STILL ALLOCATE (concatenate) up to fifteen other application libraries before the LIBDEF and system libraries:

   ISPPUSR Other application panel library.
   ISPMUSR Other application message library.
   ISPSUSR Other application skeleton input library.
   ISPFILU Other applications skeleton output library.
   ISPTUSR Other applications table input library.
   ISPTABU Other applications table output library.
   ISPLUSR Other application link libraries.

Invoking ISPF Applications

After allocating the necessary libraries, you need to invoke ISPF and the desired application. To do this, a clist either uses ISPSTART (if not in ISPF) or the SELECT command (if in ISPF). A menu (selection) panel can also do this. Here is a clist executing the correct command invoking an application based on &SYSISPF's value. &SYSISPF is a clist control variable returning either ACTIVE (in ISPF) or NOT ACTIVE (not in ISPF).

```
IF &SYSISPF NE ACTIVE THEN DO
  ISPSTART PANEL(APP@PRIM) NEWAPPL(APP1) OPT(&OPT1)
END
ELSE DO
  ISPEXEC SELECT PANEL(APP@PRIM) NEWAPPL(APP1) OPT(&OPT)
END
```

Both commands use these operands.

1. CMD(clistname) Invokes ISPF and a selected function (clist) for an application. A percent before the clist name in a SELECT command uses full-screen mode, while just the clist name uses line mode.
2. PANEL(panelname) Invokes ISPF and a specified panel. Use the OPT (option) operand for specifying an initial menu panel option. A clist symbolic variable can supply the value of OPT. The @PRIM part of the panel name commonly identifies a menu panel.
3. PGM(programname) Invokes ISPF and a function written in a compiled programming language. Use the PARM (parameters) for supplying parameters to a program function.
4. NEWAPPL(applicationname) Identifies a new application and creates the appropriate datasets. The above example prefixes the application id of APP1 to the general (APP1*PROF*) and edit (APP1*EDIT*) profile as well as the command table (APP1*CMDS*) members of the partitioned profile dataset.

Other ISPF Services Used by Applications

Once invoking ISPF and an application begins processing, then a function uses one or more of the following ISPF services. (An ISPEXEC precedes all of them.)

BROWSE	Browse a dataset.
CONTROL	Assign settings to an entire ISPF session.
DISPLAY	Show a panel or an associated message.
EDIT	Edit a dataset
FTxxxxx	File-tailoring services.
GETMSG	Retrieve a message and related information.
ISREDIT	PDF Edit Macros (see Chapter 10).
LMxxxxx	Library access services.
PQUERY	Retrieve information and settings of a panel (Version 2 Release 2 and later).
SELECT	Invoke a new application or other services.

SETMSG Set next message.
TBxxxxx Table services.
VGET Retrieve pool or profile variables
VPUT Write pool or profile variables.

Later in the chapter is more on many of these services.

ISPF CONTROL Command

Like the clist CONTROL statement, the ISPF CONTROL operands used decide the overall characteristics for an ISPF session. (Unless issuing another ISPF CONTROL command.) The following are common uses of the CONTROL command.

1. ISPEXEC CONTROL DISPLAY setting
   setting = SAVE Saves information on the current displayed screen. To avoid problems, keep track of the number of SAVEd displays. Otherwise, the application abends or displays a message about an issuing a SAVE without a matching restore.
   RESTORE Retrieves settings on a screen stored with a SAVE command.
   LOCK Temporarily locks the keyboard to display a panel. The next panel or message unlocks the keyboard.
   LINE Switches between full-screen and line mode. An integer *line number* specifying the line (row) number where to begin line mode can be placed after LINE or SM.
   SM Allows TSO Session Manager to take over for the next non-full-screen command.
   REFRESH Clears and redisplays the current screen. Use CONTROL DISPLAY LINE not REFRESH for returning successfully to full screen mode.
2. ISPEXEC CONTROL SPLIT state
   state = ENABLE Enables split-screen mode (Press PF 2 or PF 14).
   DISABLE Disables split-screen mode unless in split-screen mode when issuing this command. It is a matter of choice to turn this on or off for an ISPF session. A good compromise is disabling split-screen mode as the default (So novices with roving fingers do not get into trouble.) but provide an operand for experienced users to enable this feature:

```
PROC 0 SPLIT
IF &SPLIT = SPLIT THEN ISPEXEC CONTROL SPLIT -
ENABLE
  ELSE ISPEXEC CONTROL SPLIT DISABLE
```

3. ISPEXEC CONTROL ERRORS mode
   mode = CANCEL Ends the ISPF application session when getting a return code greater than 12. Then display an appropriate error message panel and write a message to the session log. *This is the default.*
   RETURN On getting a return code greater than 12, the application decides what to do. Usually you write no message to the system log. The system variable ZERRMSG stores the error.
4. ISPEXEC CONTROL NODISPL key—Affects only the next panel.
   key = ENTER Does not display the next panel and acts as if a user pressed ENTER. *This is the default.*
   END Same as ENTER but acts as if a user pressed END.
5. ISPEXEC CONTROL NOCMD For the next panel only, ignore any user input.

ISPF System Variables

As with clist system variables, you can retrieve and often modify the values stored in ISPF system variables. As mentioned earlier, ISPF system variables begin with the letter Z and the function, shared, or profile pools store them. An ISPEXEC VGET command obtains shared and profile system variable values and an ISPEXEC VPUT command overwrites them (if allowed). Note that many ISPF system variables duplicate clist system variables because *ISPF panels cannot access clist system variables*. There are over fifty system variables available for your use. The following are the most common system variables used.

Miscellaneous. A VGET command can get, but a user *cannot* change, the following variables. Most of these are available for all ISPF versions. Also listed are *typical values* for many of these variables.

Z	A null variable.
ZAPPLID	Application name. Value—*ISR*.
ZDBCS	DBCS characters supported? Value—*YES* or *NO*.
ZENVIR	ISPF version, type of MVS (MVS or MVS/XA), TSO mode (TSO or BATCH). Value—*ISPF 2.3MVS/XA TSO*.
ZDATE	Current date. Other system variables produce dates in other formats (e.g., ZJDATE returns julian date) or parts (e.g., ZMONTH gives current month). Value—*89/04/03*.
ZLANG	Language used by ISPF application (Version 2 Release 3 and later). Values are up to eight characters.
ZPREFIX	Default prefix (usually your userid which *ZUSER* stores). Value—*GG08*.

ZSCREENx	Screen length (ZSCREEND) or width (ZSCREENW). Values—*32* (ZCREEND), *80* (ZSCREENW).
ZSPLIT	Split screen enabled or disabled? Value—*YES* or *NO*.
ZTEMPx	File-tailoring output file name. x may be F or N. Value—*GROO.SPFTEMP1.CNTL*.
ZTIME	Current time (hh : mm). Value—*08 : 04*.

A VGET command can retrieve and a user can modify the following system variables.

ZISPFRC	Return code from a dialog started with ISPSTART (Version 2 Release 3 and later).
ZKEYS	The number of PF keys. Value—*24*.
ZPF01–ZPF24	The values of each PF key. Value—*END*.
ZTERM	Terminal type. Value—*3277A*.
ZSCROLLx	Scroll values (x may be A, N or D).
ZTDTOP	Current top row for a table. There are thirteen other "ZTD" system variables available for tables.
ZERRMSG	The error message identifier.
ZERRHM	The help panel associated with an error message.

HELP PANEL VARIABLES

ZHTOP	The top panel name. Value—*ISR00003*.
ZUP	The name of previous or parent panel.
ZCONT	The name of next panel.
ZIND	Index panel flag. Value—*Yes* or *No*.
ZINDEX	The name of top index panel. Value—*ISR91000*

MENU PANEL VARIABLES

ZPARENT	The name of previous menu panel.
ZPRIM	Primary menu panel flag. Value—*YES* or *NO*
ZCMD	Selection/command input variable.
ZSEL	Selection/command input variable up to the first period.

If enabled, PDF option 7.3 (Dialog Test - Variables.), displays and modifies many system variables.

Panels

Most of a dialog's processing takes place in the panel rather than a function. This section reviews (1) invoking a panel from a clist, (2) panel components and statements, (3) menu panels, and (4) help panels.

Invoking Panels

There are two ways to invoke an ISPF panel from a clist:

1. ISPEXEC DISPLAY PANEL(panelname)
   Panelname The panel name (up to eight characters) which is a member of one of the allocated ISPPLIB datasets.

   Other useful DISPLAY operands include:

   MSG (message identifier) Retrieves and show messages on a panel.

   CSRPOS(cursor position) Sets the position of the cursor in the panel with a default of 1. Only using the control variable .CSRPOS overrides this value.
2. ISPEXEC SELECT PANEL(panelname) Invokes another dialog while already in one. The PANEL operand says the dialog begins with a panel. Earlier mentioned was using the OPT operand for passing a value to a menu panel.

Starting to Build Panels

Before invoking a panel, a valid panel definition in a member of an ISPPLIB dataset must exist. A panel definition uses two to seven sections. Note each section name begins with a right parenthesis [i.e.,)] and starts in the first column.

)ATTR This optional section sets or overrides the panel's *attribute characters* or *attribute bytes,* marking the start or end of a field. A *field* is the area between attribute bytes used for displaying a dialog variable value/text or getting/holding a user-entered dialog variable value. Associated with these bytes are features affecting a field's processing such as justification, type of variable (input/output), color, and intensity.

)BODY Along with END is a *required* section (unless no ATTR section). This specifies how the panel appears to the user, including input and output fields and associated attribute bytes.

)MODEL Used for displaying records in a table. It selects which rows from the table for displaying in a continuous format (such as a list of names and addresses).

)INIT Although not needed, this invaluable section decides the initial values of fields (including retrieving or updating variables from shared or profile pools) and performs any other necessary processing *before* displaying a panel.

)REINIT Similar to INIT but performs needed processing before *re*displaying a panel (such as showing a message, a new value, or redisplaying a table). REINIT is not discussed in detail.

)PROC Does the necessary processing (such as data validation and transformation) *after* displaying a panel. It uses many of the same statements as INIT.

)END A *required* section ending the panel definition. (So no statements should appear after it.)

The following is a typical data entry panel:

```
)ATTR
)BODY
% ----------------------------------------------(APP10P) -
+                       ADD CUSTOMER+
+
+
+ NAME:_NAME                          +
+
+ COMPANY:_COMPANY                    +
+
+ ADDRESS:_ADDRESS                                        +
+
+ PHONE:_PHONE              +
&MSGFLD1
% ---------------------------------------------------------
)INIT
 .CURSOR = NAME
)PROC
 VER (&NAME, NONBLANK)
 VER (&COMPANY, NONBLANK)
 VER (&ADDRESS, NONBLANK)
)END
```

This example adds records to a customer database. It has a null ATTR section. The INIT section initially sets cursor to the NAME (&NAME) field. The PROC section verifies if three of the fields had something entered into them. Let us now take a closer look at the ATTR, INIT, BODY, and PROC sections and their associated statements.

)ATTR—Setting Attribute Bytes. In the above example, you may have noticed the percent (%), plus (+) sign, and the underscore (_). These are three predefined attribute bytes or *attribute characters* associated with a set of characteristics affecting the processing of a field. Three common characteristics include:

1. TYPE(value) *The type of field*:
   value = TEXT A *protected* (user cannot overwrite) field that may contain

dialog variables all prefixed with *ampersands*. The displayed panel lists the dialog variable value.

INPUT An *unprotected* (user can overwrite) field that precedes the dialog variables and thus needs no ampersand. The displayed panel shows any initial variable value and assigns all user input to a dialog variable. *This is the default.*

OUTPUT Similar to INPUT but is a *protected* field used to display dialog variables.

All other ATTR statement values can be symbolic variables except TYPE.

2. INTENS(intensity) The brightness of a displayed field—HIGH (very bright), LOW (normal), NON (no display). Any type of field can use these in Version 2 Release 3 and later. (Earlier releases could only use NON for unprotected fields.)
3. COLOR(color) The color of a field (color terminals only) color—BLUE, GREEN, PINK, TURQ (turquoise), RED, WHITE, YELLOW.

These are the default attribute characters and their properties:

% Protected text type using high intensity and white.
\+ Protected text type using low intensity and blue.
_ Unprotected input type using high intensity and red.

You can easily change the characters tied to these attributes:

```
)ATTR DEFAULT(y+*)
```

which replaces % with y and _ with *; the plus sign remains unchanged.

These are other additional attribute characteristics you can specify. *Use only with INPUT- or OUTPUT-type fields*:

1. CAPS(state) Puts a field in upper- or lowercase.
   state = ON Places all fields in uppercase before displaying or assigning them to a dialog variable. *This is the default.*
   OFF If the clist has a CONTROL NOCAPS or CONTROL ASIS active, then display or assign all fields to a dialog variable in their current case.
2. JUST(justification) Justifies a displayed field. Justification = LEFT (the default for most fields), RIGHT, or ASIS (no change and retains leading blanks when assigned to a dialog variable).
3. SKIP(state) (Use with TEXT or OUTPUT (if protected) type fields only) The cursor automatically tabs past a protected field to the next

unprotected field. State = ON enables this feature, OFF disables this feature, *this is the default.*

Place new attribute characters on a separate line.

```
)ATTR
# TYPE(OUTPUT) INTENS(HIGH) SKIP(ON)
```

Gets the user's attention and prohibits overwriting a field. The cursor tabs past this field to the next unprotected field.

```
)ATTR
¬ TYPE(INPUT) INTENS(NON) CAPS(OFF)
```

Gets a password field value in its current case and does not display it.

)BODY—The text and format of the panel.

To discuss the components of the BODY section, we must review the system-supplied parts of a panel:

1. *Messages* *Short* messages quickly tell a user information or an error. You can place them in the right-hand corner of the top line of a panel. Place *longer* messages on the panel's third line. (This is why usually you leave the *third line blank.*)
2. *Title* Uses the first line of the panel; typically holds a unique title briefly stating the panel's purpose. (This rather than a panel name is how most users identify a panel.) Use the last 26 characters of the first lines for displaying unimportant information and short messages.
3. *User input* This is usually (but not always) on the panel's second line. User input may be a valid menu option or a command field (which usually is the system variable &ZCMD.) Some panels (such as those using EDIT or BROWSE) lists a changeable scroll value.
4. *The last line* Usually blank so that a user can split a screen and quickly see the panel bottom.

These are some other guidelines in panel design:

1. Set as many default field values as possible to reduce user typing.
2. Consider standardizing panel format at your site: (a) panel titles, (b) panel identifiers, (c) field names, (d) use of short and long messages, (e) menu and

help panels, (f) panel field pointers (such as NAME ===>_NAME), and (g) use of upper- and lowercase.

3. Make the panel visually appealing;
   a. Using 4 to 10 fields per panel with plenty of white space between them (about 18 to 20 lines per panel).
   b. If possible, line up the start of fields:
   ```
   + NAME              ===> _NAME         +
   + SEX               ===> _SEX+
   + PLACE OF BIRTH     ==> _PLACE              +
   ```
   c. Place any detailed explanation on a field's values in a help panel.
   d. Place command/option input near the top of the screen and less important fields near the bottom.
   e. Use common sense when highlighting or putting color in a panel to flag a user to important text or needed fields.
   f. Use uppercase for screen titles; capitalize other important words and menu options.

The Beebe reference has many good ideas on panel design. The body consists of a combination of three parts:

1. Attribute characters determine the start and end of a field and its associated characteristics.
2. Fields and field values capture user input for assigning to dialog variables for displaying system or dialog variables values. Remember dialog variables in a TEXT type field require ampersands but INPUT type fields do not (e.g., INPUT—NAME:_NAME and TEXT—+ &TITLE +).
3. Other characters (such as text, or graphics.)

Further discussion on the BODY section without an understanding of the components and statements of the INIT and the PROC sections is pointless. So, more on the BODY section is presented when reviewing these other panel sections.

Control Variables. The INIT, REINIT, and PROC sections can use CONTROL VARIABLES for deciding how a field or panel processes. Control variables names range from two to eight characters and are prefixed by a period (.). Some common control variables are:

.ALARM Beeps at the user when the panel is displayed. For example,

```
.ALARM = YES   enables beeping
.ALARM = NO    disables beeping
```

.ATTR Changes the attribute characteristics for a field "on the fly." How long the attribute settings are in effect depends on in which section it appears—multiple redisplays if in INIT (unless overridden by another ATTR setting in the REINIT section) and only one redisplay if in a REINIT section. Also use .ATTRCHAR for associating a character with a setting applying to all fields. .ATTR cannot be a value (the right side) in an assignment statement. (These are discussed later.)

`.ATTR (&NAME) = 'INTENS(ASIS) CAPS(OFF)'`

Changes the intensity and caps values for the field &NAME.

`.ATTR (.CURSOR) = 'SKIP(OFF) COLOR(TURQ)'`

Changes the color and the automatic skip feature for the initial current position which affects .CURSOR.

.CURSOR Decides the field where the cursor appears on displaying (INIT) or redisplaying (REINIT) a panel. This overrides the DISPLAY command cursor setting. Also use .CSRPOS for setting the location of the cursor in a field. Table display panels use .CSRROW for selecting the table row (record) where the cursor appears. Place all three control variables on either side of an assignment statement. For example,

`.CURSOR = NAME`

Puts the cursor initially at the &NAME. (Place no ampersand in a .CURSOR assignment.)

.HELP Pressing PF1, PF13, or a key assigned the HELP command displays a selected help panel. For example,

`.HELP = JR2H` Display panel JR2H

.MSG Display a selected message after processing a panel. For example,

`.MSG = JR3111` Display message JR3111

.PFKEY Capture which PF key was pressed before processing a panel. Before displaying or redisplaying a panel, it has initially a null value.

`.PFKEY = 'PF03'`

Verifies if PF3 was pressed. (This does not work "as is," it must be part of an IF statement.)

.RESP Captures the type of user reply. The value is either ENTER (the usual reply) or END. (The user pressed RETURN or END.)

`.RESP = ENTER`

Used for conditional processing if giving a normal reply. (This does not work "as is"—it must be part of an IF statement.)

.TRAIL Saves the remainder after processing a TRUNC (truncate) function.

`&TWO = .TRAIL`

Places the remainder of a truncate operation in &TWO (shown later).

.ZVARS These are "dummy variables" later substituted with the variable names.

It is only important at this point that you should know what control variables are and the general functions of each one. Examples of many of these, including &TRAIL and .ZVARS, are later in the chapter.

)INIT—Initial Processing of a Panel. The INIT section has various statements that decide the initial panel processing. These statements may contain system variables, control statements, and built-in functions. (Similar to the function and syntax of clist built-in functions.) Both the REINIT and PROC sections use many of the same statements.

The most basic statement is ASSIGNMENT. An assignment statement has various forms:

```
&NAME = &NM          dialog variable = value
&NAME = ' '          dialog variable = blank
&CUR = .CSRPOS       dialog variable = control variable
.CURSOR = NAME       control variable = dialog variable
&KEY1 = PFK (1)      dialog variable = built-in function
```

Before further discussing statements used in the INIT section, let us look briefly at built-in functions. *Built-in functions* perform special operations, returning a result. The following is information about three commonly used built-in functions. (*Note:* There is usually a space between the function and the argument(s) in parentheses.)

PFKEY Retrieves the command associated with a PF key or a PF key associated with a command. For example, to get the command associated with a PF key:

```
&WHICHKY = PFK (24)
```

&WHICHKY stores the command tied to PF 24. The result is the command or blank is not found.

To get the PF key associated with a command.

```
&PRKEY = PFK (PRINT)
```

&PRKEY stores the PF key tied to the PRINT command. The result is PF01 to PF24 or blank (not found).

TRANS Assigns a value based on another variable's value. Use commas only for separating the pair of a possible valid value and the translated result. You may include 126 such pairs. For example,

```
&SEX = TRANS (&SX 1, MALE 2, FEMALE)—Assigns &SEX
              |  |       |                a value
              |  |       └─Translated     based on
              |  Valid     value for 1    &SX's
              |  value     stored in      current
              |  for &SX.  &SEX.          value.
              Variable to translate
```

or

```
&SEX = TRANS (&SX   1, MALE
                    2, FEMALE)
```

which is easier to read and maintain for long lists. Other valid arguments include MSG = message text for an unlisted value and * signifying all other values (left of comma) or do not translate (right of comma).

`&SEX = TRANS (&SX 1,MALE 2,FEMALE MSG = SX1000)`

Gives message if &SX is not 1 or 2

`&SEX = TRANS (&SX 1,MALE 2,FEMALE *,*)`

Do not translate if &SX is not 1 or 2.

TRUNC Assigns a dialog variable a substring of another dialog variable. Menu panels heavily use this for truncating user input. (An application also may nest built-in functions for truncating a translated dialog variable value.) Two formats are used. The second argument is either a number or unique character for identifying the length of the substring.

Format 1—Truncate specified number of characters.

`&NAME = TRUNC (&NM, 2)`

Assigns &NAME the first two characters of &NM's value. So Lowell becomes Lo.

Format 2—Truncate based on character location.

`&FINIT = TRUNC (&NM, '.')`

Assigns &FINIT &NM's value up to the period. Thus &FINIT stores the first initial of a name.

`&REST =.TRAIL`

Assigns &REST the rest of &NM. The following summarizes two additional statements used by the INIT, REINIT, and PROC sections.

IF Allows conditional processing. The syntax is

IF (var operator condition) action

var—dialog variable name

*operator**— = Equal ¬= Not equal,
> Greater than†, < Less than†
>= Greater than or equal†
<= Less than or equal†
¬> Not greater than†
¬< Not less than†

condition—Has various formats:

`IF (&AGE = 10,15)`

If &AGE equals 10 *or* 15.

`IF (.PFKEY = 'PF03' OR 'PF15')`

If PF3 *or* PF15 is pressed.

`IF (&AGE = 10) (&SEX = M)`

IF &AGE equals 10 *and* &SEX equals M.

* Can also use EQ, NE, GT, LT, GE, LE, LE, NG, and NL for ISPF Version 2 Release 3 and later. These cannot be in lowercase.

† ISPF Version 2 Release 3 and later.

action—An assignment statement(s) including control variables and built-in functions
`IF (&ANS = 'Y') &FLAG1 = 1`
or any valid statement(s) used by INIT, PROC, or REINIT sections (such as VER or VGET.)
`IF (&ANS1 = 'Y') VER (&ANS2,NONBLANK) --`
If &ANS equals Y then, &ANS2 must also have a value (more on VER later). Place *actions* on the same line as the IF statement or indent on the next line.
Multiple IFs—The IF statement is sensitive to indentations so carefully line up your multiple IFs. Otherwise, you may process the wrong statement. With ISPF Version 2 Release 3 and later, you can do the same thing with an ELSE statement.

Old Way

```
IF (&AUTO = "DOMESTIC") null condition
   IF (&ATYPE = "COMPACT")
      &CAR = "DC" action on separate line.
   IF (&ATYPE = "OTHER")
      &CAR = "DO"
IF (&AUTO = "FOREIGN")
&CAR = "I" action on same line.
```

New Way

```
IF (&AUTO = "DOMESTIC")
   IF (&ATYPE = "COMPACT")
      &CAR = "DC"
   IF (&ATYPE = "OTHER")
      &CAR = "DO"
ELSE
IF (&AUTO = "FOREIGN") &CAR = "I" IF must be-
under or to the left of ELSE.
```

VER Confirms if the user input matches a specified condition. The syntax is
VER (var, condition, other)
var—Dialog variable name.
condition—Only one operand per VER except NONBLANK.
The condition operands are

ALPHA Alphabetical characters (a–z in either case, @, $, and #.); *blanks do not meet this criterion.*

BIT Bit characters (0s or 1s)

DSNAME Confirms TSO dataset names.

ENUM Same as NUM plus decimals, commas, plus signs, negative number sign, leading but not trailing blanks.

HEX Valid hex characters (0–9, A–F)

LEN, operator, length Length of input for ISPF Release 2 Version 3 and later. See the IF statement listed earlier for valid operators. Length is a positive number up to five digits. You can also use a dialog variable.
VER (&N, LEN, GT, 5)
Checks if the length of &N is greater than 5.

LIST,value1. . .value2 Compares against values in a list.
VER (&Y, LIST, Y, N)
Is &Y Y or N?

NAME Verifies a valid PDS member name.

NONBLANK or **NB** Blank (no) input is not allowed and may be used with other operands (*if placed before them*).
VER (&Y, NONBLANK, ALPHA)
Required input is an alphanumeric value.

NUM numeric characters and blanks.

PICT,string Picture string (like COBOL.) *String* uses any or all of the following: A, alpha; C, any character; N or 9, numeric; X, hex.
VER (&SSN, PICT, 'NNN-NN-NNNN')
social security id.

The user input must match the length of the PICT string and cannot include trailing blanks. PICT strings can have special characters.

other—MSG (display message if not meeting a condition)
VER (&A, NONBLANK, MSG = IB02310)

Let's try to put everything together by reviewing a typical ISPF data entry panel and sections.

```
)ATTR
)BODY
%---------------PRINT FILE OPTIONS--------------(PE10P)--
+
+
+
+ 1. Do you want MAILING LABELS? ==> _YN+ (Y OR N)
+ 2. Number of Copies            ==> _COPY+ (1-99 )
+ 3. Mail Stop                   ==> _MS + (E.G. T-29)
+
% ------------------------------
%PF3/15 PREVIOUS PANEL                ENTER - NEXT PANEI
%PF4/16 EXIT APPLICATION              PF1/13 - HELP
)INIT
    .CURSOR = YN
```

```
   .ALARM = NO
   .HELP = PE10H
   &YN = N
   &COPY = 1
   &MS = T-22
   &PFKEYED = ' '
)PROC
   IF (.PFKEY = 'PF03' or 'PF15')
      &PFKEYED = 3
   IF (.PFKEY = 'PF04' or 'PF16')
      &PFKEYED = 4
   &COPY = TRUNC (&COPY,2)
   IF (&MS = 'T-28')
      &COPY = 10
      .ATTR (COPY) = 'TYPE(OUTPUT)'
   VER (&YN,LIST,Y,N)
   VER (&COPY,RANGE,1,99)
   VER (&MS,PICT,'A-NN')
)END
```

An application for printing ad hoc reports could use the above panel. Here are some of its features.

1. Body The title is highlighted (%). The panel also lists PF keys for exiting the application, looking at a previous panel, or displaying a help panel. *Remember the length of an input field does not include the attribute bytes.*
2. INIT The following takes place in the INIT section:
   a. Set the initial cursor to &YN.
   b. Do not sound an alarm when displaying the panel.
   c. If pressing PF 1 or 13, then display help panel PE10H.
   d. Set default field values: 1 copy, no mailing labels, and department T-22.
   e. Initially set &PFKEYED to blank.
3. PROC The following takes place in the PROC section:
   a. Assign a value to &PFKEYED if pressing PF3, PF4, PF15, or PF16. The sequence processing &PFKEYED in the clist looks similar to the following:

```
PA10P: -
  ISPEXEC CONTROL DISPLAY PANEL(PE10P)
  /* Go to Exit module, if pressing PF4 or PF16. */
  IF &PFKEYED = 4 THEN GOTO EXIT
  /* Display previous panel if pressing PF3 or-
 PF15. */
   IF &PFKEYED = 3 THEN GOTO PA05P
```

b. Truncate &COPY to two characters.
c. For department T-28, set the number of copies to 10 and do not allow the user to override this.
d. Verifies if &YN is Y or N, &CO is between 1 through 99. Also verifies if the input for &MS matches the pattern of an alphabetical character followed by a hyphen and two numeric characters.

In the above example, you must truncate &COPY because the length of the field name (4) is larger than the length of the maximum field value (2). An alternative approach is using .ZVARS in the INIT section. This is commonly used for displaying table values. Here is an example:

```
)ATTR
)BODY -- only part
%----------------------USE OF ZVAR----------------------+
+
+
+ 1. NUMBER OF COPIES =>_Z + (1-99)
+
+ 2. PRINTER NUMBER =>_Z+   (1-9)
)INIT
 .ZVARS = '(COPY PRNUM)'
)PROC
 VER (&COPY,RANGE,1,99)
 VER (&PRNUM,RANGE,1,9)
)END
```

The following are additional guidelines when using Z variables.

1. The BODY section uses Z as a "dummy" field instead of the actual field name. The plus sign (attribute character) decides the length of the first field is 2 and the second is 1.
2. The INIT section contains the .ZVARS statement telling ISPF the name to substitute the &Z dummy variable with. Commas or blanks separate names that are substituted *by their position* in the .ZVARS statement. Note using parentheses and single quotes for processing of the blanks. *Do not use .ZVARS in the PROC section.*
3. After the .ZVARS definition, you can refer to the Z variables in the INIT, REINIT, and PROC section by their actual names.

)PROC—Processing of Panel. Because the statements used in the INIT and PROC sections are nearly identical, little needs to be added. When a user presses a PF key (other than a scrolling key), ENTER, or RETURN, then the panel begins processing. One minor difference is that .AUTOSEL and .ZVARS do not work in the PROC section. Examples of typical PROC sections were shown when reviewing the INIT section.

Help or Tutorial Panels. The remaining part on ISPF panels focuses on two special areas: help or tutorial and menu or selection panels. Help panels can provide both a complete tutorial or context-sensitive help for a dialog using a hierarchical structure. (Like an outline, the further you are in the hierarchy, the more detailed is the information provided.) The following are some guidelines to creating a help hierarchy:

1. Place .HELP in the INIT section of a data entry, selection, or table display panel. ISPF then decides which help panel to display when a user presses the HELP key.
2. Most help panels just display text. However, there are usually two special panels in the help hierarchy—*table of contents* (really a menu panel that is usually the *top* panel in the hierarchy) and *index* (listing subjects in alphabetical order and is not required). To access either of these panels in an application, do the following:
   a. In the top panel of a dialog (usually the primary menu), include the following in the INIT section:

```
&ZHTOP = GHOO
         |______Name of top panel, usually table of contents.
&ZHINDEX = GHII
           |____Name of index panel (optional statement).
```

   b. In an INDEX panel's PROC section, include a &ZIND = YES to indicate it is an index panel.
3. Other variables to use in the PROC section of help panels:
   a. &ZCONT The next help panel *down* in the hierarchy.
   &ZCONT = IDF007
   b. &ZUP The previous help panel *up* in the hierarchy. Since ISPF keeps track of your "path" in the help hierarchy, it is not always needed. You typically use &ZUP for setting an "upward path" from a dialog's topmost help panel (usually a system help panel).
   &ZUP = IDF008
   c. &ZPARENT You may use in the last help panel to return directly to the top help panel. This results in ISPF losing track of your "path" through the help hierarchy.
   &ZPARENT = ISF001

d. &ZSEL A table of contents or index panel uses this for deciding the help panel related to the user's selection. An example of this is given later.

4. The user enters the following commands for navigating through the help hierarchy.

Command	Abbreviation	Function
TOC	T	Go to table of contents.
INDEX	I	Go to index panel.
UP	U	Go to parent panel.
Enter key		Go to next panel.
BACK	B	Go to previous panel.
SKIP	S	Go to next topic.

5. Use the ISPTUTOR program for accessing the system and application tutorials. A parameter passes the initial panel name. The primary menu panel shown below has an example of this. The following is a typical help panel.

```
)ATTR
)BODY
%----------------A HELP PANEL---------------(M0001H)
+ This is a typical help panel that is nothing more-
  than
+ text and an occasional dialog variable (&DATE.)
+
)INIT
)PROC
 &ZUP = ISP0014 Next level up (a system help panel.)
 &ZCONT = M0002H Next panel if user presses ENTER.
)END
```

Menu or Selection Panels. An important part of a dialog is the menu panel. It uses the input selection to decide which series of functions or panels to execute. Let us look at a typical menu panel:

```
)ATTR
)BODY
%---------------DIALOG PRIMARY OPTION MENU----------------
%OPTION ===>_ZCMD
%
%Select an option by letter:          +USER      - &ZUSER+
%                                     +TIME      - &ZTIME+
```

```
% A +Weekly Expense Report              +Terminal  - &ZTERM+
% S +Stock Room Inventory
% T +Accounting Tutorial
)INIT
 .HELP = ACCT10H
 &ZPRIM = YES
 &ZHTOP = ACCT10H
)PROC
 &ZSEL = TRANS ( TRUNC (&ZCMD,'.')
                 A,'PANEL(ACCT10P)'
                 S,'CMD(ST10C)'
                 T,'PGM(ISPTUTOR) PARM(ACCT10H)'
                 O,'PGM(STATS)'
                 '',''
                 *,? )
)END
```

The following are the major elements of the above panel:

1. &ZPRIM = YES This indicates a primary menu—the top menu for the dialog. Lower-level menus are nearly identical to primary menus. Including @PRIM in the panel name commonly identifies a primary menu panel.
2. &ZCMD The system variable used for command input (such as a menu selection). On primary and some secondary menu panels, users may enter options and suboptions using the format *option.suboption*. (Such as 3.4—option 3, suboption 4.) The review of &ZSEL discusses processing suboptions. You can use another dialog variable for capturing menu selections.
3. &ZSEL The other system variable used for processing command input. It follows these steps:
   a. Is a period and suboption included in the user input? If yes, then execute but not display the suboption menu. (Using NOCHECK after CMD or PGM suspends this and you can control suboption processing. The control variable .TRAIL stores the suboption.) &ZSEL only retains the option part.
   b. Translate the truncated &ZCMD to the corresponding ISPF statement and execute it. You must assign the result to &ZSEL.
      (i) PANEL(ACCT10P) Executes secondary panel ACCT10P.
      (ii) CMD(ST10C) Executes clist (function) ST10C.
      (iii) PGM(ISPTUTOR) PARM(ACCT10H) Executes ISPF tutorial program with PARM setting the first help panel.
      (iv) PGM(STATS) An option not on the menu but which invokes a program. "Hidden" options are quite common.

(v) ·· Redisplays menu with or without an *Enter Option* message because &ZCMD contains a blank string.
(vi) ? Processes invalid strings by redisplaying the panel with an *Invalid Option* message.

Other valid keyword operands for a &ZSEL statement are:

1. EXIT Exit ISPF. You do not need single quotes for EXIT.
```
&ZSEL = &TRANS ( TRUNC (&ZCMD. '.')
                 E, EXIT)
```
2. MODE(state) State is LINE (line mode) or FSCR (full-screen). Use MODE with CMD or PGM.
3. NOCHECK Allows you, not ISPF, to control suboption processing. Use with CMD or PGM.
```
&ZSEL = &TRANS ( TRUNC (&ZCMD. '.')
                 1, 'CMD(TEST10) NOCHECK'
                 E, EXIT)
        &SUBOPT = .TRAIL
```

Now that we understand what &ZSEL does, let us look briefly at its use in table of contents and index help panels. A table of contents panel is similar to any other selection panel. Because there are no suboptions, you do not need TRUNC.

```
)BODY
%------------------------Tutorial-------------------------
$OPTION ===>_ZCMD
+
+             %--------------------------------
+             %: Tutorial Selection Panel     :
+             %--------------------------------
+ The following topics will be presented in sequence, or
+     may be selected by letter:
+ %1 - Main Menu Help
+ %2 - Some Possible Problems.
)PROC
 &ZSEL = TRANS(&ZCMD
          1, APP01H
          2, APP02H
          ' ', ' '
          *,?)
)END
```

An index panel may have up to 100 indexed topics. Here is a sample panel using &ZSEL two different ways:

```
)BODY
%-------------------------INDEX-------------------------
%OPTION ===>_ZCMD
+
+            %------------------------------
+            %:          Tutorial Index       :
+            %------------------------------
+ To select a topic, enter the two character option:
+ %A1 - Allocating Data Files
+ %C1 - Copying Data
)PROC
 &ZIND = YES
 &ZSEL = TRANS(&ZCMD
        A1, APP01H
        A2, APP02H Valid: A1, A2
        ' ', ' '
        *,?)
 IF (&ZCMD = A,C) &ZSEL = APP01H If entering just A or C.

 &ZUP = APPA1H Previous help panel.
)END
```

Variables

Variables are the key to communicating between dialog elements. The VGET (retrieve a variable from a variable pool) and VPUT (place a variable in the variable pool) statements do this. Storing a variable in the dialog profile pool allows recalling of values in later sessions. Also use VGET/VPUT for passing variables between pools. If a program uses a variable, then you also need a VDEFINE statement. ISPF sites with ISPF Version 2 Release 3 and later can place VGET statements in an INIT or PROC panel sections and decide which pool to use. The following are examples of these two statements:

1. ISPEXEC VGET (PRJX,MEMX) PROFILE The clist retrieves the PRJX and MEMX variable values that the dialog profile pool stores and overwrites any values in the shared pool. ISPSTART creates a shared pool when issuing an ISPSTART statement and a NEWAPPL operand. It overwrites any existing values in a clist or panel. This is the most common format.

2. VGET (PRT1,PRT2) The panel retrieves the PRT1 and PRT2 variable values using the default ASIS operand. (Checks both shared and the dialog profile pools.) The SHARED operand searches only the shared variable pool.
3. ISPEXEC VPUT &ALIST PROFILE The clist stores the variable values assigned to &ALIST in the dialog profile pool (and deletes any shared pool equivalents). This is the most common format.
4. VPUT (PRT1,PRT2) The panel stores the current PRT1 and PRT2 variable values using the default ASIS operand. (Checks both shared and the dialog profile dataset but stores in the shared pool.) You can also use the SHARED operand. VGET and VPUT are the only way for passing variable values between a clist and a PDF Edit Macro or vice versa.

Messages

Use messages for communicating to the user an error condition occurred or an action has taken place. Display or retrieve a message any of the following ways.

- The control variable .MSG.
- The message operand (MSG) of the DISPLAY service.
  `ISPEXEC DISPLAY PANEL(MYT10P) MSG(AG100C)`
- Using the STEMSG service.
- Using the GETMSG service. This displays the contents and settings of a desired ISPF message. It is not discussed further.

Since the first two approaches were already mentioned, let us take a brief look at SETMSG. Use SETMSG for determining which message to display when *showing* the next panel or full-screen display. Display the message with symbolically substituted values. (The exception is help panels, which display values when invoking the panel and not when invoking SETMSG.) A COND keyword tells ISPF to display a message if there are no other outstanding SETMSG requests (otherwise only the last SETMSG executes). An example of a SETMSG statement in a clist is:

```
ISPEXEC SETMSG(MXY100)
```

This displays the MXY100 message (if it is the only or last SETMSG request outstanding).

After knowing how to invoke ISPF messages, it is now appropriate to review: (1) What includes a message id, (2) how messages are stored in a partitioned dataset member, and (3) the operands to use with messages. Five to eight characters compose a valid message. Up to five characters are alphabetic (such as A–Z, @,$,#), followed by three numeric characters and another optional alphabetic character (only valid if using less than five alphabetic characters). The name of the library (i.e., PDS member) where a message is stored *is the message id up to and including the second numeric character* (so MXY100 is stored in number MXY10). Messages in large dialogs are spread across several message libraries, with each library referring to one panel or one type of message (such as skeleton-related messages). Looking at a sample message library (PDS member) created with your favorite editor reveals the format of and operands used in a message library:

```
MXY100 '&R -- INVALID DATASET NAME.' .HELP = MXY10H
.ALARM = YES 'INVALID
DATASET NAME. PLEASE RETYPE YOUR CHOICE'

MXY101
'YOU CANNOT CREATE AN EXISTING DATASET'
```

Message library MXY10 stores message MXY100 through MXY109. Remember, message id is through the second numeric. Place messages on two lines separated by blanks. Reserve the end of the first line for the short message and related operands and the second line for the long message. Here is more on these three components:

- *Short message* The far right side of a panel's first line displays this message. The message is up to 24 characters enclosed by single quotes.
- *Operands* Is either *.ALARM = NO* (the default sounds no alarm when displaying a message) or *.ALARM =YES,* plus *.HELP=help panel.* (The default is *; the panel specifies the help. This operand decides which help panel to display if the user presses the help key twice.) Separate them by one or more blank spaces.
- *Long Message* This is up to 78 characters enclosed by single quotes. This message appears on the third line of a panel and only displays on pressing the HELP key.

Other guidelines for creating message libraries:

1. Message ids always start in the first column on the first line and long messages always start in the first column of the second line.
2. As in the above example, you can use a symbolic variable in either a long or short message. They also can supply values to .ALARM or .HELP. Delimit symbolic variables by nonalphabetic characters including period for concatenation. Use two special characters to produce one (such as ampersands or double quotes).

Tables

The ISPF table service (or commands starting with TB) is one of the more confusing and misused areas of ISPF. Errors result because the programmer

1. Uses tables for an application it was not meant for
2. Fails to grasp important concepts when using tables
3. Executes the wrong table command
4. Copied the program from another user who made one of the other three errors.

This section attempts to clear up some of this confusion by describing when to use tables, major table concepts and commands, and other tips. The Fosdick reference provides a complete and documented table example.

When to Use Tables

A table is a two-dimensional array composed of *rows* (each row being one unit of associated values) and *columns* (the values for all rows for a particular symbolic variable or *field*). The following is an example of this:

ROWID	COMPANY	PHONE	
0001	Nothing but Laughs	555-8576	Column values for
0002	New England Food	555-9999	PHONE field.
0003	Clair's Bridal Shop	555-9980	

Row-One unit of related variables

Knowing what a table is gives a good clue what applications to use it for.

- Data with one to three keys and no multiple instances (such as a subrecord for each course taken by a student). Keys are used all at once and so cannot be "secondary."
- Data you can represent as a "flat file," such as telephone directories or a password file.
- Data not needing a cross-reference to another file.
- Data not needing to be in a hierarchical format.
- Data you can represent in less than 65,536 bytes per row and no more than 16.7 million rows. As a guideline, use tables if less than 10,000 records.

Applications that do not fit the above criteria should consider using database software such as DB2 or FOCUS.

Concepts

This section covers the components of a table (in addition to row and column) and types of available tables.

Table Components. ISPF tables are either *keyed* or *unkeyed*. A *keyed table* uses the *unique* value of one or more fields (called *key fields*) to identify a row. If the values of the keys matches, then retrieve the corresponding row. Keyed tables use more overhead but retrieve records faster. (You can specify a sequential search on a keyed table.) Let us look at a row from the above example:

```
ROWID   COMPANY               PHONE
0001    Nothing but Laughs    555-8576
```

If ROWID is the key field, then only retrieve this row when specifying ROWID as 0001. This allows having two rows with the same company name.

An *unkeyed table* has no key fields. If the value(s) of one or more specified fields matches, then the corresponding rows are retrieved.

Each table also contains a *current row pointer* (CRP), which works similarly to the pointer of TSO EDIT. It marks the next row to access and changes every time you scroll or perform an action to a row. ISPF allows querying the value of CRP or modifying it to a desired value (location). Note that when opening a table, the CRP is located ahead of the first row. More information on the CRP is given later in this section.

Types of Tables. In addition to being keyed or unkeyed, tables also have two other general attributes. They are either temporary or permanent. A *temporary table* exists only for the run of the dialog. You cannot write to the PDS libraries associated with the ISPTABL concatenation (using virtual storage instead). A *permanent table* is saved in a PDS library associated with the ISPTABL concatenation and future ISPF sessions can use it.

Table Commands

Use the following common commands (Table 9-1), system variables (Table 9-2), and control variables (Table 9-3) associated with ISPF tables. Do note that each new release of ISPF *greatly* enhances table capabilities so that some problems you are having may be resolved in a later release. For example, reading an empty table is difficult with ISPF Version 1, but later releases use TBDISPL to do this easily. Check to see if TB commands listed in Table 9-1 are available for your release.

System Variables. There are 13 system variables with the prefix ZTD that ISPF table services uses. They can decide when and which rows to display by scrolling up or down when displaying a table with TBDISPL. They are listed in Table 9-2. Control variables are listed in Table 9-3.

Table 9-1. Common Table Commands

Command	Function
	General Table Commands
TBCLOSE	Closes and saves a permanent table if marked.
TBCREATE	Produces and opens a new table. You can also specify the type of table to create.
TBEND	Closes the work copy (virtual storage) of the table. The permanent version of the table remains unchanged.
TBERASE	Clears a permanent table.
TBOPEN	Opens a permanent (not temporary) table.
TBQUERY	Assigns information about a table to dialog (symbolic) variables.
TBSAVE	Saves a permanent table while keeping the table open.
TBSORT	Sorts a table by one or more fields. You can save this sort information for future sessions.
TBSTATS	Assigns statistics on a table to dialog (symbolic) variables.
	Row-Oriented Commands (Pointer Location)
TBTOP	Sets the CRP to the start of the table.
TBBOTTOM	Sets the CRP to the end of the table.
TBSKIP	Sets the CRP to a table location ahead or behind a specified number of rows from the current location. TBSKIP also can retrieve the assigned row.
	Row-oriented Commands (Row Actions)
TBADD	Places a new row in a table at a specified location.
TBSARG	Assigns value for use by TBSCAN or TBDISPL searching for a record.
TBDELETE	Removes a specified row.
TBDISPL	Displays specified rows (may use TBSARG.)
TBEXIST	Returns if a row with one or more specified values exists (keyed tables only).
TBGET	Retrieves a specified row.
TBMOD	Always adds a specified row with new values for unkeyed tables and keyed tables. (If the user value does not match the key field value for any row, then add the record. Else if a match occurs, then update the row with the new values.)
TBPUT	Always updates a specified row with new values for unkeyed tables. But a specified row only updates when the user value matches the key field value for the row pointed to now.
TBSCAN	Searches for a row with a specified value. TBSARG also can use TBSCAN.
TBVCLEAR	Assigns a null value to dialog variables used in a table as columns. This is useful before doing a TBSCAN.

Table 9-2. Table System Variables

Variable	Function
&ZTDADD	Returns YES or NO, indicating if needing more rows before scrolling a table. If yes, use &ZTDCRP, &ZTDAMT (how many rows to add), or &ZTDSIZE (how many rows to place in a scrollable area).
&ZTDMARK	Sets the end of table marker from BOTTOM OF DATA &ZTDMARK to whatever string you specify (including none). However, it must be smaller than the maximum screen size.
&ZTDMSG	Sets the message id used for marking top of the table. See the message section earlier for what is a valid message id.
&ZTDRET	Decides when to return control to the clist for adding more rows. This may be when reaching the top (UP) or bottom (DOWN) of a table or both (VERTICAL).
&ZTDROWS	Returns number of rows displayed. This value may have leading zeros and is up to six characters.
&ZTDSCRP	Sets or returns value of CRP after scrolling. This is up to six characters and may have leading zeros.
&ZTDSELS	Returns number of rows selected by user. This value may have leading zeros and is up to four characters.
&ZTDTOP	Current value of CRP is up to six characters and may have leading zeros.

Table 9-3. Control Variables

Variable	Function
.AUTOSEL	Enables automatic selection. The INIT and REINIT panel sections of a TBDISPL, but not a DISPLAY panel, can use it. This overrides the AUTOSEL operand of TBDISPL. YES enables automatic selection when the TBDISPL operand CSRROW has a valid value and overrides any user input. NO disables automatic selection. BLANK value enables automatic selection.
.CSRROW	The value of CRP (cursor location) when displaying a table model. (Part of panel definition used in displaying a table.) Unless setting the AUTOSEL control variable or TBDISPL operand to NO, this row is automatically selected. Use .CSRROW in the INIT, REINIT, or PROC sections of a TBDISPL, not a DISPLAY panel.

Table 9-4. How Table Commands Affect CRP Location

Command	CRP Location after Command.
TBADD	After row added.
TBBOTTOM	After last row.
TBCREATE	Before first row.
TBDELETE	Before deleted row.
TBEXIST	Before first row.
TBDISPL	Before first row but can be changed.
TBGET	The retrieved row.
TBMOD	The added/updated row.
TBOPEN	Before first row.
TBPUT	Unchanged.
TBSCAN	Row matching user value.
TBSKIP	The location after moving behind or ahead a certain number of rows from the present location.
TBSORT	Before first row.

Additional Table Guidelines

The following are additional table guidelines:

1. Compressing table partitioned datasets improves performance and reduces future problems.
2. Because TBOPEN reads the entire table from disk and TBCLOSE writes the entire table to disk, generally use one statement per session.
3. For larger tables, submit the ISPF dialog to background.
4. Generally, use a TBVCLEAR before using TBSARG and TBSCAN.

Table 9-4 shows how table commands affect the CRP.

Skeletons

ISPF provides a file-tailoring facility for creating customized sequential files (up to 255 characters). This includes creating output files based on symbolic variable values and ad hoc substituting of symbolic values in output statements. Although this facility is traditionally used for creating JCL programs, it also can create clists and other language programs. To produce and execute an output file, a dialog uses the following:

- A skeleton (input file)with a length up to 255 characters. It is composed of the *input records* (the information) used to create the *output records* and *skeleton statements*. (Decides when to include certain input records.)

- "FT" dialog manager statements. The *FT* prefix notes use of the file-tailoring service for opening/closing an output file or processing a skeleton.

Here is more on these file-tailoring components along with a brief example.

Skeleton (Input File)

Input records may contain any of the following.

1. Symbolic variables starting with an ampersand that translate to no larger than the length of the output record. An ampersand followed by a blank fails to process. Symbolic variables can also use a period for allowing concatenation with a text string.
2. Using two of special characters to produce one. Some of these are & (for clists), !, ., and |.
3. A question mark in the last column continues an input line.
4. Use the)BLANK skeleton statement for retaining blank lines in an output record.

The syntax of skeleton statements is *)operand values*. Each statement may include one or more operand values (separated by blanks), which are some combination of symbolic variables or their possible values. Note the operand is always in uppercase and each statement must start in column 1. Common skeleton statements include:

)BLANK num Adds one (the default) or blank lines to the output file. *Num* is a number or symbolic variable marking the number of blank lines to add.

)CM text Comments your input files. It is not symbolically translated or added to the output file.

)DOT tablename–)ENDOT Iteratively assigns each row's values to dialog variables. Then, other skeleton statements within a)DOT–)ENDOT block can use them. You can nest up to four)DOT–)ENDOT blocks (using different tables). Unless issuing a TBOPEN, the table closes after the skeleton ends processing. Otherwise, place the current line pointer (CRP) before the first row in the table.

)ENDEL Ends a)SEL–)ENDSEL block. See)SEL for further explanation.

)IM skeletonname options Nest up to three skeletons. Options include *NT* (include but no further processing [tailoring])) and *OPT* (continue processing whether or not the nested skeleton exists).

)SEL condition Conditionally include input records until finding a required)ENDSEL. This means include input records only if the condition is true (such as a symbolic variable in a certain range or having a certain value). These conditions may include ANDs (&&), ORs (|), and most clist relational operators (such as GT or >). You may nest up to eight)SEL–)ENDSEL blocks. You may use any other skeleton statement in a)SEL–)ENDSEL block.

)SET dialogvar = value . . . Assigns a value to a dialog variable *which uses no ampersand*. You can have a nearly infinite number of dialog variable assignment pairs for one)SET statement. Note *value* may include adding or subtracting subvalues (e.g.,)SET ADDIT = 1 + 2) but must not have a string with embedded blanks (e.g., New York).

After FT dialog manager statements is an example of an input file (skeleton).

FT Dialog Manager Statements

Use the following framework in creating your clist FT statements for processing a skeleton and producing a permanent output dataset.

```
1. ISPEXEC FTOPEN TEMP
2. ISPEXEC FTINCL MYSKEL
3. ISPEXEC FTCLOSE
4. ISPEXEC VGET (ZTEMPF)
5. ALLOC DD(MYCOPY) DA('&ZTEMPF') SHR
6. ALLOC DD(PERMCOPY) DA(PERM.DATA) NEW.....
7. COPY '&ZTEMPF' PERM.DATA
```

Explanation. An explanation by statement number follows.

1. Opens a temporary sequential dataset (because of TEMP operand; otherwise assigned dynamically to a dataset associated with the ISPFILE ddname). Assign ISPF system variable &ZTEMPF the eight-character name of this dataset. See statement 4 on retrieving &ZTEMPF.
2. Include and process the MYSKEL (or any specified) skeleton. The name used must be a member of a partitioned dataset in ISPSLIB concatenation. Note that placing NOFT after the skeleton name just copies the file without any symbolic substitution. Also, a &LASTCC of 8 means the skeleton does not exist.
3. Close the file. Placing a NOREPL operand after the FTCLOSE operand stops any overwriting of existing output files. Common nonzero return codes include:
   4 File not overwritten because of using NOREPL operand.
   8 Forgot to use FTOPEN so file was never opened.
   12 Try again later. The input (skeleton) or output file is being used by someone else.

16 Forgot an ALLOCATE for the input or output files.

4. Retrieve the temporary file name (&ZTEMPF) from the shared profile pool. Use this for submitting the output file (if JCL) or copying it to a permanent dataset.
5. Allocate the temporary output file so you can copy it in statement 7.
6. Allocate the permanent output file. See Chapter 2 for ALLOCATE statement examples.
7. Copy the temporary output file to a permanent one. You may have to make sure no one else is using either dataset.

The following is an example of a simple skeleton generating a clist. It includes the appropriate statement depending on &OPT's value.

SIMPLE SKELETON

```
)BLANK 2
)CM ***OPT = A***
)SEL &OPT = A
)SET &&A = 1 + &B——
                       | Perform symbolic substitution. &B
)ENDSEL
                       | becomes 3 and &&A becomes &A. Note
)CM ***OPT = B***
                       | the clist, not the skeleton,
)SEL &OPT = B
                       | assigns a value to &A.
)SET &&A = &B + &B___
)ENDSEL
WRITE &&A -- Used by both options
```

CLIST

```
WRITE Supply a NUMBER
  READ B
WRITE SELECT AN OPTION:
WRITE A - ADD 1 to &B
WRITE B - ADD &B to itself
  READ OPT
ISPEXEC FTOPEN TEMP
ISPEXEC FTINCL SIMPLE
ISPEXEC FTCLOSE
ISPEXEC VGET (ZTEMPF)
EXEC '&ZTEMPF'
```

Output File

```
                    Assuming &B = 2
      OPT = 1                          OPT = 2
(2 blank lines)                  (2 blank lines)
SET &A = 3                       SET &A = 4
WRITE &A                         WRITE &A
```

Using Clists with ISPF

The following are additional guidelines on using ISPF Dialog Manager with clists.

1. Clists and ISPF:
   a. ISPF halts on a null command:

   ```
   SET &NULLS = &STR( )
   &NULLS - causes end of dialog.
   ```

   The exception is a NULL command in an ATTENTION routine ends the routine. You cannot issue TSO commands or call another clist.

   b. Do not use the following with ISPF:
   - LOGON, LOGOFF (unless with the TSOEXEC command described in Chapter 5)
   - Global variables
   - Clist variable names longer than eight characters (TSO Version 1 Release 4 and later)
   - Invoking ISPF from an ATTENTION routine
   - ATTENTION routines unless using ISPF Version 2 Release 3. This includes using the PA1 key. (See the "ATTENTION Routines" section of Chapter 4 for further information.)
   - TERMIN
   - ISPF control variables saved by CONTROL DISPLAY SAVE (nested clists only)

   c. You can use &SYSOUTLINE and &SYSOUTTRAP for capturing TSO commands and their output if executing after invoking an ISPF service.

   d. You can place a field on a panel so the clist, not ISPF, issues messages.

   Panel

   ```
   )BODY
   &MSGFLD1
   )INIT
   &MSGFLD1 = ' '
   ```

Clist

```
IF &LASTCC = 4 THEN SET & MSGFLD1 = &STR(I or O-
only)
GOTO PANEL 100  /* Redisplay panel.  */
```

e. Using clist control variable &LASTCC tells the clist how the dialog executed.

```
ISPEXEC DISPLAY PANEL(MY200)
  IF &LASTCC = 4 THEN EXIT CODE(4) /*enter END or-
 RETURN*/
  IF &LASTCC = 12 THEN DO
    WRITE FIELD NOT FOUND...TRY AGAIN
    GOTO PANEL100  /* Redisplay panel.
  END
  IF &LASTCC = 16 THEN GOTO PROB1 /* TRANS or TRUNC
                                  /*error
  IF &LASTCC = 20 THEN DO
    WRITE SERIOUS ERROR. CALL 555-9000
  END
```

f. Use .PFKEY and a clist variable to go back to a previous panel or exit the dialog. Remember that .PFKEY holds the value of the last pressed PF key.

Panel

```
)PROC
IF (.PFKEY = 'PF03' OR 'PF15') &PFKEYED = 3
```

Clist

```
IF &PFKEYED = 3 THEN GOTO NEXTPNL
```

Debugging Applications (ISPF Test)

ISPF contains complete facilities for testing and debugging your dialogs. There are two methods you can use: (1) enter test or trace mode or (2) PDF's Dialog Test Option. If available, use Dialog Test because it has more features and is easier to use. Let's look a little closer at each approach.

Test/Trace Mode

The test/trace mode is similar to normal ISPF processing except it supplies additional information. Placing *only* one of the following four keyword operands in an ISPSTART statement invokes test or trace mode:

1. TEST Enables test mode:
   - Always keeps latest changes to panels and messages because they are retrieved an extra time.

- Panels printed with the PDF PRINT command include line numbers and panel and message ids.
- Helps panels show previous panel and message ids.
- Any errors or pressing the PA1 key ends the ISPF application. (Unless issuing CONTROL ERRORS CANCEL. then the dialog continues processing.)

2. TESTX — Same as TEST but also displays messages sent to the ISPF log.
3. TRACE — Same as TEST but also writes to the ISPF log when invoking any ISPF service.
4. TRACEX — Same as TRACE but displays the additional messages written to the ISPF screen.

PDF's Dialog Test (Option 7)

Use the Dialog Test Facility for interactively testing and debugging nearly any ISPF service "in action" without invoking an entire dialog. It includes the following options:

- *Functions* Test clists and programs, the trace mode mentioned earlier (logging ISPF service messages), and *breakpoints* (a preassigned place to stop a clist or program to examine symbolic variables values or use other ISPF services).
- *Panels* Test panel appearance, INIT/REINIT/PROC logic, related help panels, split screens.
- *Variables* Display variables from all pools including user and system dialog variables. You can also create new variables or modify existing ones.
- *Tables* Display, modify, or delete table rows. Table statistics and other information are also available. Table creation is also accessible.
- *Log Display ISPF log. This is useful for trace mode.*

See the Maurer reference or the *PDF Guide* SC34-4118 for further information.

Customizing ISPF—How to Get More ISPF Dialogs

This section briefly discusses customizing ISPF and PDF at your site and offers suggestions on places to get more ISPF dialogs.

Customizing ISPF

Most ISPF/PDF customization is modifying IBM-supplied panels, functions, tables, and messages by adding new options such as a foreground compiler or modifying the edit screen or a JCL (background) skeleton. This involves typical ISPF Dialog Manager commands; the *ISPF Installation and Customization* (SC34-4117) details any unusual aspects of doing this.

You can also create extensions of existing services using VDEFINE exits. (Although its official use is defining dialog variables when having unusual program variable types.) The Stewart reference offers good advice on doing this, including pitfalls, undocumented features, and several examples. Also, read the section on VDEFINE in *ISPF Dialog Management Services and Examples* (SC34-4113). This is done for creating new panel validation statements such as telephone numbers, social security numbers, or decimal points (integers), or appending a percent sign when displaying a value. Once created, these VDEFINEd panel statements and dialog variables are identical to user and system-supplied equivalents. Other uses include invoking TEST based on a VDEFINEd variable value, and writing to the log any VDEFINEd values.

How to Get More Application Dialogs

Here are some places beyond the usual IBM manuals to turn to for ideas in creating IBM dialogs:

1. Three unusual IBM manuals filled with good advice and user's experiences with ISPF.

   GG24-3080 *ISPF and ISPF/PDF Version 2 for MVS Implementation and Use Experiences*

   GG24-1706 *ISPF Version 2 for MVS: Installation and Use*

   GG24-3286 *ISPF and PDF Version 2 Release 3 Experiences*
2. The ISPF projects of SHARE, SEAS, and GUIDE, the IBM Users' Groups. Chapter 5 gives their addresses. These groups have newsletters, coordinate talks, and publish the proceedings of their semiannual conferences, and provide IBM with input for future ISPF enhancements.
3. Several Connecticut Bank and Trust (CBT) tapes (see Chapter 5 for the address) are on ISPF dialogs.
4. Other software used with ISPF also provide good examples (such as DB2, SAS, and others) in their documentation and user-group proceedings.
5. Periodic articles in magazines such as *Mainframe Journal*.

THE DEMO DIALOG EXAMPLE

This example was developed and documented by Charles Hoffman of GTE Laboratories Inc. It is a simple dialog showing many of the ISPF Dialog Manager services this chapter discusses.

Dialog Overview

The Demo clist (DEMO) invokes the primary option panel (DEMOP01). The user may select one of four options:

- Learn more about the dialog by pressing HELP. This displays panel DEMO-H01 (a tutorial selection panel.) Option T will invoke the main ISPF tutorial panel.
- Invokes the ISPF parameter options selection panel (Option O). The user can change terminal settings, display the list/log dataset defaults, and review current PF key settings.
- Invokes the demo utility application (Option U) that reads user input from the panel and writes it back to the screen. This is Option U.
- Entering X ends the dialog.

Figure 9-2 is a flow diagram of the dialog. The following are the panels, clists, messages, and programs for the dialog:

$CONCAT (Run before DEMO clist)

```
PROC 0
CONTRO NOFLUSH
/*
    FREE DD(SYSPROC)
    ALLOC DD(SYSPROC) DSN('HHG1.DEMO.DIALOG'             +
                          'SYS1.CMDPROC'     ) -
                          SHR BLKSIZE(6160)
  FREE DD(ISPPLIB)
  ALLOC DD(ISPPLIB) DSN('SYS1.ISPF.ISRPLIB'              +
                        'SYS1.ISPF.ISPPLIB'              +
                         'HHG1.DEMO.DIALOG')-            +
                         SHR BLKSIZE(6160)
  FREE DD(ISPMLIB)
  ALLOC DD(ISPMLIB) DSN('SYS1.ISPF.ISRMLIB'              +
                         'SYS1.ISPF.ISPMLIB'             +
                         'HHG1.DEMO.DIALOG')-            +
                         SHR BLKSIZE(6160)
EXIT CODE(&MAXCC)
```

Figure 9-2. Demo Utility Dialog

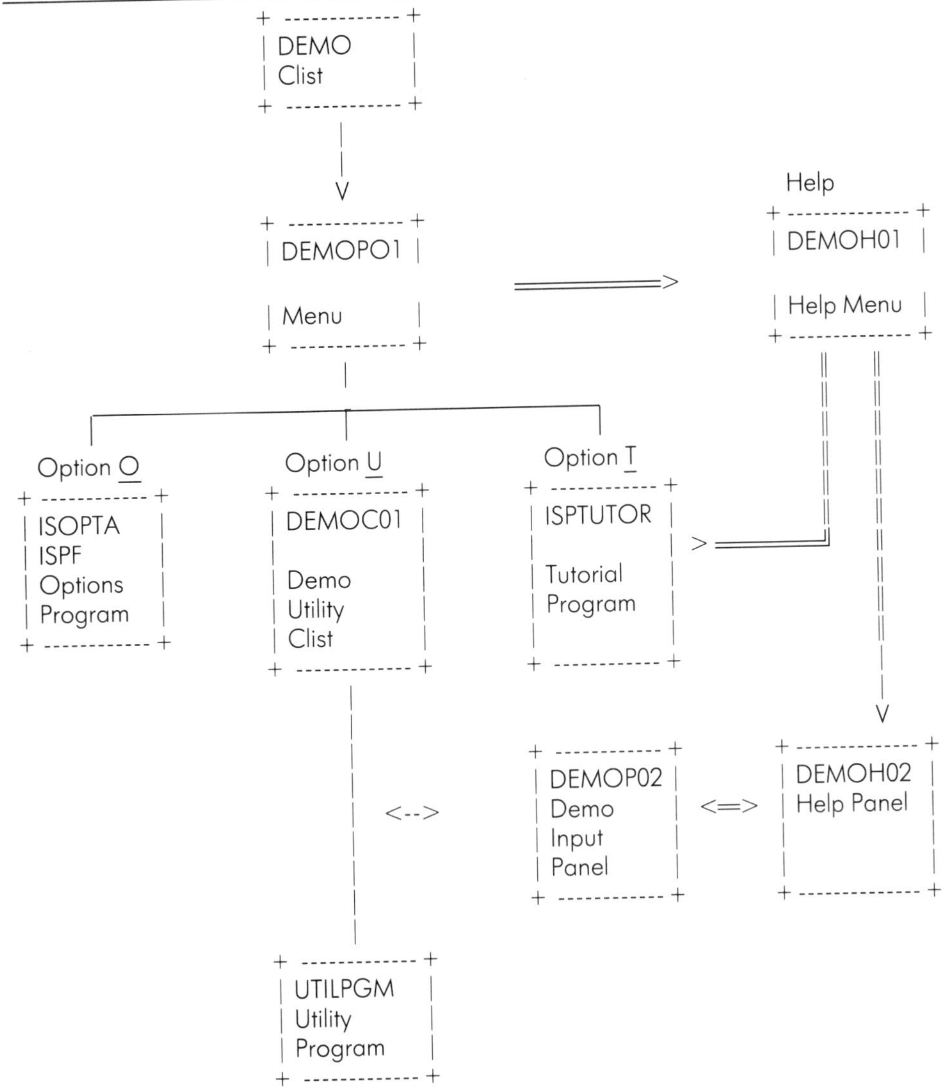

DEMO Clist

```
PROC 0
/*********************************************************/
/*                                                       */
/*  INVOKE THE APPLICATION DIALOG WITH A CLIST.          */
/*                                                       */
/*********************************************************/
INITIAL: +
   CONTROL MSG
MAINLINE: +
  IF &SYSISPF EQ ACTIVE THEN ISPEXEC SELECT PANEL(DEMOP01)
  ELSE DO
    ISPFPROF
    ISPSTART PANEL(DEMOP01)
END
ENDING: EXIT CODE(&MAXCC)
```

DEMOC01 Clist

```
PROC 0
/*********************************************************/
/* DATA ENTRY FROM A PANEL TO A CLIST.                   */
/*********************************************************/
INITIAL: +
    CONTROL NOMSG
      FREE DD(SYSOUT)
      ALLOC DD(SYSOUT) DSN(*)
    CONTROL MSG
MAINLINE: +
    ISPEXEC DISPLAY PANEL(DEMOP02)
    ISPEXEC VPUT (UTILPARM) PROFILE
    CALL 'HHG1.DEMO.LOAD(UTILPGM)' '&UTILPARM'
ENDING: EXIT CODE(&MAXCC)
```

DEMOM01 Message Library

```
DEMOM011 'Parm field is blank'   .HELP=DEMOH01 .ALARM = YES
'Fill in a value for the parm.'
```

UTILPGM COBOL Program

```
ID DIVISION.
PROGRAM-ID. UTILPGM.
*
ENVIRONMENT DIVISION.
*
DATA DIVISION.
LINKAGE SECTION.
01 INPUT-PARM.
   05 IPARM-LEN        PIC S999  COMP SYNC.
   05 IPARM-VALUE      PIC X(10).
   05 FILLER           PIC X(90).
*
PROCEDURE DIVISION USING INPUT-PARM.
  DISPLAY ' '
  DISPLAY 'This is a simulated utility program.'
  DISPLAY ' '
  DISPLAY 'You passed me an input parm of: ',IPARM-VALUE
  DISPLAY ' '
  GOBACK.
```

DEMOP01 Panel

```
%-----------------Demo Primary Option Menu-----------------
%OPTION ===>_ZCMD                                          +
%                                          +USERID   -&ZUSER
%  0 +ISPF PARMS  -Specify user parms      +TIME     -&ZTIME
%  U +UTILITY     -Invoke Demo Utility Program
%  T +TUTORIAL    -Display information on this application
%  X +EXIT        -Terminate ISPF using list/log defaults
%
+Enter%END+command to terminate application.
%
)INIT
  .HELP = DEMOH01      /* Help for this panel              */
  &ZPRIM = YES         /* This is a primary option menu    */
  &ZHTOP = DEMOH01     /* Help table of contents for appl */
```

```
)PROC
 &ZSEL = TRANS( TRUNC (&ZCMD,'.')
               0,'PANEL(ISPOPTA)'
               U,'CMD(%DEMOC01) NEWAPPL(DEMO)'
               T,'PGM(ISPTUTOR) PARM(ISP00000)'
              ' ',' '
               X,'EXIT'
               *,'?')
)END
```

DEMOP02 Panel

```
)BODY
%-----------------------INPUT PANEL-----------------------
%COMMAND ===>_ZCMD
  + Fill in the following value to be passed to the
   utility program UTILPGM:

     Parm%===>_UTILPARM +


                                                  %Press ENTER

)INIT
 .CURSOR = UTILPARM
 .HELP = DEMOH02
)PROC
 VER (&UTILPARM,NB,MSG = DEMOM011)
)END
```

DEMOH01 Panel

```
%----------------------Demo Tutorial----------------------
%OPTION ===>_ZCMD                                        +

              %  ----------------------------

                |  Tutorial Selection Panel  |
                 ----------------------------

+ The following topics will be presented in
  sequence, or may be selected by number.
```

```
    % I+- Demo input panel.
      The following topic will be presented only if
      explicitly selected by number.
    % E+- Edit
Type%END+on the Option line, or press%PF-3,+to end-
tutorial.
)PROC
  &ZSEL = TRANS( &ZCMD
                 I,DEMOH02
                 E,*ISR20000
                ' ',' '
                 *,'?')
)END
```

DEMOH02 Panel

```
%---------------Tutorial for Demo Input Panel---------------
%OPTION ===>_ZCMD

                        %  --------------------
                          |  Demo Input Panel   |
                           --------------------

+   This panel is for data capture. Data on the input line
   will be verified before it is accepted.
)END
```

Explanation

$CONCAT CLIST This executes before anything else, allocating the necessary clist, panel, and message datasets. Note that application clists are allocated before the system clists, but the system panel and message datasets are allocated before the application datasets. This order determines which dataset ISPF searches first. (Thus an application panel with the same name (id) as a system panel does not display.) The BLKSIZE operand specifies the maximum block size for libraries in the concatenation.

DEMO Clist This clist uses &SYSISPF to detect if you are in ISPF. If not, then invoke ISPF and display the DEMO primary option menu panel (DEMOP01).

DEMOC01 Clist This clist executes if selecting option U (Utility) on the DEMO primary option menu panel (DEMOP01). It suppresses informational messages from the TSO commands used in allocating an output dataset to the terminal. The DEMO input panel (DEMOP02) then displays to read the user's input parameter. It then saves this parameter to the profile variable pool (VPUT statement). Next, call the COBOL load module and pass this input parameter. Exit the clist after completion.

DEMOM01 Message Library   If the user enters no input parameters on the DEMO input panel (DEMOP02), then display the DEMOM011 message prompting the user for a parameter.

UTILLIB Program   This is the source for the load module that just writes to the screen what the input parameter was.

DEMOP01 Panel   The DEMO primary option panel that is identical to the selection panels presented earlier in the chapter. Note that option O displays the system ISPF parameter option selection panel (you can mix system and application panels together). Option U invokes the DEMOC01 (DEMO utility program) clist in full-screen mode (because of the %). Note that you can use NEWAPPL in the PROC section as well as ISPSTART for establishing an application id. Selecting option T invokes the ISPTUTOR program, which calls the ISPF tutorial panel hierarchy. It passes the first panel's name (ISP00000) as a PARM.

DEMOP02 Panel   The DEMO input panel with associated panel DEMOH02. The PROC section verifies that the user has entered an input parameter. Else, a message appears prompting the user for a parameter.

DEMOH01 Panel   An example of a help selection panel. Option I is an application help panel and option E is a system help panel. Note the highlighting of END and PF3.

DEMOH02 Panel   The help panel associated with DEMOP02. It explains what the DEMO input panel does.

THE FUTURE OF ISPF

ISPF Version 3 was announced February 1989. It includes the major features necessary to implement SAA (Systems Application Architecture) under MVS. SAA is a set of *evolving* software user interfaces and standards announced in March of 1987. (SAA will never be cast in stone—expect its components to be constantly updated.) This change coupled with the lack of a uniform SAA compliance certification system has some critics charging that few know what SAA really is and that this limits its chances for becoming a popular standard. This allows IBM mainframes, minicomputers, and microcomputers (using OS/2) all to operate in nearly the same manner.

One part of SAA is common user access interface (CUA), which provides a consistent screen format on all IBM machines. (However, it was announced in

1989 that CUA screens may have differences between operating systems.) *In fact, just using CUA screens means an application is SAA-compliant!* Users of OS/2 already have CUA windows each with title, action, scroll bars, function key area, and screen text. Pull-down menus and multiple windows are also featured in CUA-based applications. This means your present terminals will soon include input devices taking advantage of CUA. (A mouse, trackball, touch screen, or . . . ?) Also, IBM and Microsoft are working together so you can easily port CUA screens to UNIX and other operating systems. This should be out in late 1990. At about that time, you will be able to port CUA screens to the X Windows environment (a graphical interface capable of running on *any* operating system.)

Two other major trends are also taking place. The first is DISTRIBUTED, or COOPERATIVE, PROCESSING (meaning an application will be displayed and executed on one or more machines simultaneously or nearly simultaneously). Some time during 1990, you will be able to port CUA Screens to the X Window System (a public domain windowing interface which supports distributed processing by allowing an application(s) running on other networked computers look like it is running on your own terminal). SAA-compliant Office Vision is another example of distributed computing for office automation software. DISTRIBUTED PROGRAM DEVELOPMENT will also increase. Both IBM & Sage Software provide packages to help develop ISPF applications in a MS-DOS or PC-DOS, and OSZ environment.

The second trend for CUA applications is supporting *object-oriented programming,* which uses and modifies predefined blocks of code rather than creating programs line by line (so that a block defines "color" or "menu" and does not have to be created from scratch). It is a good guess that object-oriented programming will someday come to ISPF. What this eventually means is strong portability and ease of development.

Version 3 uses the new Dialog Tag Language (DTL) to create a dialog in a CUA format. You can then convert your existing dialogs to a CUA format using the utility explained in IBM's *ISPF Conversion Utility User's Guide and Reference* (SC34-4216.) *However, you can continue using ISPF Version 2 panels and services under Version 3 without modification.* Other related IBM user guides include GC26-4341 *SAA: An Overview,* and SC26-4351 *SAA Common User Interface.*

The other major feature of ISPF Version 3 is the ability to write dialogs in C and REXX. (See Chapter 11 for more on REXX.) REXX is the interpetive language that SAA uses and will eventually replace clists for TSO.

SUGGESTED READINGS

Arnold, Jonathan, 1989. "The X Window System," *MIPS*. December 1989, pp 82–87.

Azevedo, Joey A., 1986. ISPF Dialog Management. *SHARE 66 Proceedings,* pp. 2350–2418.

Azevedo, Joe A., 1986. ISPF Dialog Management Tutorial. *SHARE 66 Proceedings,* pp. 2339–2348.

Balsly, Charles S., 1989. The State of SAA. *Systems User.* April 1989, pp. 5–6.

Beebe, Caroline, 1988. Developing Screen Design Standards. *Proceedings of the Digital Equipment Computer Users Society USA Spring 1988,* pp. 77–84.

Colonna, Jerome D., Michael Puttre, and Charles Pelton, 1989. "IBM's Wheeler Clarifies SAA," *Information Week.* July 17, pp. 12–13.

Eskrow, Dennis, 1989. "SAGE Brings ISPF Interface to Workstation," *Information Week.* May 22, p. 14.

Fosdick, Howard, 1987. *Using IBM's ISPF Dialog Manager Under MVS, VM, and VSE.* New York: Van Nostrand Reinhold.

German, Hallett, 1987. *Clist Tips.* Unpublished document. GTE Laboratories.

Hakenewerth, Skip, 1987. ISPF Made TSO/E-ASY. *SHARE 69 Proceedings,* pp. 1–27 (handout).

Hoffman, Charles A., 1987. *ISPF Dialog Management Services.* (Course notes).

IBM Corporation, 1988. *INFO/SYSTEM Database.* Various notes.

IBM Corporation, 1987. *Interactive System Productivity Facility Version 2 Release 3 Dialog Management Guide.* SC34-4112.

IBM Corporation, 1987. *Interactive System Productivity Facility Version 2 Release 3 Dialog Management Services and Examples.* SC34-4113.

IBM Corporation. 1987. *Interactive System Productivity Facility (ISPF) and Program Development Facility Version 2 Release 3 Installation and Customization.* SC34-4117.

IBM Corporation, 1987. *Interactive System Productivity Facility (ISPF) and Program Development Facility Version 2 Release 3 Primer.* SC34-4122.

IBM Corporation, 1987. *Interactive System Productivity Facility Version 2 Release 3 Services.* SC34-4119.

IBM Corporation, 1989. *Interactive System Productivity Facility Version 3 Announcement.* MVS 5685-054.

Joslin, P. H., 1981. System Productivity Facility. *IBM Systems Journal.* 20(4), pp. 388–406.

Kerr, Susan, 1989. "Cooperative Processing Part One: The Host Perspective," *Datamation,* September, pp. 45–47.

Majkiewicz, Jane, 1989. "A Test for SAA?," *Datamation.* October 15, pp. 37–40.

Martin, James, 1989, "SAA's Presentation, Dialog Interface Fuse Programming," *PC Week,* August 14, p. 68.

Maurer, M. E., 1983. Full-Screen Testing of Interactive Applications. *IBM Systems Journal.* 22(3), pp. 246–261.

Stewart, Eric A., 1987. ISPF Advanced Dialogs. *SHARE 69 Proceedings,* pp. 1–30.

Veilleux, Joe, 1984. SPF Hints. Examples, and Tricks. *SHARE 62 Proceedings,* pp. 2450–2451.

10

ISPF/PDF and PDF Edit Macros

This chapter continues reviewing the features of ISPF. In particular, it discusses the Program Development Facility (PDF), PDF EDIT, and PDF EDIT Macros.

WHAT IS PDF?

As stated in Chapter 9, PDF (Program Development Facility) is a system supplied dialog. You use PDF to edit or browse data, compile and test programs in foreground operation, and other dataset operations. All discussed features are available in ISPF Version 2 Release 2 and later.

Table 10-1 lists popular ISPF options and suboptions. Some of these may be different at your site.

ISPF provides a JUMP feature for quick movement between panels. For example, putting =3.4 and pressing ENTER or PF4 (RETURN) in the *COMMAND* ===> or *OPTION* ===> area of a panel moves to the dataset list utility screen (or option 3, suboption 4). The exceptions are SDSF (system log display and search facility, see Chapter 2) if installed and ISPF dialog test. Any entered JUMP commands pertain only to SDSF or dialog test panels, not the main ISPF panels.

PDF easily does some functions that otherwise require a clist or JCL program. With foreground/background compiling and link-editing capabilities, and a complete ISPF dialog Manager test facility, PDF provides high programmer productivity. The rest of the chapter examines the most powerful editor of those reviewed so far—PDF EDIT.

Table 10-1. Popular ISPF Options and Suboptions

Option/Suboption		Function
0		Set terminal, PF key, and list/log dataset characteristics
	0.1	Set terminal characteristics (number of PF keys, and terminal type).
	0.2	Set list/log dataset characteristics (e.g., keep or delete, sysout class.)
	0.3	Display and change PF key values.
1		Browse a sequential or partitioned dataset (or member).
2		Edit a sequential or partitioned dataset (or member). Also can process an edit macro.
3		Utilities (system-supplied and local).
	3.1	Browse, delete, print, or rename partitioned dataset member(s).
	3.2	Allocate, display information, print or rename sequential or partitioned datasets.
	3.3	Move or copy datasets or members.
	3.4	Dataset list utility. Combines 3.1 and 3.2
4		Foreground compiling and link editing for assembly and other languages.
5		Background compiling and link editing for assembly and other languages.
6		TSO command processor (and optionally Session Manager).
7		ISPF Dialog Manager test (see Chapter 9).
9		IBM products (available in ISPF Version 2 Release 3 and later. This includes the INFO/SYSTEM database.)
C		Tutorial on changes and enhancements in current ISPF release (including latest documentation order numbers).
T		PDF tutorial.
X		Exit PDF (usually return to TSO).

PDF EDIT

Overview

EDIT Features

PDF EDIT is a full-screen editor with the following features:

- Ability to edit fixed/variable-length, blocked/unblocked, partitioned, or sequential datasets. The first column can have carriage control characters. Maximum logical record length for an edited dataset is 255 (fixed length) and 259 (variable). Browsed datasets can be longer.

- EDIT has two types of commands. Line commands are entered in the line number area. They affect a line or a block of lines. Primary commands affect the entire dataset and are entered in the COMMAND ===> field of a panel.
- EDIT is very much a WYSIWYG (what you see is what you get) editor. To add or change text, generally just enter it.
- Processing can include EDIT macros (new or changed EDIT primary or line commands.)
- PF keys provide dataset scrolling and perform the most common edit tasks.

Starting and Ending EDIT

After entering a 2 on the primary option menu panel, you see the EDIT–ENTRY panel. A simplified version is listed below (reprinted by permission from Interactive System Productivity Facility [ISPF] and ISPF/Program Development Facility, Version 2 Release 3 Primer © 1987 by International Business Corporation, p. 403):

```
---------------------EDIT-ENTRY PANEL---------------------
COMMAND ===>
ISPF LIBRARY:
  PROJECT ===> HHG1
  GROUP   ===> YR88
  TYPE    ===> CLIST
  MEMBER  ===> CLIST1
OTHER PARTITIONED OR SEQUENTIAL DATASET:
  DATA SET NAME ===>
  INITIAL MACRO ===>
```

Here are some more comments on the EDIT–ENTRY panel:

1. Enter one or more TSO commands in the *Command* ===> field.
2. Enter three-qualifier dataset names in the *project, group,* and *type* fields. If a partitioned dataset and not specifying a member, then a member list displays. The user places an *S* next to the desired member name or adds a member name in the *member* field.
3. Enter other names in the *data set names* field of the *other partitioned or sequential dataset.*
4. One way to invoke an EDIT macro is placing the macro name in the *INITIAL MACRO* ===> field.

If HHG1.YR88.CLIST(CLIST1) is an existing dataset, then you see something similar to the following:

```
EDIT ---- HHG1.YR88.CLIST(CLIST1) - 01.09 ---COLUMNS 001 072
COMMAND ===>_                                  SCROLL ===> HALF
**********************************************************
000001  PROC 0 CTEST
000002  IF &CTEST = CTEST THEN CONTROL CONLIST LIST
  (more clist code)
000010  EXIT CODE(&MAXCC)
```

The following are the components of the above screen:

1. *Header* contains the edited dataset name, its version number (the ninth), and the starting and ending columns on the screen.
2. *Command* ===> field for TSO commands (preceded by TSO commands) or *edit primary commands*. This is the initial cursor position.
3. *Scroll* ==> field for screen scrolling. Values are *half* (half a screen), *page* (an entire screen), and *cursor* (places the current line first on the screen. This is my favorite scrolling value.).
4. Six-digit *line numbers* (e.g., 000001 through 000010) usually in increments of 1, 10, or 100, tell the position of a line in a dataset. Also enter here any *EDIT line commands*. If in insert mode, then six dots appear instead.
5. *Text area* for adding or writing over text.

Keep these components in mind when we review EDIT primary and line commands.

To end an EDIT session, enter END or RETURN in the *COMMAND* ===> field. You can also press PF3 (END) or PF4 (RETURN). If not wanting to save your EDIT session changes, then enter CANCEL in the *COMMAND* ===> field. This cancels all changes from the start of the EDIT session or the last time the dataset was saved. (SAVE allows saving of your edit session changes without leaving edit.)

Since EDIT macros perform the equivalent of both primary and line EDIT commands, it is necessary to review them.

Primary Commands

EDIT primary commands affect usually the entire dataset or particular columns in a dataset. Enter them on the *COMMAND* ===> line or by pressing a PF key. Table 10-2 lists the edit commands to be discussed.

Since ISPF Version 2 Release 1, you may assign one or more lines a *label* (or line marker). The power of labels is that they help perform edit operations without entering the exact line number. This is invaluable for our later discussion of EDIT macros. *Valid label names start with a period and are up to five alphabetical*

Table 10-2. Primary EDIT Commands

Command	Function
	String Operations
CHANGE or CHG	Changes a text, numeric, or mixed string to a specified modification.
FIND or F	Searches for a character, numeric, or mixed string.
	Profile Operations
CAPS	Converts new text to uppercase.
HEX	Displays dataset in hexadecimal format.
NULLS or NUL	Decides what the keyboard does when inserting new text at the end of current text.
	Member Operations
COPY	Places another member into the current edited dataset but retains the original.
MOVE	Places another member into the current edited dataset but deletes the original.
	Other Commands
CANCEL or CAN	Cancels EDIT session changes.
END	Ends an EDIT session and save changes.
RECOVERY or REC	Saves data if EDIT session unexpectedly ends.
RESET or RES	Clears the screen.
SAVE	Saves EDIT session changes without leaving EDIT.
SORT	Sorts the dataset (ISPF Version 2 Release 2 and later).
SUBMIT or SUB	Submits a batch program.

characters. Note that EDIT macros can have up to eight character labels and only system labels can start with a Z. System labels include .ZCSR (current cursor location), .ZFIRST (relative first line), and .ZLAST (relative last line). To assign a label, simply type the name in the line number area of a data line. Just remove the name to erase the label. *By using labels, many EDIT primary commands can specify line ranges in addition to column ranges*. These are CHANGE, COPY, FIND, DELETE, MOVE, SORT, and SUBMIT.

String Operations

The following are common uses of the FIND and CHANGE commands:

1. FIND 'test' Finds the next instance of the character string test in *any* case and moves the cursor there. (NEXT is the default for both FIND and CHANGE.) Other values are ALL, FIRST, LAST, and PREV (previous). This searches all columns because there is no column specifier. The found string can be in upper-, lower-, or mixed case—the CAPS MODE setting has

no effect on the match. Enclose in single or double quotes search strings containing special characters (including blank or comma). A simple character string like *test* does not require quotes.

2. F' ' ALL 1 2 Searches for all instances of a blank space between columns 1 and 2.

3. FIND P',' LAST 1 1 Searches for the last occurrence of a nondisplayable character in column 1. The P',' is a picture string available for use by the FIND and CHANGE commands. Here is the complete list:

   P'=' All characters
   P'¬' All nonblank characters
   P'.' All nondisplayable characters
   P'$' All special characters
   P'−' All nonnumeric characters
   P'@' All letters
   P'<' All lowercase letters
   P'>' All uppercase letters
   P'#' All numeric characters

   You can use more than one picture string combined with text (e.g., P'<>#'—a lowercase letter followed by an uppercase letter and a numeric such as sP2). Also prefix text with a C for character (for exact mataches) or H for hexadecimal searches. (e.g., C'TexT' matches *only* TEXT.)

4. CHANGE 'TEST' 'TEXT' Changes the next instance of TEST to TEXT in any column and moves the cursor to the end of the replaced text. CHANGE can use any of the operands or picture strings listed above for FIND. However, the length of the "from" and "to" strings must be the same. You may use these special characters in "to" picture strings: = (no change), > (uppercase only if in lowercase, else no change) and < (lowercase only if in uppercase, else no change). For example, CHG 'TEXT' P'<<<<' converts all four characters to lowercase.

Profile Operations

EDIT maintains up to 25 "profiles" for each user, which store tab and other session settings. The dataset type decides the profile used (such as FORT, DATA, CLIST). Entering PROFILE 7 displays the current (usually default) profile settings on the top dataset lines. Using RESET clears the profile display. PROFILE LOCK "freezes" the current profile settings until issuing a PROFILE UNLOCK or entering a command to change a profile setting. Three special display modes are commonly used—CAPS, HEX, and NULLS. The EDIT profile stores the current settings of each mode. The following are guidelines for using them:

1. CAPS ON This is the default that converts all existing and added (input) text to uppercase (double-byte characters are unchanged). However, the CAPS setting changes if entered data does not match the setting. (Such as entering all lowercase text with a CAPS ON setting.) It is the usual setting for program source.
2. CAPS OFF Leaves all existing and added (input) text unchanged (i.e., lowercase stays lowercase). This is the usual setting for text datasets.
3. HEX ON Enables hexadecimal mode for displaying a dataset. (The default in HEX OFF.) This is useful in debugging programs and examining object datasets. One line in "normal" display uses four lines in hexadecimal display. (The first line is the normal or EBCDIC display of text or data, the next two lines are the hexadecimal representation of the text or data, and the last line is a divider.) You may display HEX characters vertically (HEX ON VERT, which is the default for HEX ON) or horizontally with HEX ON DATA. Here is an example of both types of displays:

```
 HEX ON VERT              HEX ON DATA
-------------             ----------------------
TEXT 987654               TEXT 987654
ECEE4FFFFFF44             E3C5E7E340F9F8F7F6F5F4
3573098765400             4040404040404040404040
```

   T has a hex value of E3. With HEX ON VERT, you just read the value under the normal charcter (T). HEX ON DATA displays the data in a more compact format but is harder for new users to understand. To change or add a normal or hex value, just overwrite it with valid characters.
4. As mentioned earlier, your NULLS setting decides if you can insert text. If NULLS OFF (the default), then EDIT inserts blank spaces instead of null (no) spaces after the last character. This means the INSERT key locks up when adding text because something (a blank) occupies a space. To add text, go one space past the last character and press ERASE EOF to delete all blank spaces. Then go back to where you want to insert text and press the INSERT key again. One advantage to NULLS OFF is that spaces between text are retained:

```
000100  TEXT WITH SPACES                           RETAINED
```

   The following shows what happens with NULLS ON:

```
000100  TEXT WITH SPACES RETAINED
```

5. NULLS ON (the default) makes it easier to insert text by placing null, not blank, spaces after the last character. However, by removing blank spaces, text shifts to the left. NULLS ON STD (the default) replaces all blanks after the last character with a null space. The exceptions are the first blank after the last character and blanks up to the cursor. Therefore, a blank line locks up unless following the approach suggested under NULLS OFF. NULLS ON ALL is the same as NULLS ON STD except only blanks up to the cursor are unchanged.

Member Operations

During an editing session, you often need to manipulate or include text from other members or datasets as well. COPY duplicates part or all of a dataset or member in the edited dataset and retains the original, whereas MOVE relocates an entire dataset or member in the edited dataset and deletes the original. The following are guidelines in using the COPY and MOVE commands:

1. Entering COPY or MOVE and no other operands, the EDIT–COPY or EDIT–MOVE panel appears. (It is nearly the same as the EDIT–ENTRY panel shown earlier.) Then you may enter the name of any sequential dataset or partitioned dataset member. The EDIT–COPY screen also can set the number of lines to copy and the copying mode of *STANDARD* (use line numbers), *COBOL,* or *RELATIVE.* (Ignore sequence numbers and use position in the dataset such as the tenth line rather than 000001.) Most of the time you will use RELATIVE. Put a B (before) or an A (after) on the *appropriate line numbers in* the edited dataset to place correctly the copied or moved dataset. (A and B are line commands.)
2. To copy or move another member of the same partitioned dataset into an edited dataset, enter COPY membername or MOVE membername on the command line.

Other Commands

Most of these commands deal with exiting EDIT. Here is a summary of each one:

1. CANCEL and END both finish an EDIT session. CANCEL, or CAN, does not save any changes unless you have previously issued a SAVE. This is a handy "escape route" if you entered something accidentally. END just ends the session. Enter SAVE;END to save the EDIT session changes and end the session. (This is required if disabling automatic saves. AUTOSAVE OFF is the default EDIT profile setting.) SAVE stores the EDIT session changes in the same dataset or member and does not end the session.

2. RECOVERY ON, or REC ON, enables PDF to save your editing session changes in a table called ISREDRT and recall them later if a session unexpectedly ends. (A temporary backup dataset stores the changes until the EDIT session ends. SPF saved changes in a temporary backup dataset called 'yourid.SPFEDITA.BACKUP.') If this happens, PDF prompts the next time you access the dataset to do one of the following:

- Press *ENTER* to recover the last EDIT session changes and edit the dataset.
- Type in *CANCEL* to edit the dataset without recovering the last EDIT session changes.
- Type in *DEFER* to edit the dataset and recover the last edit session changes at another time.

   Although RECOVERY ON is a useful feature, it does use more space and memory and can slow your response time. It is quite common to run out of temporary backup space for a frequently edited dataset.

3. Messages appear in the line numbers area after processing some EDIT line and primary commands (such as CHANGE). To remove any or all of these messages, issue a RESET or RES command. The following are examples of RESET:
   a. RESET   Clears all messages in a dataset. If you assigned a label to one or more lines, this retains the label message.
   b. RESET LABEL CHANGE ERROR   Clears all label (LABEL or LAB), changed lines (CHANGE or CHG), and error (ERROR or ERR) messages. Use each of these operands (i.e., LABEL, CHANGE, ERROR) together or separately.
4. Since ISPF Version 2 Release 2, EDIT contains a SORT primary command that is ideal for simple sorts on small datasets. The sorting sequence used depends on your installation and display mode. You can find more on sorting tables and customizing PDF in the *ISPF Installation and Customization Guide*. Hexadecimal mode sorts by hex values while normal-mode sorts use a table for your particular written language. Here are some sort examples:
   a. SORT   Sorts the dataset in ascending order (the default) based on the line's value (usually just the first field).
   b. SORT D 1 10   Sorts columns 1 through 10 in descending order (D). You may specify up to five such pairs of sort order and range (column numbers).
5. SUBMIT or SUB places a job for processing in background (batch) mode. No other operands are usually necessary. (None are available in SPF and ISPF Version 1.)

PF Keys

As mentioned earlier, ISPF has assigned many EDIT primary commands to PF keys. Table 10-3 lists the PF keys and their default settings. Unless otherwise marked, they can be used elsewhere in PDF:

Table 10-3. EDIT PF Keys

PF1/13	PF2/14	PF3/15	PF4/16
HELP Access tutorial.	SPLIT SCREEN Split the screen.	END End panel and more up in hierarchy.	RETURN End panel and more to the previous menu.
PF5/17	**PF6/18**	**PF7/19**	**PF8/20**
FIND or RFIND (EDIT) Search/continue searching for string.	CHANGE or RCHANGE (EDIT) Modify/continue modifying string.	SCROLL UP Scroll toward top of screen.	SCROLL DOWN Scroll toward bottom of screen.
PF9/21	**PF10/22**	**PF11/23**	**PF12/24**
SWAP Move cursor between two screens in split screen mode.	SCROLL LEFT Move to the left of the screen.	SCROLL RIGHT Move to the right of the screen.	CURSOR Move the cursor usually to the COMMAND ===> or OPTION ===> area.

With ISPF (not SPF), you can press the RFIND or RCHANGE keys to process a series of searches or changes. There are also other settings that you can assign to any PF key. Use the PF Key Setting Panel (PDF 0.3) to assign any of the following:

- Multiple commands separated by semicolons. SORT ;FIND 'X'
- Precede an edit line command with a colon. :D Without the colon prefix, PDF assumes it is an edit PRIMARY command.
- Settings not assigned to any PF key like PRINT (puts a copy of the screen in the session log).
- Labels to be used with PF keys.

Line Commands

While EDIT primary commands usually affect the entire dataset or particular columns in the dataset, line commands affect one or more specified lines. One or more line commands (if not conflicting) may be typed in the line number area of the edit screen. *Then press the ENTER key to process.* Use the RESET command to clear any error messages. To process a set of contiguous lines or a block, enter a block version of the line command. (Which usually just repeats the command letter so D (delete) becomes DD.) Another option is using a single letter followed by a number. (For example, D5 deletes the next five lines, including the line where the command appears. A DD at the start and end of the block does the same thing.) Table 10-4 lists common EDIT line commands:

The following are guidelines in using EDIT line commands:

1. Here is an example of using a direction command with a M (MOVE) block command. This is nearly identical for the C (COPY) command.

Table 10-4. Common EDIT Line Commands

Command	Block Command	Function
		*Location Commands**
A	An†	Perform operation after this line.
B	Bn	Perform operation before this line.
O	OO	Overlay (copy or move) columns to another location.
	On	
		String Operations (Version 2 Release 2 and Later)
LC	LCC	Converts text to lowercase.
	LCn	
UC	UCC	Converts text to uppercase.
	UCn	
		Line Commands
C	CC	Copy one or more lines to another location.
	Cn	
D	Dn	Delete one or more lines.
	DD	
I	In	Insert one or more blank lines.
M	MM	Move one or more lines to another location.
	Mn	
R	RR	Repeat one or more lines.
	RRn	
	Rn	
TE	TEn	Enables typing without boundaries.
TF	TFn	Reformats (wraps) text.
TS	TSn	Insert new text.
		Other Commands
COLS		Gives a header with column numbers.
)	))n	Shifts text right.
)n		
(	))	Shifts text left.
(n		

* Use these commands with C (Copy) or M (Move).

† n is any valid integer.

```
Before (or use M2)                        After
MM0001  This is line one.    000001  This is line
                                     three.
MM0002  This is line two.    000002  This is line one.
A00003  This is line-        000003  This is line two.
        three.
```

Do not use A and B or COPY and MOVE together.

2. For data entry and text manipulation, the COLS command is invaluable by giving a header with column numbers:

```
COLS> ----+----1-----+----2----+----3----+----4-----+-
  |     |                  |                        |
 Cols Column 1          Column 15                Column 40
Message
```

   Entering a D or RESET primary command removes the header.

3. I (INSERT) adds one or blank lines, saves any entered text or data, and renumbers the dataset. Otherwise, pressing ENTER removes the blank line.

4. The O (OVERLAY) command allows one or more columns of data to be moved up or down:

```
Before                                    After
M00001  This is                000001  This is moved up.
000002  Lots of text.          000002  Lots of text.
O00003          moved up.      000003
```

   This overwrites any text that currently appears in the "to" location.

5. The text commands (TE, TF, and TS) provide word-processing capabilities to PDF EDIT:
   a. TE (Text Entry) Like INSERT, you can add text but in one contiguous area rather than distinct lines. After pressing ENTER, the text wraps (flows together).
   b. TF (Text Flow) Enables the flow of a paragraph until finding a period, colon, or ampersand in the first column. TFn specifies the last column to wrap text up to. Here is a text flow up to column 15.

```
Before
TF1501 Text Flow works great. Here is an example.
000002
After
COLS> ----+----1----+----2----+----3----+----4----+-
000001 Text Flow works
000002 great. Here is
000003 an example
```

c. Use TS (Text Split) for inserting text easily in a paragraph. Just type in TS on the desired line, place the cursor at the insert point, and press ENTER. All text after the split starts on a new line. TSn indicates how many blank lines to insert.

Before

```
TS2001  Let us split text right here_. And
more text.
                                    |
                                    Cursor
```

After

```
000001  Let us split text right here_.
 ......
 ......                                  — 2 blank lines
 000004  And more text.
         |
         Remaining text
```

6. Use),)), (, and ((for shifting text/data left or right in a line. However, it does overwrite existing text or data in doing this. (Unlike its counterpart >> or <<.)

EDIT MACROS

What Are Edit Macros?

PDF EDIT macros have been available since ISPF Version 2 Release 1. An *EDIT MACRO* is an ISPF/PDF primary EDIT command consisting of one or more clist-like statements performing some specified edit task (usually repetitively). These clist statements reside as a member of a partitioned dataset part of the SYSPROC (clist) concatenation. You can create EDIT macros with clists, EXEC2, and REXX. These are called *command language macros* or *command macros* and all EDIT macro commands begin with ISREDIT. (The name of the ISPF service for edit macros.) Or you can use these programming languages: APL2, Assembler, C, COBOL, FORTRAN, PASCAL, and PL/I. (Check if they are available for your release.) These are called *programming language macros* or *program macros*. Access EDIT macro commands used by program macros by CALL ISPEXEC or ISPLINK. FORTRAN and Pascal use ISPLNK or ISPEX instead. The emphasis of this section is on command language macros. (We will briefly look at program macros near the end of the chapter.)

The following are the major capabilities of EDIT macros:

1. Override EDIT primary commands with your own.
2. *Initial macros,* which execute before displaying a dataset.

3. *Recovery macros,* which restore the EDIT profile of a dataset after an EDIT session's unexpected end.
4. Extend EDIT's capability:
   - Draw simple graphics or process simple games.
   - Set up your own EDIT profile.
   - Perform simple sorts.
   - Pass one or more lines in a dataset to a clist.
   - Edit two datasets or members at once.
   - Customize FIND or DELETE primary EDIT commands.
   - Change a few lines in a dataset and submit it for background execution.
   - Query DCB information about the edited dataset (or use the TSO command LISTDSI instead).
   - List all members of a partitioned dataset.
   - List when the last changes to PDS members were made.
   - You are only limited by your imagination and hardware!
5. Faster to use than all line editors (such as TSO EDIT or QED).
6. Can use other ISPF services. This includes VGET and VPUT to pass values between a clist and an EDIT macro.
7. Can nest up to 255 EDIT macros.
8. Mixing clist or REXX statements, TSO commands, and EDIT macro commands without error.

The following are common problems or disadvantages with EDIT macros.

- There is no built-in function to pass values between clists and EDIT macros or the reverse. However, using VGET and VPUT is an indirect means to do this.
- EDIT macros are slow for datasets with 5000 or more records. One solution is to run the macro in background or use a program macro. Before TSO/E Version 1 Release 4, program macros had additional advantages, including better flow control statements and the ability to process double-byte or mixed-character strings. Since then, the major advantages of program macros continue to be speed and language features.
- There are no validations to verify if passed symbolic variable values are out of order (being positional) or not entered.

How to Invoke EDIT Macros

Before discussing how to invoke command language macros, let's briefly review macro name syntax. As stated earlier, an EDIT macro is stored as a member of a partitioned dataset part of the SYSPROC concatenation and follows the same rules for valid member names. Usually, the member name is also the name of the EDIT macro. (Using the edit macro ISREDIT DEFINE command, you can also assign an alias.) Do not use a macro name that can be confused with a EDIT primary command. (How to override an EDIT primary command is discussed later.)

You can invoke an EDIT macro by any of the following four methods:

1. Do one of the following for specifying an *initial* macro to process before displaying a dataset:
   a. use the *IMACRO macroname* primary EDIT command.
   b. Use the EDIT macro command *ISREDIT IMACRO* = macroname.
   c. Type in the initial edit macro name in the *INITIAL MACRO* ===> area of the EDIT–ENTRY panel (PDF option 2.)

   Only approaches *a* and *b* save the initial macro name in the EDIT profile. This becomes the initial macro for *all* edited datasets in this and *future* EDIT sessions. Use a macroname of NONE to clear a stored initial macro.

2. Specify a *recovery macro,* which restores an edit profile if an EDIT session unexpectedly ends. One of the following methods assigns a recovery macro to automatically execute before displaying a dataset.
   a. Use the *RMACRO macroname* primary edit command.
   b. Use the EDIT macro command *ISREDIT RMACRO = macroname.*

3. Invoke an EDIT macro from a clist within ISPF or after invoking ISPF.
   ```
   ALLOC F(Filename) DSN(datasetname) SHR
   ISPEXEC EDIT DATASET(datasetname) MACRO(macroname)
   ```
   Where *datasetname* is a valid sequential or partitioned dataset (member) name. The dataset is displayed after program completion. Any informational or warning messages appear in the top right corner. The EDIT macro in this case is really a one-time initial EDIT macro but cannot pass any symbolic variable values. I recommend adding a code sequence to check if the macro and the edited dataset exist.

4. After the *COMMAND* ===> part of the EDIT screen. An information or error message displays after macro processing. PDF EDIT thinks that any unknown text in this area is a user-defined command (not program) macro—so beware! This is the only approach that directly passes *positional* symbolic variable values. (Use the ISPEXEC VGET and VPUT commands for initial and recovery macros.) Use as many variable values as needed, separated by blanks or commas. Use single or double quotes to pass symbolic variable values with special characters such as blanks.

EDIT Macro Basics

This section takes a closer look at EDIT macros by reviewing the macro structure, major concepts, and basic statements.

The Macro Skeleton

EDIT macros always begin with an *ISREDIT MACRO* statement, which identifies the partitioned dataset member as an edit macro. Here are some examples of the ISREDIT MACRO statement:

1. ISREDIT MACRO(LASTNAME) Defines an EDIT macro with one symbolic variable. (Always enclose variables in parentheses.) If the macro name is NAMECHG, then enter at *COMMAND* ===> area of the EDIT screen NAMECHG GERMAN. Then assign &LASTNAME the value of GERMAN. Here is some other information about passing symbolic variable values.
   - PDF assigns a null value if there is no symbolic variable value. You must code a sequence to check if a value was entered—the macro does not do this!
   - A macro ends if you pass one or more symbolic variable values to a macro that does not have any values defined (such as ISREDIT MACRO.)
   - You may pass multiple symbolic variable values to an EDIT macro, but *beware*! EDIT macro symbolic variable values are positional, so PDF assigns the first value to the first variable regardless if it is valid or not. It is up to you to add a sequence to check if you are entering a symbolic variable value out of order. If there are more symbolic variable values than defined, it assigns all remaining values to the last symbolic variable. (So if entering DAYWEEK MON TUES WED THU and the macro is defined by ISREDIT MACRO (DAY1 DAY2), then *&DAY2* has the value of *TUES WED THU*.)
2. ISREDIT MACRO NOPROCESS Define a macro without a symbolic variable value. EDIT macros cannot issue an EDIT line command but can duplicate many of their functions. Using PROCESS or NOPROCESS decides when to accept line EDIT commands from the keyboard and process them. PROCESS automatically processes user-entered line EDIT commands before executing the next edit macro statement. (Since this is the default, it is almost never used.) Use the ISREDIT PROCESS command instead to reinvoke an EDIT macro after an ISREDIT MACRO NOPROCESS command.

   Other operands to use in an ISREDIT PROCESS command are DEST and RANGE. DEST detects if a user enters an A or B line EDIT command, which it assigns to the .ZDEST label; otherwise it is assigned to the last line. RANGE specifies up to two characters (really special line commands) for processing if the user types them in the line number area. To capture what line commands a user entered, assign a value to a symbolic variable using the RANGE_CMD command. To retrieve the line numbers of a user-specified range, examine the values of the labels .ZFRANGE (start of range) and .ZLRANGE (end of range).

NOPROCESS delays processing of user-entered line commands until the macro ends or finds an ISREDIT PROCESS command. Some reasons to use NOPROCESS are (1) to examine a line before and after processing a line EDIT command, (2) to check if all statements are correct before executing a line EDIT command, (3) to allow other statements and commands to process before executing the line EDIT commands, (4) to stop processing temporarily for issuing an ISREDIT PROCESS command with new DEST and RANGE operand values.

Usually one of the following ends an EDIT macro:

1. A clist EXIT statement with or without a CODE operand:
```
ISREDIT MACRO
(edit macro statements)
EXIT CODE(&LASTCC)
```
2. An ISREDIT END command ends the edit session and usually saves the dataset unless AUTOSAVE is off. Only TSO commands or clist statements can appear after an ISREDIT END—an ISPEXEC or ISREDIT command ends the macro with an error.
```
ISREDIT MACRO
(EDIT macro statements)
ISREDIT END
```
3. You must have an ISREDIT MEND statement for batch edit processing on a MVS/370 computer, but it is optional for MVS/XA. It is disabled for foreground EDIT macros. An EXIT command or clist statement can follow an ISREDIT MEND.
```
ISREDIT MACRO
(edit macro statements)
ISREDIT MEND
EXIT
```
4. An ISREDIT CANCEL statement stops the EDIT session and does not save any changes made during the session. Usually, only an EXIT statement appears after an ISREDIT CANCEL.
```
ISREDIT MACRO
(edit macro statements)
ISREDIT CANCEL
```

Variables, Values, and Assignment Statements

Important parts of any EDIT macro are ASSIGNMENT statements that tie a value to a symbolic (dialog variable). Before discussing ASSIGNMENT statements, let us briefly review symbolic variables and their values.

Symbolic variables used by EDIT macros are identical to those used in clists. This includes using the period for concatenation. Use eight-character names for portability between different TSO versions. Remember, clist system variables are unavailable to ISPF/PDF. Two important differences between the two are symbolic substitution methods and how to control them. PDF EDIT and the clist interpreter both perform symbolic substitution before PDF EDIT processes a statement. (Program macros use only PDF EDIT.) Placing parentheses around the variable name and omitting the ampersand stops symbolic substitution of the name. (Somewhat like &NRSTR or &SYSNSUB for clists.) However, depending on where it appears in an ASSIGNMENT statement, the variable's value may still change.

You can also stop symbolic substitution of primary EDIT commands used in edit macros by using an ISREDIT SCAN OFF statement. (ON is the default that has PDF edit perform one substitution pass.) An ISREDIT FIND &&X with SCAN OFF has the clist interpreter remove the first ampersand, but the PDF EDIT retains the second.

Symbolic variable values are one of the following:

Unquoted (simple) strings A continuous string without a blank or comma such as MOUNTAIN. Enclosing the string with single or double quotes is optional.

Quoted strings A continuous string containing blanks, commas, or other special characters enclosed in either single or double quotes, such as "TOM'S NAME."

Symbolic variable A dialog variable enclosed in parentheses to prevent symbolic substitution, such as (RCMD).

ASSIGNMENT statements are a crucial part of EDIT macros before they provide the temporary part (the value) of an EDIT macro command. PDF EDIT uses this value in processing the EDIT macro. If an operand appears on the right side of an ASSIGNMENT statement, then usually its value is passed to a symbolic variable. Otherwise, a setting or value is assigned to an operand. You may use these assignment formats:

1. *Command = Value/Command Setting* Assigns the value/command setting on the right side to the command on the left side.
   `ISREDIT SCAN = ON`
   Assigns setting (ON or OFF) to a command.
   `ISREDIT IMACRO - INITMAC`
   Assigns value (macro name) to a command.
2. *(Variable) = Command* Assigns a command setting to a symbolic variable.

```
ISREDIT (RCMD) = RANGE_CMD
```
Assigns the last line command entered to &RCMD.

3. *(Variable,Variable) = Command* Assigns two variables the current command setting. Commands that use this format are AUTOSAVE, BOUNDS, CHANGE_COUNTS, CTL_LIBRARY, CURSOR, EXCLUDE_COUNTS, FIND_COUNTS, FLOW_COUNTS, HEX, LABEL, NULLS, PROFILE, SEEK_COUNTS, and TABS.
   ```
   ISREDIT (TABS1,TABS2) = TABS
   ```
   Assigns &TABS1 ON or OFF and &TABS2 ALL or STD. Together they contain the complete TABS setting.

The following are additional guidelines for assignment statements:

1. They must always contain at least one command.
2. For multiple variable assignment statements, use a comma to assign only the second variable. At least one variable is required.
3. You cannot have mathematical expressions in assignment statements. Another way is using SET or GET statements.

Labels

When reviewing PDF EDIT, we discussed labels as a way to provide the relative position of a line. Thus performing an EDIT operation without either hardcoding the line number or knowing the actual line number is possible. *Valid label names start with a period and then have up to five alphabetical characters.* Note that EDIT macros can have up to eight-character labels.

Only system labels can start with a Z and cannot be changed by an EDIT macro. Table 10-5 lists the six system labels available for your use. All values are six characters with leading zeros retained. Retrieving a label without a value ABENDS the macro.

Table 10-5. ISPF/PDF System Labels

Name	Function	How Determined
.ZCSR	Current cursor line	Always changes to reflect current line.
.ZDEST	The "to" line for edit operations	Set to last line if not entered by user. Set by user to line before "to" line and retains value until overriden.
.ZFIRST or .ZF	Relative first line	Always changes to reflect relative first line.
.ZFRANGE	Starting line in range	Set by user and retains value until overriden.
.ZLAST or .ZL	Relative last line	Always changes to reflect relative first line.
.ZLRANGE	Ending line in range	Set by user and retains value until overriden.

As mentioned earlier, you can set .ZDEST, .ZFRANGE, and .ZLRANGE with the DEST and RANGE operands of the ISREDIT PROCESS command. IN PDF EDIT, you type the label name in the line number area to assign a label. Because a macro cannot directly enter a line EDIT command, you must use an ISREDIT LABEL statement instead. The following are some typical examples of assigning labels:

```
SET &XX = A
ISREDIT LABEL.ZCSR = .SS&XX
  IF &LASTCC = 0 OR &LASTCC = 8 THEN WRITE Label Set.
```

This assigns the current cursor position to label .SSA. Note that the clist SET statement can change a label name. .ZCSR is a line marker of the line to be labeled. Other valid markers include other system labels, user labels, and a symbolic variable with the line number as a value. Use the LINENUM command shown a little later to do this.)

```
ISREDIT (POSIT) = LABEL .LBLA
```

Assigns to &POSIT the label name .LBLA. *Remember, if the LABEL operand appears on the left side, it helps set a label. If appearing on the right side, it passes the label name to a symbolic variable.*

The following are some of the commands using labels: CHANGE, COPY, FIND, DELETE, LINE, LINE_AFTER, LINE_BEFORE, LOCATE, MOVE, SORT, and SUBMIT. Once setting the label, use the LINENUM command for retrieving its location. Here are two ways to find the number of lines in a dataset.

"Subtraction" Method

```
ISREDIT (LN) = LINENUM .ZCSR /*Assigns to &LN the
                             /*current line number.
ISREDIT (FIRST) = LINENUM .ZF /*Starting line of range.
ISREDIT (LAST) = LINENUM .ZL /*Ending line of range.
SET &DIFF = &LAST - &FIRST /*Use clist statements for-
                           /*math.
WRITE Number of lines in range is &DIFF
```

"Go-to-Last-Line" Method

```
ISREDIT (END) = LINENUM .ZLAST /*Number of lines in-
dataset.
  SET & RCD = &LASTCC
  IF &RCD = 0 THEN WRITE Label Found
  ELSE IF &RCD = 8 THEN WRITE Label Not Found
```

```
    ELSE IF &RCD = 4 OR &LASTCC = 12 THEN -
      WRITE  Check Line Number of Label
WRITE Dataset has &END Lines. /*ex. &END = 000001
```

Edit Macros with Clist Statements and other ISPF Services

The power of a command language macro increases through using clist statements and other ISPF services. The following are some guidelines for doing this:

1. You may use nearly all clist features (except system variables) with edit macros. These clist features are especially useful:
   - Clist trace facility—*CONTROL LIST CONLIST SYMLIST* particularly. *LIST* displays TSO and ISPF (including edit macro) commands and subcommands after symbolic substitution. *CONLIST* shows clist statements after symbolic substitution while *SYMLIST* shows before.
   - Clist *labels* can distinguish between different EDIT macro code sequences.
   - *SET* assigns a value to a dialog value. Here are some typical examples:

     Assign a Label Value

     ```
     SET &A = A
     ISREDIT LABEL .ZCSR = .LAB&A /* Assigns current -
                                     cursor
                                  /* position to label -
                                     .LABA.
     ```

     Assign a Line or Column Number

     ```
     SET &A = 10
     SET &B = 20 + &A /* Perform math in SET not macro -
                         edit
                      /* statements.
     ISREDIT CHANGE 'TIRED' 'HIRED' &A &B
     ```

     Changes the next instance of TIRED to HIRED in columns 10 through 30.
   - Any clist flow control statement—*IF-THEN-DO, DO-WHILE-END, Iterative and Compound DO, DO UNTIL, SELECT.*

     ```
        SET &COUNT = 1 /* Initialize counter
        DO WHILE &COUNT <= 10 /* Find first ten -
        instances of
         ISREDIT FIND 'A STRING'   /*A STRING.
            SET &RCD = &LASTCC     /*Get return code of FIND
            IF & RCD = 0 THEN DO   /*IF found A STRING.
               ISREDIT LABEL .ZCSR = .SSA
     ```

```
/* Then label the line. This is a crucial part of -
   many                                             */
/* edit macro operations:                           */
/* 1. Find a line.
/* 2. Was the line found or not found. (Check-
   & LASTCC. )                                      */
/* 3. If SUCCESSFUL:
/*    Then assign a label to the current cursor
      position.                                     */
/*    (In our example, assign a label to the line -
      with A                                        */
/*    STRING. ) Then you can perform another -
      operation on                                  */
/*    that line such as change or delete.           */
           ISREDIT DELETE .SSA .SSA /* Delete line
           SET &COUNT = &COUNT + 1 /* Bump counter
        END /* End found string loop
/* IF NOT FOUND :
/*   a. Decrement the counter by 1.
/*   b. Write number of strings found.
/*   c. End edit Macro and clist.
         IF &RCD > 0 THEN DO /* If not found A
           STRING.
           ISREDIT END /* End macro and save
           dataset.
           SET &COUNT = &COUNT - 1 /* # of times
           found.
           WRITE FOUND STRING &COUNT TIMES /*
           Message
           EXIT CODE(&RCD) /*Exit with return code
           END /*End not found string loop
END /* End DO loop
```

- *EXIT statement, IF &LASTCC, WRITE &LASTCC* Passes return code (to clist and executes statements based on values). All EDIT macro statements give a return code. Note a return code of 4 or 8 indicates a simple error or partly successful execution. Usually these can be easily fixed. A return code of 12 or higher notes a serious error that may take some time to debug.

Macro

```
EXIT CODE(&RCD)
```

Clist

```
ISPEXEC EDIT DATASET(DATA.CURRENT) MACRO(AMACRO)
 SET &RCD = &LASTCC
```

```
WRITE LASTCC -- &RCD /*Can also write return code.*/
                      /* Also could use SELECT */
IF &RCD = 0  THEN WRITE MACRO WORKED/DATASET SAVED
   ELSE IF &RCD = 4 THEN -
        WRITE MACRO WORKED/DATASET NOT SAVED
   END
   ELSE IF &RCD = 14 OR &RCD = 16 THEN -
        WRITE MEMBER NOT FOUND OR IN USE
   ELSE IF &RCD = 20 THEN WRITE FATAL ERROR
```

Also use WRITE statements with *READ* for obtaining a value. The screen clears temporarily to do this.

- *Built-in functions* (such as &DATATYPE, &LENGTH, &STR, &SUBSTR) can be useful in string operations. The example below retains a blank and a pair of single quotes.

```
SET &NAME = &STR('HALLETT GERMAN')
ISREDIT FIND 'HAL GERMAN'
        IF &LASTCC = 0 THEN DO
           ISREDIT CHANGE ALL 'HAL GERMAN' &NAME
        END
        ELSE EXIT
```

2. You also may use many other ISPF services with EDIT macros. Here are some that are particularly useful.
   - *Message services* to issue messages for invalid macro processing. If you wish to set EDIT macro messages "on the fly" rather than creating a message library, then use ISRZ000, ISRZ001, ISRZ002. Assign the short message to &ZEDSMSG and the long one to &ZEDLMSG. The following is an example of setting a message. (See Chapter 9 for an explanation of message libraries and how to set messages.)

```
ISREDIT MACRO
IF &LASTCC = 8 THEN DO
  SET &ZEDSMSG = &STR(MACRO HAS NO PARAMETERS)
  SET &ZEDLMSG = &STR(PLEASE REINVOKE MACRO)
  ISPEXEC SETMSG(ISRZ002) /* Or use ISPEXEC DISPLAY
                          /* MSG.
  ISREDIT CANCEL /*Cancel macro and save no changes.
END
```

   - Error control handling. *ISPEXEC CONTROL ERRORS RETURN* expects the EDIT macro to process all errors. The default of *ISPEXEC CONTROL ERRORS CANCEL* ends the macro on any return code of 12 or higher.
   - Pass values to and from clists and EDIT macros using ISPEXEC *VGET* and *VPUT* statements. The macro does not "pick up" clist variable values

in the function pool. The following is an example that tells number of lines in a dataset.

Macro

```
ISREDIT MACRO  /* How many lines in dataset.
ISREDIT (LAST) = LINENUM .ZLAST /* Value of last -
line.
ISPEXEC VPUT (LAST) /* Stores in shared pool.
ISREDIT END
```

Clist

```
  ISPEXEC EDIT DATASET(CURRENT.DATA) MACRO(LASTMAC)
     IF &LASTCC = 0 THEN DO
        ISPEXEC VGET (LAST)
        WRITE NUMBER OF LINES IN CURRENT.DATA IS &LAST.
        /* Write out value from edit macro
     END
```

- Use *skeletons* (file tailoring) to create a customized EDIT macro based on user values. Here is a skeleton that adds a statement to convert everything to upper- or lowercase. A later example expands on this EDIT macro. See Chapter 9 for more information on ISPF skeletons.

Skeleton

```
  ISREDIT MACRO
)CM UPPERCASE selected. Convert all to uppercase.
)CM Setting picture strings to variables allows -
reuse.
)SET &LC = P'<'
)SET &UC = P'>'
)SEL &OPT = UC
   ISREDIT CHANGE &LC &UC ALL
)ENDSEL
)CM LOWERCASE selected. Convert all to lowercase if
)CM enabled.
)SEL &OPT = LC
 ISREDIT CHANGE &UC &LC ALL
)ENDSEL
  ISREDIT END
```

Clist

```
WRITE SELECT AN OPTION
WRITE UC - UPPERCASE
WRITE LC - LOWERCASE
READ OPT
ISPEXEC FTOPEN TEMP      /* Open temporary dataset
ISPEXEC FTINCL HALSKEL  /* Include skeleton
```

```
ISPEXEC FTCLOSE           /* Close temporary dataset
ISPEXEC VGET (ZTEMPF)     /* Obtain name of tempo-
                          rary dataset.
COPY '&ZTEMPF' CLIST(EDMAC) /* Save macro into per-+
                               manent
                            /* SYSPROC PDS member.
```

Uppercase File

```
ISREDIT MACRO
ISREDIT CHANGE P'<' P'<' ALL
ISREDIT END
```

Edit Macro Statements

Most EDIT macro commands are identical to PDF primary and line EDIT commands, except that they are prefixed by ISREDIT. See the section earlier in the chapter for a review. This part focuses on commands unique to EDIT macros or used somewhat differently in an edit macro. Table 10-6 lists them.

Table 10-6. EDIT Macro Commands

Command	Function
	Enable/Disable Setting
CAPS	Convert new text to uppercase.
HEX	Turn on hexadecimal display.
NULLS	Modify end of line to nulls or blanks.
	Query Setting
BLKSIZE	Obtain block size of a dataset.
CHANGE_COUNTS	Obtain number of changed and unchanged straings.
DATA_CHANGED	Obtain if data was changed or not.
DATA_WIDTH	Obtain logical width of data.
DATASET	Obtain name of current edited dataset.
DISPLAY_COLS	Obtain first and last column number of screen.
DISPLAY_LINES	Obtain current first and last line number on screen.
FIND_COUNTS	Obtain number of strings found.
LRECL	Obtain the logical record length of the edited dataset.
	Set/Query Setting
CURSOR	Modify or obtain the cursor position.
LINE	Modify or obtain a specified line.
	Other Commands
COPY	Copy one or more lines from another member to the currently edited dataset.
LOCATE	Set cursor to a specified line.

The following are guidelines to using the above commands:

1. *Enable/disable setting* commands have two common formats:
   - *Modify* setting without assigning it to a variable:
     `ISREDIT CAPS ON`
     CAPS ON (the default) converts new text to uppercase. ISREDIT CAPS OFF disables this.
     `ISREDIT HEX ON VERT`
     HEX ON (the default) displays hexadecimal characters vertically under each character. The earlier discussion of EDIT primary commands shows examples of HEX ON DATA and HEX ON VERT.
     `ISREDIT NULLS ON`
     NULLS ON (the default) sets all trailing blanks in a line to nulls, making it easier to insert. Earlier in the chapter is a more complete discussion of nulls.
   - *Retrieve* current setting and store it in a symbolic variable.
     `ISREDIT (CAPSVAR) = CAPS`
     Assigns current CAPS setting of ON or OFF to &CAPSVAR.
     `ISREDIT (HEXFLAG,HEXTYPE) = HEX`
     Assigns the current HEX setting of ON or OFF to &HEXFLAG. &HEXTYPE also stores the current setting of DATA or VERT (HEX ON only). You can also assign the current NULLS setting to one or two variables. The first is ON or OFF and the second is ALL or STD (if ON).

2. *Other commands* simulate EDIT line or primary commands.
   - COPY command to duplicate one or more lines from another dataset into the currently edited one.
     `ISREDIT COPY OTHERMEM BEFORE .HERE`
     Copy the entire member OTHERMEM before the .HERE label. (An AFTER keyword is also available and you can also use system labels such as .ZFIRST.)
     `ISREDIT COPY OTHERMEM AFTER .HERE 10 20`
     Copies lines 10 through 20 of member OTHERMEM after the .HERE label. Note you must specify two line numbers. A return code of 8 or 16 notes premature end of file, while 12 or 20 is a syntax error or mistake in the command. (Such as bad member or label name.)
   - LOCATE moves to a specified line.
     `ISREDIT LOCATE 1 OR ISREDIT LOCATE .ZFIRST`
     `ISREDIT LOCATE NEXT LABEL`
     Locate next labeled line. Other direction keywords are PREV (look backward), FIRST (look from first line to bottom of dataset) or LAST (opposite of FIRST). Other search keywords besides LABEL are CHG (line that changed) and ERROR (last line with error).

3. *Query settings* obtain the current EDIT session settings and optionally store the values in a symbolic variable.
   - One powerful feature of PDF EDIT macros is the ability to retrieve the number of times a string was found or changed. Then assign this value to a symbolic variable. This saves capturing the return code of a CHANGE or FIND command.

     ISREDIT (CHANGED,FAILED) = CHANGE_COUNTS

     Assigns to &CHANGED the number of times the string changed. All values retrieved from CHANGE_COUNTS or FIND_COUNTS are eight character numbers with leading zeros. Also assign &FAILED the number of times the string failed to change.

     ISREDIT (CHANGEFL) = DATA_CHANGED

     Assign &CHANGEFL the status of a dataset. This is either YES (dataset probably changed) or NO (the value at the start of an edit session or after a SAVE command). This value does not absolutely tell if a dataset was changed or saved.

     ISREDIT (HOWMANY,NUMLIN) = FIND_COUNTS

     Assign to &HOWMANY the number of times finding a specified string and to &NUMLIN how many lines finding the string. All values retrieved from a CHANGE_COUNTS or FIND_COUNTS command are eight-character numbers with leading zeros. You can use these variables in a DO loop:

```
ISREDIT FIND 'A STRING'
ISREDIT (FCOUNTS) = FIND_COUNTS
SET &CNT = 1
DO WHILE &CNT LE &FCOUNTS
  (other commands)
  SET &CNT = &CNT + 1
END
```

   - Edit macros retrieve information about the dataset being edited and assign it to a symbolic variable. Or use the LISTDSI command outlined in Chapter 5.

     ISREDIT (BLCKSIZE) = BLKSIZE

     Assigns &BLCKSIZE the block size of an edited dataset. This is a six-character value with leading zeros.

     ISREDIT (DNAME) = DATASET

     Assigns &DNAME to name of the edited dataset. The name contains no quotes and includes your userid or default prefix.

     ISREDIT (ACTCOL) = DATA_WIDTH

     Is the actual number of columns available for data. For unnumbered datasets, this is the same as the logical record length value from an ISREDIT LRECL. For numbered datasets, it is the logical record length minus the sequence number size (8 for STD and 6 for COBOL). The result is a three-character value with leading zeros.

`ISREDIT (RLENGTH) = LRECL`

Assigns &RLENGTH the logical record length of the edited dataset. This is a three-character value with leading zeros.

- EDIT macros also can capture which columns and lines the user is viewing or processing.

  `ISREDIT (STARTCOL,ENDCOL) = DISPLAY_COLS`

  Assigns &STARTCOL the starting data (nonsequence number) column and ENDCOL the ending data column the user is viewing. Both values are three characters with leading zeros.

  `ISREDIT (STARTLIN,ENDLN) = DISPLAY_LINES`

  Assigns &STARTLN the starting data line and &ENDLN the ending data line the user is viewing. Both values are six characters with leading zeros.

4. *Set/query setting* modifies or obtains the current line or cursor setting. Note many EDIT primary or line commands can modify this location.
   - ISREDIT CURSOR obtains both the current line and column numbers of the cursor if in the data area.

     `ISREDIT (LN,CN) = CURSOR`

     Assigns &LN the current cursor line number, which is a six-character value with leading zeros. Also assigns &CN the current cursor column number, which is a three-character value with leading zeros. Special column values to note are 0 (line number area or nondata line) and 1 (command area or first column).
   - ISREDIT LINE can store or modify (not discussed) a line's contents and assign it to a variable.

     ```
     SET &A = 2
     ISREDIT (LINE2) = LINE &A
     ```

     Assigns the contents of the entire second line to &LINE2. You can use a system or user label after the LINE keyword. LINE without anything else means the current line.

Sample Macros

Here are two macros reinforcing what was just discussed.

MONITOR MACRO

```
1. ISREDIT MACRO
2. /* Function: This shows the current settings of an -
              edit
```

```
/*            session. It can help in debugging a -
/*            macro.
/*Current label settings. .ZDEST, .ZFRANGE, and -
/*.ZLRANGE
/* may ABEND when you access it!
LBLSET: -
   ISREDIT (ZC) = LINENUM .ZCSR
   ISREDIT (ZF) = LINENUM .ZFIRST
   ISREDIT (ZL) = LINENUM .ZLAST
   WRITE                                        LABEL SETTINGS
   WRITE .ZCSR (Current Position)                  -- &ZC
   WRITE .ZFIRST (First Line No.)                  -- &ZF
   WRITE .ZLAST (Last Line No.)                    -- &ZL
/* DCB characteristics and name of edited dataset.
DCBSET: -
   ISREDIT (BS) = BLKSIZE
   ISREDIT (DN) = DATASET
   ISREDIT (DW) = DATA_WIDTH
   ISREDIT (LL) = LRECL
   ISREDIT (DC) = DATA_CHANGED
   WRITE                                   DCB CHARACTERISTICS
   WRITE Block Size                               -- &BS
   WRITE Dataset Name                             -- DN
   WRITE Data Width                               -- &DW
   WRITE Logical Record Size                      -- &LL
   WRITE Dataset Changed ?                        -- &DC
/* Settings for all three modes.
MODESET: -
   ISREDIT (CA) = CAPS
   ISREDIT (N1,N2) = NULLS
   ISREDIT (H1,H2) = HEX
   WRITE                                       MODE SETTINGS
   WRITE Caps Mode                               -- &CA
   WRITE Nulls Mode                              -- &N1 &N2
   WRITE Hex Mode                                -- &H1 &H2
/* Other miscellaneous settings
OTHSET: -
   ISREDIT (SC, EC) = DISPLAY_COLS
   ISREDIT (SL,EL) = DISPLAY_LINES
   ISREDIT (LN,CN) = CURSOR
   WRITE                             MISCELLANEOUS SETTINGS
```

```
42.     WRITE Columns on Screen          -- &SC through &EC
43.     WRITE Lines on Screen            -- &SL through &EL
44.     WRITE Cursor Position (r,c)      -- &LN , &CN
45. ISREDIT END
```

Explanation. Following is an explanation of the preceding monitor macro by statement number.

- 1–13. List the values of labels set by the system. Accessing .ZDEST, .ZFRANGE, and .ZLRANGE may ABEND a clist.
- 14–26. List the DCB characteristics of the currently edited dataset.
- 27–35. Place the settings of all three modes in one or two variables and then display them.
- 36–45. Display other miscellaneous settings. You could also add FIND_COUNTS and CHANGE_COUNTS.

CASE MACRO

```
ISREDIT MACRO (CASE)
/*Function: To show how a macro can do the same -
   thing as
/*          the skeleton shown earlier. Symbolic -
            variable
/*          value checking is also included:
  IF &CASE = THEN DO
     MENU100: WRITE SELECT AN OPTION
              WRITE LC = LOWERCASE
              WRITE UC = UPPERCASE
              READ OPT
             IF &OPT NE LC AND &OPT NE UC THEN GOTO -
             MENU100
  END
  IF &CASE = LC OR &OPT = LC THEN DO
     ISREDIT CHANGE P'>' P'<' ALL
  END
ELSE IF &CASE = UC OR &OPT = UC THEN DO
     ISREDIT CHANGE P'<' P'>' ALL
END
ISREDIT (CH1,CH2) = CHANGE_COUNTS
WRITE Number of STRINGS Changed: &CH1
WRITE Number of Change ERRORS: &CH2
ISREDIT END
```

Explanation. Following is an explanation of the case macro by statement number.

1. Also statements
2–4. This shows that a macro does processing nearly identical to the macro and clist example shown earlier.
5–11. Invoke the macro. If the user hasn't entered a value, then prompt for one. (Note that the screen clears to display the menu.) Reprompt the user if an invalid value is entered.
12–17. If passing a value indicating an uppercase (UC) or lowercase (LC) on invoking the macro or after prompting the user, then process the appropriate statement. Therefore, a skeleton is not always necessary to conditionally process a macro statement.
18–21. List the number of strings changed and errors. Then end the EDIT macro and save the changes.

Advanced and Miscellaneous Topics

Before concluding this chapter, let us take a brief look at the following topics:

- Special macros (initial, built-in, and recovery)
- Program macros
- Other places to get edit macros
- Miscellaneous tips

Special Macros

In addition to the general-purpose macros shown during the chapter, there are three other specialized macro types.

1. Initial macro This macro executes before displaying a dataset. The *IMACRO macroname* edit macro statement or EDIT primary command invokes the macro. (Other ways are shown earlier.) Typical statements used by initial macros are:
   * Mode setting (NULLS, CAPS, HEX)
   * PF key or ISPF system variable setting
   * Initial cursor setting
   * Any macro definitions or macro aliases
   * Any nested macros (such as MONITOR)

- *Built-in macros* are macros that you have created that override another EDIT macro or EDIT primary command of the same name. To invoke a built-in macro, issue an *ISREDIT BUILTIN macroname* from an EDIT macro or

BUILTIN macroname EDIT primary command. Issuing a *DEFINE ALIAS aliasname* statement sets up the necessary alias for a built-in macro. To override the built-in macro with another user macro, issue a *DEFINE* EDIT primary command or an *ISREDIT DEFINE* command in an EDIT macro. Built-in macros can do the following:
  * Have one macro to save or cancel an EDIT session complete with extensive error-handling capabilities. It can decide what EDIT session settings to save.
  * Create a customized FIND or CHANGE macro capturing and displaying FIND or CHANGE counts or does specialized changes.
  * Create a NULLS mode placing exclamation points instead of blanks or nulls at the end of a line.
- *Recovery macros* restore an edit profile if an edit session unexpectedly ends. The *RMACRO macroname* EDIT macro statement or EDIT primary command invokes the macro. (Other methods are shown earlier.) This macro processes before displaying a dataset for *all* recovered datasets. Usually, recovery macros are nearly identical to initial macros.

Program Macros

A chapter on EDIT macros is incomplete without at least an overview of *program macros,* or macros compiled in a programming language. Advantages of program macros over command language macros and supported languages are discussed earlier. Here are some guidelines for using program macros:

1. Program macros must be explicitly defined, commands macros do not. Use an *ISREDIT DEFINE macroname MACRO PGM* or a *DEFINE macroname MACRO PGM* EDIT primary command to do this. If the macro name is up to seven characters, you can also prefix an exclamation point before the macro name on the ===> *COMMAND* line such as *!PGMMAC*. (The exclamation point is optional for reinvoking the same macro.) The load module (compiled macro) must reside in a STEPLIB, LINKLST, or ISPLLIB concatenation dataset.

2. Variables must be explicitly defined for program macros using an ISPEXEC VDEFINE command. (Use VDEFINE for specifying different variable formats and lengths.) This is not necessary for command language macros. *Note that clists convert all variable values to uppercase*. This is not true for program macros, so a case conversion sequence may be necessary.

3. Creating a command language version of the EDIT macro first before developing the program version can save significant time. It may be easy to write a program or develop an ISPF skeleton converting an edit macro to a programming language.

4. EDIT macro statements in program macros have two formats:

```
CALL ISPLINK ('ISREDIT',length,command)
CALL ISPEXEC (length, 'ISREDIT command')
```

   Note that all operands are positional. *Length* is the length of an EDIT macro or TSO command stored in a full-word fixed binary number. (Note ISPEXEC is for ISPF or PDF commands only.) Do not use ISPLINK with APL, FORTRAN, and Pascal programs. Instead, FORTRAN and Pascal use ISPLNK (same format as ISPLINK) and ISPEX (same format as ISPEXEC). The maximum length of a command is 512 characters.

5. The following ISPF commands are only available to dialogs and EDIT macros written in a programming language:
   - ISPEXEC VCOPY assigns the value of one or more existing variables to new program variables.
   - ISPEXEC VDEFINE defines one or more program variables used by a dialog or EDIT macro.
   - ISPEXEC VDELETE removes one or more variables.
   - ISPEXEC VREPLACE assigns new values to one or more program variables.

6. Take advantage of a programming language's features when creating EDIT macros. You can then create a feature far beyond the normal capabilities of edit such as DRAW by Dan Dirkse (1987). This program draws flowcharts and organizational diagrams all while in PDF EDIT!
   - Flow control statements
   - Ability to read mixed data and real numbers
   - More system functions
   - More powerful subroutine and user function features
   - More powerful formatted output
   - More powerful array manipulation (especially APL)

7. Program macros executed in background generally provide the fastest execution time.

See *Edit and Edit Macros* and *Dialog Management Services and Examples* for more details on program macros.

Other Places to Get Edit Macros

User guides such as *Edit and Edit Macros* have a sufficient number of EDIT macro examples including program macros. (The older versions are more generous with examples.) Each SHARE and GUIDE IBM user's group meeting has at least one presentation on edit macros (usually program macros), so poring through past SHARE and GUIDE proceedings may be useful. Most system clist libraries that are part of the SYSPROC concatenation have good command language macro examples. And always ask other programmers in your department and company for ideas.

Edit Macro Tips

The following are additional guidelines, concepts, and tips when using edit macros:

1. Type in the following to enter an alias:
   `ISREDIT DEFINE macroname ALIAS aliasname`
   Command language macro.
   `ISREDIT DEFINE macroname ALIAS aliasname MACRO PGM`
   Program macro.
   Do not attempt to nest an alias, it cannot be done. Also useful are:
   `ISREDIT DEFINE macroname DISABLED`
   Stops the use of the macro and a related alias for the rest of the PDF edit session.
   `ISREDIT DEFINE macroname NOP`
   This temporarily disables a macro until issuing an
   `ISREDIT DEFINE macroname RESET.`
2. Each macro has an associated macro level between 0 (highest) and 255 (lowest). Most macros operate at 0 (keyboard input), 1 (an user-invoked macro), and 2 (a nested macro in an user-invoked macro). ISREDIT LABEL allows setting of the level before assigning or retrieving a label. The default is finding a label on the current or a higher level. To obtain the macro level, issue the following (or place them in the MONITOR program):
   ```
   ISREDIT (LVL) = MACRO_LEVEL
   WRITE Current Macro level is &LVL.
   ```
3. To debug edit macros, use the following:
   a. ISPEXEC CONTROL and TSO CONTROL statements to learn as much as possible on which statements executed and the results of symbolic substitution.
   b. ISPF test facility or test/tract mode. Chapter 9 describes this.
   c. WRITE statements to capture variable values and PDF edit and edit macro return codes. Also use WRITE to see how far you got in the program.
   f. The Monitor EDIT macro to view current PDF edit session and profile settings.

g. Examine ISPF system variable values. Chapter 9 gives a list of useful variables. The ISPF test facility also displays this list.

h. Use your language debugger for program macros to resolve language syntax or other problems.

SUGGESTED READINGS

Dirkse, Dan, 1987. *Advanced ISPF/PDF Edit Macros*. Share 69. (Handout).

German, Hallett, 1987. *An Overview of ISPF Edit Macros*. Handout from May 6 presentation to the Boston Area SAS Users' Group.

IBM Corporation, 1988. *INFO/SYSTEM Database*. Various/Notes.

IBM Corporation, 1987. *Interactive System Productivity Facility Version 2 Release 3 Dialog Management Services and Examples*. SC34-4113.

IBM Corporation, 1987. *Interactive System Productivity Facility Version 2 Release 3 Edit and Edit Macros*. SC34-4121.

IBM Corporation, 1987. *Interactive System Productivity Facility Version 2 Release 3 Installation and Customization*. SC34-4117.

IBM Corporation, 1987. *Interactive System Productivity Facility Version 2 Release 3 Services*. SC34-4119.

IBM Corporation, 1987. *Interactive System Productivity Facility Version 2 Release 3 What's New in ISPF*. GC34-2172.

Shein, David, 1989. "Raising Your IQ (ISPF Quotient): ISPF Techniques for Advanced Users." *Mainframe Journal*, October, pp. 13–18.

11

REXX: The Next Command Language Generation

In 1987, IBM announced that their present and future mainframes, minicomputers, and microcomputers would adhere to a set of procedures and standards called System Application Architecture or SAA. An important part of SAA was selecting a subset of REXX (REstructured eXtended eXecutor) as the SAA programming language (or SAA/PL). So, programs and system utilities written in SAA/PL can easily export to other operating systems. In the MVS operating system, this means REXX runs both under TSO and non-TSO areas (such as IBM's network management product, Netview). Although you can continue to run clists without change, it is clear REXX, not clist, is the focus of IBM future developments.

I believe the following reasons are why REXX was selected over clists:

1. It was becoming hard to develop enhancements of the clist language which were consistent with existing clist syntax. The language had developed as far as it could go without a major revision.
2. REXX is far easier to learn and maintain. REXX supports structured programming and other good programming practices better than clists, including having no GOTO statement.
3. Generally, REXX is more powerful than clists. This includes processing a greater variety of data (including decimal integers) without always relying on built-in functions and stronger flow-control structures.
4. The clist language can only work in a TSO area of MVS, while REXX is system- and hardware-independent. Clists cannot easily export to another operating system, whereas REXX can.

The chapter gives an overview of REXX and its major features under TSO/E. This is needed before using REXX execs and converting your clists to execs.

(REXX programs are called *execs*.) It also compares the clist and REXX languages and takes a brief look of REXX for TSO/E Version 2 Release 1 and later.

WHAT IS REXX?

IBM's computing research facilities are always looking into the area of *human augmentation*, or what will help computer users work smarter. Mike Cowlishaw, in spare time at IBM Laboratories in Hursley, England, developed REXX as a *personal* computer language for human beings, not computers. He then placed a note in the "Tools" (dealing with tools development for the VM/SP or Virtual Machine/System Product Environment) area on IBM's internal network called VNET during 1979. The note asked for opinions on what was the first version of REXX. Many replies came back and he developed over 30 different versions between 1979 and 1982. (This makes REXX the only language developed by electronic reviewers!) Since then, REXX has become the most popular programming language used at IBM, with over 3 million lines of execs in existence. In 1983, after four years of rigorous internal testing and development, a REXX interpreter became available in the VM/SP environment. It soon replaced EXEC and EXEC2 as the preferred interpreted command language for the VM environment. In 1985, IBM and Mansfield Software released REXX interpreters for the PC DOS operating system. How good a personal language REXX is becomes clearer with the following review of the major characteristics and common uses of REXX.

MAJOR REXX CAPABILITIES

The REXX language seeks to meet the following aims.

1. To be a language for users rather than computers by minimizing typing and creating easy-to-understand programs. REXX does this in the following ways.
    - It reduces the number of situations requiring statement delimiters and terminators. The result is fewer statement syntax errors.
    - REXX statements can use mixed, lower-, and uppercase. Later in the chapter are recommendations on when to use each.
    - REXX statements are more English-like than other programming languages, with words you commonly use.
    - REXX is designed to work with your particular style—so you can place one statement on several lines or multiple statements on one line. Combined with the free-formatting nature of REXX, this allows generous use of blanks; the REXX language is extremely flexible.

- You do not need to initialize variables with a value before use. If initialized, it provides additional documentation at the start of a program or assigns a flow-control statement with an initial loop counter value. *Note all variables also have the default value of the variable name in uppercase,* so uninitialized variables are less frequent.

2. REXX allows structured programming and features from other languages without the difficulty of use. This includes the absence of a GOTO statement, the inability to enter the middle of a loop, and controlled exit from a loop for both normal and abnormal processing.

3. REXX provides other desirable features to promote flexibility, ease of use, and portability:
   - It minimizes the use of data types. Each REXX value is a variable-length character string with the maximum length decided by your REXX interpreter. REXX provides a good set of string operators and functions. In addition, REXX does not distinguish between integer, single-digit, and double-floating-point numbers. They are all the same type of "looks like a number, so do a numeric operation." REXX also allows arrays and boolean-like values.
   - REXX passes a non-REXX command to the operating system or environment specified. The REXX interpreter does not check the syntax of the statement. This reduces the system-specific information that the REXX interpreter has to "know."
   - Allows your REXX interpreter and not the language to determine the maximum variable value size and other limitations. However, Cowlishaw (1985) specifies several lower limits for the language and gives guidelines for setting upper limits.

The following are common uses of REXX:

- Preprocessor for a compiler performing parsing and string manipulations.
- System utilities and commands, including operating system or commands for a different environment (such as PDF EDIT macros shown in Chapter 10).
- "Quick-and-dirty" prototypes for application front-ends and system utilities.
- Front-ends to applications (such as an ISPF dialog).
- Startup files that execute when first logging on.
- Anything requiring simple read/write operations, mathematical operations, or string manipulation.

Major Concepts

Although REXX is easy to use, you must still understand certain concepts about the syntax and the language features before using it.

Clauses

REXX execs (programs) consist of one or more *clauses*. A clause is similar to a TSO command or clist statement. Let us hold off for a little bit on what actually is in a clause. There are five types of clauses:

1. *Comment* or *Blank* A clause which has a comment or is all blank (a comment starts with /* and ends with */). Blanks or comments do not affect REXX exec processing and are also called *null clauses*.
2. *Assignment* This assigns a value to a variable and is identical to the assignment statements used by clists and EDIT macros. (A SYMBOL in REXX is a variable, label, or array name.)
   ```
   name = 'HAL'
   Assigns symbol (variable name of name) a value of HAL
   ```
3. *Label* The same as a clist label, it marks a location in the program. Labels consist of a name ending with a colon. You may place one or more labels before a REXX statement (or *instruction*). If two labels have the same name, then process only the first one. A comment may follow a label name.
   ```
   CATALOG: /* A LABEL NAME followed by a comment. */
   ```
4. *Instructions* One or more clauses with REXX statements starting with a *REXX keyword* (or statement name). Some flow control instructions (i.e., a DO loop) may have nested instructions. The following sequence has the REXX keywords ARG, IF, DO, SAY, CALL, and END. Note SAY and CALL are nested in the DO structure.
   ```
                  arg option /* Pass the option value on*/
                             /* invocation. */
                  if option = "DATABASE" then do /* -
                  IF keyword*/
   nested            say 'DATA to be processed' /* Write -
                                                    text to*/
   instructions                                 /* screen. */
                     call db /* Call database routine*/
                  end /* End DO structure. */
                  db: Say 'Got to db' /* Db label, */
                                      /* start of */
                                      /* routine. */
   ```
5. *External Command* A character string in single or double quotes passed to an environment (such as ISPF or TSO) for immediate processing.
   ```
   'TIME' /* Executes TSO TIME command from a REXX -
   exec.*/
   ```

To end a clause, use any of these characters.

6. *Implied end of line* This marks the end of a line, but REXX implies the terminator character of semicolon (;). So semicolons at the end of clauses are optional. You *only need* them to separate more than one clause on the same line.
   / Marks the end of a comment (starting with a /.)
   , Marks a long clause continuing on the next line.

Tokens

In addition to REXX keywords, TSO/E/ISPF commands, and delimiters, REXX clauses are made up of tokens and expressions. *Tokens* are the different forms of data, constants, and variables a REXX clause uses. All tokens are essentially character strings with maximum lengths defined by your REXX interpreter. *Expressions* are tokens with operators performing a mathematical, logical, or string operation. The following are the different types of tokens a REXX clause can use.

Number or Numeric Value. A number or numeric value that is a *character string* may begin with a plus or minus followed by leading blanks and a numeric value. The numeric value may contain a decimal point and trailing blanks. However, blanks in a numeric value are invalid (i.e., 38 5), but scientific (exponential) format or expressing a number as a power of 10 is not. This makes it easier to represent large numbers. Some valid numeric values are:

1	*Whole number no decimal.*
2.85	*Integer number with decimal.*
−88	*Negative whole number with leading space.*
88e5	*Number in scientific format. E (exponent) can be in upper- or lowercase.*

Rounding may occur for mathematical operations unless using the *numeric digits* instruction for controlling the level of precision. (The default is nine digits.) All REXX interpreters must be able to represent all numbers up to 999,999,999 (optionally in scientific format). Numbers cannot be variable names.

Literal String. A literal string is one or more valid EBCDIC characters including numbers contained in single or double quotes. Using two single quotes creates one for a string enclosed in single quotes. The same doubling rule also applies to double quotes. (But not to single quotes within a double-quoted string or double quotes within a single-quoted string.) REXX instructions cannot change this character string or continue it on another line. It also allows null strings such as ''. The maximum string length is usually 250 characters. Some valid literal strings are:

```
"A single quote in a double-quoted string'"
'A double quote within a single-quoted string "'
'1'
'That"s good news'
"Here's two double quotes to make one"" "
```

Hexadecimal String. A hexadecimal string is any literal string followed by an upper- or lowercase X. Valid hexadecimal characters include 0–9 and a–f in any case. You usually add Blanks between bytes to improve clarity, but they are not processed. Note ''X is still a null string. You may set OPTIONS EXMODE for enabling double-byte characters. Some examples of valid hexadecimal characters are:

```
'a1 d8'x
"bacd"X
```

Comment. Any valid EBCDIC characters enclosed by /* and */. Use comments for creating "exec flowerboxes" to describe the current exec and related programs. You may nest comments but keep track of your /*s and */s. Your interpreter, not the language, sets the length of comments. The interpreter ignores comments during exec processing.

Symbol/Variable. A symbol is a series of valid EBCDIC characters that are the names for variables, labels, arrays, and certain REXX keywords. These characters include:

a–z (any case)
0–9
@, #, $, ¬, !, ?, ¢, £, ., _ (underscore)

If it is a variable name, a symbol cannot begin with a number or a period. *Note lowercase letters convert to uppercase. The default value for a symbol is the symbol name in uppercase*—so uninitialized variables are unlikely. There are four types of symbols:

A *constant symbol* may include alphabetical characters (always converted to uppercase) and starts with a period or number. No assignment statement or REXX instruction can modify it. Some valid constant symbols are:

88 a numeric symbol
.aconstant a character symbol

A *simple symbol* is a variable name including no period and it may have a value.

Variable names may begin with alphabetical or other valid EBCDIC character (besides 0–9.) Some valid simple symbols are:

`hal` same as HAL
`@al`

REXX has some reserved variable names, each initially set to null. You may modify their values or allow the interpreter to set them after processing an instruction. These are RC, RESULT, and SIGL (more on them later). In addition, do not use THEN as a variable name.

Compound symbols are several simple symbols joined by a period. Use them to build arrays or variable lists. The *stem* is the variable up to the period and the *tail* is the rest of the symbol name. (The stem is also the fourth symbol type.) Alphabetical or numerical characters make up the tail and do not indicate array size. A powerful feature is that assigning the stem a value gives all compound symbols with that stem that value. (So if *x.* equals 20, then *x.1* also equals 20 unless assigned another value.) DROP clears all current array values for a specified stem and PROCEDURE EXPOSE lists all values for a specified stem. Note the default name of a compound symbol is the symbol name in uppercase. You may also use compound symbols in mathematical operations.

Operators. REXX includes a rich variety of operators for use in mathematical, logical, and string operations. An *expression* has at least one *term*, such as symbols, function, or subroutine results, and subexpressions or expressions enclosed in parentheses. Examples of expressions are c=b−2, a=(g*7)−8, and if 'g' == 'H'. The following are valid REXX operators:

MATHEMATICAL

+	Add
−	Subtract
*	Multiply
/	Divide
%	Return only integer part of division.
//	Return positive or negative remainder.
**	Exponential
Prefix −	Negate the number.
Prefix +	Positive number (keep as is)

STRING CONCATENATION

(*blank*)	Place blank between concatenated strings
|| or (*abuttal*)	Place no blanks between concatenated strings.

BOOLEAN OR LOGICAL OPERATORS

(*Note*: Use these operators with character strings having values of 0 (false) and 1 (true). All other values are invalid. Each operator returns a 0 or 1.)

&	AND returns 1 (true) when both terms are true.
|	INCLUSIVE OR returns 1 if at least one term is true.
&&	EXCLUSIVE OR returns 1 if only 1 term is true.
Prefix ¬	LOGICAL NOT, which converts 1 to 0 and 0 to 1.

RELATIONAL OPERATORS

(*Note*: All relational operators result in 1 (true) or 0 (false). The operators compare a combination of two numbers, characters, symbols, functions, or subexpressions (which are expressions in parentheses). These two items are the *terms* of an expression. There are no character equivalents (such as EQ for =) for these operators.)

=	Tests if two terms are equal.
¬=	Tests if two terms are not equal. >< and <> are also valid.
>	Tests if one term is greater than another.
<	Tests if one term is less than another.
>=	Tests if one term is greater than or equals another term.
<=	Tests if one term is less than or equals another term.

The following relational operators are only for character strings. These are *strict relational* operators because they compare strings character by character for exact match or not exact match.

==	True only if terms exactly match.
¬==	True only if terms not exactly match.

Unless using parentheses or finding another operator with higher precedence, an expression (including terms and operators) processes left to right. Figure 11-1 shows the descending precedence of operators.

Delimiters and Other Characters. We have already talked about most delimiters and other special characters that are part of a token: the comma (continuation), semicolon (clause delimiter), colon (label indicator), and parentheses (for subexpressions and subroutines or functions). Since we have reviewed all of the components of a clause, let's see an example of one.

Figure 11-1. Precedence of REXX Operators

Highest ↑	+, −, ¬ (Prefix operators)
	**
	*, /, %, //
	+, − (Addition and subtraction)
	(blank) | | (abuttal)
	=, ==, >, <, >=. ¬> (all relational operators)
	&
↓ Lowest	| , &&

```
         expression              expression
       ┌───────────┐             ┌─────┐
IF  VAR_IN == "?"        |  A.1   =20      THEN DO;
    term       term         term   term
k   ss      so ls       b   cs    o n      k     k d
```

where
- *b* = boolean (logical) operator
- *cs* = compound symbol
- *d* = delimiter
- *k* = REXX keyword
- *ls* = literal string
- *n* = number
- *o* = operator
- *so* = strict operator
- *ss* = simple symbol (variable)

We will discuss clauses when examining REXX instructions and other components a little later in the chapter.

REXX Compared to Clist

Although the clist language will continue to be popular for the next several years, it is time to start thinking about converting clists to execs. This requires a good understanding of the differences between REXX and clists. This section gives help in that area by discussing (a) conceptual differences between the two interpreted languages, (b) the REXX equivalent of clist statements, and (c) suggestions for converting from clists to REXX execs.

REXX and CLIST Conceptual Differences

This subsection discusses differences between the clist and REXX language in overall design, use of variables and operators, stack operations, built-in functions, debugging, and user-written functions and subprograms.

Overall Design

Both languages are interpreted rather than compiled. However, the clist interpreter uses two phases to process a clist, with execution occurring during the second phase. In contrast, the REXX interpreter interprets the entire exec in one phase, which is more efficient.

Clists offers less rigorous enforcement of structured programming concepts. The clist language includes a GOTO statement, allowing a clist to enter the middle of a DO loop or exit the DO loop before normal completion. REXX offers more controlled branching. REXX also has slightly more flow-control structures. Clist statements are slightly less flexible than REXX instructions. They are always in uppercase (except built-in function names), whereas REXX instructions can use any case. Both languages allow generous use of blanks and rarely need terminator characters. Because REXX can run on any operating system, it offers a major advantage over the clist language, which is dependent on TSO/E.

Use of Variables and Operators

This is one area where REXX is far stronger than clists. REXX can process a greater variety of data than clists, including numbers, characters, decimals, hexadecimal strings, and exponents, without the need of built-in functions. This increases flexibility and reduces chances for errors.

REXX variable names can be in any case and have a default value of their name in uppercase. In contrast, clist symbolic variables initially have a null value and can have their name in any case. Many clist sequences require the use of double-ampersand variables, which go through several levels of symbolic substitution. Double-ampersand variables are especially useful for building arrays. On the other hand, only when dynamically creating statements with the INTERPRET instruction is nested symbolic substitution used. All other REXX instructions have one level of scanning. You can easily assign a value to dynamically allocated arrays and all related variables. These arrays can have a subscript (tail) that uses either letters or numbers.

REXX operators are identical to clist operators with the following exceptions. REXX operators do not have character equivalents of relational operators. Also REXX has the powerful strict relational operators for character-by-character comparison of two character strings and boolean (logical) operators for certain types of data. Additional concatenation and mathematical operators also exist in REXX.

Stack Operations. One major differences between REXX and clist languages is their stack structure and operation. To take full advantage of REXX, the TSO stack was changed to a superset of the CMS stack structure. (The TSO section includes a brief discussion on the new TSO stack structure.) Let us briefly compare TSO and CMS stack operations.

Chapter 4 reviewed the TSO input stack, showing how the stack stores TSO commands or clist for processing using a "pushdown" format (i.e., the most recent command placed on top of the stack). If an ATTENTION or ERROR routine is invoked, the default action is to flush the input stack. When reaching the first record of the input stack, then the stack is empty and the interpreter reads more input from the terminal.

Although not part of the REXX language, the CMS data stack is becoming a standard extension. See the "File I/O" section later for an alternative approach. The CMS stack retains user input until processed. Using the CMS MAKEBUF command, you can set up a reserved area called a *buffer*. The interpreter creates two markers to "remember" the boundaries of the buffer and places new elements on top of the buffer. You can *easily* manipulate and query the buffer through REXX instructions and CMS commands. This gives REXX a big advantage over clists. If an error occurs, the program abnormally ends and the stack clears unless a SIGNAL instruction is in effect. Later in the chapter, we will take another look at stack operations and REXX.

Built-in Functions. REXX shines over clists with its built-in functions. It offers over 60 standard built-in functions versus 15 for TSO clists. These additional functions include string manipulation (e.g., CENTER a string), bit operations (bit OR, Exclusive OR, and AND), data-type conversion (C2D—character to decimal), utilities (ERRORTEXT returns the matching error message for a certain error message), and date/time operations (DATE can return the day of the week). REXX also makes it far easier to parse strings.

Debugging. Both languages offer a trace facility for debugging errors, including symbolic value resolution, displaying only statements and TSO commands executed, and conditionally turning trace on or off. Table 11-1 compares trace options. Both trace facilities are adequate, but the REXX trace instruction has greater flexibility. A list of REXX error codes appears in Appendix C.

Subprograms. Although the clist language always supported nesting clists, it was only in TSO/E Version 1 Release 4 that support was added for subprocedures. Subprocedures are *always* in the "main" clist and identified with a label. You may pass them a value or variable name. They can also give the "main" clist a return code or, using SYSREF, a result. Variables defined in a subprocedure default to local (not known by main clist). However, with SYSREF, a subprocedure can modify the value of a variable in the main clist. Using the REXX CALL instruc-

Table 11-1. REXX Trace Options and Their Clist Equivalents

CMS	Function	Clist Equivalent
TRACE !	Suppress TSO commands.	CONTROL NOLIST NOSYMLIST.
TRACE ?	Turn trace on.	IF &TRACE = ON THEN – CONTROL CONLIST LIST.
TRACE A	Trace the exec before execution.	CONTROL CONLIST but after symbolic substitution.
TRACE C	Trace TSO commands before execution and display greater than zero return codes.	CONTROL CONLIST but only displays return codes if clist traps &LASTCC.
TRACE E	Trace TSO commands with greater than zero return codes.	CONTROL CONLIST and if clist traps &LASTCC.
TRACE I	All clauses traced with all levels of symbolic substitution.	CONTROL CONLIST SYMLIST and WRITE/SET statements.
TRACE L	Trace only labels executed.	None. Labels not displayed in trace. Could use WRITE statements to show if label processed.
TRACE N	Trace TSO command with greater than zero return code after execution.	None.
TRACE O	Turn trace off.	CONTROL NOCONLIST, etc.
TRACE R	Trace exec before execution with symbolic substitution.	CONTROL CONLIST.
TRACE S	Trace remaining exec but do not execute.	None.

tion, an exec can process a subprocedure with or without values. (All variables in the subprocedure are global, unless the subprocedure is in a different exec or using PROCEDURE EXPOSE.) Another choice is creating *user functions* to return a result. Both types of subprograms can be in a same (internal identified by a label) or different (external) exec.

Table 11-2 shows the differences between the two languages.

REXX Instructions and their Clist Equivalents

Although a clist and REXX statement comparison can be misleading, it may be helpful in learning REXX and converting your clists to execs. Table 11-3 offers such a comparison. The TSO REXX guides provide an appendix on converting clist statements to their REXX equivalents. (A little later we will see what these REXX instructions do.)

Table 11-2. A Comparison of REXX and Clist Languages

Feature	REXX	Clist
System design	One-phase interpreter	Two-phase interpreter
	More flow-control structures	
	Statements in any case	Statements in uppercase
	Independent of operating system	TSO-dependent
	Freeform syntax	Freeform syntax
Variables and operators	Greater variety of data types	
	Names any case	Names any case
	More powerful operators, including boolean and a string	Has character equivalents of relational operators
Stack operations	Pulldown stack which can be easily queried and manipulated	Pulldown stack with no easy manipulation
Built-in functions	60+ functions, including string, bit, date/time, and utility	15 functions
Trace facility	Has more flexible trace facility	Has adequate trace facility
Subprograms	Internal/external subprograms and functions	Internal only subprograms

Table 11-4 lists a few REXX built-in functions with clist equivalents. As stated in Chapter 6, parsing and other string operations are possible in clists, but only writing lengthy sequences which combine &SYSINDEX, &LENGTH, &STR, and &SUBSTR. Also included are REXX functions which are only available for TSO/E.

Guidelines on Converting Clists to Execs

Although many sites continue using clists, you need to begin thinking about converting them to execs or another language. The following is one approach for the conversion and also includes specific things to watch out for.

Step 1 Evaluate Your Situation (3–6 months)

1. Start to program all new utilities and front-ends in REXX rather than clist to eliminate future conversion. If time is an issue, start with smaller ad hoc utilities to gain experience.

Table 11-3. A Comparison of REXX and Clist Statements

REXX Instruction	Clist Equivalent and Comments
ADDRESS	TSO/E command or TSOEXEC, ISPEXEC and ISREDIT statements, LINK command
ARG	PROC when invoking clist or subprocedures not as powerful
CALL	SYSCALL for subprograms or clist name for nested (multiple) clists
DO-END	Same
DO-TO-BY-FOR-END	Iterative DO but no FOR operand
DO FOREVER	DO-WHILE or DO-UNTIL
DO number	DO-WHILE
DO-WHILE	DO-WHILE
DO-UNTIL	DO-UNTIL
DO TO..WHILE	DO TO..WHILE (Compound DO)
DO TO..UNTIL	DO TO..UNTIL (Compound DO)
DROP	SET &X = ' ' but still exists
EXIT	EXIT but passes return code not result
IF-THEN-ELSE-DO-END	Same
INTERPRET	SET &SYSSCAN = 2 and process statements
ITERATE	None—GOTO to leave loop and go to label. Not as clean.
LEAVE	None—GOTO to leave loop and go to label. Not as clean.
NOP	None
NUMERIC	None because only whole numbers
OPTIONS	None—CONTROL closest
PARSE	None—have a sequence with &SYSINDEX and &SUBSTR. PARSE ARG like PROC on invoking clist.
PROCEDURE	All variables defined in subprocedure or nested clist default to local, so not usually needed.
PULL	READ but PULL is more powerful
PUSH	None—but &SYSDVAL closest
QUEUE	None—cannot perform queue operations
RETURN	Same but only passes return code or whole number. REXX can pass a result.
SAY	WRITE
SELECT-WHEN-OTHERWISE-END	Same in TSO/E Version 1 Release 4. REXX cannot specify condition on SELECT statement.
SIGNAL	ERROR—error routines. But REXX offers cleaner processing.
TRACE	CONTROL—see discussion earlier

Table 11-4. REXX Built-in Functions and Clist Equivalents

REXX Function	Clist Equivalent and Comments
ADDRESS	No one variable—&SYSENV, &SYSISPF
ARG	PROMPT 0 VAR1 IF &VAR1 NE ' ' THEN SET &COUNT = 1
COMPARE	IF &STR(&X) = &STR(&Y)
DATATYPE	&DATATYPE but less powerful than REXX
DATE	No one function—same as &SYSJDATE, &SYSDATE, &SYSSDATE, and using &SUBSTR with a date value. REXX is far more flexible.
DELSTR	SET &A = &SUBSTR(1:3,&A) or similar but not as clean
INSERT	SET &A = &SUBSTR(1:2,&A)&STR( )&SUBSTR(3:5,&A) or similar but not as clean
LASPOS	&SYSINDEX
LEFT	&SUBSTR optionally with &SYSINDEX or &LENGTH(&STR( ))
LENGTH	&LENGTH
LISTDSI	LISTDSI statement (*for TSO/E only*)
MSG	Same as CONTROL MSG (*for TSO/E only*)
OVERLAY	See INSERT
OUTTRAP	Similar to &SYSOUTTRAP and &SYSOUTLINE (*for TSO/E only*)
POS	&SYSINDEX
PROMPT	Similar to CONTROL PROMPT (*for TSO/E only*)
RIGHT	&SUBSTR optionally with &SYSINDEX or using &LENGTH(&STR(var))
STRIP	Using &SYSINDEX to find blanks and then reassign variable with SET statement.
SUBSTR	&SUBSTR
SUBWORD	&SYSINDEX with &SUBSTR
SYSDSN	&SYSDSN (*for TSO/E only*)
SYSVAR	The appropriate clist system variable (*for TSO/E only*)
TIME	No one function; same as &SYSTIME, &SYSSTIME, and using &SUBSTR with a time value. REXX is far more flexible. Elapsed time similar to subtracting &SYSCPU.
TRACE	No one function; similar to &SYSSYMLIST, &SYSCONLIST, &SYSLIST, &SYSMSG.
TRANSLATE	&SYSCAPS, but far more in REXX
VALUE	WRITE &A—write current value.
VERIFY	IF &SYSINDEX(a, 'abc') = 1 THEN. . .

2. Review private and public clists. Decide the following:
   - Which clists to drop or not convert.
   - Which clists are critical (convert last) and noncritical. Another decision is which clists can take immediate advantage of REXX features (such as decimals, bit operations, and string operations) and which cannot.

- Which clists to write in assembly language, C, FORTRAN, or other languages.

3. Develop your conversion plan, realizing this can take up to one-third of your staff's time.
4. Keep users informed of progress.
5. An interim solution is to convert certain parts of a clist to a REXX exec (really an external function or subprogram) and then call the exec from a clist. This gives you the best of both worlds.

Step 2 Getting Your Feet Wet (6–18 months)

1. Convert simple clists to REXX to gain experience.
2. Build new utilities in REXX if appropriate.
3. Set site REXX standards.
4. Investigate conversion aids (none now exist).
5. Provide REXX training.
6. Write conversion guide based on initial experiences.

Step 3 The Real Thing (1 year–?)

1. Convert noncritical clists then critical ones.
2. ALL new application and utility development should be in REXX instead of clists.

Here are some specific things to look out for converting from clists to execs:

1. Using the clist features of TSO/E Version 1 Release 4 will make it easier to convert to REXX. Many of these require little or no conversion including:
   - Compound DOs
   - Iterative DO
   - SELECT
   - Subprograms (Watch out for internal subprogram variables now being global!)
2. Watch out for GOTOs:
   - Can you write the sequence in one module?
   - Can you eliminate GOTOS in and out of DO loops?
3. Watch out for the following, which REXX does far easier.
   - A multiple (nested) clist that should really be a subprogram (or a REXX function).
   - Clist sequences that do date or time math.

- Clist sequences that perform string operations or parsing.
- Clist sequences that convert a whole number to a decimal. An example is the money sequence mentioned in Chapter 5.
- Clist sequences that simulate exponents and scientific formats.

4. Start using the relational operator (e.g., =) rather than the character equivalent (EQ). This will make it easier to convert your clists.

5. Error handling
   - Determine which SIGNAL conditions your ERROR routines compare to and perhaps convert them to look more like a SIGNAL sequence.

GETTING STARTED WITH REXX

Major Statements (Instructions)

This section is both a reference and tutorial on REXX statements (instructions). The REXX Language is composed of the following components:

1. Interface to foreign environments (such as TSO or ISPF)

2. Instructions
   - Parsing
   - Flow control
   - Subprograms/Functions
   - Error handling
   - Stack manipulation
   - General statements

3. Trace Facility

4. Functions (User and Built-In)

5. System Variables

Table 11-5 lists the major REXX instructions. Let us take a closer look at each of these instructions.

REXX Environment Model and Non-REXX Commands

The *REXX environment model* explains how REXX interfaces with foreign environments. The REXX interpreter uses the following sequence:

1. Get the "instruction."
2. If it is a REXX instruction, then continue to process.

Table 11-5. Major REXX Instructions

Clause	Command to Send to a Non-REXX Environment Such as TSO/E
	Interface to Foreign Environments
ADDRESS	Sends command to a specified environment.
SUBCOM (CMS)	Makes a program an environment.
	Parsing
ARG	Parses input into variable values.
PARSE	Parses input (from a variety of sources) into variable values.
PULL	Parses queue input into variable values.
	Flow Control
DO	Sets up looping operation.
END	Ends the DO structure.
IF	Conditional processing
ITERATE	Bypasses one DO iteration.
LEAVE	Ends DO loop.
NOP	"Do nothing" instruction.
SELECT	Complex conditional processing.
	Stack Manipulation
DROPBUF (CMS)	Erases one or more buffers in the stack.
EXECIO (CMS)	Writes lines to stack or file.
MAKEBUF (CMS)	Creates a buffer in the stack.
PUSH	Puts a value on the stack.
PULL	Retrieves a value from the stack and parses it into variable values.
QUEUE	Places a value on the stack.
	General Statements
DROP	Eliminates one or more variables.
EXIT	Ends the exec and gives a return code.
INTERPRET	Performs symbolic substitution and processes dynamically created string.
NUMERIC	Sets numeric precision and format.
OPTIONS	Specifies global options.
SAY	Writes a line to the screen (or other location).
	Error Handling
SIGNAL	Specifies that there is an available sequence to process a certain type of error condition successfully.
	Subprograms/Functions
CALL	Calls a subprogram or function.
PROCEDURE	Retains existing variable values after processing a subprogram.
RETURN	Returns from a subprogram.

Table 11-5. *(continued)*

Clause	Command to Send to a Non-REXX Environment Such as TSO/E
	Trace Facility
TRACE	Enables trace facility.
	System Variables
RC	Return code from SIGNAL, ADDRESS, and non-REXX commands.
RESULT	A value from a subprogram.
SIGL	Line number of instruction that caused a skip to a label.

3. If not a REXX instruction, then pass it after symbolic substitution (as a character string) to the Command Processor or CP (TSO/E or what REXX is running under).
4. The CP evaluates and processes the instruction.
5. The return code of the instruction (stored in the system variable RC) passes back to the REXX interpreter and the exec continues processing. A zero return code means successful processing.

It is this "passing and not knowing non-REXX commands to the CP" procedure that makes REXX portable. CMS and TSO/E also provide a SUBCOM command that allows an application or software package to become a valid (subcommand) environment. (You may pass commands to it with ADDRESS.) Capturing the return code from a SUBCOM environment command tells you if the specified subcommand environment is now active. (With environment being the environment name.) TSO/E also supports the SUBCOM command. Obviously, if an environment is inactive, then its commands are ignored.

The following are guidelines for sending commands to a non-REXX environment:

1. The interpreter passes any clause not seen as a REXX instruction to the active environment (usually the Command Processor). After processing, the exec resumes control and places the command's return code in the system variable RC. *Always place the clause in single or double quotes*. Some valid TSO examples are:

```
'TSO ALLOC F(DATA1) DA(TEMP.DATA) SHR';
'TIME' /* Assumes CP is the current environment. */
'TSO SEND "HOW IS IT GOING?" US(GTY7)'
```

2. The more powerful way of sending non-REXX commands to any valid foreign environment is the ADDRESS instruction. ADDRESS temporarily or permanently overrides the current foreign environment. Once done, control returns to the REXX interpreter and assigns the command return code to the system variable RC. To avoid problems with how the selected environment resolves a command, be as explicit as possible. REXX retains the current environment setting even after processing functions and subprograms. The following shows common uses of ADDRESS.

```
address TSO "TIME"
  if RC = 0 then say 'TIME command succeeded.'
```

Note the syntax: *ADDRESS environment 'command.'* Write a message to the screen if the command works. If in TSO, it is the default environment for the ADDRESS command. This is a *temporary* override.

This is a *permanent* override until meeting the ADDRESS command in the same format or just ADDRESS with no other operands (restores previous environment).

```
address ISPEXEC
  "SELECT PANEL(GXH100) OPT(6)"
  address ISREDIT
  (edit macro statements)
```

General Commands

The following are guidelines in using these general commands.:

1. **DROP** clears any existing value for a variable. It also restores variables to the default value of the variable name in uppercase. You can specify a stem for clearing all values of an array and include more than one variable. A DROP statement with a nonexistent variable does not abnormally end.
   `drop Town. Street`
   Clears value of Town array and Street variable.
   Value is then variable name in uppercase.

2. **EXIT** immediately ends an exec and returns to the environment REXX was invoked from. You may place it at the end of an exec, but it is implied if absent. EXIT can pass a numeric or character return code from either the system variable RC, a user-created variable, or the result of a mathematical operation. If you are not using internal subprograms, you may also use RETURN.

```
exit
exit Exitvar
exit 3+i
exit rc
```

3. **INTERPRET** performs an additional level of symbolic substitution and then executes the created instruction. Flow-control statements must be complete and include END instructions. You may have LEAVE and ITERATE instructions for DO loops. (However, do not use them with other instructions.) Ending semicolons are implied. Labels can not be part of an instruction created by INTERPRET, but additional single and double quotes can be. The following are examples of INTERPRET:

```
INTERPRET "SAY "What"s is your name'"
ifvar = 'x > 25'
INTERPRET 'if' ifvar /* Result:  if x > 25 */
INTERPRET "Y = 1;DO WHILE Y < 3;SAY 'Y IS' Y;Y =
Y + 1;END"
```

Using the debug facility (especially TRACE I and TRACE R) is extremely useful in understanding how REXX symbolic substitution operates.

4. **NUMERIC** sets the precision of mathematical operations and determines how data formats. Functions and subroutines retain these settings. The following are examples of the NUMERIC instruction.
   a. **NUMERIC DIGITS** expression sets the numerical precision for all instructions (including DO loop counters). The default value is 9 and your interpreter, not REXX, sets the upper limit. (When exceeded, abnormal exec termination occurs unless exception handling is enabled.) A value greater than the set precision always rounds. Expression is any symbolic variable or mathematical result resolving to a whole number. REXX retains trailing zeros, except in exponential and division expressions. Larger values can slow down execution processing. The DIGITS function (not yet in TSO/E) returns the current precision setting. In the following statement, If precision is less than 9 digits, then set to 9.

   ```
   IF DIGITS() <= 9 THEN NUMERIC DIGITS 9
   ```

   b. **NUMERIC FORM** sets how REXX displays exponents. **NUMERIC FORM SCIENTIFIC** (the default) places a 0 before decimal point, while **NUMERIC FORM ENGINEERING** places the number as a decimal followed by an E and the exponent. Here are some valid examples:

   4.0E+2 400 (If NUMERIC DIGITS 2, SCI = 4.0E+2)
   (ENG = 400)
   .001e+3 1
   12,000,000
   1.2E+8
   12E+7

c. **NUMERIC FUZZ** expression is useful when comparing numbers with decimals with whole numbers. It has a default value of 0. It temporarily overrides the NUMERIC DIGITS by decreasing it by the FUZZ value. (Therefore, the FUZZ value cannot be larger than the DIGITS value.) Here is an example using NUMERIC FUZZ.

```
NUMERIC DIGITS 2
NUMERIC FUZZ 1 /*So 5.66 = 6*/
```

5. **OPTIONS** 'options' enables or disables one or more settings affecting processing for the entire exec, including settings specific to your REXX interpreter. Options are one or more keywords separated by blanks. Some possible options are:

```
EXMODE/NOEXMODE Enables processing of double-byte
                characters (TSO/E only).
TRACE/NOTRACE Enables trace.
```

6. **SAY** expression displays text or a value to the screen (not to any other device). It does not affect the current setting of the RESULT system variable. The expression may be the result of one level of symbolic substitution and mathematical/logical operations. The previously discussed rules about single and double quotes apply.

```
Say 'What''s your name' /*Displayed: What's your n,
ame*/
val = 2+2
Say 'The result is' val /*Displayed: The re,
sult is 4*/
```

System Variables

We have already mentioned that there are four useful system variables that you can use for processing. They have no initial value. You may modify their values or allow the interpreter to set them after processing an instruction.

RC is the return code from an operating system or environment command (such as TSO or ISPF). This includes using the "foreign clause" or ADDRESS instruction. It can also return an error code of 1 through 99 after the SIGNAL instruction used for exception (or error) handling. *Like &LASTCC in clists, you must assign its value to another variable to preserve it for future use.*

RESULT is the value optionally passed by the RETURN instruction in a subprogram.

SIGL The line number of the instruction that caused a skip to a specified label.

Stack Operations

As mentioned earlier, manipulating and querying the data stacks is an important extension of the REXX language. Later the chapter discusses how TSO further extends stack operations.

1. **MAKEBUF** (no other operands) is a CMS command creating a buffer (reserved area of the data stack) or partition with the boundaries set by a TOP and BOTTOM MARKER. The system variable RC holds the buffer (initially 0, then 1 after the first MAKEBUF, etc.). Once created, use PUSH or QUEUE to put lines in this buffer and PULL to retrieve them.

2. **DROFBUF** *buffernumber* is a CMS command that removes specific buffers by erasing buffer markers.
   a. To remove buffers 6 and higher.
   ```
   DROPBUF 6
   ```
   b. To remove only the buffer from the last MAKEBUF.
   ```
   DROPBUF
   ```
   c. To remove all buffers. Place at the end of a stack operation, leaving the stack as you found it.
   ```
   DROPBUF 0
   ```

3. **EXECIO** is a CMS command transferring lines from a file and placing them on the stack. It executes from the TSO/E or MVS area. For TSO/E, enter an ALLOCATE command before using EXECIO. The TSO/E version is far more limited than the CMS counterpart.
   a. Use the **DISKR** operand to read from a file. the syntax is
   ```
   EXECIO tlines DISKR filename startline (options
   ```
   Where *tlines* is the total number of lines to read, *filename* is the logical dataset name (ddname), *startline* is the beginning line in the file to read (default is first line), and *options* are keywords further customizing the operation. (These are preceded by a parenthesis. Valid options for TSO/E's EXECIO are (1) *LIFO* or *FIFO* is the order to read lines—last in, first out or first in, first out (the default for DISKR). (2) *STEM stemname* to assign one or more lines to a series of array variables starting with stem name. (3) *FINIS* closes the dataset but is always implied. An asterisk used for *tlines* means read until reaching the end of file.
   ```
   ADDRESS TSO 'ALLOC F(MYFILE) DA(HHHH.TXT) SHR'
   EXECIO * DISKR MYFILE 10 (FINIS
   ```
   Reads all lines in the file (*) starting with the tenth line. Close the dataset

on completion. Use REUSE operand for ALLOC if dataset part of a concatenation.

```
ADDRESS TSO 'ALLOC F(MYFILE) DA(HHHH.TXT) SHR'
EXECIO 2 DISKR MYFILE 10 (STEM RECVAL FINIS
```

Assigns two lines to the stem variable RECVAL. Line 1 is assigned to RECVAL1, line 2 to RECVAL2. It starts reading with the tenth line. You could include a DO loop with a *PARSE* instruction for additional processing.

b. **DISKW** always writes to the end of a file. The syntax is

EXECIO tlines DISKW filename (options

Tlines are the total number of lines to write out, *filename* is the logical dataset name (ddname), and *options* are keywords further customizing the operation (previously listed).

```
ADDRESS TSO
'ALLOC F(MYFILE) DA(HHHH.TXT) NEW CATALOG DSORG(PS),
LRECL(80) RECFM(F B) BLKSIZE(19040)'
EXECIO * DISKW MYFILE (FINIS
```

The above keeps writing until finding a blank line (*). If doing a DISKR to get the lines to write, you need two ALLOCATE commands. The file is closed on completion.

```
ADDRESS TSO "ALLOC F(MYFILE) DA(HHHH.TXT) OLD"
EXECIO 1 DISKW MYFILE (STEM WRVAL FINIS
```

The above writes the value of WRVAL array (WRVAL1 – WRVALn) to file. Note dataset disposition of OLD. You could include a DO loop with a PARSE instruction for additional processing.

c. TSO/E also has **DISKRU** for reading and updating a dataset in one step.

4. **PUSH** *expression* places a string on the top of the data stack using a LIFO (last-in, first-out) approach. PUSH and nothing else puts a null expression on the stack. Another option is **QUEUE** *expression*, which places a string at the bottom of the data stack using a FIFO (first-in, first-out) approach. Specifying QUEUE alone puts a null expression on the stack. QUEUE is commonly used for writing to a file. The built-in function QUEUED( ) returns the number of lines in the data stack. Table 11-6 shows the effect of PUSH and QUEUE when values are PULLed off the stack.

5. **PULL** *variables* reads a string from a data stack and places it in one or more variables. It converts all input to uppercase. Use **PARSE PULL** for reading mixed-case strings. If not specifying variables, then do not use the string. The string up (but generally not including) to the first blank is assigned to the first variable and so forth. When there are more values than variables, assign them to the last variable, including leading and trailing blanks.

Table 11-6. Order of Two Values When Pulled

First Value	Second Value	
	QUEUE	PUSH
PUSH	1,2	2,1
QUEUE	1,2	2,1

Sample Execs

Let us review some of the instructions just discussed by looking at two simple execs:

```
1. /*REXX*/
2. say 'Enter First Number:'
3. pull num1
4. say 'Enter Second Number:'
5. pull num2
6. addit = num1 + num2
7. say 'Your result is:  ' addit
```

Explanation. Following is an explanation by line number, of the preceding exec.

1. Many REXX interpreters (such as TSO/E) use the first line for identifying a REXX exec. Including this line and using the EXEC operand (for TSO/E's EXEC command) ends the possibility of falsely identifying an exec as a clist.
2. Display the result to a screen. You may have text of a large length or have "null text."

3–5. Place the user input in NUM1. Repeat this sequence in statements 4 and 5.

6. Add the two numbers together and place the result in addit.
7. Display result (not in single quotes) and text.

STACK OPERATIONS EXEC

```
1. /*REXX*/
2. MAKEBUF
3. BUFF = rc
4. QUEUE 'This is statement 1'
5. QUEUE 'This is statement 2'
6. PUSH 'This is statement 3'
7. SAY 'Number of lines in the stack:' QUEUED( )
```

```
 8. PULL X
 9. SAY X /* This is statement #3 . . . LIFO */
10. DROPBUF BUFF
```

Explanation. Following is an explanation by line number of the above exec.

2–3. Creates buffer and stores buffer number in system variable RC. Assign the buffer number to BUFF.

4–5. Place two lines on the data queue. QUEUE is often used to write out to files.

6. This is the first line out if issuing a PULL.
7. Use the QUEUED function for retrieving and displaying the total number of lines in the stack. A DO loop with a counter value based on QUEUED is commonly used in reading multiple lines from a stack. The above example returns a value of 3 since no lines are yet PULLed.
8. Since there are more values than variables, place all lines in the variable X. The order is lines 6, 4, 5.
9. Write the line out, or use the following for writing the lines to a file with lines stored in X1, X2, and X3.
   ```
   EXECIO 3 DISKW MYFILE (STEM X FINIS
   ```
10. Clears the specified buffer (and all later buffers).
11. Good REXX programmers follow these tenets of "stack discipline."
    - Leave the stack as you found it—use MAKEBUF and DROPBUF.
    - To avoid reading or writing the wrong line, do not include any more QUEUE, PUSH, or PULL instructions than necessary.

Flow-Control Statements

The REXX language has a rich assortment of flow-control statements. Since most of them were reviewed in Chapter 4, they are only briefly mentioned. Use these guidelines for creating REXX flow-control structures.

The following flow-control statements are nearly identical to their clist equivalents:

- SELECT WHEN..OTHERWISE..END
- IF-THEN-ELSE-DO
- DO-WHILE
- DO-UNTIL

However, NOP, not an extra semicolon, is how REXX correctly executes a null clause. Do not use THEN as a variable name. Some additional notes and important differences follow.

SELECT

1. No condition can be set on SELECT line. All WHEN conditions must result in 0 or 1.

```
SELECT /* No condition on this line */
WHEN OPT = "A" THEN DO
  (instructions)
END
WHEN OPT = ''B'' THEN DO
  (instructions)
END
OTHERWISE
  (instructions)
END
```

2. Blocks are set with the following logic:

```
WHEN condition THEN DO /* Clist has no THEN. */
OTHERWISE
  (One or more instructions)
END /* Ends entire SELECT structure.*/
```

3. Like clists, once meeting a WHEN condition, then perform the selected action and move the exec to END.

IF

1. The IF part executes only if the result resolves to 1 (true).
2. Consider an IF-THEN as one clause. When using ELSE on same line, then place a semicolon after the THEN sequence (e.g., IF .. THEN ..; ELSE ..).
3. You can have multiple tests.

```
IF OPT == 'DELETE' & VARA = 1 THEN . . .
```

4. Use as many ELSEs as needed or include a SELECT or DO structure.
5. Use SIGNAL for handling errors.

DO

There are far more REXX formats of the DO instruction than found in most languages (including clists). Table 11-7 lists common formats of REXX's DO instruction.

Here are some additional guidelines for DO loops:

- You may use whole number or decimal increment/decrements and starting/ending values.
- Place TO, BY, and FOR in any order.

Table 11-7. Common REXX DO Formats

Format	Example

IF-THEN-DO-END	`IF AG = ''26'' THEN DO`
	`  SAY 'Are you lying?'`
	`END`

DO-FOREVER-END	`DO FOREVER /* Loops until IF is true.*/`
	`  IF AGE = 25 THEN LEAVE`
	`END /* This is same thing as */`
	`     /* DO FOREVER UNTIL AGE = 25*/`
	`     /* or DO FOREVER WHILE AGE ¬ = 25*/`
	`     /* or DO WHILE AGE ¬ = 25 */`
	`     /* or DO UNTIL AGE = 25 */`

DO expression (expression resolves as whole number)	`DO x  /* x = 6*/`
	`SAY x /* Display 6 six times.*/`
	`END`

DO-TO-END	`DO x = 1 to 6 /* Previous x values*/`
	` SAY x         /* ignored. Writes 1–6.*/`
	`END`

DO-TO-BY-END	`DO x = 1 TO 6 BY 1 /* Same as last,*/`
	` SAY x              /* writes 1–6.*/`
	`END`

DO-TO-BY-FOR-END	`DO x = 1 TO 6 BY 1 FOR 2`
	` SAY x /* Do entire loop 2 times.*/`
	`END   /* Writes 1,2.*/`

DO-TO-BY-WHILE*	`DO x = 1 TO 6 BY 2 WHILE ANS = 1`
	`  SAY X`
	`  IF X = 3 THEN ANS = 2`
	`END /*Writes 1,3*/`

DO-TO-BY-UNTIL*	`DO x = 1 TO 6 BY 2 UNTIL ANS = 2`
	`  SAY X`
	`  IF X = 3 THEN ANS = 2`
	`END  /*Writes 1,3*/`

* Other combinations of DO-TO-BY-FOR-UNTIL, DO-TO-BY-FOR-WHILE, and the unforgettable DO-TO-BY-FOR-WHILE-UNTIL are also valid.

- Use **LEAVE** for leaving a DO loop before it completely ends, especially for a DO FOREVER. **LEAVE** *var* ends the loop and goes where *var*. *Do not use SIGNAL for this purpose!*
- Or use **ITERATE** to skip to the next iteration of a DO loop. **ITERATE** *var* increments or decrements *var*.
- The default BY increment is 1. A DO-TO-BY (and any similar formats) can increment or decrement a counter variable.

String Manipulation and Parsing

String manipulation and parsing are a major strength of the REXX language. Parsing is the process of decomposing a string into smaller units. The three instructions used in parsing are ARG, PARSE, and PULL (already discussed.) The main part of this process is specifying a template. A TEMPLATE instruction specifies into which variables a parsed string goes.

Use ARG to process operands (strings) from an EXEC command or specify operands with a function/subroutine. ARG provides the simplest parsing mechanism by reading values and assigning them to a matching variable in uppercase (so that the first value up to a blank is assigned to the first variable, and so forth). When there are more values then variables, then assign the remaining values to the last variable. If there are more variables than values, then assign the extra variables a null value. Specify a period to bypass a variable. Here are some examples.

1. At TSO/E READY prompt: (EXEC says it is REXX EXEC.) fewer values than variables.
   `EXEC REXX1 'ONE TWO THREE' EXEC`
   In REXX EXEC:
   ```
   /*REXX*/
   ARG A B . D /* A = ONE, B = TWO C = C and D = null.*/
   ```
2. At TSO/E READY prompt: more values than variables
   ```
   /*REXX*/
   EXEC REXX2 'ONE TWO THREE' EXEC
   ```
   In REXX EXEC:
   ```
   ARG A B /* A = ONE, B = TWO THREE.*/
   ```
3. Invoking REXX Function:
   ```
   TWIN('A STRING',18) /* Function passing two values.*/
   ```
   Later in REXX EXEC:
   ```
   TWIN: ARG chval,numval /*chval = 'A STRING', -
   numval = 18*/
   ```

The PARSE instruction offers the greatest flexibility for parsing a string. Parsing criteria can be by blanks, substrings (character patterns), column number, or a combination of the other three. The following are popular parsing combinations:

1. **PARSE UPPERCASE PULL** is identical to the PULL instruction shown earlier, which parses by blanks between values. The more flexible version is PARSE PULL, which retains the current case of a value. It can be used with QUEUE and PUSH shown earlier. You may build sophisticated templates to retrieve information.
   ```
   SAY "What is your phone number?"
   ```

```
PARSE PULL '(' AREA ')-' EXCHANGE '-' EXTENSION
SAY 'area is' AREA    /* area is 914*/
SAY 'exchange is' EXCHANGE /*exchange is 555*/
SAY 'extension is' EXTENSION /*extension is 1212*/
/* Input Format: (914)-555-1212. You can use other*/
/* characters besides blanks in your templates. If*/
/* pattern does not match, then assign variables to*/
/* the left of pattern the remainder of string and */
/* assign variables to the right, null values.*/
```

2. **PARSE UPPER ARG** is the same as the ARG instruction. PARSE ARG is more flexible because it retains the current case of a value. Like the above example, you can include character strings in a template.

   ```
   PARSE ARG '(' AREA ')-' EXCHANGE '-' EXTENSION
   ```

   From TSO:

   ```
   EXEC EXECA (914)-555-1212
   ```

3. **PARSE VALUE** performs a logical, mathematical, or string operation before parsing a string. You must include the string to parse (optionally using built-in functions) in the PARSE VALUE instruction. VALUE usually uses the WITH keyword for assigning the variables for holding the parsed string. You can also parse multiple strings, separated by commas. REXX drops leading and trailing blanks for all but the last variable. Here are some examples of PARSE VALUE.

   a.
   ```
   /* SQ1 = a , SQ2 = real, SQ3 = string.*/
     PARSE VALUE 'a real string' WITH SQ1 SQ2 SQ3
   ```

   b.
   ```
   /* YEAR = 89, MONTH = 09, DAY = 01.*/
     /* Parse result from a built-in function.*/
     PARSE VALUE DATE(O) WITH YEAR '/' MONTH '/' DAY
   ```

   c.
   ```
   /* Split string at column 7. SP1 = (cols 1-6).*/
     /* SP2 = (cols 7-21) trims leading blank.  */
     /* SP1 ='A LONG', SP2 ='STRING TO SPLIT'.*/
     PARSE VALUE 'A LONG STRING TO SPLIT' WITH SP1 7 SP2
   ```

   d.
   ```
   /*Relative position*/
     /* SP1 ='A LONG', SP2 = ST, SP3 = RING TO SPLIT*/
     PARSE VALUE 'A LONG STRING TO SPLIT',
       WITH SP1 7 SP2 +3 SP3
   ```

4. **PARSE VAR** *varname* stores the parsed string in a variable named *varname*. It can use the UPPER keyword for converting the parsed string to

uppercase. Several parse operations can occur in the same instruction. Here are examples of PARSE VAR.

a.
```
/*Relative (e.g., +7) or absolute (10) column. */
/*can be used. A = A ST, B = RING TO PARSE. */
STR = 'A STRING TO PARSE'
PARSE VAR STR A 5 B /*Split String A =-
columns 1-4.*/
                    /*B = Columns 5-17.*/
```

b.
```
/* Multiple operations on same string.*/
VARA = 'A STRING' /* No trailing blanks for A.*/
PARSE VAR VARA A 2 B 1 C /*A = 'A', B = 'STRING'*/
                         /*C = 'A STRING'*/
```

5. Use **PARSE SOURCE** for retrieving information about the current exec and placing it in seven variables. (But only the first three are commonly used.) (a) ENVIRONMENT (usually TSO or ISPEXEC if ISPF), (b) EXEC TYPE (COMMAND, FUNCTION, or SUBROUTINE), and (c) DATASET NAME. You could then invoke an EDIT macro with the dataset name captured by a PARSE SOURCE.

```
/* Ignore last 4 values*/
/* ENV = TSO, TYP = COMMAND, DNAME = EXECA*/
PARSE SOURCE ENV TYPE DNAME ....
ADDRESS 'ISPEXEC EDIT DATASET(DNAME) MACRO(TEST1)'
```

This is a brief introduction to parsing with the REXX language. Check the references for additional information.

Error Handling

The SIGNAL instruction decides what a label processes after abnormal processing instead of the exec abnormally ending. Here are some common uses of SIGNAL.

1. The syntax is SIGNAL *labelname*. SIGNAL can also be part of a DO, IF, or SELECT. It ends the loop if used.

```
SIGNAL LABA
```

or

```
IF X = 25 THEN SIGNAL LABA
  (later in the exec)
LABA: SAY 'Bad value'
      EXIT 100
```

2. SIGNAL ON condition turns on error condition and SIGNAL OFF turns it off.

```
SIGNAL ON ERROR    /* For nonzero return codes.*/
SIGNAL ON HALT     /* If pressing attention.*/
SIGNAL ON NOVALUE /* Uninitalized value*/
SIGNAL ON SYNTAX   /* REXX syntax error*/
```

The interpreter then goes to the label with the same name as the exception. System variable RC stores the syntax error number (1–99) after a SYNTAX ON ERROR, FAILURE, and SYNTAX. (See the list in Appendix C.) All SYNTAX ON exceptions in a subprogram are local and do not affect the main exec. They are also set off during use of the trace facility. Use the system variable SIGL for displaying the line that caused an exception. Here is an example of an exception routine:

```
SIGNAL ON ERROR
(later in the exec)
ERROR:
say 'Your error was' errortext(rc) /*lists error text*/
say 'The error was on line' sigl
EXIT 200 /*Optionally add SOURCELINE returning line*/
         /*causing the error.*/
```

Built-in Functions

There are over 60 built-in REXX functions for your use. The following are guidelines for using the common functions available for TSO REXX.

String Operations

To better show what built-in string operation functions can do, let us use the same string ''typical string.''

1. ABBREV returns 1 (true) if a string (argument 1) includes a substring (argument 2) *and* if the substring is equal or greater than the length of the optional third argument. Otherwise returns 0 (false.)

```
ABBREV('TYPICAL STRING', 'TYP')   /*Returns 1.*/
ABBREV('TYPICAL STRING','TYP',5) /*Returns 0 due to*/
                                   /*length less than,
                                     5.*/
```

A null string with no length argument always matches. But a substring in a different case than the compared string always will not. You may use ABBREV with user input so that D, DE, DEL, or DELE are all valid forms of DELETE.

2. CENTER or CENTRE returns centered text (argument 1) of a certain length (argument 2 and always greater than 0) with specific pad characters. (Optional argument 3 with a default of blank.) This is useful in displaying option menus created by SAY. Truncation of pad characters may occur to center a string.

   CENTER('@TYPICAL STRING',16,@) /**Returns: '@TYPICAL, STRING@*/*

3. COPIES returns a string (argument 1) copied a set number of times (argument 2). REXX places no spaces between "copies." Use COPIES to draw patterns such as a row of asterisks.

   A = COPIES('TYPICAL STRING',1) /**Returns 'TYPICAL STRINGTYPICAL STRING'.*/*

   A = COPIES('TYPICAL STRING',0) /**Returns null.*/*

4. DELSTR deletes a substring appearing in a string (argument 1) starting with a specific character position (argument 2) up to the optional substring length (argument 3). The default length is the remaining string—*beware!*

   A = DELSTR('TYPICAL STRING',4) /** Returns 'TYP'*/*

   A = DELSTR('TYPICAL STRING',4,3) /** Returns 'TYPL, STRING'*/*

5. LENGTH returns the length of a string including blanks.

   LENGTH('TYPICAL STRING') /** Returns 14*/*

   LENGTH('') /**Returns 0*/*

6. POS finds the location of a substring (argument 1) in a string (argument 2) starting with the first character. The default can be overwritten with optional argument 3. Some people get in trouble with POS because it is more natural for the first argument to be the string and not the substring to search for.

   POS('TYP','TYPICAL STRING',6) /** Returns 0 not, found.*/*

   POS('TYP','TYPICAL STRING') /** Returns 1.*/*

7. SUBSTR returns the substring found in a string (argument 1) starting with a specific location (argument 2) of a set length. (The default is the entire string, which argument 3 overrides.) An optional fourth argument is padding characters with a default of blank.

   SUBSTR('TYPICAL STRING',14,1) /** Returns 'G ' */*

8. There are other string-oriented functions as well.

COMPARE	Compares two strings.
INSERT	Inserts a substring into a string.
LEFT	Returns left-most characters of a string.
OVERLAY	Overlays one string over another.

REVERSE	Reverses a string (only argument).
RIGHT	Returns right-most characters of a string.
SPACE	Pads characters in a string.
STRIP	Deletes any leading or trailing blanks in a string.
TRANSLATE	If string only argument, then converts string to uppercase.
VERIFY	Does a string contain only characters used in substring?

9. REXX also provides built-in functions for words as well as strings:

DELWORD	Delete word in string. Same syntax as DELSTR.
SUBWORD	Returns substring including certain words
WORD	Returns a specified word in a string.
WORDINDEX	Returns starting position of word in a string.
WORDLENGTH	Returns length of a word in a string.
WORDS	Returns number of words in a string (only argument).

Data Manipulation

The REXX language provides a variety of functions for manipulating data into different types, including the following listed in Table 11-8. (Usually the argument is just the data/string.)

There are additional functions for manipulating numbers. Usually arguments are in single or double quotes.

ABS Returns absolute value of a number (only argument).

FORMAT Rounds a number or converts argument to scientific format.

MAX Returns the largest number from a group of numbers delimited by commas.

MIN Returns the smallest number from a group of numbers delimited by commas.

SIGN Returns −1 if the number is negative, 0 if equals zero, or 1 if positive.

Table 11-8. Conversion Function Names

	ASCII	Decimal	Hexadecimal
ASCII	na	C2D	C2X
Decimal	D2C	na	D2X
Hexadecimal	X2C	X2D	na

TRUNC Truncates a number up to an optional number of decimal points. (The default is 0 for this argument 2.)

Some functions are available for bit/byte manipulations of data:

BITAND ANDs two hex strings.
BITOR ORs two hex strings.
BITXOR XORs two hex strings.
TRANSLATE Converts characters to a different value.
XRANGE Returns all 1-byte characters between two positions.

Other Functions

These are other useful functions:

ADDRESS Returns the current environment which ADDRESS instructions go to (no arguments).

ARG Returns information about values which ARG passes. Argument 1 specifies which ARG value to return (as null or if a whole number. If not included, then return the total number of ARG values.) Optional argument 2 tests if a specific ARG value was passed. Its values are E or e (returns 1 if exists) and O or o (returns 1 if not exists.) This function is only useful for subprograms and functions; it always returns 1 for EXECs.

```
CALL FUNC ,3,4
```

In subprogram:

```
ARG() /*Returns 3 (3 values)*/
ARG(1) /*Returns '' (null)*/
ARG(1, 'E') /*Returns 0 (ARG value 1 is null)*/
```

DATATYPE Returns or verifies the datatype of an argument. In this case, returns NUM for a number in any valid numeric format; otherwise it returns CHAR.

```
DATATYPE('12')
```

The following returns 1 (true) if a string is in mixed case.

```
DATATYPE('Ac',M)
```

Other values are A (A–Z, a–z, 0–9), B (only 0 ,1), L (a–z), N (numbers), S (valid symbol name), U (A–Z), W (whole number), X (hex).

DATE Displays current date into various formats. Argument can be the following: D (Julian), E (dd/mm/yy), M (mixed-case month), N (dd Mmm yyyy), S (yyyymmdd), U (mm/dd/yy), W (mixed-case day of week)

```
DATE('U')  /* Returns 07/04/89 */
DATE('W')  /* Returns Wednesday */
DATE('N')  /* 4 Jul 1989 or default format*/
```

ERRORTEXT Returns the matching text for an error number. (The only argument with a value from 0 to 99.) See Appendix C for REXX error messages.

QUEUED Number of lines left in the data stack and has no arguments.

RANDOM Random number generator useful for games and statistical analysis. Returns whole numbers only.

```
RANDOM() /*No argument returns a value 0-999*/
RANDOM(0,1) /*Argument 1 is smallest number,
              returned and*/
            /*argument 2 is the target.*/
            /*Returns a value between 0 and 1.*/
RANDOM(,,2000) /* Argument 3 is the seed. Always,
                  returns*/
               /* 430. */
```

SOURCELINE With no argument, returns the last line of the program. Otherwise returns the specified line. You often use this in error sequences.

```
SAY 'The line with error:' SOURCELINE(SIGL)
```

SYMBOL Returns if an argument is BAD (not a symbol), VAR (a symbol), or LIT (a constant).

```
SYMBOL(A = 3) /*returns LIT*/
```

TIME Places current time in a specified format (only argument.)

```
TIME('N') or TIME() /* Default 24-hour format---
Returns 18:22:35*/
```

Other formats are (hh : mmcc) with cc = am or pm. E (elapsed time from *first* E or R in seconds) or R (elapsed time from *last* E or R), H (hh—hours since midnight), M (mm—minutes since midnight), and S (ss—seconds since midnight).

TRACE If no arguments, returns current trace setting. With arguments, then override current trace settings. The argument cannot be a number.

```
A = TRACE() /*Returns ?0 (current trace,
setting of OFF).*/
TRACE('?L') /*Turns on tracing of labels. Enter,
TRACE OFF*/
            /*to turn it off.*/
```

VALUE Returns value of a variable (in uppercase.) The argument in quotes performs one level of symbolic substitution, no quotes does two.

```
A = 22
G = 'A'
VALUE(G) /* Returns 22 .*/
VALUE('G') /* Returns 'A'.*/
```

TSO also has some additional functions returning userid and other information. These are presented later.

Subprograms and Functions

With REXX, you can easily build a series of subprograms doing one or two tasks and optionally passing a return code or result. There are two major types of subprograms, both of which are functionally equivalent. Both types of subprograms can be in the same program as the "main" exec (called *internal functions* or *subroutines*. Internal subprograms may invoke other subprograms including itself) or a different exec (called *external functions* or *subroutines*). The system variable SIGL stores the line number in the "main" exec that is calling the internal subprogram.

Functions are invoked with the same format as built-in functions. The returned result substitutes for the function call and can be assigned to a variable.

Subroutines are invoked by CALL. They place the returned result in system variable RESULT.

Let us briefly look at each type of subprogram.

Function

A function call usually takes one of two formats:

```
X = addit(a,b) /* X equals result, otherwise equals,
null.*/
```

```
Say addit(a,b) /* Use as part of another instruction and*/
               /* substitute the result for addit(a,b). */
```

A function call consists of (1) result variable name, (2) function name, and (3) up to ten function operand values. Separate each operand value by commas and process them in order (left to right). We have seen that you can use the ARG/PARSE instruction or ARG built-in function for retrieving and manipulating these values. For internal functions, the exec then looks for a label with the same name as the function. (*Note*: an EXIT instruction appears before the label to avoid processing the subprogram twice!) You can use RETURN for giving a result to the main exec. Even RETURN " " is valid.

```
a=1;b=2; /*Assign values to both variables.*/
X=addit(a,b) /*Assign X the result of d+c.*/
(later in the same exec)
/* Looks for ADDIT label in any case. */
EXIT /* End exec avoids reprocessing subprogram. */
ADDIT: ARG d,c /*Uses different variable names.*/
       RETURN d+c /*Assigned to X.*/
```

If you wish to use an external function or subprocedure, then place the name in quotes and uppercase. This overrides the default search order of internal subprogram, built-in functions, and then external subprograms. The external may also use an EXIT instruction to return to the main exec.

```
X = 'ADD'(a,b) /* Uses external not internal function.*/
```

Subroutines

The other approach is using subroutines with the following calling format:

```
a = 1; b = 1; /* Assign values. */
CALL ADDIT a,b /* Look, no parentheses! */
SAY a '+' b '=' result /* Display 1 + 1 = 2.*/
EXIT /* End exec avoids reprocessing subprogram. */
ADDIT: ARG d,c /*Identical to function.*/
       RETURN d + c /* Place sum in system variable
       RESULT */
```

Do not confuse the CALL instruction with the TSO CALL command, which invokes load modules.

The following are additional guidelines for both types of subprograms:

1. SIGNAL sequences affect the internal subprogram it appears in, not the main exec. This also applies to the numeric settings, current address environment, any elapsed time results from the time function, and trace settings.
2. Do not call your subprogram ON or OFF—these are reserved.
3. Variables in an external subprogram do not know the values of the main exec and are always *local* (hidden). This is also called *scoping*. Beware that internal subprograms include all variables from the main exec and are always *global* (which the main exec can overwrite). To make internal subprogram variables local, use PROCEDURE EXPOSE *var1,varn*. Only *var1* through *varn* then pass to the main exec on completion—all others are dropped. Note that exposing the stem exposes the entire array.

```
A = 1
B = 2
C = 3
CALL EXAMP
SAY 'A' = A, 'B' = B, 'C' = C /* A = 22, B = 33,
C = 3*/
EXIT
EXAMP: PROCEDURE EXPOSE A,B
A = 22
B = 33
C = A + B /* Not passed back to main exec. */
RETURN '' ''
```

File I/O

We have already discussed EXECIO and stack operations for reading and writing to a file, but most of these are CMS extensions and are not part of the REXX language. Instead, REXX provides its own set of I/O built-in functions that are not used by most implementations including TSO/E (and so is briefly discussed). These built-in functions manipulate input and output streams (which you may name) by character or lines. They include

CHARIN Returns a string of a given length from an input stream
CHAROUT Writes a string to an output stream.
CHARS Returns the number of characters in input stream.
LINEIN Returns the number of lines read from input stream.
LINEOUT Returns if a line was written to an output stream.
LINES Returns number of lines in character input stream.

Debugging Execs

When comparing the REXX and clist language, we briefly looked at the REXX trace facility invoked by either the TRACE built-in function or instruction. The following are the most commonly used TRACE settings.

TRACE A Traces all clauses before execution.
TRACE C Traces just external environment commands before execution and nonzero return codes.
TRACE E Traces just external commands after execution with nonzero return codes.
TRACE I Shows intermediate and final symbolic substitution for all clauses.
TRACE L Just traces labels processed. Useful for subroutines and saves writing SAY 'GOT TO LABEL X'.
TRACE N The default displays just external environment commands with nonzero return codes.
TRACE O Turns off all tracing.
TRACE R Shows just final symbolic substitution for all clauses. This is used for most symbolic substitution debugging.

REXX also has a powerful interactive trace mode not discussed here. Instead we will look at what the TRACE facility displays. This display uses the following codes:

- The REXX clause in your exec before symbolic substitution.
>>> The result of a variable after parsing or symbolic substitution. >.> also shows the result of a variable after parsing.
++ A trace message, return code.

If Trace I is specified, these also may be displayed.

>C> Name of compound variable after symbolic substitution.
>F> This line is the result of a subprogram.
>L> This line is a character literal.
>O> This line is a result of a mathematical, logical, or relational operation.
>P> Result from a prefix operation.
>V> This line is the value of a variable.

Let us look at the result of a trace display:

EXEC

```
/*REXX exec*/
TRACE AR
'TIME'
```

```
a = 1; b = 2
X = addit(a,b)
say X
EXIT
ADDIT: ARG d,c
RETURN d + c
```

TRACE

```
3 *-* 'TIME' /* trace and comments not shown*/
  >>> ''TIME'' /*after symbolic substitution*/
4 *-*a = 1;
4 *-*b = 2
5 *-*X = addit(a,b)
8 *-*ADDIT :
8 *-*ARG d,c
9 *-*RETURN d + c
5 *-*X = addit(a,b)
6 *-*say X
3 /*Result from say*/
7 *-*EXIT
```

REXX Tips, Tricks, and Traps

Here are some additional guidelines in using REXX.

1. Avoid these common traps:
   a. Thinking the default length for string operations is one character—usually it is the end of string.
   b. Using SIGNAL as a GOTO to normal end of a loop.
   c. Thinking internal subprograms have local variables and not using PROCEDURE EXPOSE.
   d. Confusing a subprocedure and a function—they basically do the same thing.
   e. Assuming the default environment is the one you want, or thinking the ADDRESS command is set to one environment when it is set to another.
   f. Reversing the first two arguments in the POS built-in function.
   g. Thinking system variables retain their values after processing an instruction. When in doubt, assign the value to another variable.

2. There are plenty of places to find examples of REXX execs. However, they may need changes to work under TSO/E.
   a. IBM Users' Groups: SHARE, GUIDE, and SEAS (Share Europe) proceedings and meetings.

b. The Miscellaneous Language Section of the IBM Programming Languages (GO IBMPRO) of Compuserve. Also Mansfield Software under Software Vendors (GO PCVEN).

c. For UNIX users, comp.lang.rexx newsgroup of Usenet. There are also two REXX lists on BITNET. REXXLIST and TSO-REXX both @OHSTVMA.BITNET or @POLYGRAF.BITNET.

d. User group proceedings for software products used with REXX (such as FOCUS, SAS, etc.).

e. Periodicals such as *Mainframe Journal.*

3. Here are some guidelines to using REXX:

a. Get in the habit of quoting arguments in functions and certain instructions. This may save you from certain "wrongful symbolic substitution" errors.

b. Use flowerboxes in your execs. Here is a sample skeleton:

```
/ ************************************************/
/* Exec: SAMPLE                                  */
/* Purpose: This is a sample exec.               */
/* Internal Subprograms: aa - erases a line      */
/* External Subprograms: bb - sin of x           */
/* Arrays: A.0-A.99                              */
/* History:                                      */
/* Date      Person       Change                 */
/* 07/01/88 Mark Jackson Production Version      */
/ ************************************************/
```

c. Always "clean up" during an exec. Use DROPBUF to clear unused buffers and DROP to remove unused variables.

d. REXX style issues:

(i) Standards on label, exec, and subprogram names and use.

(ii) Indenting flow-control blocks and use of white space.

(iii) Use of comments: (flowerbox, on same line as instruction).

(iv) Use of case in an exec. A common practice is placing TSO commands entirely in uppercase, REXX instructions (especially keywords) in lowercase, and capitalize REXX variable names (Age).

(v) Variable names with underscore (Array_Var) or joined together (ArrayVar). My personal preference is to use the underscore because it is easier to read (but not type).

e. The PARSE instruction works well with EXEC positional operand values but cannot easily process keyword operand values (e.g., DATASET('HHG1.TEMP.DATA').) You will have to create your own sequence do to this or use one created by someone else (such as on the REXX discussion group on BITNET).

REXX Under TSO/E

The rest of the chapter looks at how the REXX interpreter operates under TSO/E and discusses TSO/E extensions to REXX. Much of this emphasis is on conceptual areas since they are a source of potential confusion. The following are TSO/E extensions to the REXX language:

- Expansion of ADDRESS instruction:
  ```
  ADDRESS ATTACH ''module'' /*Invoke module,
  as a subtask. Exec waits for completion.*/
  ADDRESS ISPEXEC ''SELECT service operands''
  /*Any ISPF command once enabling ISPF.*/
  ADDRESS ISREDIT ''command operands''
  /*Any EDIT Macro command if under PDF EDIT.*/
  ADDRESS LINK ''module value1..valuen''
  /*Access load modules anytime. ISPPLIB and the
  Linklist*/
  /*libraries are searched.*/
  ADDRESS MVS ''command value1..valuen'' /*Any MVS com-,
  mand anytime. This is the default if in a */
  /* MVS area.*/
  ADDRESS TSO ''command operand1..operandn'' /*Any TSO/,
  E command only if in a TSO/E area. This is the*/
  /*default if in a TSO/E area.*/
  ```
- CMS data stack commands plus extensions (see below).
- A limited EXECIO command (presented earlier).
- New functions (Only STORAGE can be used in a non-TSO area.)

  LISTDSI Like LISTDSI statement in TSO/E, gives information about a dataset.

  MSG Enables/disables informational messages display during processing. Same as CONTROL MSG in clist. Argument is ON or OFF.

  ```
  MS = MSG(''ON'')
  ```

  OUTTRAP Saves command output into system variables. This is the equivalent of clists's &SYSOUTTRAP and &SYSOUTLINE. Arguments are ON or OFF, variable names, and whether or not to concatenate variables.

  PROMPT Turns on or off command prompting if no operands. Same as CONTROL PROMPT with an argument of ON or OFF.

  ```
  PR = PROMPT(''ON'')
  ```

  STORAGE Reads or writes data into virtual storage. Arguments include address space and length.

SYSDSN   Same as clist's &SYSDSN built-in function. Returns the same text return codes.

```
IF SYSDSN('HHG1.DATA.DATA') = ''OK'' THEN. . .
```

SYSVAR   Displays values for 17 of the 37 clist system variables. (These are SYSCPU, SYSENV, SYSHSM, SYSICMD, SYSISPF, SYSLRACF, SYSLTERM, SYSNEST, SYSPCMD, SYSPREF, SYSPROC, SYSRACF, SYSSCMD, SYSSRV, SYSTSOE, SYSUID, SYSWTERM.)

```
SAY 'Your userid is' SYSVAR(''SYSUID'')
```

- IRXEXCOM Programming Services   creates, passes, and deletes the values of a REXX variable similar to IKJCT441 for clists and some execs (both TSO/E and non-TSO/E areas). You can also use IRXEXEC to store but not process an exec, IRXIC enables the TRACE facility, and IRXJCL runs an exec in batch (background) mode.
- CMS SUBCOM command supported. As said before, this allows an application to be seen by the REXX interpreter as an environment and is how many commercial software packages interact with REXX.

```
SUBCOM NEWENV /*Creates an environment called NEWENV.*/
  IF RC <> 0 then say ''NEWENV environment not-
  created''
```

- You can process REXX execs in foreground or background. For background processing, the JCL is the same as clists running in background discussed in Chapter 7 with these exceptions:

  1. Instead of executing IKJEFT01, use PGM = IRXJCL.
  2. Include a SYSEXEC DD statement instead of SYSPROC DD to point to exec PDS.
  3. Use one parameter per PARM field, but these can include many tokens.

- Ability to customize your environment using new exits. You can apply these exits to any stage of processing. You may also use replaceable routines, which replace, not override, a system routine. Some canned replaceable routines are.

  GETFREER   Tasks concerning storage.
  IRXINOUT   Record I/O.
  IRXLOAD   Load an exec and later free it.
  IRXMSGID   Enable displaying message id.
  IRXSTK   Tasks concerning the data stack.
  IRXUID   Capture userid.
- Grouping external subprograms (both subroutines and functions but not execs) into a load library called a *package*. The major advantage of doing this is faster execution time because the entire package is always available in storage. Packages may be *private* (also called *user-level*, and also searched first),

that is, hidden from other users, or *local* (for department or division packages) and SYSTEM (usually for commercial software and always searched last).

- Support CMS immediate commands to override exec processing. These can be invoked from the EXECUTIL command (see "Allocating Execs" later in the chapter), the IRXIC programming service, and immediately after pressing the attention key. Note these are not included in the SAA Programming Language version of REXX. Immediate commands include:

  Trace Enable/Disable
  Call areas)

  TS—Enable exec trace facility
  TE—Disable exec trace facility

  Exec Processing
  (TSO area and IRXIC
  programming service)

  HI—Disable symbolic substitution
  HT—Disable typing (display off)
  RT—Enable typing (display on)

Allocating EXECS

This section looks at allocating and invoking execs. You may store EXECS in datasets allocated to a SYSPROC or SYSEXEC concatenation. (SYSEXEC is just for execs. Some execs must be in SYSEXEC. Remember TSO also searches SYSEXEC before SYSPROC. However, ADDRESS TSO 'EXECUTIL SEARCHDD(NO)' overrides this. EXECUTIL also supports immediate commands mentioned earlier, can close a SYSEXEC dataset after use (EXECDD CLOSE) or rename external functions (RENAME to deactivate an external function and use a different one instead).

Another option is using the new ALTLIB command to dynamically define exec and REXX libraries while in TSO. This is similar to the ISPF LIBDEF command used to dynamically allocate ISPF libraries and can speed up exec/clist search time.

Execs may be both implicitly (*The exec name* or *the exec name preceded by a* %, which says search only the SYSPROC and SYSEXEC concatenation) and explicitly invoked (*Using EXEC. This must be done for all execs in a SYSEXEC dataset and will not work in an MVS area*). Using the EXEC (not CLIST) operand with the EXEC command and having the first line of your exec as an identifier (e.g., /* REXX */) guarantees that your exec will not be incorrectly processed as a clist. In addition, REXX execs may also call clists and vice versa.

Stack Operations

As mentioned earlier, the TSO/E data stack was created as an a superset of the CMS data stack. New capabilities and commands were added as well. Note that this stack is also available for the non-TSO/E address spaces of MVS/XA but not to clists. The two major areas of extension of stack operations was (a) allowing an exec to simultaneously process several tasks, and (b) allowing an exec to enable or disable sharing a stack with other execs processing at the same time. This is done by creating *secondary stacks* that can be shared with other execs but not with external environments. (Primary stacks do the reverse.) There is only one active secondary stack at any one time, although allowed multiple secondary stacks. You may use QUEUE, PULL, and PUSH to manipulate the primary or secondary stack. (The primary stack also uses MAKEBUF and DROPBUF.) TSO/E added these instructions and built-in functions were added to take advantage of the new capabilities:

DELSTACK Removes secondary stack, otherwise clears current primary stack.

NEWSTACK Creates secondary stack with RC as number of available stacks after creation. (Value initially same as QSTACK.)

QBUF A function returning the number of buffers in a primary stack not including the initial buffer. RC stores this value.

QELEM A function returning how many elements (lines) are the primary stack's current buffer. RC stores this value.

QSTACK A function returning how many stacks exist. RC stores this value.

SUGGESTED READINGS

Adesse Corporation, 1988. *Program Development Using REXX*. Adesse Corporation.

Cowlishaw, M. F., 1984. The design of the REXX Language. *IBM Systems Journal*. 23(4), pp. 326–335.

Cowlishaw, M. F., 1985. *The REXX Language: A Practical Approach to Programming*. Englewood Cliffs, NJ: Prentice-Hall.

Doherty, W. J., and W. G. Pope, 1986. Computing as a Tool for Human Augmentation. *IBM Systems Journal*. 25:(3/4), pp. 306–320.

Englebart, Doug, 1988. *The Future of Computing*. Notes from a talk given at GTE Laboratories Inc. on November 15.

Gleason, Chapman, 1989. A CMS VM Batch Facility REXX Exec for the SAS System. *Proceedings of the Fourteenth Annual SAS Users Group International Conference*. (Forthcoming).

Heavener, Zeiva. 1989. TSO/E REXX: An Overview. *Mainframe Journal*. IV:10 (October), pp. 69–72.

Hoernes, G. E. 1989. REXX on TSO/E. *IBM Systems Journal*. 28(2), pp. 274–293.

IBM Corporation, 1988. *Introducing TSO Extensions Version 2*. GC28-1868.

IBM Corporation, 1988. *TSO Extensions (TSO/E) Version 2 Announcement*. 5685-025.
IBM Corporation, 1988. *TSO Extensions Version 2 REXX Reference*. SC28-1883.
IBM Corporation, 1988. *TSO Extensions Version 2 REXX User's Guide*. SC28-1882.
IBM Corporation, 1988. *Using REXX in Practice EXEC 2 to REXX Conversion Experiences*. GC24-1615.
Kusnierz, Thomas E., 1989. REXX in MVS. *SEAS 89 Proceedings*. pp. 1–23 (Handout).
Lovelace, M. "REXX Techniques" 1986. *SEAS Spring 1986 Proceedings*. pp. 1215–1224.
Mansfield Software Group, 1988. *Personal REXX User's Guide*. Storrs, Ct: Mansfield Software.
Ohara, Robert, and David Gomberg, 1985. *Modern Programming Using REXX*. Englewood Cliffs, NJ: Prentice-Hall.
Russell, Scott, 1989. *Letter on Compuserve*. July 3rd.
Stolz, Otto, 1989. *Letter on Bitnet Electronic Group REXXLIST*. June 20.
Stolz, Otto, 1989. *Letter on Bitnet Electronic Group REXXLIST*. Dec. 1.
Tran, Kha, 1989. *Letter on Bitnet Electronic Group REXXLIST*. June 19.

Appendix A

Related Software

The following is a sample of additional software available for the TSO and TSO/E environments with one exception. The author makes no endorsement of any of these products.

1. MVS/Quick Ref—an online reference to JCL, JCL Utilities, clist, and REXX statements running under ISPF. The company also makes Help/D, which proposes solutions to TSO and JCL problems.
   Cost: $5000 or more.
   Vendor: Chicago-Soft Ltd.
   738 N. LaSalle Street
   Suite 2
   Chicago, Illinois 60610
   (312) 525-6400
2. pCLIST—Clist interpreter for the PC. Includes many of the features of TSO/E Version 1 Release 4.
   Cost: Trial Disk $10, Registration $39.
   Vendor: Robert Jones
   3534 Hawkwood Road
   Diamond Bar, California 91765
   Compuserve: 72047,1154
3. DB/CLIST—Access DB2 and build DB2 applications using clists.
   Cost: $3800.
   Vendor: Updata Software Company
   Holmdel, New Jersey
4. PDSFAST—Faster version of IEBCOPY/SPFCOPY.
   Cost: $6000 and higher.
   Vendor: Software Engineering of America
   2001 Marcus Avenue
   Lake Success, New York 11042
   1-800-272-7322

5. ISPFVSAM Utility—Menu utility to perform operations on VSAM and non-VSAM files
   Cost: $1295.
   Vendor: Mackinney Systems
   2740 South Glenstone, Suite 103
   Springfield, Missouri 65804
   (417) 882-8012
6. Almost TSO_{TM}—Edit files of any select LRECC. They also make the superset utilities which supply COPY, LIST, and other TSO extensions.
   Cost: Not available.
   Vendor: Applied Software Inc.
   840 US Highway 1, Suite 250
   North Palm Beach, Florida 33468
   (407) 626-4818

Appendix B

Common TSO Clist Error Messages

The following table lists return codes by clist statements when trapping &LASTCC. It is reprinted by permission from *OS/VS2 TSO Terminal Monitor Program and Service Routines Logic*. Copyright © 1984 by International Business Machines Corporation. (The order and format of material has been slightly modified and updated for TSO/E Version 1 Release 4.)

Statement	Return Codes
TSO Command	0 (*Author's Note*: Can be higher.)
ATTN, CONTROL, ELSE, END, ERROR, WRITE	4
CLOSFILE	4, 368
DO	4, 500, 502, 504, 800 series
EXIT	304, 308, 964
GETFILE	4, 352, 356, 400, 408
GOTO	4, 948, 952, 956
IF	4, 800 series from evaluation
OPENFILE	4, 16, 336, 340, 348, 904, 944
PROC	528, 532, 536, 540, 544, 548, 552, 556, 560
PUTFILE	4, 360, 364, 372, 404
READ, READDVAL	324, 976 (READ)
RETURN	4, 512
SET	16, 800 series, 904, 940, 944
SYSCALL	508
TERMIN	4, 16, 316, 328, 972

The following are lists of common clist return codes by category. Check if they are available for your release.

SYNTAX ERRORS

304 EXIT has invalid operand.
308 EXIT has CODE operand with no value.
316 Too long a TERMIN delimiter.
328 Too many TERMIN delimiters.
332 File name does not follow TSO naming conventions.
500 DO has invalid TO value.
502 DO has invalid FROM value.
504 DO has invalid BY value.
512 RETURN has an invalid operand.
528 PROC has invalid positional operand.
532, 536 PROC has invalid operand name.
540 User entered more positional operands than PROC defines.
544 PROC without positional or keyword operands.
548 PROC used positional or keyword operand twice.
552, 556 PROC has invalid keyword operand value. Check if second quote needs to be added for a 556.
840 Supplying less operands than required.
940 Invalid symbolic variable.
944 Label processed as a symbolic variable.
948 GOTO has an invalid label.
952 GOTO label nonexistent.
956 GOTO without a label.
968 DATA PROMPT block has no prompts.
972, 976 Using TERMIN (972) or READ (976) in a batch job.
980 Clist statement is too long. This is checked after doing symbolic substitution.
Sxxx, Uxxx System (Sxxx) or User (Uxxx) abend code. This is a hexadecimal value.

MATHEMATICAL OPERATIONS

800 Had a value instead of an operator.
804 Had an operator instead of a value.
808 Relational operator in a SET.
816 Statement ends with an operator.
820 Invalid expression.
832 Result of mathematical operation too large to process.
844 Invalid operators.
848 Tried to treat a number as a character value.
852, 856, 860, 864 Tried to add (852), subtract (856), multiply (860), or divide (864) a character value.

BUILT-IN FUNCTIONS AND SYSTEM VARIABLES

708 Invalid &SYSINDEX expression.
712 Invalid starting position in search string argument(s) for &SYSINDEX.
716, 724 Invalid number of symbolic scans argument (np) for &SYSNSUB. 724 is for built-in functions supplying a value for np argument.
720 &SYSNSUB has one or more missing arguments.
912, 916, 932 Invalid &SUBSTR range. 932 is a substring range longer than the search string.
920 &SUBSTR has zero or negative range argument.
924 &SUBSTR substring argument is invalid.
936 Missing an argument for a built-in function.
960 &SYSSCAN has an invalid value.
964 &LASTCC has an invalid value.

QSAM FACILITY AND FILE I/O

340, 344 Invalid OPEN statement. For 344, check OPEN operation operand.
348, 368 File unopened. Check allocation status.
352, 360 Did a GETFILE (352) or PUTFILE (360) on an unopened file.
356, 364 File closed during a GETFILE (356) or PUTFILE (364).
372 Forgot to do a GETFILE before a PUTFILE.
400 Unexpected end of file during a GETFILE.
404 Write to an INPUT file.
408 Read from an OUTPUT file.
412, 416 Tried to update after end of file (412) or while it was empty (416).

SUBPROCEDURES AND DOUBLE-BYTE CHARACTERS

508 Unknown subprocedure name used by SYSCALL.
516 Subprocedure processed as a symbolic variable.
572 SYSREF operands not processed.
576 SYSREF operand has no matching PROC operand.
580 Nested ERROR routine in subprocedure.
584 Nested ATTN routine in subprocedure.
588 Character not in valid double-byte range.
592 Missing one or more bytes.
596, 600 Missing at least one SHIFT-IN character.
620 &SYSTWOBYTE has invalid argument.

Appendix C

Common REXX Error Messages

Here are some common generic REXX error messages which are between 1 and 99 and stored in system variable RC only if SIGNAL ON SYNTAX is enabled. The wording may be different for your release.

Keyword	Return Code
ADDRESS	29
DO/END	10, 14, 27
IF	8, 14, 18
LEAVE/ITERATE	28
Subprograms	17, 40, 43, 44
PARSE	38
SELECT	7, 9, 10, 14
SIGNAL	16
TRACE	24

TYPE ERRORS

13 Invalid character.
15 Invalid hexadecimal value.
19, 20 String or symbol expected.
22 Invalid character string.
26 Invalid whole number.
30 Name or string longer than allowed.
31 Name begins with a period or a number.
34 Logical value not equal to zero or one.
41 Mathematical conversion failed.

SYNTAX ERRORS

6 Missing /* or ending quote.
7 SELECT is missing WHEN or OTHERWISE.
8 Missing IF or WHEN for THEN or ELSE.
9 Missing SELECT for WHEN or OTHERWISE.
10 Missing SELECT or DO for END.
12 Clause longer than allowed.
14 Missing END for DO/SELECT or THEN for IF
16 Nonexistent label
17 Procedure missing CALL or invocation
18 IF or WHEN has no THEN.
21 Invalid token at end of clause.
24 Invalid TRACE statement.
25 Invalid subkeyword.
27 Invalid DO structure.
28 Invalid LEAVE/ITERATE.
29 ADDRESS environment too long.
33 Invalid expression after processing.
35 Invalid expression before processing.
36 Missing right parenthesis.
37 Extra right parenthesis or invalid expression.
38 Invalid parsing template.
40, 43 Nonexistent or invalid routine.
44 External function gives no result.
45 Internal function RETURNs no result

OTHER ERRORS

4 User pressed ATTENTION or program stopped.
5 Out of work space.
11 Stack full.
48 System service failed.
49 Symbolic Substitution failed.

Index